TEJANO TIGER

José de los Santos Benavides and the Texas-Mexico Borderlands, 1823–1891

JERRY THOMPSON

THE TEXAS BIOGRAPHY SERIES | NUMBER 5

A Joint Project of the Center for Texas Studies at TCU
and TCU Press / Fort Worth, TX

Library of Congress Cataloging-in-Publication Data

Names: Thompson, Jerry D., author. | Center for Texas Studies at TCU, issuing body.
Title: Tejano Tiger : José de los Santos Benavides and the Texas-Mexico borderlands, 1823–1891 / Jerry D. Thompson.
Other titles: TCU Texas biography series ; no. 5.
Description: Fort Worth, Texas : TCU Press, [2016] | Series: Texas biography series ; number 5 | «A Joint Project of the Center for Texas Studies at TCU and TCU Press / Fort Worth, TX." | Includes bibliographical references and index.
Identifiers: LCCN 2016042738 (print) | LCCN 2016045851 (ebook) | ISBN 9780875654072 (alk. paper) | ISBN 9780875656656
Subjects: LCSH: Benavides, Santos, 1823-1891. | Confederate States of America. Army—Officers—Biography. | Politicians—Texas—Biography. | United States—History—Civil War, 1861-1865. | Texas—History—Civil War, 1861–1865. | Southwest, New—History—Civil War, 1861-1865. | Laredo (Tex.)—History—19th century. | Mexican-American Border Region—History—19th century.
Classification: LCC E467.1.B395 T46 2016 (print) | LCC E467.1.B395 (ebook) | DDC 976.4/46205092 [B] —dc23
LC record available at https://lccn.loc.gov/2016042738rd tk>

TCU Press
TCU Box 298300
Fort Worth, Texas 76129
817.257.7822
www.prs.tcu.edu

To order books: 1.800.826.8911

Text design by David Timmons

For my wife,

Sara Amparo Cabello

A cotton train. *Drawing by Gary Zogby*.

CONTENTS

Editor's Foreword VII

Acknowledgments IX

Introduction 1

CHAPTER I: Revolutions Without End 5

CHAPTER II: "Mexico Has Lost Laredo Forever." 35

CHAPTER III: Secession and Civil War 80

CHAPTER IV: Cotton and Blood 135

CHAPTER V: Forsaken Corner of the Confederacy 159

CHAPTER VI: Peacemaking on the Border 208

CHAPTER VII: Ballots and Bullets 230

CHAPTER VIII: Beyond the Memory of Living Men 279

CHAPTER IX: International Diplomat 311

Epilogue 325

Notes 333

Bibliography 379

Index 393

EDITOR'S FOREWORD

Through its rich and colorful history, Texas has been home to countless fascinating figures. Some of the state's great works of historical literature, such as Eugene C. Barker's biography of Stephen F. Austin and Marquis James's study of Sam Houston, have chronicled the lives of Texas's larger-than-life leaders. Yet there remain many important personalities who have not yet found their biographer, and many more whose stories are in need of fresh examination in a scholarly biography. The Texas Biography Series, jointly published by the TCU Press and the Center for Texas Studies at TCU, offers a venue for telling their stories. Another major goal of the series is to broaden the body of biographical literature in Texas historiography beyond its traditionally heavy emphasis on the "great men" (which in practice has often meant "great white men on horseback"). While the series certainly includes biographies of nineteenth-century political and military leaders, it also strives to encourage biographers to examine the full range of historical actors who have shaped the destiny of the Lone Star State, including women; members of racial and ethnic minorities; and figures from the worlds of business, the arts, science, religion, and even sports. In doing this, the series aims to keep the field of Texas history vital and relevant in the twenty-first century.

The fifth volume in the series, Jerry Thompson's biography of José de los Santos Benavides fulfills several of these goals. Benavides was a towering figure in the history of the South Texas borderlands for half a century, yet he has had no biography until now. As a Tejano who served the Confederacy, his role in Texas history is complicated. As a political leader, he successfully negotiated both the Mexican American-majority world of the Texas border and the broader Anglo-majority world of the state. A patriotic American who nonetheless maintained deep ties south of the US-Mexico border, his story is also a transnational one, reminding us that the Rio Grande has always been something of an artificial dividing line. In short, the fascinating story of his life speaks not only to the Texan past but to its present and future.

This book and its predecessors in the Texas Biography Series owe their existence to several important institutions. TCU Press and its staff continue to furnish the editorial and production expertise to create books equal to those of the leading national publishing houses. The Center for Texas Studies at TCU is a critical partner in launching, funding, and publicizing the series. And finally, Houston Endowment, the Summerlee Foundation, and the Carl and Florence King Foundation have provided generous grants to underwrite the costs of the series. As editor of the series, I am grateful to all of these partners who continue to make the series a success.

Gregg Cantrell
Erma and Ralph Lowe Chair in Texas History
Texas Christian University

ACKNOWLEDGMENTS

I am grateful to a large number of individuals who helped to make this biography of Santos Benavides possible. When I first came to Laredo in 1968, Luciano Guajardo at the Laredo Public Library graciously offered a helping hand. Later Luciano's successor at the library's special collections, Joe Moreno, made available many of the municipal records that had previously been at city hall. Henry Flores, county clerk at the time, was most helpful with Webb County records. Henry's successor, Margie Ramirez Ibarra, whose brother Manuel was a dear friend, was always friendly and helpful, despite the pressures of public life. More recently, Rene LaPerriere, special collections librarian at the Laredo Public Library, was also helpful. I must also thank George Farías, author of an authoritative book on the history of the Farías family, who graciously made available documents relating to the life of Benavides. In Laredo, Hector Farías, a political tiger himself, shared photographs and rare family documents. My colleague at Texas A&M International University for many years, Stanley Green, an authority on the early history of the Mexican republic as well as José de Escandon's Villas del Norte, was always encouraging and willing to share the results of his extensive forays into the small municipal archives in northeastern Mexico and the larger depositories in Mexico City.

I will always be grateful to Luis Munoz, who diligently labored to translate a number of barely legible documents. In Monterrey, Manuel Gonzales retrieved valuable letters from the Santiago Vidaurri papers at the *Archivo General del Estado de Nuevo León* and was helpful in the search for the grave of Santos's daughter, Agustina Garza Ayala de Benavides. In Mexico City, Ruben Emilio Gutierrez Primental helped locate records at the *Archivo General de la Nación*, the *Archivo de la Defensa Nacional,* and Benavides letters in the Porfirio Díaz papers at the *Biblioteca Francisco Xavier Clavigero* at *Universidad Iberoamericana.* In Laredo, Lily Perez shared large numbers of legal documents showing how Santos Benavides's properties and large land holdings were lost to the family following his death. Olivia "Olee" Rodriguez, an authority on Darío Gonzales and Laredo genealogy, went out of her way to help locate a number of obscure yet significant genealogical records. At the Texas State Archives, Donaly Brice was always gracious and prompt in locating records. Various archivists at the National Archives in Washington, DC, especially in the Old Military and Civil Reference Department, were supportive in locating and retrieving numerous valuable documents, as were archivists at the Library of Congress. Several individuals in the Interlibrary Loan Department of the Killam Library at TAMIU were prompt and professional. I am also especially grateful to Kathy Walton of TCU Press for her editorial expertise. And I must thank the indefatigable and always helpful Ana Clamont at the Office of Public Relations at Texas A&M International University for her assistance with a number of illustrations. Finally, I need to thank Gregg Cantrell, Lowe Professor of Texas History at Texas Christian University, for his patience and encouragement.

Portions of this study rely on several previously published books and articles of mine. Some of the narrative relating to the Civil War in South Texas is drawn from *Sabers on the Rio Grande* (1974), *Vaqueros in Blue and Gray* (1976, 2000), and from the far more definitive *Civil War and Revolution on the Rio Grande Frontier: A Narrative and Photographic History* (with Lawrence Jones, III) (2004). Parts of Benavides's political career are discussed in *Laredo: A Pictorial History* (1986) and *Warm Weather and Bad Whiskey* (1991). Benavides's bloody and decisive fight with Juan Nepomuceno Cortina at Carrizo (Zapata) at the beginning of the Civil War is thoroughly covered in *Cortina: Defending the Mexican Name in Texas* (2007). A detailed account of

Benavides's gallant defense of Laredo against Union forces in March 1864 originally appeared as an article in *Civil War Times Illustrated* (1980).

My interest in Santos Benavides and the Tejanos who fought and died in the Confederate and Union armies during the Civil War began when I first arrived in Laredo, Texas, fifty years ago. After years of research, it became evident that Benavides and his brothers played a far more significant role in the war and the nineteenth-century history of the Texas-Mexico border than what historians had thought. As my research and focus intensified, I contemplated writing a dual biography of Santos and one of his Civil War adversaries—the wily and indefatigable Juan Nepomuceno Cortina. Both men were fascinating, partly because they came from very similar backgrounds and went on to lead adversarial, yet parallel lives. Benavides was born into one of the more influential families in Laredo, while Cortina came from one of the more formidable families in Camargo. In fact, Cortina's mother was one of the heirs to the largest land grants in the Lower Rio Grande Valley. What was so fascinating was that the two men, caught in the vortex of American expansionism and hegemony, became polar opposites and went in such opposite directions. Benavides became the die-hard defender of the status quo and a colonel in the Confederate army while Cortina started a revolution against what he called "flocks of vampires in the guise of men."[1] The "vampires" were a political clique of lawyers and judges in Cameron and Hidalgo counties who were complicit in unprecedented legal chicanery that resulted in Tejanos being relegated to second-class citizenship, and in some instances, dispossessed of their land.[2]

When the dual biography proved difficult, I turned to Cortina first. After all, he was one of the few men in history to have a war named after him and was the classic "social bandit." Cortina fought the Texas Rangers and blatantly defied authorities in Texas for two decades. He battled the US Army, harassed the Confederate Army, ambushed foreign and Mexican Imperialists, attacked Juárez's beleaguered Liberals, hanged countless unnamed bandits, and fought anyone who dared get in his way. His undaunted courage and feistiness were just too appealing. But Santos Benavides, the struggling young merchant, the mayor and county judge, the loyal Confederate and obstinate state representative, the international diplomat, was always there, lurking in the background, his striking and impressive story begging to be told.

INTRODUCTION

Geographically, South Texas is a giant wedge, an alluvial plain, thrust inland from the sea into the heart of the Lone Star State. This immense and uncompromising land is unlike any other region of Texas, physiographically, demographically, and historically. Stretching from the Balcones Escarpment and the Guadalupe River on the north to the Rio Grande on the south and the Gulf of Mexico on the east, South Texas comprised over thirty-nine thousand square miles, an area the size of Kentucky. The long hot summers, mild winters, and arid climate make the region nearly unique. It was on the vast sandy plains, along the banks of the Rio Grande and the Wild Horse Desert, where vast herds of bison and wild mustangs once roamed freely. Along the Guadalupe, San Antonio, and Nueces rivers, but especially along the Rio Grande, the fourth longest river in North America, the region's rich and fascinating history took shape. Eight decades before the Pilgrims arrived at Plymouth and seven before the first Englishman walked ashore at Jamestown, Spanish explorers, many of them from Estremadura in western Spain, an arid land similar to South Texas, roamed the parched landscape and came in contact with the native peoples of the region, the Coahuiltecans and Karankawas. In this clash of races and cultures, the Native Americans perished by the thousands.

A half century before the United States existed as a nation, Franciscan priests in search of gold and souls built missions along the waterways of South Texas. Here settlers established the first cattle ranches in what would eventually become the United States. Along the banks of the Rio Grande, a series of nineteenth-century wars helped determine the boundaries of two nations and the destiny of two peoples. One war would begin here in 1846, and another war would end here in 1865.

In this wild and vivid land on November 1, 1823, only a stone's throw from the banks of the Rio Grande at the small village of Laredo, José de los Santos Benavides was born to José de Jesús Benavides and Margarita Ramón. Although living conditions were rough and life was difficult, Santos came of age as part of the mercantile class and landed elite of the community. Dating back to the early Spanish era, the Benavideses took pride in being one of the pioneer families of José de Escandón's province of Nuevo Santander. Among the first to arrive in the region was Francisco Baez Benavides Lópes, who came to Mexico from the Canary Islands in 1594 and traveled north to establish several mines in what became the state of Nuevo León. Benavides settled at Cerralvo, but by 1620 he had moved on to become *alcalde* of Monterrey. Members of the family would later settle at Revilla on the Rio Grande, and it was from these Benavideses that Santos could trace his ancestry.[1]

Riding the rough and sometimes bloody peaks and canyons of border politics, Benavides's rise to prominence was largely due to the influence and careful mentoring of his well-known uncle, Basilio Benavides, who served several terms as alcalde of Laredo and chief justice of Webb County. When the Civil War erupted in 1861, Basilio was one of only two Tejanos in the state legislature. During Santos's lifetime, five flags flew over the small community he called home—that of the sometimes chaotic and struggling Republic of Mexico, the ill-fated Republic of the Rio Grande, the upstart Republic of Texas, an expansionist United States, and in March 1861, the rebellious and backward-looking Confederate States of America. It was under the Stars and Bars of the Confederacy in the disputed Texas-Mexico borderlands that Benavides reached the pinnacle of his military career as a regimental commander and the highest-ranking Tejano in the Confederate Army. In the decades that followed the Civil War, he became an esteemed political leader, highly respected on both sides of the border.

At the pinnacle of his political career in 1879 he held the distinction of being the only Tejano in the Texas legislature. Through strife, sweat, blood, and heroism in defense of the border, Benavides rose to economic and political heights few could dream of. As a friend and confidant of two Mexican presidents, he was one of the single most influential individuals in the nineteenth-century history of the border. His life was one of endless struggle, difficult adaptation, and enduring perseverance, as well as binational leadership and skilled diplomacy. He was without doubt the single most important individual in the long and often violent history of Laredo. The niche he carved in the tumultuous transnational history of the Texas-Mexico borderlands seems secure.

CHAPTER 1

REVOLUTIONS WITHOUT END

He was with his Uncle Bracilois [sic] in much of the Revolution; was generally employed in harassing the enemy on their march, by waylaying them in the defiles, and firing on them at night.

—Mirabeau B. Lamar interview with Santos Benavides, Summer 1847.

After a tedious and exhausting trek across the desert from Monterrey, the French botanist Jean Louis Berlandier and a party of the Mexican Boundary Commission reached the Rio Grande at the small and forlorn-looking village of Laredo on a frigid day in February 1828. The inhabitants of the forsaken rock and adobe settlement were in large part, Berlandier said, shiftless, lazy, fun loving, and prone to frivolity. The bleak and dreary treeless village included several thatched, one-story huts perched perilously on both sides of the river. Besides a lively song and dance by a band of fierce-looking Lipan Apache warriors, menacingly camped on the outskirts of the hamlet, there was little of interest for the travelers. It was unlikely that anyone from Laredo would ever amount to much or go anywhere. But a five-year-old boy named José de los Santos Benavides lived there at the time, and he probably gave more than just a curious glance at Berlandier and his companions, who were soon back in the saddle and headed north for San Antonio de Béxar.

José de los Santos Benavides's Creole great-great-grandfather, Tomás

Sánchez Barrera y de la Garza, founded the small and often troubled community of La Villa de San Agustín de Laredo on the north bank of the Rio Grande in 1755, as part of José de Escandón's province of Nuevo Santander. Named after a Cantabrian coastal village on the Bay of Biscay in northern Spain, Laredo was the last of Escandón's Villas del Norte and his only successful settlement on the north bank of the river. Both of Santos's parents were born in this small river community. Not long before Mexico made its break from the Spanish empire, on July 6, 1821, Santos's older brother José del Refugio was born to Margarita and José de Jesús. Two years later, on November 1, 1823, José de los Santos, as he was christened, came into the restless Laredo world. The infant was christened eight days later in the small rock church on the east side of a barren and treeless San Agustín Plaza by Fr. José María García, with Teodocio Treviño and María del Patrocinio Benavides, sister of Basilio, as *padrino* and *madrina*.[1] Three years after Santos's birth, a daughter, María Ricarda, followed, and four years after that, another daughter, María Seferina, was born. Tragedy struck the family when Santos's mother died at an early age.[2] At the time of her death, Margarita owned a sizeable herd of 635 sheep, along with a few other animals. Personal possessions included household items valued at 675 pesos. Debts, including that owed to relatives such as Basilio, amounted to 369 pesos. After Santos's father had taken his half of the estate, the boy was given thirty-eight pesos.[3] It was not much, but through time and hard work Santos would turn his meager inheritance into one of the largest and most profitable mercantile firms in the community.

Santos's father, José de Jesús, was not long in taking a second wife, Tomasa Cameros. From the second marriage, five children were born: María Andrea, María Juliana, José Cristóbal, María Francisca, and José Eulalio.[4] At the time of his father's death in late 1844, when Santos was twenty-one, José de Jesús was deeply in debt and listed only two mules on his last will and testament. Knowing he was near death, José de Jesús, being a "good Christian" as most people thought they were at the time, left his mules and his debts to his wife. In his last will on September 28, 1844, he asked that his remains be placed in the parish cemetery without ceremony.[5] It was said that few individuals did as much for the growth and development of Laredo as José de Jesús, who was remembered years later as a "frontiersman of high character and boldness."[6] In the difficult years that followed, Tomasa struggled to raise her family and through time, she and her stepson grew close.

Two years prior to Santos's birth, in September 1821, exciting news reached the river village. A Créole general in the Mexican army, Agustín de Iturbide, had taken control of Mexico City, and centuries of Spanish rule were at an end. Hoping to protect the country from the disintegration of vice regal authority and the Radical Republican rule that had swept across Latin America in its wake, Iturbide declared Mexico independent in his Plan de Iguala, which set up a provisional junta to govern the country until a national congress could be established.[7] Mexico was to be a constitutional monarchy with Roman Catholicism as the sole religion. Moreover, all citizens of the new state would enjoy equal political and social rights. With considerable political maneuvering culminating in the stroke of a pen, Iturbide achieved what eleven years of barbarous ferocity and bloodshed had not. Not surprisingly, Iturbide was asked to preside over the junta, and shortly thereafter on July 21, 1822, the congress declared him Agustín I, Emperor of Mexico. A pompous coronation presided over by the archbishop of Mexico at the national cathedral in Mexico City followed. The new emperor created a red, white, and green flag representing the three guarantees of the Plan de Iguala: freedom, religion, and union. In place of the old Spanish emblem, Iturbide resurrected the old Tenochtitlán symbol for Mexico City, a golden eagle perched on a prickly pear cactus devouring a snake.

It was not long before revolutionaries demanding a more republican government forced Iturbide into exile in Italy and then England. Less than a year later, in July 1824, a courier reached Laredo with the news that Iturbide, thinking conditions had deteriorated so badly that upon returning he would again be hailed as a liberator, had returned to Mexico. The deposed emperor landed at the port of Soto la Marina on the coast of Nuevo Santander, now Tamaulipas, where he was warmly received at first—but

German-born naturalist and artist Arthur Carl Victor Schott sketched "Las Isletas: The Falls on the Rio Grande near Presidio del Rio Grande" for the United States Boundary Commission in 1851. Sixty-two miles above Laredo and forty miles below Eagle Pass, the falls prevented boats from passing upriver from Laredo except during high waters. The pristine Rio Grande frontier that Santos Benavides came to know and love in the nineteenth century scarcely resembles the Texas-Mexico border of the twenty-first century. Steel engraving. *From William H. Emory,* Report of the United States and Mexican Boundary Survey (1857–1859). *Courtesy of the Center for American History, University of Texas at Austin.*

then arrested and shot by a firing squad and buried at the parish church at the village of Padilla.

On the northeastern frontier of the Mexican republic, the vast province of Tejas y Coahuila proved worrisome and almost ungovernable. On March 21, 1822, a twenty-eight-year-old, dust-covered Virginia-born traveler rode into Laredo from the north and identified himself as Stephen F. Austin. The journey-weary Austin said he was on his way to Mexico City to petition the Mexican government to affirm a large land grant his father had received from the Spanish government. Riding south from the Rio Nueces with only a small escort, the aspiring *empresario* was twice confronted by large bands of hostile Comanches who took his possessions. When the Comanche realized the travelers were not Mexican, however, Austin persuaded them to return his belongings.[8] Austin said the land south of the Nueces was the poorest he had ever seen; it was "nothing but sand, entirely void of timber, covered with scrubby thorn bushes and prickly pear." Laredo, Austin told his brother, was "as poor as sand banks, and drought, and indolence can make it."[9] Told that the area south of Laredo was infested with bandits, Austin remained in the small village for several days until he could join a larger party and resume his travels south to Monterrey and Mexico City.

The creation of a new government in Mexico City did not measurably influence the frontier villages like Laredo in the far northeast. Citizens struggled to eke out an existence on the raw Rio Grande frontier, and decrees from afar were less concerning than the fear of attack from hostile Lipan Apaches or Comanches. When fragile years of peace collapsed, as they did fairly frequently, the pugnacious mounted fighters swept down on the Rio Grande with a fury, seizing livestock, killing settlers, and carrying off captives. Santos came of age in a time when the citizens of Laredo greatly feared being killed or captured by the raiding Native Americans. All of his life, Santos felt a deep disdain for Indians, a hatred inherited from Uncle Basilio that was embedded in his soul.

In 1829, six-year-old Santos was listed as a student in the all-male town school.[10] It was here in his formative years that he learned the essential tenets of reading, writing, religion, rudimentary math, and basic geography. Just as Santos was finishing his elementary education, revolution again swept over the village of Laredo. In December 1835, when he was only eleven, Santos had watched as the defeated and demoralized army of Gen. Martín Perfecto de Cos limped through Laredo on their way south. General Cos had been ordered to suppress a revolt by restless Anglo-Americans that Antonio López de Santa Anna, president of Mexico, had denounced. Santa Anna was determined to punish the disloyal insurgents in Texas just as he had done in Zacatecas and in the Yucatán. After landing on the Texas coast, General Cos arrived in San Antonio only to find himself besieged and overwhelmed, and on December 11, 1835, he signed disgraceful capitulation terms agreeing not to oppose the federal Constitution of 1824 and to retreat with his army to the interior of Mexico. Cos's ragged and demoralized army reached Laredo on a somber Christmas Day in 1835, and as Santos watched, the village was again stripped of animals and food.[11] Hearing of Cos's humiliating retreat, Santa Anna was soon on the march.

During the Texas Revolution that followed, civil affairs in Laredo continued much as they had before the conflict, and in January 1836, Santos watched as Basilio was elected alcalde. The great-grandson of Tomás Sánchez, Basilio was young, energetic, and a born leader whom many in the community looked to for guidance and protection. Born on April 15, 1800, Basilio had been selected as the village postmaster at the age of sixteen, a position he held for almost a decade. In February 1822, he wed María Encarnación García, daughter of José Antonio García and María Gertrudis Martínez, who represented one of the more prominent families in the community.[12] Basilio was reelected alcalde twice more, in 1843 and again in 1848, at the end of the war between the United States and Mexico.[13] His tenure as head of the community would span some of the most tumultuous and eventful years on the frontier. With his influence and prestige rising steadily, Basilio also served at various times as military *comandante*, fighting what seemed to be a never-ending and frequently losing battle with the Lipan and Comanches.[14]

Only four days after Basilio became alcalde in 1836, a small convoy of six soldiers and several civilians carrying a supply of corn were on their way from Laredo to the villages upriver when they were suddenly attacked by a band of Comanches, and the commanding officer, Esteban de León, was killed. As had long been the custom, the church bell atop San Augustín Church sounded out the call to arms, and reinforcements were soon in the saddle. The small army found the Comanches camped on a high bluff overlooking the Rio Grande. Surprisingly, the Indians were caught off guard, and several were killed. With their retreat cut off, a number of the warriors jumped from the bluffs into the river and swam to the south bank where they scurried off into the dense underbrush. Trails of blood leading into the mesquite indicated that several of the Comanches had been seriously wounded.[15]

On March 24, 1836, Comanches attacked several farms in the river bottom near Laredo, killing three citizens and carrying off a twelve-year-old boy. Forty citizens and the small military garrison in the community gathered early the next month and rode out to confront the Indians. One "savage" was killed, but Cesario Gil, a prominent citizen, also died. "The hostilities of the barbarians are increasing day by day in a horrible way," Basilio wrote. "The troops which guard this village are destitute," he complained.[16] The few soldiers in the community, he went on to say, spent all their efforts guarding wagon trains along the San Antonio-Laredo trail.

After the Comanches sent out scouts "to ascertain the conditions of the country and the presence of troops," they would move in a body, John S. "Rip" Ford wrote years later of the Comanche raids on the middle Rio Grande.[17] The Indians "fall upon ranches boldly during daytime, kill, plunder, and carry off women and children prisoners." When the Comanches sensed danger, they divided into smaller groups and descended on different ranches. If the Indians were pursued, they would "move day and night, very often not breaking a gallop except to exchange horses (which they do several times) and to water the *cavallado*, until they deem themselves safe," Ford continued.[18] In their flight, the raiders were known to cover at least seventy miles a day.

With the community under siege from the Comanches, there was talk in Laredo, as there had been in the past, of abandoning the village. It was an age of great fear and uncertainty, a time of trepidation that Santos would never forget. The suffering of relatives and friends remained ingrained in his psyche and influenced his thoughts and actions for decades. Speaking on behalf of the desperate citizens, Basilio pleaded with the governor of Tamaulipas, José Antonio Fernández Izaguirre, for assistance. "The savages," he told the governor, "declared war in the year 1813 and up to the present time there has been only three years that have been more or less peaceful; the rest has been a perpetual continuance of hostility and has resulted in the loss not only of wealth but of persons of both sexes and of all ages."[19] In the midst of this "prolonged suffering" there was little left to hope for. If only the governor could come to Laredo to "hear the weeping of the grieving widow, the laments of the disconsolate father, and the wails of the abandoned orphan." A long list of *vaqueros*, *labradores*, *pastores*, and prominent citizens had been killed and captives carried off. Citizens were subsisting on meat, since the supply of flour and corn from Mexico had been cut off. There were a few wagons in Laredo but not enough horses or mules to pull them. Only a few cows and horses remained on the farms and ranches near Laredo, and they were certain to starve or be lost since citizens were afraid to venture beyond the outskirts of the village unless escorted by soldiers. Citizens were desperate for relief, Basilio said, and if the community could not be protected, he was sure they would starve or be forced to abandon the town. If they were forced to leave, the towns south of the Rio Grande would be exposed to the "barbarous Indians." Benavides asked Fernández Izaguirre to forward his letter to Gen. Antonio López de Santa Anna, who Basilio knew was deep in Texas, having crossed the Rio Grande near Presidio del Rio Grande in February with a large army on his way to San Antonio de Béxar.

The day before Benavides's letter appeared in *El Mercurio del Pueblo de Matamoros*, unbeknownst to the alcalde, General Santa Anna had suffered a crushing and epic defeat along the banks of the San Jacinto River, deep in the bayou country of southeast Texas. In eighteen bloody minutes, Santa Anna lost a large part of his army and the general himself, dressed in the uniform of a private, was captured the next day. Although they did not realize it at the time, the destinies of Benavides and the citizens of Laredo had been radically altered. Starting in the year 1836, the political winds in Laredo seemed to always blow from the north.

In Laredo there was more to worry about than barbarous Indians and the ineptitude of the Mexican government. The political and economic future of the twelve-year-old, bright-eyed José de los Santos Benavides, neph-

Arthur Schott's sketch "Military colony opposite Fort Duncan." The small settlement on the south bank of the river in Coahuila opposite Eagle Pass would grow to become the city of Piedras Negras. *Emory,* Report of the United States and Mexican Boundary Survey (1857-1859). *Courtesy of the Center for American History, University of Texas at Austin.*

ew of the alcalde, was changing rapidly. From the time Santa Anna signed the Treaty of Velasco, the Republic of Texas claimed all the land north and east of the Rio Grande.

In the months and years following the battle of San Jacinto, a defiant Mexico refused recognition of the Republic of Texas and remained determined to regain the lost province. Although forced to eventually realize that Texas was probably lost, Mexico continued to assert control over the Nueces Strip, that wild and immense land between the Rio Grande and the Rio Nueces. Despite the fact that Laredo was on the north bank of the river and claimed by Texas, the community remained in the hands of the Mexican military.

Many veterans of the Texas War for Independence sought every opportunity to strike at Mexico. Envisioning a Texas that would rival the United States in size and economic clout, there were those in the Republic of Texas who dreamed of annexing large swaths of Mexico. One such individual was the well-known Erastus "Deaf" Smith. Smith had come to Texas as early as 1817, hoping the climate would restore his health and hearing. He was a man of few words, and when he did speak it was usually in monosyllables. Smith had served admirably under Gen. Sam Houston at San Jacinto, and he was admired by many for his bravery and knowledge of the Texas frontier.

In March 1837, one year after the declaration of Texas independence, Deaf Smith, John Coffee Hays, and twenty men rode south from the Medina River with the intention of "raising the flag of independence on the spire of the church" at Laredo.[20] Ten days after leaving the Medina River, Smith and Hays were in camp at the San Ygnacio ranch on Chacón Creek, only five miles northwest of Laredo, where they encountered five scouts from the Laredo garrison who were watching the wagon road to San Antonio and who galloped back to San Agustín Plaza to sound the warning. As a young adult, Santos would certainly have been caught up in the excitement. Within minutes the garrison galloped out to give battle. Although Smith and his men were able to fall back and take a defensive position in a mesquite thicket, the Mexicans advanced in good order, firing as they pressed forward. From the thicket, Smith and his men opened fire, killing several of the Mexicans. A fierce forty-five minute firefight ensued, in which several more Mexican soldiers were killed or wounded before the Laredo garrison finally withdrew to the town. A captured soldier told Smith that a sizeable force remained in the town and that any attack would be suicidal. Certain that the man was telling the truth, Smith and Hays drew off and were soon in retreat. Although they had technically won the "Battle of Chacón Creek," since they had forced the garrison to retreat, Laredo remained securely in the hands of the Mexican army. Hoping to avoid an all-out war with Mexico, President Sam Houston, who had not authorized the raid on Laredo, told a friend that Smith and his men had "acted badly."

In the months and years that followed the creation of the Republic of Texas, the area between the Rio Grande and the Rio Nueces became a "no-man's land." In this vast semi-arid wilderness of mesquite, prickly pear, rolling plains, and unbearable heat, only the daring dared venture, and the Comanche and Lipan reigned supreme. Yet trade along the old Camino Real that stretched across the Rio Grande from San Antonio to Monclova, Saltillo, and beyond, as well as commerce along the wagon road from San Antonio to Laredo, remained lively. Leather items, saddles, shoes, beans, flour, and sugar could be found in Mexican caravans heading north, while wagons with tobacco, calico, and various hardware tools were frequently seen heading south for the border. At the same time, the Nueces Strip remained a lawless land of death. Bandits from the border raided north, stealing horses and cattle, while Texas "cowboys" struck ranches along the Rio Grande, stealing livestock. In many instances peaceful citizens of Laredo came to suffer from the transgressions and expansionist ideas of others.

In Laredo, there was only a brief respite before the small community was engulfed in a struggle between Centralists and Federalists—the latter being individuals who hoped for a full restoration of the liberal Constitution of 1824 and who aspired to political freedom and autonomy from what was perceived to be as an oppressive centralist government in distant Mexico City. Geographically isolated on the northeastern frontier, most political leaders in small communities such as Laredo generally aspired to the Federalist cause. Basilio Benavides, for example, was a strong supporter of the Constitution of 1824 and a Federalist at heart. He was largely responsible for a *pronunciamiento*, a proclamation, at Laredo in November 1838 in support of the Constitution of 1824.[21]

Downriver at Guerrero on November 5, 1838, a prominent lawyer and land-holding *Tamaulipeco*, Antonio Canales, issued a pronunciamiento calling for opposition to the central government. Canales succeeded in sparking a bloody struggle that swept like a wildfire over Laredo and the Rio Grande frontier. Critical to the Federalist cause was the daring Guerrero sheep man and celebrated Indian fighter, the mulatto José Antonio de Za-

Basilio Benavides was the much beloved uncle of Santos Benavides. Born on April 15, 1800, he became one of the most influential political leaders in Laredo and was deeply admired and emulated by Santos. Basilio was postmaster at the age of sixteen and served in that capacity for eleven years. He also served as alcalde during the difficult days of the Texas Revolution. Joined by his young nephew, he became a staunch Federalist in the struggles with the Centralists in the early 1840s. On the eve of the Civil War, he was elected State Representative, the second of five Tejanos in the nineteenth century. He died in 1864. *Jerry Thompson Collection.*

pata, for which Zapata County, at Basilio Benavides's suggestion, would be created and named in 1858. Both Santos and Basilio were loosely associated with Zapata, and may have at times actually ridden with him. There is little doubt that Zapata was highly respected by Santos and Basilio.

From what Santos told Mirabeau B. Lamar seven years later, it is evident he was with Basilio in the struggle, although exactly where and in what capacity is uncertain. Santos simply said that he joined his uncle in much of the revolution and was employed in "harassing the enemy on their march" and "waylaying them in the defiles, and firing on them at night."[22] It was perhaps Santos's first taste of combat. He took great pride in being with his uncle, who set a lasting example of bravery and dedication. To defy the federal government as the Federalists did was inspiring, but daring and dangerous.

Years later Santos would remember how Antonio Canales was indecisive and shied away from combat, while Zapata "always wanted to fight."

Santos may have even witnessed a nasty scene when Zapata threatened to kill Canales if he compromised or abandoned the Federalist cause. "I will as surely kill you," Santos remembered Zapata saying. "Death shall be certain—my vengeance shall be more speedy and terrible, than that which you apprehend from the foe."[23] Santos remembered Zapata telling his men that they were fighting against great odds and could expect "hard fighting" and "much suffering." Santos recalled how Canales was always intimidated by Zapata, who had a reputation on the Rio Grande as a fierce Indian fighter.

As Zapata realized from the beginning of the struggle, the Federalists were fighting against great odds. By the winter of 1839 they had retreated north to a wooden picket fort on the lower Rio Nueces called Lipantitlán. Canales, a conspirer by nature, was hoping to win support from the new president of the Texas Republic, Mirabeau B. Lamar, and recruit Texans into his beleaguered army. Not wanting an all-out war with Mexico, Lamar refused support, although more than two hundred Texan volunteers rode south to join Canales. Even some poorly equipped Carrizo Indians from the Reynosa area went over to the Federalist cause. With more than a thousand men, the Federalists again advanced on the Rio Grande, seizing Guerrero and Mier and pursuing the Centralist garrison south into the desert, where a fierce fight with heavy casualties ensued.[24]

On the Rio Grande opposite Guerrero, in January 1840, leading Federalists from the frontier called for a convention to organize a government for what came to be called the Republic of the Rio Grande. Largely based on the Constitution of 1824, delegates selected a lawyer from Reynosa, Jesús Cardenas, as president. Although Laredo was selected as the capital for the new republic, it was decided the government should remain at Guerrero, where a printing press was available. By early February 1840, the Guerrero press was turning out an official federalist newspaper, the *Correo del Río Bravo del Norte*. But in a major offensive, the Centralists seized both Mier and Guerrero.

In March 1840, the end came for Zapata at Santa Rita de Morelos in the state of Coahuila, upriver from Laredo, when the insurgents under

Gen. Mariano Arista were decisively defeated and Zapata's small force was surrounded. Although Zapata and his men put up a fierce fight, they eventually ran out of ammunition and had no choice but to surrender. Defiant to the end, Santos remembered Zapata saying he had "taken up arms against the tyranny of the government and I will never lay them down, except in death, until the wrongs of my people are redressed and their rights secured."[25] Tried before a hastily summoned court-martial, he was found guilty of treason, sentenced to death before a firing squad, shot, and then beheaded. With his triumphant but ragged army, the Cuban-born Gen. Pedro de Ampudia, who had been with Santa Anna at the siege of the Alamo, marched through Laredo where Zapata's severed head was exhibited in San Agustín Plaza as a warning against disloyalty. Ampudia had Zapata's head preserved in a cask of brandy and ordered the gruesome trophy of war taken downriver to Guerrero, where it was displayed on a pole on the plaza for the citizenry to see.[26] Santos was certain to have been in Laredo at the time and would later say that Zapata "fell a martyr to his fidelity and patriotism."[27] He would always remain a hero to young Santos, but it was his uncle Basilio who became his mentor and role model.

With the death of Zapata and the disintegration of his small army, what was left of the Federalist army limped back across the Rio Grande where Canales eventually set up his headquarters at Lipantitlán. Santos watched again as Centralist forces occupied Laredo and Canales hurried north to the newly established frontier capital of Austin to visit with Mirabeau B. Lamar, then moved on to Houston and Galveston, seeking recruits and support from the Texas Republic. In July 1840, a small ragtag army of 150 recruits rode southwest from Lipantitlán and were able to surprise the Centralist garrison at Laredo, seizing the military barracks on the plaza, before retreating back to the Rio Nueces. Two months later, a larger Federalist army crossed the Rio Grande, this time moving as far south as Ciudad Victoria, plundering as they went, before being turned back by an even larger Centralist army. Repulsed at Saltillo, many in the Federalist army deserted or went over to the Centralists, and the few downhearted men who remained staggered back to the Rio Grande in late October. On the north bank of the river opposite Camargo, Canales agreed to surrender. The last of the beleaguered Federalists stacked their arms at Laredo, and the Republic of the Rio Grande was no more. It had lasted for 283 violent and tumultuous days and proved to be one of the pivotal events in Santos's life.

As the Centralists tightened their hold on northeastern Mexico, aspirations of regaining Texas by the Mexican government reached new heights. By 1841, rumors of Mexican armies marching north to regain the lost lands were common. Texas was equally determined to control the bloody borderlands, and the two republics entered a new period of what one historian characterized as "attack and counterattack."[28] Once again, marauders struck north to the Nueces, stealing horses and cattle, and retreating back to the Rio Grande. At the same time, companies of Texas Rangers, whom the Hispanics on the Rio Grande learned to fear and hate, were organized to defend the frontier. Perhaps no Ranger was better known than John Coffee Hays. Hays had first served as a spy for Sam Houston in the days after San Jacinto, had ably fought Comanches, and had been in the 1837 "Battle of Chacón Creek" with Deaf Smith. In January 1841, Hays rode south to spy on the Mexican troops on the Rio Grande. Reaching the vicinity of Laredo, the Rangers were surprised to learn the town was guarded by only a small detachment of soldiers, who upon learning that Hays and his men were approaching, fled across the river. The Rangers triumphantly galloped into Laredo, where they took some horses and tried to intimidate the populace by galloping up and down the dusty streets, shouting their defiance of anything Mexican. Early the next morning most of the stolen horses were returned, and Hays gave José María Ramón a note saying the Rangers had no intention of harming the citizens but only outlaws and robbers such as the notorious Capt. Agatón Quinoñes. Quinoñes had been a resident of San Antonio until he was driven out by the Texans after San Jacinto. He had tried to associate himself with the Mexican military and frequently operated against the Texas frontier from a base near Laredo, although he was known to set up camp as far north as the Medina River. In early 1841, Quinoñes

Santos Benavides's half-sister Francisca Benavides Farías (1842–1909) was married to Francisco Farías (1833–1915). Farías Elementary School in Laredo honors his memory today. *Courtesy Hector Farías.*

and his men attacked a mule train of two *Bexareño* traders, Antonio Herrera and Francisco Ganado, just north of Laredo, and carried off a considerable amount of valuable cargo. In response, residents of towns as far away as Bastrop vowed to "burn Laredo and drive off all cattle, horses, and mules that could be found."[29] In the post-San Jacinto years, a number of Mexican trading caravans were plundered on the Laredo-San Antonio Road.

San Antonio merchants demanded protection, and President Mirabeau B. Lamar, with the congress of the Republic of Texas acquiescing, sent the Rangers into action. With twenty-five men, including thirteen Tejanos under Capt. Antonio Pérez, Hays again started for Laredo. Learning the Rangers were on the march, a force of forty men from the Laredo garrison led by Capt. Ignacio García intercepted the Rangers ten miles northeast of Laredo, just east of the Laredo-San Antonio Road near the San Ignacio Ranch. When they discovered the larger Mexican force was on their flanks and moving to encircle them, considerable panic ensued among the Rangers. When Hays and Pérez finally restored order, Hays ordered a frontal attack across a deep ravine and through several small mesquite motts. Although the Mexicans seemed to retreat, they quickly dismounted and formed a battle line. Several times the Mexicans retreated, only to dismount and fight again. In one final stand, the Rangers overran the small army, capturing twenty-five men, killing three, and wounding several.[30]

Hearing that the Rangers were again on the outskirts of the small community, many of the citizens fled across the river to the safety of Nuevo Laredo, as they had done in times past. Not long after the battle, a small delegation of citizens under a white flag met with Hays, offering rations but asking that Laredo be spared from any plunder or violence. Well into the twentieth century, long after Santos's death, the Rangers were still viewed in Laredo as racist ruffians.

Continued antagonisms between the Republic of Texas and the Republic of Mexico did little to lower tensions on the border and in Laredo. Riding north from his camp on the Rio Grande in September 1841, Agatón Quiñones struck the small village at the mission of Nuestra Señora del Refugio, on the coastal plain, far to the east of Laredo. After plundering the settlement, Quiñones and his raiders took several men from the community, tied their hands to the tails of their horses, and galloped off toward the border at a brisk trot. Those who survived the ordeal were taken to Laredo and then on to Lampazos de Naranjo, where Gen. Ráfael Vásquez ordered their release.

Perhaps more destabilizing was the fact that in 1841, Antonio López de Santa Anna again assumed dictatorial powers over Mexico, and any hope of peace between the two infant republics disappeared into the wind. Santa Anna was again determined to regain the lost province of Texas. His decision to send an army into Texas was largely provoked by the support that Texas provided the rebellious province of Yucatán, even going as far as to send the Texas Navy to support the insurgents.

In June 1841, in hopes of securing control over the lucrative Santa Fe

Trail and extending the authority of the Republic of Texas west to the Rio Grande, President Lamar sent a caravan of some twenty-one wagons escorted by three hundred men across the vast Llano Estacado to Santa Fe, in what is now New Mexico. After weeks of seemingly endless travel across a vast and uncompromising landscape, the Texans were greeted as enemy combatants, forced to surrender, and were hustled off to Mexico City in chains where they were imprisoned in the fortress at Perote.[31]

By late 1841, when Santos was eighteen, Santa Anna had completed his plans for an invasion of Texas. On February 24, 1842, with orders to occupy San Antonio, Gen. Ráfael Vásquez splashed across the Rio Grande at Presidio del Rio Grande with 399 men. At the head of Vasquez's small army of seven hundred men rode twenty-five men of the Laredo Presidials, commanded by Capt. Calixto Bravo Villaso. Not everyone on the Rio Grande frontier identified with Mexico or the Mexican army, however. From the time Vásquez crossed the river, a Laredo native, José María García, whom Benavides had known from the time he was a child, was spying on the Mexican army and reporting their every movement to the Texas authorities. There was little doubt, García said, that Vásquez was intent upon marching on San Antonio.

With the Mexican army across the Rio Grande and striking north, three-fourths of the residents of San Antonio fled. When Vásquez and his small army appeared before San Antonio early on the morning of March 5, six years after Santa Anna had raised his blood-red flag over the town and demanded the surrender of the Alamo, only one hundred men could be found to defend the place, and the town was easily occupied. Once again, to the disgrace of the Republic of Texas, the Mexican National flag could be seen waving over the town. While several Mexican Texans hastened to swear allegiance to the Mexican Republic, the stores and homes of those who had fled were looted. But Vásquez and his men only held San Antonio for two days before retreating back to the Rio Grande. Within days, as many as 3,500 angry Texans, all vowing revenge, were camped in and around San Antonio.

One of the tragic consequences of the Mexican invasion was the wrath, scorn, and racial animosity that many Anglo Texans piled on Tejanos, many of whom were seen as second-rate citizens in a land that had once been theirs. The degree to which Basilio Benavides was influenced by this animosity is a matter of conjecture, but it is certain his young nephew felt it to some degree. One such individual who came to be hated and ridiculed was the Tejano hero of the Texas Revolution, Juan N. Seguín. Many of the Anglos in Texas who blamed Seguín for the failure of the Santa Fe Expedition now blamed him for the Vásquez invasion. Fearing for his life, Seguín and his family fled for the border only to be imprisoned in Mexico by the Mexican authorities.[32]

Only weeks after Vásquez marched on San Antonio, a second column of Mexican soldiers commanded by Lt. Col. Ramón Valera crossed the Rio Grande at Mier, where they were joined by Agatón Quiñones and fifty of his men. Although forced to march over seventy miles without water, leading their horses much of the way and encountering a hostile band of Lipan Apaches along the way, Valera was able to seize the presidio at Goliad. Unable to make contact with Vásquez and his horses badly jaded, Valera decided to retreat back to the Rio Grande, only to be attacked again by as many as three hundred hostile Native Americans. With the Mexican army back across the river, relations between Texas and Santa Anna continued to spiral downward. The Vásquez and Valera expeditions into Texas were evidence of the vulnerability of the southern border claimed by Texas. Yet at the same time, the inability of the Mexican army to sustain itself in Texas was readily evident. Displeased with both Vásquez and Valera, Santa Anna was already making plans for yet another invasion of Texas.

By August 1842, French-born Gen. Adrián Woll assembled a Mexican army of over a thousand men at Presidio del Rio Grande. Woll was an experienced veteran who had served as aide-de-camp and quartermaster to Santa Anna during the ill-fated invasion of Texas in 1836. Woll pushed his army north along the old Camino Real much as Vásquez had done a few months earlier. In a heavy fog on September 11, the Mexican army appeared on the outskirts of San Antonio, where Woll celebrated his arrival with the Mexican band playing a lively "La Cachucha." After only thirty minutes of sporadic fighting, the Mexican flag once again floated over the "city of Bexar." Following a fierce fight along Salado Creek outside San Antonio and rumors of Texan reinforcements arriving daily, however, Woll and his men began the long march back to the Rio Grande. As many as two hundred Tejano families, all fearing retaliation by Anglo Texans, followed the Mexican army, streaming out of the town in a long train of 150 carts and wagons carrying furniture and household items, alongside hundreds of animals. After a skirmish on the Rio Hondo, Woll's army reached the Rio Grande on September 30, and by late that afternoon the last soldier had safely crossed to the south bank.[33] For ten days the Mexican flag had fluttered over San Antonio, and although it would never again fly over the town, Woll had struck a dagger into the heart of the struggling Republic of Texas, where there developed an uncontrolled thirst for revenge.

Besides the armies he watched cross the Rio Grande and tramp through the dusty streets of Laredo, other events came to impact the life of young Santos. In the summer of 1842, he watched anxiously as the Rio Grande spilled over its banks as it had done before. This time, however, the floodwaters kept rising, and the small jacales and brush huts near the riverbank were soon engulfed. The floodwaters first poured into the homes on the south bank of the river and then those on the higher north bank. It was the worst flood anyone in the community, including Basilio, could remember. Before the waters had receded days later, much of the town was in ruins. Some of the adobe buildings had melted away and had become little more than mounds of mud. Only those houses constructed of stone or those on high ground survived.[34]

In the midst of the chaos and uncertainty on the border, Santos fathered an illegitimate son, Petronilo, with Felipa Vargas. According to baptismal records at San Agustín Church, Petronilo came into the world on April 28, 1842, but lived for only seven days.[35] Six months later, on Thursday, October 27, 1842, nineteen-year-old Santos married twenty-year-old

Santos Benavides and Agustina Villarreal de Benavides. This is the only surviving photograph of the couple. The financially independent Agustina survived her husband by seventeen years. Before her death in February 1908 she had lost the vast landholdings her husband had spent a lifetime accumulating. *Courtesy of Hector Farías.*

Agustina Villarreal in a grand ceremony at San Agustín Church, with Fr. José Trinidad García presiding. As was the tradition at the time, the wedding had been announced at mass the three previous Sundays.[36] Agustina, like Santos, came from one of the more influential families in the community, and the wedding was one of the social highlights of the year. One year older than Santos, Agustina was described as a "great beauty and belle."[37] Three years later, Santos and Agustina are listed on the census as living on Calle Vallesillo, with Santos making a living as a *criador* or *ganadero*, a cattle raiser or breeder.[38]

At the same time, Mexican soldiers continued to gather on the Rio Grande for yet another invasion of Texas. Thirty-one men from Laredo were recruited to serve under Capt. Francisco Castañeda in a battalion named after Santa Anna. There is no evidence that Santos joined or was inclined to join such a unit. It is possible that Basilio sensed the turning of the tide and dissuaded him. Moreover, diehard Federalists such as Basilio tended to see the Mexican military as an oppressive instrument of the dictatorial Centralists regime in distant Mexico City. If Santos did participate in the struggle in one way or another, his service went largely unrecorded. If he was indeed involved, he may have later, perhaps for political reasons, chosen to ignore this chapter of his life.

On a frigid winter morning early in December 1842, Santos and the citizens of Laredo awoke to learn that more than seven hundred angry Texans had deployed around Laredo. The Texans were part of what has been called the Somervell Expedition, one of the most controversial armies to ever descend on the Rio Grande during the decade-long history of the Texas Republic. Not long after General Woll evacuated San Antonio, as many as 1,200 Texans met in front of the Alamo, where they swore to revenge the "outrages of the Mexicans."[39] In a retaliatory expedition against Mexico, the Texans were hoping to capture prominent Mexicans who could be exchanged for leading San Antonio citizens Woll had previously carried off to Mexico. By late November 1842, more than seven hundred men were in camp along the San Antonio River near Mission Concepción. Sam Houston, president of the Republic of Texas, appointed Alexander Somervell, a Maryland-born veteran of San Jacinto, to head what was called the "Southwestern Army of Operations." One of the young recruits, John Henry Brown, said the army "embraced more than one preacher, many church members, a full array of Texas farm boys and every variety of the genus homo."[40] Although the original objective of the expedition was Presidio del Rio Grande, it was decided that the army would strike Laredo instead.

Gen. Alexander Somervell was under orders from President Sam Houston to "proceed to the most eligible point on the western frontier of Texas and concentrate with the men now under your command, all troops who may submit to your orders, and if you can advance with a prospect of success into the enemy territory you will do so forthwith. You will receive no troops into your command, but such as will march across the Rio Grande under your orders if required by you to do so. If you cross the Rio Grande, you must suffer no surprise."[41] Feinting toward Presidio del Rio Grande to mislead any Mexican spies, the army crossed the Medina River and took the road to Laredo. Crossing a rain-swollen Nueces River, the army was hit by a severe "norther" of driving rain and high winds. The bad weather continued as the army assembled around Laredo on the night of December 7.

Once again, Santos Benavides and the citizens of Laredo were to become innocent victims of the warring republics of Mexico and Texas. Florencio Villarreal, a wealthy rancher with lands on both sides of the Rio Grande, was alcalde of Laredo at the time, while Col. Calixto Bravo commanded an eighty-man military garrison. From the time the Texans left San Antonio, the Mexican military, through a series of spies, was well aware that either Laredo or Presidio del Rio Grande was the target. Learning the Texans were across the flooded Rio Nueces and moving toward Laredo, and realizing it would be senseless to try to defend the town, Colonel Bravo began preparations to evacuate Laredo. As many as one hundred citizens also fled, some seeking refuge with relatives in Nuevo Laredo, while others took their animals and belongings downriver to Guerrero. Santos watched as a thousand animals, horses, mules, sheep, goats, and cattle were all herded across the Paso de los Indios west of town and then downriver or south into the interior. The animals were barely across when the river began to flood from the recent rains. Other animals were taken into the dense chaparral nearer the town. Fearing that not only would their animals be taken but that the town would be plundered, townspeople either hid valuable foodstuffs and supplies in the mesquite or ferried them across the river.[42]

At sunset on December 7, 1842, after following the San Antonio-Laredo Road, little more than a wide path through the dense chaparral, the Texan Army neared the river and began their final descent on Laredo. Not knowing the Mexican military had already fled, six companies of cavalry were sent across the river to cut off any retreat by the Laredo garrison. Finding the Rio Grande as badly flooded as the Rio Nueces, the men were fearful of crossing and instead deployed between the town and the river, where they huddled together in the winter cold and waited for daylight. In the first light of morning, a small boy who was leading a mule came down to the river from the north bank and was seized by the Texans. The boy revealed that Colonel Bravo and the Mexican military had evacuated the town. A few minutes later, two women came to the river's edge, saw the Texans, began screaming, and fled back into the town. Once a woman in a canoe started to cross the flooded river from the south bank, but upon seeing the Texans, she quickly paddled back across the river, dragged the canoe up the riverbank and fled. Realizing their position was revealed, the men scrambled up the steep river embankment and raced into the streets of the town. Not a shot was fired. Minutes later, after the remainder of the army entered the town from the north, the Lone Star flag could be seen fluttering in the early morning light from the small steeple of San Agustín Church.[43]

As General Somervell and the main army entered Laredo from the north, those citizens who had not fled—mostly women, children, and elderly men—gathered on the streets. "¡Buenos dias caballeros! ¡Nosotros [somos] amigos de los Americanos!" one soldier remembered the citizens saying. The *pan dulce* and *piloncillo* held out for the Texans by the Laredo populace came more out of fear than friendship, however.[44]

General Somervell had calculated it would take seven days to march from San Antonio to Laredo. It had taken seventeen, and the army was out of food. The general wasted no time in levying a requisition on the town. As white flags of submission fluttered about, once again the community was forced to pay the consequences of the war between the two republics. Already impoverished, many in Laredo deeply resented such impositions, which also included demands for clothing, but were fearful of the consequences should they resist. At noon several cattle were driven into the Texan camp and slaughtered. At the same time, several sacks of flour were found in caches in the brush outside of town. Seeing tracks from carts and wagons leading downriver, the Texans concluded that even more supplies were hidden elsewhere. At the Texan camp at the mouth of Chacon Creek, just downriver from Laredo, several of Somervell's men began consuming mescal they had seized in Laredo. Others were content to rest and smoke something similar to tobacco they found in town, something that made them feel light-headed and at ease. Although Somervell issued strict orders prohibiting the Texans from leaving camp, on the morning of December 9 as much as one-third of the army, having little respect for Somervell or military rules and regulations, left camp for the purpose of "visiting" Laredo. What the Texans did in the next few hours would be debated by leading diplomats in Austin, Mexico City, London, and other world capitals for decades. It was something that young Santos would never forget.

Without leadership the men became a mob. Many were intoxicated and thirsting for revenge for the Mexican raids on San Antonio. The disorder started when several of the Texan ruffians rode up to the town jail on the south side of San Agustín Plaza and demanded all prisoners be freed. When the jailer hesitated, the mob pushed him aside, forced their way into the jail, and quickly liberated twenty prisoners. Other Texans rushed into the office of the alcalde, Villarreal, and threatened to hang him if he did not reveal where he had hidden the silver he was reported to have in his possession. When Villarreal refused, several of the drunken Texans placed a noose around his neck and threatened to hang him before some of the saner Texans rode up and freed him.[45]

Many of Somervell's men were angry there were so few horses, and they began seizing any animal they could find. Others began breaking into homes and stealing anything they deemed valuable. Stores that were broken into and pillaged of their inventory included that of Santos and Basilio. Citizens hid in terror as groups of men were seen going up and down the streets with huge battering rams, smashing doors regardless of size or thickness. For hours the drunken and disgraceful pillage continued. Many of the victims were women whose husbands had fled and who were helpless at the hands of the hooligans. The Texans went into "houses and stores and took a great many such things as they could lay hands upon and took them by force and carried them off by violence," it was said, "breaking down doors, opening boxes, and trunks and taking off blankets wherever they could find them, even from the beds of women, leaving them to weep the fate of their unhappy lot."[46]

Santos later testified that he lost "a silver mounted saddle valued at one hundred pesos," along with clothing and bedding.[47] Basilio said the Texans took from him "one hundred and fifty pounds of flour, nine wool rugs, a pistol and a gentle horse."[48] Former alcalde Ildefonso Ramón, Santos's maternal grandfather, said the Texans stole from his store "four loads of flour, one hundred and fifty pounds of sugar, ten pounds of chocolate, a silk shawl, eighteen pairs of shoes, one set of silverware, a musket, a silver decorated powder box, a saber and one gentle horse." Another former alcalde, José María Gonzales, lost from his mercantile business "four hundred pounds of pepper, six pairs of shoes, a carbine, three silk umbrellas, two silk crepe dresses and two dozen sets of harnesses." The Texans stole from Agustín Dovalina "one fully equipped saddle, a change of clothes, and a fine rope." In the pillage, Bartolomé García, Santos's first cousin, came up missing "two new saddles, a new quilt, two good shawls and two blankets." From Vivian Díaz, the Texans took "women's apparel, two pairs of silk stockings, a fine linen dress, one ladies jacket, three silk umbrellas and an embroidered sidesaddle." Lorenzo Gil lost "a set of jewelry, one fine quilt, three fine blankets, two hundred pounds of sugar, two bedspreads, three embroidered sheets, two new napkins and twenty-five pounds of coffee." And the pillage went on and on.

A few of the terrified citizens lost their life savings. One of the Texans later boasted that he stole from a Laredo family one hundred doubloons as well as four of the finest blankets he had ever seen. One of the blankets "had the rising sun in the center and its rays terminated to its outer parts with brilliant colors of the rainbow."[49] The unnamed Laredoan who lost the blanket was said to have wept, claiming his sister in Monclova had taken three years to weave the blanket and that it was the pride of his family. Once the floodwaters of the Rio Grande subsided, the Texans were able to cross to the south bank, and the plunder continued. Crossing the river, Thomas Jefferson Green and five of his men planted the Texas banner in the plaza and demanded five mules from the frightened and bewildered citizens.[50]

Realizing the extent of the looting, Somervell immediately called a council of war and ordered all the stolen items returned. With two-thirds of his men still in camp and under military control, a company was ordered to seize the plunder. Once the loot had been collected from the drunken mob, it was placed in a pile that grew to become the size of a large house. Many of the Texans claimed they had purchased the goods while others argued their items had been given freely by the inhabitants of Laredo. The pillage included "blankets, beds and bed clothes; cooking utensils of various design; horses, mules, and asses; beeves, veals and muttons; poultry of every genus of ornithology; honey bread, flour, sugar, and coffee; saddles and bridles; boots, hats, and . . . apparel known amongst the gentler sex that our blushing muse forbids us to catalogue." For decades, citizens would never forget being "left as poor as church mice."[51]

Somervell scribbled out a letter apologizing for the actions of his men. "I regret to learn that some bad men belonging to the army under my command have committed acts of outrage in your town. The army is composed of volunteers and is difficult to control. But I am to state to you that these acts have excited the indignation of a large portion of the army and are utterly reprobated by myself and officers under my command. We will make you all the reparation in our power, by returning all such articles are not essential to the army."[52] Although Laredoans drove several carts and wagons to the camp of the Texans and recovered much of what had been stolen, almost all of the foodstuffs were kept by the army and consumed. Certainly most of the Texans did not approve of what happened in Laredo. "Here was a town," one soldier wrote, "on the soil claimed by Texas; its inhabitants, claiming to be Texans, and opened their doors to us, as to friends—had received the soldiers of Texas as deliverers, and yet, those inhabitants, were not safe in the possession of their private property."[53] Yet others somehow tried to defend what happened in Laredo. Thomas Green later wrote a book defended the sacking of Laredo. "Did not the Texans have a clear right by the *lex talionis* [law of retaliation] of war . . . to lay every Mexican town upon the border in ashes? Did not the burning of our towns in 1836, and the subsequent plunder of Refugio and San Antonio, give them this right?" Green wrote.[54]

Sam Houston, president of the Republic of Texas at the time, was appalled at what happened in Laredo, and he placed most of the blame on Green. In a speech on the floor of the United States Senate in 1854, Houston called Green a dog, a loafer, and a dastardly coward. "Laredo was inhabited by Mexicans," Houston said, "but they were Texan citizens, and as such, entitled to its protection. They were citizens of Texas and none but an enemy of Texas could raise his hand against them or molest one of them."[55] Eight years after that terrible day in 1842, after Laredo had become part of the United States, Basilio Benavides, who was mayor at the time, formed a committee seeking reparations. The committee estimated the value of the stolen items at 12,681 pesos. In the Texas legislature, Hamilton P. Bee attempted to obtain compensation for the victims, but the legislature never appropriated any money.

Although most of the Texans under Somervell returned home after the sacking of Laredo, several hundred soldiers refused orders and continued downriver. At Mier, they suffered a resounding defeat, and 248 of the men were marched off to prison in Mexico.[56] After being paraded through the

Lipan Warrior by Arthur Carl Victor Schott. Although Spain and Mexico frequently made peace with many of the Native American tribes in the Texas borderlands, Benavides spent much of his early life warring with raiding bands of Lipan, Comanche, and other Native Americans. When at peace, the Lipan were frequent visitors to Laredo, often camping on the outskirts of the city. *Emory,* Report of the United States and Mexican Boundary Survey (1857–1859). *Courtesy of the Center for American History, University of Texas at Austin.*

streets of many of the towns on the Rio Grande in chains, the men were taken to Monterrey and then Saltillo. At Salado in the Chihuahuan Desert, 110 miles south of Saltillo, the Texans made a daring break. Most of the escapees were recaptured and returned to Salado for the infamous "Lottery of Death" or "Black Bean Incident." Seventeen black beans were placed in an earthen jar along with 159 white beans. A white bean meant life, while a black bean meant death. Those who survived the Salado executions were first imprisoned near Mexico City and later Perote Prison, 160 miles to the east, on the road to Veracruz. Although a few escaped, the remaining Texans were held until September 14, 1844, when Mexico agreed to their release.

In the presidential election of 1844, the annexation of Texas to the United States became a major political issue. The Democrat candidate, James K. Polk of Tennessee, running on an expansionist platform calling for annexation, swept into power. The lame-duck president, John Tyler, seeing the election as a clear mandate, pushed through Congress a joint resolution calling for annexation. In February 1846, Anson Jones, the last president of the Republic of Texas, lowered the Lone Star flag in Austin and raised the Stars and Stripes as hundreds cheered and bands played. Mexico, which had previously agreed to recognize the Republic of Texas if the infant nation would remain independent, broke relations with the United States. With the United States inheriting the Texas claim to the Rio Grande, President Polk ordered Gen. Zachary Taylor to head an "Army of Observation" and take a position on the Nueces River at the small trading and smuggling village of Corpus Christi. Rumors reached Laredo that General Taylor's 2,400-man army was intent on attacking Laredo. Posing as merchants, five men were sent to the coast to spy on Taylor's army. According to one rumor, the American Army numbered as many as 50,000 infantry and 200,000 cavalry.[57] After months of waiting, on March 8, 1846, the United States Army, now the "Army of Occupation," marched for the Rio Grande. As Santos watched anxiously from Laredo, the two nations held their breath, and then rushed headlong into the bloody cauldron of war.

CHAPTER II

"MEXICO HAS LOST LAREDO FOREVER."

"I have been unable to travel to see you because of difficulties one encounters on the road of life."

—SANTOS BENAVIDES TO SANTIAGO VIDAURRI, JANUARY 25, 1861

It was warm in Laredo on the morning of March 13, 1846, when a cloud of dust was spotted northeast of town on the road to San Antonio. On the dung-peppered, barren main plaza, a small thirty-man Mexican garrison scurried about as soldiers grabbed their weapons and personal belongings. At the stables near the plaza, the commanding colonel hastily saddled his horse and rode off toward the river and the ferry. Only minutes later, a ragtag, buckskin-clad company of forty Bexar County Rangers, who were on their way to join Gen. Zachary Taylor's army in the lower valley, emerged from the *brasada* and galloped into the narrow streets of the sun-baked town.[1] Without a shot being fired, those who remained of the small Mexican garrison surrendered. The soldiers were hastily paroled and their muskets "delivered to the civil authorities for protection against the depredations of the Indians."[2]

As Capt. Richard Addison Gillespie and his men raised the Lone Star flag over San Agustín Plaza, one era was ending in Benavides's life and another was beginning. For the last forty years the town had experienced epidemics, droughts, and floods, while at the same time, the armies of the Spanish empire, the Mexican Republic, the Republic of the Rio Grande, and the Republic of Texas had occupied and abused the community. Several times in the early years, Native Americans had come close to destroying the town, as they had the river villages of Palafox and Dolores.

Captain Gillespie was received by Alcalde Andrés Martines and the population of the town "in a very friendly manner."[3] At a hastily called meeting of the *ayuntamiento* (town hall), Alcalde Martines pleaded with the Texans for protection against the barbarous Comanches. The next morning, however, the Ranger captain and his men reined their horses downriver, despite being told that two hundred Mexican soldiers awaited them at Guerrero and another eighteen hundred at Mier. Seven months later, the Tennessee-born Gillespie would lie dead on the bloody battlefield at Monterrey.

In October 1846, not long after the Mexican-American War erupted in the lower valley, news reached Laredo that a strange-looking rectangular boat that belched black smoke like a dragon, the likes of which Santos and the citizens of the river village had never seen, was slowly making its way upriver. Couriers brought word from Guerrero that a group of Americans was "coming in a thing that split the rocks in two, forcing a passage for itself."[4] A few days later, citizens lined the riverbanks as the *Major Brown*, a 150-foot-long, 125-ton side-wheeler with a draft of three feet, came into view. The steamer was commanded by Capt. Mark Sterling and manned by Lt. Bryan P. Tilden Jr. and twenty men of the Third US Infantry. Although Captain Sterling was under orders to take the *Major Brown* as far upriver as possible, the level of the Rio Grande began dropping as soon as the soldiers arrived, and the steamer was stranded in Laredo for over a year. For weeks the *Major Brown* remained a great curiosity to Santos and the citizens who hurried onboard to examine the vessel.

Two weeks later, on November 8, 1846, after the bloody battle for Monterrey and General Taylor's army of occupation had taken possession of Saltillo, seventy-three men of the Texas Mounted Volunteers arrived in Laredo. In command was the former president of the Republic of Texas, Capt. Mirabeau Buonaparte Lamar, a poet, politician, and diplomat turned soldier, who was under orders to "extend protection to the settlements . . .

[and] check particularly the incursions of the Indians."[5] As a result of unprecedented flooding in 1842, Lamar found Laredo to be "little more than a heap of ruins" with "scarcely a comfortable home in the place." The town was, Lamar wrote, "divided into two distinct villages by the Rio Grande, both, however, bearing the common name of Laredo and being governed by the same local authorities." Lamar went on to say that the town was isolated and "much exposed to the ravages of the Indians. Seven hundred of its inhabitants have been killed within the last twenty years."[6]

One of the first things Lamar did upon arriving in Laredo was to declare martial law, and shortly thereafter, on July 13, 1847, he issued orders for an election to select two justices of the peace, one constable, and a county commissioner, all to represent Laredo as part of the newly created Nueces County.[7] All male "free persons" twenty-one years of age or older were eligible to vote between the hours of 9:00 a.m. and 4:00 p.m. in the office of the alcalde, Andrés Martines.[8] With the community under martial law and a new form of government, only forty residents came forth to cast ballots. They were the social and economic elite of the community and included Basilio Benavides, who was a candidate for justice of the peace but who lost to L. T. Tucker and Agustín Soto. Among the forty voters was Santos's older brother Refugio, but not Santos himself.[9]

The first six months of American rule were generally uneventful and peaceful. Except for making the usual reports of Comanches passing near the town, Lamar spent most of his time complaining of boredom and scheming to obtain a command in the Mexican interior, where he and his men could make a name for themselves. When the newly elected alcalde, Florencio Villarreal, and the city council learned that Lamar was eager to leave, they drafted a letter to General Taylor asking that the "Laredo Guard" be allowed to remain in the town and arguing that Laredo was badly in need of protection from the "hostilities of the barbarians" and the "plunder of bandits," both of which had plagued the town for decades.[10] Undoubtedly, they were also interested in the small revenue flow the military brought to the community.

Capt. Mirabeau B. Lamar, the second president of the Republic of Texas, and forty-two men of the First Texas Cavalry occupied Laredo from 1846 to 1848. In many ways Lamar was the town's first oral historian, recording valuable recollections of Basilio and Santos Benavides and others. *Jerry Thompson Collection.*

Lamar spent a lot of time policing the consumption of "spirituous liquors," compiling a census of the town, drafting an ordinance outlawing peonage, creating a list of municipal officers dating back to 1767, and cursing and demeaning his bigger-than-life political rival, the hero of San Jacinto, Sam Houston. Lamar also interviewed several leading citizens, including young Santos, with whom the captain seemed impressed. Santos told Lamar that during the violence that had swept over the Rio Grande in 1840, Basilio had been one of the first to take up arms for the Federalists. Although only an impressionable teenager at the time, Santos had joined Basilio and about thirty other men in fighting the Centralists.[11] During the struggle, Santos had come to admire Antonio Zapata, the hero of the Republic of the Rio Grande who had been executed and decapitated during the conflict. Lamar also interviewed Basilio, who vividly recalled the epic Federalist-Centralist struggles and how the capital of the Republic of the Rio Grande had been located in a small rock and adobe building on the south side of the main plaza.[12]

When news of the American victory at Buena Vista, southwest of Saltillo, reached Laredo in March 1847, the mood of the town changed. The garrison at Laredo was not needed any longer, and Lamar complained bitterly of being forced to "slumber on . . . while the flag of our country is yet to [be] borne in triumph on other fields." His men were demanding that they be transferred to a "sphere of more active and useful operations."[13]

In the early summer of 1847, the political atmosphere in the community abruptly changed again when news reached Laredo that Gen. Winfield Scott had suffered a decisive defeat in his march toward Mexico City. "This has greatly altered the tone of the populace," Lamar wrote. "Citizens of this town of some intelligence and who are thought to be altogether friendly to our cause have since then exhibited a very unexpected opposition to us."[14] In April 1848, three of the most influential citizens—Basilio Benavides, José María Ramon, and José María Gonzales—wrote the American commander in Monterrey to protest American rule over their town. Laredo had not prospered under American rule, as Lamar would have everybody believe.

Instead, Lamar's Laredo Guard had committed unnamed "oppressions of great magnitude." One citizen had been assaulted in his home, whereas others complained of their property being stolen and their cattle carried off by the hungry soldiers.[15]

If the conduct of the Laredo Guard was an example of American rule, the three men wanted no part of it. But Lamar was unwavering. "Texas extends from the Sabine to the Rio Grande, and no portion within these limits has belonged to Mexico since the year 1836 when Texas won her independence," he lectured the townsmen.[16] "The government of Mexico has not employed you to sustain its rights; it pays you nothing for your assistance, and the vindication of its cause cannot benefit the town of Laredo," he continued. According to Lamar, the citizens of Laredo were "contented and happy." Their "personal rights have been protected and their families have been defended from the Indians."[17] In reality, he argued, they had "enjoyed the greatest liberty, prosperity and peace under the laws and institutions of the United States." "I am sorry that it is my duty to state that you can never realize your desires for the re-establishment of the authority of Mexico on this side of the Rio Grande. I have often told you this truth. Such a thing is impossible. Whatever you may believe to the contrary, Mexico has lost Laredo forever."[18]

Lamar gave the leaders of Laredo three choices: they could "submit to the laws of the United States . . . leave the country, or . . . take up arms." If they chose the first, Lamar was sure that "great good" would "result to them and to their children." "But if contrary to reason and experience, they should choose the last, then inevitably a thousand misfortunes will flow, and they will approach their total destruction." Three days later, when Lamar learned the three leaders were intent on sending a courier into the Mexican interior "for the purpose of invoking the aid of the public authorities," he warned the men they were "leading the people of their country into trouble."[19]

On January 28, 1848, several months before the ratification of the Treaty of Guadalupe Hidalgo, the Texas legislature moved to create Webb County, with Laredo as its county seat. The county was named after Virginia-born

James Webb, Lamar's close friend and adviser, who had served in the Republic of Texas as secretary of the treasury, secretary of state, and attorney general. After consolidation with Encinal County four decades later, Webb County would become the largest county east of the Pecos River and the sixth largest in the Lone Star State.[20]

In the hot summer of 1848, the reality of what Lamar had been saying was emphasized once again. General Scott had not been defeated, as had been rumored, but had won a series of bloody battles and marched triumphantly into the *zócalo* of Mexico City after one of the most brilliant military campaigns in American history. A treaty of peace between the two warring republics, the Treaty of Guadalupe Hidalgo, had been signed, and the Rio Grande had become the permanent boundary between them. Laredo was now divided. Citizens on the less populous south bank of the river were forced to form a new municipal government under the leadership of Andrés Martines. Although citizens living on the north bank of the river could retain their Mexican citizenship, a few families decided to relocate to the south bank, although never as many as later described by local myth.[21]

The end of the war between the United States and Mexico brought a great deal of anxiety and uncertainty to Laredo. In July 1848, a "robbing party" of sixty Texas Rangers who were on their way out of Mexico plundered Sabinas, Coahuila, 170 miles to the west, and the community feared that they would turn east and sack Laredo, as the Somervell Expedition had done in 1842. The forty men from Lamar's First Texas Cavalry who were still in the town were no match for the six-shooter-wielding Texas Rangers commanded by Walter P. Lane and Gideon K. "Legs" Lewis. After killing a "Mexican" on the south bank of the river, however, the Rangers continued north, and the citizens breathed a sigh of relief.[22]

There was even more insecurity over the ability of the Tejano population to hold on to their lands. In February 1850, there was even talk in Brownsville that the Americans would annul all the land titles in the Nueces Strip, or that to defend their property the landowners would be forced into expensive litigation and ruinous lawsuits. One prominent American in the lower valley advertised in the *Brownsville American Flag* on June 2, 1847, that "Mexican law and authority are forever at an end" in the Nueces Strip, and that "by the laws of Texas no alien can hold real estate within its limits."[23] Several individuals in the lower valley went as far as to propose a territorial government that would be allowed to form a provisional government and quickly adjudicate land titles. The separatist movement never gained either momentum or legitimacy, however. Senator Thomas J. Rusk denounced the separatists on the floor of the United States Senate on March 11, 1850, for their dirty intentions, and Gov. Peter H. Bell and the Texas legislature moved to establish a commission to investigate and recommend for confirmation to the state legislature all land claims. William H. Bourland and James B. Miller, experienced public officials, were appointed to what came to be known as the Bourland Commission. Claimants were asked to submit evidence of title and a description of the land they claimed. An affidavit was also to be submitted, stating that their documents were not forged or antedated.[24]

After several delays, the Bourland Commission arrived in Laredo in the heat of July 15, 1850. At first Laredoans were suspicious of the commissioners and their attorney, Robert Jones Rivers, but County Clerk Hamilton P. Bee assured the landowners of the commission's honest intentions, and fifteen claims, including all the lands the Benavides family had inherited through decades of Spanish and Mexican rule, were eventually submitted. Sensing the urgency of the situation, Bourland hurried back to Austin and submitted the list to Governor Bell. On September 4, 1850, the legislature confirmed the rancheros' fifteen claims and a giant sigh of relief could be felt all the way to the border.[25]

With the end of the Mexican-American War and the departure of Captain Lamar's Laredo Guard, county judge James Wilkinson complained that Laredo was constantly being "annoyed by the Indians, who prevent[ed] the people from cultivating their ranchos." No soldiers of any kind lived within 140 miles of the town, and the people were yearning for "suitable protection." Hoping to nudge Governor George Tyler Wood into action,

Ringgold Barracks and Rio Grande City.

Following the war between the United States and Mexico, the army established a chain of military posts along the Rio Grande from Fort Brown at Brownsville to Fort Duncan at Eagle Pass, and then along the San Antonio–El Paso road all the way to Fort Bliss in far West Texas. Seen in the distance is Ringgold Barracks, a half-mile below Davis's Ranch, or what became Rio Grande City. Col. Santos Benavides established his headquarters at the post in the latter months of the Civil War. *Emory,* Report of the United States and Mexican Boundary Survey (1857–1859). *Courtesy of the Center for American History, University of Texas at Austin.*

Wilkinson pointed out that the area around Laredo had at one time sent one hundred thousand head of sheep to Mexico City, but that fewer than five thousand now remained in the entire county. Everyone in the area suffered constantly from the "external dread of being killed by the Indians at their ploughs."[26]

On March 3, 1849, Santos watched as the US Army arrived in Laredo to establish a permanent military post. Thirty-three blue-clad men of the First US Infantry commanded by 2nd Lt. Egbert Ludovicus Vielé came trampling into Laredo from Ringgold Barracks at Rio Grande City. Camp Crawford, named for James Madison's secretary of war, William Harris Crawford, was established less than a mile west of the town in a big bend of the river, just below the Paso de los Indios.[27] Unfortunately, Second Lieutenant Vielé and his men arrived in the midst of a terrible cholera epidemic that ultimately killed half of his small command and devastated the community. Decades later, Vielé also remembered having to "repress the forcible enlistment of recruits for the Mexican army, which was several times attempted at midnight."[28] Vielé recalled how the community was constructed mostly of stone, including the "quaint old Spanish Catholic church" on the east side of San Agustín Plaza. Wearing his ethnocentrism on his shoulder, and still bitter at being sent at Laredo, Vielé remembered how the inhabitants of the town "led a primitive life, counted their beads, and contented themselves with a very small allotment of worldly goods." The entire region, Vielé went on to say, was "desolate in the extreme, and it sometimes remains unvisited by rains for a whole year." "On the whole, it is the most worthless part of the United States, and always will be."[29]

In 1850 a more permanent military presence was established at Laredo. Camp Crawford was renamed Fort McIntosh to honor Col. James Simmons McIntosh, who survived being bayoneted at the battle of Resaca de la Palma only to be mortally wounded at the battle of Molino del Rey outside of Mexico City. Early the same year, the mail rider from Corpus Christi who was scheduled to arrive at Fort McIntosh went missing, and around that time Tonkawas stole fifty horses near Laredo. Kentucky-born lieutenant Walter W. Hudson, a respected officer who had risen through the ranks, along with a mounted detachment of Company G of the First Infantry Regiment, went in pursuit. The trail of the stolen animals led northeast through the brasada toward the Nueces River. On the fourth day out of Fort McIntosh, the trail of the Indians split, and the men agreed that Lieutenant Hudson would follow one trail while West Point lieutenants Egbert Vielé and Samuel Beckley Holabird would follow the other. On April 7, 1850, after a close pursuit covering several miles, Hudson's bluecoats recovered most of the stolen horses. The lieutenant decided to continue the pursuit only to become involved in a fierce fight with the Indians, who had taken refuge in a mesquite thicket. As Hudson and his men galloped up to the mott, bullets and arrows flew. One private was killed instantly, while a sergeant and two other enlisted men were wounded, the sergeant seriously. Although hit in the leg with an arrow, Hudson chased after one of the Indians who was on foot and killed him instantly with his six-shooter. No sooner had the lieutenant dismounted than several Indians rushed up and shot him with three arrows.[30] The badly bloodied lieutenant managed to grab his saber and slash about before he collapsed. Although the soldiers captured several rifles and horses from the Indians and recovered the saddle and saddlebags belonging to the Corpus Christi mail rider, any further pursuit was called off so the wounded could be cared for.

In critical condition, the young lieutenant and the other wounded were carried back to a water hole where the soldiers rested through the night and cared for the injured. Of Hudson's ghastly wounds, the most serious had been made by an arrowhead buried deep in his chest. The next morning the group was met by the post surgeon with an ambulance. Eleven days later, at Fort McIntosh, Hudson died of his wounds and was buried after a somber ceremony in the newly designated post cemetery.[31] He was the first regular army officer killed in the Indian wars in Texas and the only officer stationed at Fort McIntosh ever to die in combat. Seven years later, a remote outpost on the Devils River was named in his honor.[32]

On September 24, 1850, a twenty-eight-man company of Texas Rangers commanded by Capt. John S. "Rip" Ford arrived in Laredo, having been sent to South Texas by Governor George T. Wood. It was Santos's first glimpse of Ford, who would become his commander and adversary in a bloody conflict a decade later.[33] Like most Mexicans and Anglos on the frontier at the time, Ford saw the Indians as impediments to civilization. He thought they were savages, and if they did not surrender, he hoped to kill every single one of them. "An aggressive policy is the only one which will force the Indians to sue for peace," Ford wrote. "They should be made to feel the iron hand of war upon their hunting grounds, and within their lodges. Whip them and then talk of peace."[34]

Reaching Laredo, the Rangers went into camp at Fort McIntosh to rest and resupply. The Rangers, who were said to prefer "intoxicating liquors" to other forms of recreation, offered a striking contrast to the more disciplined army regulars at the post. The Texans looked down on the bluecoats for their lack of riding skills, and in one instance the Rangers deliberately spooked the troopers' horses "to see the mounted infantrymen go to the ground like so many bags of sand." Ford blamed the army for the increasing violence on the frontier, since he believed they had not done a proper job of confronting the Comanches and other hostile tribes. Moreover, the bluecoats "did not understand or appreciate the Indians' mode of fighting."[35] At the same time, the army regulars looked down on the Rangers as uncouth and uneducated frontiersmen who possessed little sense of civility.

Despite the presence of the garrison at Fort McIntosh, in August 1852 forty-four Laredo citizens petitioned Governor Peter H. Bell for more protection from raiding Native Americans. The Laredoans asked that officers and other men be recruited from among "those who have been the sufferers." Such men would be better received on the border than "Rangers brought from a distance."[36] Help came in August when a company of Rangers commanded by Capt. Owen Shaw and Lt. Edward Burleson arrived in Laredo before going into camp about thirty miles upriver, where they requisitioned supplies from Hamilton P. Bee.[37] Shaw had left Austin with only twelve men and had enlisted more recruits as he rode south, although he discharged two of the recruits for otherwise unspecified "misconduct of the worst kind."[38] In San Antonio he had obtained enough supplies to last his men until they reached Laredo. Plenty of beef was available in Laredo, although Bee was forced to supply the Rangers with corn from Mexico.

Although Captain Shaw and his men brought some semblance of order to the area, by December 1852 citizens from the small community of Bellville (Zapata) were complaining that the Rangers were keeping the animals they had seized from the raiding Indians instead of returning the animals to their owners. Governor Bell promised Henry Redmond, a leading merchant at San Bartolo, just upriver from Carrizo, that any animals taken from the Indians would be returned to their legitimate owners. Some of the stolen goods recovered from the Indians could be kept by the Rangers, however.[39]

At Fort McIntosh, the Fifth US Infantry and local laborers spent the first two months of 1853 constructing a small star-shaped earthen field fortification. Maj. Richard Delafield of the Corps of Engineers, who had graduated first in his West Point class of 1814, was in charge of construction. The earthwork was located on high level ground that overlooked the Paso de los Indios, a favorite low-water crossing on the river. Opposite Mexico and fifty feet above the river, the earthen fort was approximately one hundred by one hundred feet in size, with the longest points of the star jutting out toward the northeast and southwest. A large magazine overlaid with earth, complete with descending steps, arched roof, and iron doors, was built in the southeast part of the fort. But the fort was built with the Mexican army in mind, not raiding Comanches; within a few years the earthwork had been abandoned, and the wind swept it away.[40]

During the antebellum period, the number of soldiers at Fort McIntosh varied from a high of 444 in 1854, when the entire Fifth Infantry, complete with regimental band, was stationed at the post, to a low of twenty-six in 1858, when only one company of the First Infantry was present.[41] Nine men who commanded Fort McIntosh in this era would become generals during the Civil War (six Federals and three Confederates) and command vast armies. One Confederate, Virginia-born James Edwin Slaughter, a young lieutenant who helped supervise the building of the star-shaped earthwork at Fort McIntosh in 1853, would become Santos's controversial commander on the Rio Grande in the waning days of the war.

The army brought a degree of protection to the town that was much appreciated by the Benavides family and other townsmen. Consequently, there was little animosity between the Anglo military and the majority Tejano populace. The military boosted the local economy, and Santos's store near the plaza prospered, despite the fact that most of the soldiers bought their personal items from the post sutler. Although the army freighted supplies from San Antonio, Corpus Christi, and Brownsville, a considerable amount of foodstuffs was purchased locally. Citizens of Laredo helped supply the post with forage for the army's horses and mules, and as many as 140 tons of hay were bought annually by the army at sixteen dollars per ton. Soldiers bought corn, beans, and onions from townsmen, as well as wood and beef. Tejano teamsters, wheelwrights, and blacksmiths were also employed. The army needed scouts, guides, and interpreters, and the Tejanos proved particularly adept. Washerwomen and seamstresses were always needed, and prostitution near the post and San Agustín Plaza flourished.[42]

At least once during the antebellum period, the army helped to restore civil order in Laredo. On June 24, 1854, a delegation headed by Basilio Benavides asked Col. Gustavus Loomis of the Fifth Infantry to assist the locals in arresting the vagrants and other lawless elements who frequented the town.[43] A year later, Lt. James E. Slaughter, quartermaster at the post, complained of the large number of filibusters in Laredo who were threatening the stability of the border. They had already assaulted one of the officers at the post and threatened to kill another.[44]

However, the degree of lawlessness in Laredo in the decade prior to the Civil War is best exemplified by a nasty incident from June of 1854, two years before Santos became mayor. Both the citizens and the garrison at Fort McIntosh were on edge after several days of temperatures over 115 degrees and the hanging of a murderer on San Agustín Plaza. Nowhere was the heat worse than at the fort, where many of the soldiers lived in canvas tents. Conditions in the town, where alcohol flowed freely, were said to be "choleric." A special correspondent to the *New York Daily Times*, who wrote under the moniker "Texas," described Laredo: "Bad people sell bad brandy, which drives bad men mad, and they devour each other." Not a "single thing . . . agreeable to see, hear, smell, touch taste or tell" could be found in Laredo, according to Texas.[45]

In the heat of the early summer, a Mexican circus owned by Pedro Carrera arrived in town. One of the acts that drew large crowds featured several rope dancers, and present at one of the performances was Achilles Centro, band master of the Fifth Infantry at the fort, along with a former assistant surgeon from the US Navy named Linton. The surgeon was said to have been at one time a talented physician of "manly and gentlemanly bearing" who had lost his way and drifted to the Rio Grande frontier, where he had led a "chequered life" for several years. In a state of obvious inebriation, Linton made sexual advances toward Centro's attractive wife, after which the bandmaster angrily warned the surgeon to stay away. Linton left the scene but returned a few minutes later and threatened to shoot Centro. In an attempt to arbitrate the dispute, Carrera stepped between the two men, only to be shot dead by Linton. The intoxicated surgeon then turned the pistol on Centro and killed him, too. Realizing what he had done, Linton fled across the river to Nuevo Laredo, where he became involved in another row and was promptly disarmed and arrested.[46]

In the meantime, angry soldiers and a few citizens had gathered on the north bank of the river to demand justice. A committee was appointed, and its members crossed to Nuevo Laredo, where they persuaded the alcalde to turn Linton over to them. Linton was bound and ferried across the river. At least twenty angry soldiers waded into the Rio Grande to seize Linton and drag him up the riverbank to San Agustín Plaza, where a gallows had already been erected. Within minutes, a judge and jury had been selected, witnesses heard, and Linton found guilty. The box on which he stood was kicked from under him, and the errant surgeon was left swinging in the darkness. After several hours his body was cut down and mutilated and the corpse thrown into a shallow grave.[47]

Soldiers were certain Fort McIntosh had to be the most undesirable post in Texas, if not the entire West. Lydia Spencer Lane, wife of one of the officers at Fort McIntosh, arrived in Laredo in 1854, just in time for a hot and dreadful summer. "The houses were mere shells, entirely exposed to the baking sun all day long," she wrote. "Not a green thing was to be seen but a few ragged mesquite trees. Here and there a blade of grass attempted to grow in the scorching sandy soil, but it was soon burned up by the hot sun. Back of our quarters was quite a large yard, but there was not a living thing in it, except tarantulas, scorpions, and centipedes, with an occasional rattlesnake for variety."[48]

Two years later, during another very hot summer, Capt. Randolph

Barnes Marcy of the Fifth Infantry assumed command of the post. A noted cartographer, geographer, trailblazer, and soon-to-be author of the best-selling *Prairie Traveler: A Handbook for Overland Expeditions*, Marcy hated army life at Laredo. With the thermometer at 110 degrees on July 14, 1856, the captain sat in his shanty and wrote his daughter: "I am perspiring from every pore although I have neither coat or vest on and there are ten thousand flies that are continually biting and annoying me so that between fighting flies and trying to keep cool my time is pretty well occupied." Marcy walked the one mile to Laredo several times a week to study Spanish for two or three hours and to try to understand the local culture. The people of Laredo were the "most co[u]rteous people in the world," he wrote. The captain was amazed at the freedom of the women in the community. Once, when his Spanish teacher was absent, the man's wife took a guitar from the wall of their home and sang to Marcy in Spanish. The community frequently held dances to which the officers from the post were invited. The women in Laredo were fashionably dressed and danced "polkas, quadrilles, and waltzes . . . with great grace," Marcy said. On other occasions dances would be held at the post with members of the community invited. But the drudgery and weariness of army life weighed heavily on the soldiers and led them to desert in record numbers. "There is nothing new here from one month to another. We lead a life of monotony and quiet and have but little to excite or interest us except the arrival of the mails," Marcy concluded.[49]

Capt. Albert Brackett also complained of the summer heat in Laredo. "This country is a miserable apology and the thermometer in the daytime stands generally at from 102 to 108 in the shade and 125 in the sun," Brackett told his brother. "This is the truth and no romance. We have no rain, no grass and corn is worth $1.50 cents per bushel," the captain went on to say. "Our mail arrives but once a week and we are too far out on the frontier for people at a distance to feel much interest in our position or the state of affairs."[50]

In March 1856, in the same year that Santos Benavides became mayor of Laredo, Lipan Apaches swept down on the Rio Grande with a viciousness that had not been seen in decades. Beginning in late February, the "wicked Lipan," Santos said, struck the outskirts of the town and stole valuable horses, although the troops at Fort McIntosh were only a stone's throw away. The horses that were not stolen were shot full of arrows, as was the Lipan custom.[51] Two days later, the raiders made off with more horses, this time from Santos's ranch on the river, fourteen miles above town. One of his vaqueros, Victor Botello, was violently assaulted, stripped naked, stabbed, and otherwise "horribly treated." Bleeding profusely, he was left for dead but was later found and carried to Laredo.[52] Botello told Santos he had been approached by three Lipan warriors and a Mexican man led by Chief Castro, who complained that soldiers had taken their horses. In all, seven people from Laredo, including the wealthy and prominent Crisento Vela, were killed by the Lipan Apaches. Once again, church bells pealed into the morning air. Fresh graves were dug in the churchyard, and fear swept through the community. Recently planted cornfields as far as twenty miles upriver and downriver had to be abandoned.

Although the troops from Fort McIntosh, along with sixty men raised in the town by Santos and Basilio, went galloping off after the raiders, they were only able to recover a few of the stolen animals. Realizing they were being pursued, the Lipans rapidly crossed the river into Mexico and, after gaining the south bank, turned to mock the troops.[53] In a lengthy letter written on March 9, 1856, Santos pleaded with Santiago Vidaurri, governor of Nuevo León, for assistance. He was hoping that Governor Vidaurri would allow forces from Texas to cross into Mexico in pursuit of the hostile Apaches. Authorities in Texas, as well as Governor Juan José de la Garza in Tamaulipas, Santos anticipated, would do more to halt the unremitting Indian raids.[54]

For two months, the Apache incursions were "incessant and disastrous," Hamilton P. Bee wrote. The Lipans were frequently seen less than a hundred yards from the outskirts of town. In fact, at noon on March 12 they were brazen enough to attack one of Bee's wagon trains on the Corpus Christi road, in sight of the town. One of the cartmen was wounded while the others fled into the chaparral.[55] The entire wagon train would have been plundered had not several citizens rushed out to save the supplies. A mounted patrol from the Fifth Infantry at Fort McIntosh led by Lt. Henry F. Witten trailed the Lipans for fifty miles but was unable to overtake them. Bee had just returned from a session of the legislature in Austin, and he immediately wrote Connecticut-born governor Elisha Marshall Pease to plead for assistance. If Bee and Santos could just get some help, Bee promised they would "exterminate the race" on their own.[56]

On the evening of the raid on Bee's wagon train, seventy-eight of the town's prominent merchants, ranchers, farmers, and political leaders assembled in the Webb County Courthouse to draft a petition to Governor Pease. One of the town's leading attorneys, Edmund J. Davis, was selected to chair the committee, and Tómas Treviño was made secretary. Santos and Davis were selected for the Committee of Correspondence to assist in drafting a bilingual document to send to the governor. As the result of the "late outrages," they wrote, a "panic prevails [in the community]. The solemn church bell, [tells] us that another and another of our citizens have been murdered. The shrieks of the wife and children over . . . a corpse with arrows still resting in the wounds" were lamentable, they wrote. Citizens of Laredo were driven "almost to despair," and if something was not done soon, the county would be "completely depopulated."[57]

"Very many of the citizens have been murdered from time to time by the Indians," Capt. Albert G. Brackett wrote from Fort McIntosh in June 1857. "A certain band of Comanches with a few straggling Lipans and Carrizos infest the country, and some of them had the audacity to come into the fort one night and steal two horses," Brackett told his brother.[58] Fort McIntosh had only twenty horses at the time, and the infantrymen were helpless against the Lipans and Comanches. A company of Mounted Rifles was stationed upriver at Fort Duncan, but by the time they had been notified there was little hope of any pursuit.

Once again, the townsmen demanded that Governor Pease send a mounted force to protect them. They wanted a rapid and decisive retaliation against the Lipans, even if it meant the "destruction of the whole tribe." No less than two hundred men from the counties of Nueces, Bexar, Starr, Hidalgo, and Cameron should be formed into a frontier regiment to fight the Lipans and Comanches. To help detect who was guilty, Robert S. Neighbours, the agent for the Lipans who was supervising the distribution of rations at Fort Inge at Uvalde, should compile a list of all Indians who were absent from camp for "more than a few days at a time."[59]

Within weeks, Governor Pease promised to redress the "citizens in their distress." The governor wrote to Secretary of War Jefferson Davis asking that a cavalry unit be stationed at Fort McIntosh. Hoping to spur Davis into action, the governor included a copy of the minutes of the Laredo meeting. Pease pointed out that the infantry stationed at Fort McIntosh was "entirely inadequate" for the defense of the middle border. He also sent a similar letter to the commander of the Department of Texas, Gen. Persifor Smith. Pease asked Indian agent Neighbours to undertake an investigation to determine if the Lipans were indeed to blame, as the leaders of Laredo were asserting.[60]

Santos also sent a petition with the names of "various residents" of Laredo to Governor Vidaurri, outlining the scarcity of basic foodstuffs, especially flour and corn, and begging him for assistance. Farmers had planted their crops along the river as they had for decades, but the intensity of Indian raids had prevented the men from irrigating and tending to them. Santos was hoping the governor would forgo any export duties so Laredo could more easily be supplied with goods from the Mexican interior. "You know how much we have suffered," Santos told the governor. As "Mexicans don't we deserve something from the government?" he asked.[61] In times of crisis, Santos and the citizens of Laredo looked more to Vidaurri and Mexico for assistance than to Austin or Washington, DC.

With only a few brief pauses, the war with the Lipans and Comanches dragged on for the remainder of the decade. In 1857, following a raid near Laredo, Santos, along with twenty-five citizens, was reported to have ridden 250 miles in pursuit of a raiding band of Native Americans. He and his men caught up with the raiders near Roma, dispersed them in a running battle, and recovered the goods they had stolen.[62] The villages on the Mexican side of the border, weakened by the large percentage of young men being conscripted in the struggle against the federal government in Mexico City, had been under increased threats from the Native Americans in Texas. To his credit, it was Governor Vidaurri who took the cries of the border communities seriously, and with Santos's blessing and encouragement, declared war on the Lipans. The governor's highly organized local military, including the cavalry under Col. Mariano Escobedo and Capt. Julian Quiroga, was decidedly effective against both the Comanches and Lipan Apaches.

When a band of Seminoles stole a herd of horses near Laredo in February 1859, Santos gathered a party of men and followed the Indians all the way to Santa Rosa (Muzquiz), Coahuila, where he sought the assistance of Jesus Garza, a local jefe who had influence with the Seminoles. Garza was able to summon the Indians and urge them to give up the horses. In a letter to Vidaurri, Santos apprised the governor of his activities and was highly complementary of Garza.[63] As it turned out, however, the Seminoles had already traded the horses to a band of Comanches for several buffalo robes. In his letter, Santos expressed the hope that Vidaurri would draft a proclamation that would appeal to people on both sides of the border and persuade authorities in Texas and Mexico to make a concerted effort to castigate the Indians. Raids by Native Americans had become frequent, and both the "multitude of thieves on both sides of the river" and the "evils" they were committing had motivated Santos to take action.[64]

In September 1859, a raiding party of forty Comanche warriors struck south across the Nueces River into Webb County. After killing a young herder near the abandoned village of Palafox, upriver from Laredo, they moved east, and on the night of September 12 camped only a few miles from the town. Early the next day, at least twenty warriors rode east along the Laredo–Corpus Christi road, killing a citizen from the town, mortally wounding another, and stealing several horses from the mail station at Los Ojuelos. Turning south toward the Rio Grande, the raiders plundered sev-

From the south bank of the Rio Grande, Fort Duncan at Eagle Pass can be seen in the distance. Following the Union occupation of the lower valley in late 1863, vast amounts of cotton crossed into Mexico at Eagle Pass and Laredo. During the Civil War, Eagle Pass and Fort Duncan were frequently harassed and attacked by Union guerillas operating out of Mexico. Unknown artist. Wood engraving by Louderback and Hoffmann. *Emory,* Report of the United States and Mexican Boundary Survey (1857–1859). *Courtesy of the Center for American History, University of Texas at Austin.*

eral ranches, including that of Juan Farías. "Exhibiting no fear whatsoever," they continued down the river, where they took 250 horses from one of the large ranches. "[The raiders] have now been in our midst eighteen days . . . and not a gun fired at them," a correspondent for the *San Antonio Herald* complained from Laredo.[65] Refugio Benavides gathered twenty-five citizens and tracked the raiders all the way northwest to the headwaters of Los Moros Creek near Fort Clark, where they found and secured the Comanche *cavallado*, or horse herd.[66] Another party of eighteen men led by Santos Benavides had taken the field to join Refugio, but by this time the party of warriors was said to have grown to seventy men, all of whom were well armed, and the Laredoans were reluctant to attack them.

Finally, in 1861, after five years of ceaseless raids and counterattacks,

Governor Vidaurri bragged that the Lipans, in particular, had been "punished severely and exemplarily" and reduced to "a mere handful of impoverished Indians, without horses."[67] Indeed, Vidaurri brought the Lipans to their knees, and with their defeat came a degree of peace and stability on the Rio Grande that had not been felt for many years.

In the decade before the Civil War, Santos and the rest of the Benavides family began to excel in politics. At first, they watched from the sidelines as the Texas legislature agreed to incorporate Laredo. The town was divided into six wards, with each ward entitled to one councilman; the charter further called for a mayor, six aldermen, a town clerk, and a marshal to be elected annually on the second Monday of December. Both the mayor and aldermen were to "assess and collect a tax on all property . . . establish free schools, erect public buildings, improve the streets, . . . organize a patrol or city guard . . . call out the citizens for the defense of the place, collect fines not to exceed ten dollars, and establish ferries."[68]

In the first Webb County election on August 6, 1849, James A. Wilkinson, a veteran of the borderlands who had served as Lamar's interpreter, was elected county judge. At forty-two, the North Carolina–born Wilkinson had been on the border for over a decade and was well respected by the Benavides family and other prominent Tejanos in the community.[69] In reporting his own election to the secretary of state, Wilkinson told Austin that the "entire population of Webb County" was composed of "Mexicans": "but one of whom in the whole county can speak the English language." Wilkinson wanted the laws of Texas translated into Spanish, saying that the people of Laredo "[cannot be] expected to comply with the requirements of laws that they cannot read."[70] He was hoping that since Laredo had no newspaper, the laws could be published in Spanish in the *Western Texian*, a weekly newspaper in San Antonio. For several years following Laredo's incorporation, official business in the fledgling town and in Webb County was conducted in both English and Spanish, which frequently required hours of translation.

The first elected county clerk was South Carolina–born Hamilton P.

Gen. Hamilton P. Bee (1822–1897) came to Laredo as a young man with Capt. Mirabeau B. Lamar during the Mexican-American War. Bee stayed on after the war, opened a store, worked as sutler at Fort McIntosh, and became the first county clerk of Webb County. He served in the Texas House of Representatives from 1849 until 1859 and was elected speaker. Bee rose to the rank of brigadier general during the Civil War, first in command of forces along the Rio Grande, and then in Louisiana during the Red River Campaign. He and Benavides were close political allies and he staunchly defended Benavides following Santos's seizure of Nuevo Laredo in March 1863. Bee's brother, Barnard, was killed at First Bull Run. *Courtesy Texas State Library and Archives.*

Bee, who had been a lieutenant in Lamar's Laredo Guard. After the war with Mexico, the twenty-seven-year-old Bee was selected as the sutler at Fort McIntosh. At the same time, he opened a small store in Laredo, and was known to travel as far away as New York to purchase goods for the Rio Grande market. He rose rapidly in Texas politics, first as secretary to the Texas Senate, then as state representative, and then, in 1855, as speaker of the Texas House of Representatives. During his rise, he formed a lasting political alliance with the Benavides family. Like Bee, other men who came to Laredo as members of the Laredo Guard stayed on after the war and were elected to county office. But native Laredoans, such as the well-to-do farmer and rancher Nicolás Sanchez, were elected to office as well. These local elections represented a watershed in the rough and troubled political evolution of the community.

After the war with Mexico, the Post Office Department worked to establish mail routes from Laredo to Brownsville, Corpus Christi, San Antonio, and Eagle Pass. In February 1849, William Leslie Cazneau obtained a contract for a biweekly mail route to Corpus Christi at $1,250 per annum. At the same time, Cazneau also received the contract to carry the mail to San Antonio and back twice every month. A biweekly mail service using a buckboard was also established between Laredo, Brownsville, and Brazos Santiago.[71] In 1851, Hamilton Bee received the contract for a weekly mail run to Eagle Pass.[72] Three years later, Bee was awarded a four-year contract to carry the mail on the 150-mile, six-day route to San Antonio at $1,200 per annum.[73] At the same time, Bee outbid seven others including E. J. Davis, for the 140-mile, $1,100 per annum, weekly mail route to Corpus Christi. Francis M. Campbell, a Louisiana-born clerk who had settled on the border with his Mexican wife, Dolores, was able to beat out both Bee and Davis for the 285-mile, once-a-week, four-year contract for the mail route to Brownsville. In 1855, Davis did receive a four-year contract for the route to Eagle Pass, however.[74]

Santos, Refugio, and Basilio quickly adapted to the American form of government, and in less than a decade they had come to govern Laredo and

Webb County politics. Unlike other communities on the border, such as Brownsville, where the Anglos dominated politics and racism was rampant, Laredo was full of Spanish-speaking natives who rapidly mastered the system and came to govern. If outsiders in Laredo hoped for meaningful influence in the political structure of the community, they had to learn Spanish and acculturate to Mexican customs. Marrying into one of the influential Laredo families, as Raymond Martin and John Z. Leyendecker did, was also of great economic advantage.

In the first municipal election following incorporation in June 1850, Basilio picked up where he had left off under Mexican rule and was elected mayor, while Refugio was selected as an alderman.[75] At the time, only the economic elite and the educated, including the few Anglos in town, voted. Less than fifteen votes could decide an election. In 1852 Basilio became county judge and Refugio was elected mayor. The city council rented a room from Basilio on Plaza Real for six dollars a month and set out to pass ordinances that would, for example, keep hogs from running wild in the streets and limit families to having no more than one dog without paying a small fee.[76] All official documents continued to be recorded in both English and Spanish. As patriarch of the powerful Benavides clan, Basilio belonged to an older generation of townspeople who traced their origins to the last decade of Spanish rule. He carefully mentored the younger members of the family, especially Refugio and Santos, and in time his nephews came to the forefront of local politics.

In 1856 and again in 1857, Santos was elected mayor. One of his primary responsibilities as mayor was to preside over the municipal court that tried both civil and criminal cases, even those for capital murder. Another responsibility was leading the city council, which passed ordinances to regulate Laredo's traditionally rowdy and frequently violent fandangos. Licenses were required of all dance halls, and the presence of a town marshal to keep the "public peace" was mandatory.[77] The council also passed an ordinance prohibiting the firing of weapons within the city limits after seven at night, unless in self-defense. Pistols could be discharged on private property during the day but not on the two public plazas or in the streets.[78] Beginning in January 1856, no "filthy garbage" of any kind was to be thrown on the streets or public roads but was to be dumped in one of the arroyos beyond the city limits.[79] For the first time, crops produced from communal lands near the town could be sold or consumed by those growing the food. The council also passed ordinances regulating and taxing the lucrative sale of cowhides. All hides were to be registered and a small fee of one *cuartilla* paid.[80] As mayor, Santos had the opportunity to employ friends, political allies, and relatives such as Lorenzo Benavides, who became town marshal. Nepotism laws were a thing of the future, and political patronage grew unchecked.

Santos continually sought to improve the physical condition of Laredo. Of primary concern was the miserable state of the streets. After Santos stepped down as mayor in early 1858, he joined merchants Raymond Martin and John Z. Leyendecker, as well as other prominent citizens, in petitioning the city council to improve the roads. As if echoing similar complaints from the next century, Santos and the citizens sought to bring attention to the problem: "the miserable state [that] our public streets and thoroughfairs [*sic*] are in at present . . . every time we are visited by a rain of but a few hours duration. Indeed, so numerous are the mud holes in the different parts of the streets of the city that not only is locomotion both [on] foot and per carriage greatly impeaded and very often dangerous to both man and beast wandering about but on account of the stagnant water and rotten debris found therein."[81]

There was no doubt the "public health was greatly endangered . . . producing at least the cause of the long durations of sickness amongst the population of the town." The streets were a "disgrace" to the city and "only fit homes for hogs," the petitioners concluded.[82] Two years after serving as mayor, when Basilio became a state representative, Santos was easily elected county judge, and Refugio became mayor.[83]

While the Benavides family was dominating Laredo and Webb County politics, Santos enlarged his mercantile business and maintained his extensive ranching interests. Largely due to his growing political influence, he was awarded the lucrative ferry franchise that connected Laredo to Nuevo Laredo. Although a number of *chalanes*, or small boats, operated freely on the river, a larger hand-pulled ferry carried not only passengers but carriages, freight wagons, horses, and mules, and generated the most revenue. Santos profited from a growing commerce with the interior of Mexico and with Laredo's sister community of Nuevo Laredo.[84]

But both Santos and his town experienced a serious economic setback in January 1859, when the commander of the Department of Texas, the aging and infirm general David E. Twiggs, issued orders closing Fort McIntosh and other border posts and transferring the soldiers to forts along the San Antonio–El Paso road.[85] Local commerce ground to a halt, and revenues from the ferry fell accordingly. Santos complained of the "total decline" of the city and asked for a reduction of his rent, saying that for the first time his debt exceeded his revenue.[86] Although the city council was sympathetic, considerable confusion and seemingly endless litigation developed over who would control the ferry, a debate that would span more than two decades and drag leading attorneys from Austin and San Antonio into the controversy.

Basilio's position in Austin gave the Benavides family additional political clout and influence in both Texas and Mexico. During the tumultuous decade of the 1850s, Santos and Basilio maintained their correspondence with José Santiago Vidaurri y Valdez, the powerful governor of Nuevo León and Coahuila. Born in Villa Punta de Lampazos, on the road from Laredo to Monterrey, Vidaurri had taken advantage of the revolt against the dictatorship of Santa Anna in 1855 to seize control in Nuevo León. Within a few years he was also in control of Coahuila and a large part of Tamaulipas. By the time of the American Civil War, *el caudillo del noreste mexicano* had emerged as one of the most powerful military and political figures in Mexico. In one of his first letters to the governor, Basilio congratulated Vidaurri for his endorsement of the Plan de Ayutla and his opposition to the administration of Santa Anna.[87] Although Vidaurri despised the extent of Mexican centralism in Mexico, the government he created in Nuevo León and Coahuila was not so different.

From Austin and Laredo, Basilio provided Vidaurri with the latest news from Texas and frequently offered the governor political advice. Vidaurri admired the government of the United States and saw American federalism as a model for his northern states. Sharing a unique borderlands history and a cultural identity as Mexicans, Vidaurri, Basilio, and Santos had a common understanding of the problems facing the border, especially those related to banditry and the seemingly endless Indian raids. All three sought economic and political stability and aspired to become prosperous in a sea of violence, poverty, and despair.[88] Basilio also understood the problems Governor Vidaurri was having with the Catholic Church and sympathized with him. Both men believed that the church imposed "suffering onto the innocent."

In late December 1859, with the Cortina War raging in the lower valley, Basilio encouraged Vidaurri to raise a regiment of troops to patrol the border. People in Texas were very satisfied with Governor Sam Houston, the hero of San Jacinto, Basilio told Vidaurri. He also said that Santos had recently been to Austin and had more details on the politics in Texas, should the governor desire to consult him.[89] As their friendship grew, Vidaurri had Mexican newspapers sent to Basilio in Austin. In response, Basilio forwarded Texas newspapers to Vidaurri in Lampazos or Monterrey, although he regretted that he did not know what they said since he could not read English. Writing from Laredo in May 1860, Basilio told the governor that everything in Laredo, as opposed to the lower valley, was surprisingly peaceful. There had been no Indian raids in months, and the only problem was the terrible and prolonged drought that killed cattle and dried up watering holes.[90]

Unlike his older half-brothers, Cristóbal, who was thirteen years younger than Santos, took little interest in local politics. Although well educated in Laredo and Corpus Christi and fluent in English, Cristóbal neither aspired nor rose to the political heights of his two brothers. As Santos's junior partner, however, he did become wealthy from his mercantile business and from his sprawling sheep and cattle ranch.[91] The youngest brother, José Eulalio, also became a wealthy sheep rancher.

One of the most talented individuals with close ties to the Benavides family was José María Rodríguez, who married Basilio's daughter Feliz. Having attended the finest schools in New Orleans, Rodríguez was fluent in French, English, and Spanish, and his linguistic eloquence contributed to his success in Laredo and in Texas politics. Rodríguez bragged that "not a drop of Indian blood" ran through his veins; he was a proud Isleño, a descendant of the Canary Islanders who settled San Antonio in 1731.[92] As a restless young adventurer, Rodríguez had been lured to the border as part of José María de Jesús Carvajal's filibustering expedition in 1851–1852 and had stayed on to teach school in Laredo. When Basilio was elected to the state legislature, Rodríguez rode north to Austin as his father-in-law's official interpreter.[93] After the Civil War he would serve as judge of Webb County for thirty-five years.

But it was John Zirvas Leyendecker, a Texas immigrant from the German state of Nassau, whom Santos would come to trust and to whom he grew the closest. With other members of his family and 138 passengers on the schooner *Riga*, Leyendecker had sailed from Antwerp, Belgium, in November 1845. After fifty-eight days on the cold North Atlantic, the family arrived in Galveston. They made their way inland to New Braunfels and eventually to the German frontier community of Fredericksburg, which had been established the previous year. John's father, John (Johann) Leyendecker, was a veteran of the Battle of Waterloo and led the Catholic services in the small community until a priest arrived.

During the Mexican-American War, the restless and ambitious John Zirvas came south from the Hill Country to Matamoros, then traveled upriver to Laredo. Working as a clerk for Bartholomew J. DeWitt, Leyendecker sold goods at Fort McIntosh and other frontier posts such as Fort Chadbourne and Fort McKavett. In 1855 he established a small store of his own in Laredo and formed a partnership with Cristóbal Benavides to buy and sell Mexican horses and corn. Besides animals and corn, Leyendecker sent beans, leopard skins, and blankets from the border to be sold in San Antonio. After his store was robbed in 1858, Leyendecker described Laredo as "rough country," but by July he had become postmaster.

In 1858, Santos obtained a $1,550 per annum, three-year contract for the twice-weekly stage and mail run to Corpus Christi that had previously been held by Fred Belden. The lowest of nine bidders, including friends E. J. Davis, Hamilton P. Bee, Charles Callaghan, and even Refugio, Santos was officially awarded the contract on April 24. The stage left Laredo promptly every Sunday and Thursday at one in the afternoon for the four-day, 140-mile ride through the brush country and across the coastal plain to the mouth of the Nueces River at Corpus Christi.[94] Santos was also awarded a three-year contract at $720 per annum for the weekly, one hundred-mile route along the river to Eagle Pass. Every time the stage failed to arrive, a fine of $6.92 was levied by the Post Office Department.[95] At the same time, Charles Callaghan outbid Davis and Bee for the weekly Laredo to San Antonio route. Early every Monday at six the stage left Laredo for the six-day, 168-mile ride to the Alamo City.[96]

With Santos's blessing, Leyendecker married Santos's younger sister, María Andrea, in an elaborate ceremony on June 1, 1857, in San Agustín Church.[97] Mixed marriages like this one, between Tejana women and Anglo and European males, were common in Texas before, during, and after the war, especially in places such as Brownsville and San Antonio. Only two months after her marriage to Leyendecker, María Andrea developed an excruciating pain in her abdomen, and five days later, she miscarried. Although frequently ill and separated from her husband for long periods of time, she gave birth to four children over the next five years. In an effort to escape the long and unbearable Laredo summers, Andrea would spend the months with her husband in Fredericksburg in the heart of the Texas Hill Country, where he also ran a store and continued to serve as a contractor with the army for the western frontier. The couple adopted an orphan in Fredericksburg on December 24, 1861.[98]

María Andrea Benavides Leyendecker, younger half-sister of Santos Benavides, and her six-month-old daughter Isabella. Andrea died of tuberculosis in September 1863, shortly after this image was made. Two years later, in August 1865, John Z. Leyendecker married Andrea's sister Juliana. *Courtesy Leyendecker Family.*

From north of the border, Santos and Basilio watched as Governor Vidaurri struggled with President Ignacio Comonfort for sovereignty over Nuevo León and Coahuila. Some in the government feared that the powerful caudillo would also seize San Luis Potosí and Tamaulipas to create a republic of the Sierra Madre that would either be independent or possibly annexed to the United States. In fact, by October 1856 Governor Vidaurri had already taken Mier and Camargo.[99] Shortly thereafter, however, he negotiated a peace treaty with the federal government in which he agreed to recognize the authority of President Comonfort and would receive eight thousand pesos a month from Mexico City as compensation for his war on the Lipans and Comanches.[100] In Monterrey, the state capital, there was considerable celebration among the *nuevoleonés*. But the struggle in northeastern Mexico had so weakened the liberals that uprisings in Guanajuato,

Morelia, Aguascalientes, and even Mexico City soon erupted. Despite the treaty with Comonfort, in January 1857 Coahuila voted overwhelmingly for union with Nuevo León, effectively coming under Governor Vidaurri's control. Vidaurri had defied the federal government and gotten away with it. In the years to come, his fierce independence would prove to be a constant irritant to Comonfort's successor, Benito Juárez, in his efforts to centralize the Mexican government. In the end, it would lead to Vidaurri's catastrophic undoing.

At the same time that Basilio and Vidaurri commenced their correspondence, Santos, too, began to communicate regularly with the governor. Over a decade, the two men became close confidants and at various times depended on one another for personal favors. When Santos became mayor in 1856, Vidaurri was ascending to power in Nuevo León and Coahuila, and the correspondence between the two intensified. On rare occasions Vidaurri made his way north to visit Santos and Basilio in Laredo, and at other times Santos rode south to see the governor at his spacious home in Lampazos or at his headquarters in Monterrey. In one of his first letters, Santos was so audacious as to tell Vidaurri that several of the political authorities in Nuevo Laredo should be removed, especially Andrés Martines, the former alcalde of Laredo who was now the customs agent and collecting tariffs without reporting the revenue to the governor.[101] In another letter, Benavides bluntly told Vidaurri that the individual the governor had sent to recruit soldiers on the border was not reliable and that the Texas expatriate Juan N. Seguín, who was living in Nuevo Laredo, was far more dependable.[102]

Lucrative business deals, usually involving the sale of arms or the buying and selling of horses and mules, became common between the two. For example, Santos assisted the governor in selling a herd of mares that was being kept on Vidaurri's vast Mesa de Cartujanos, southwest of Lampazos and north of Candela, near the Nuevo León–Coahuila border.[103] And Santos always managed to keep Vidaurri apprised of the latest news from the border, especially events in Tamaulipas that might pose a threat to the governor. Several times, Santos asked the governor for special favors. One such

Santos Benavides formed a close political alliance with the fiercely independent governor of Nuevo León and Coahuila, Santiago Vidaurri. The two men corresponded regularly and shared a common aim of peace and prosperity for the border. During a serious drought and near famine in Laredo in the fall of 1862, Vidaurri sent supplies to the beleaguered town. On several occasions during the Civil War, Benavides seriously contemplated crossing into Mexico with his small army to join the powerful caudillo. Vidaurri's execution in Mexico City in June 1867 was shocking and demoralizing for Santos. *Courtesy Lawrence Jones III Collection, DeGolyer Library, SMU.*

request was on behalf of Juana Garza, a widow who, Santos claimed, had been cheated out of $140 in silver. Vidaurri, for once, had larger concerns and wrote that he was reluctant to get involved.[104]

By 1856 Santos was actively buying weapons in Texas and selling them to Vidaurri. On March 1, 1856, Benavides was only able to deliver thirty of the one hundred rifles he was hoping to purchase for the governor, along with forty boxes of gunpowder, although Santos promised more weapons in the weeks to come.[105] Santos anticipated no problem crossing the rifles at Laredo. If necessary, he would use his influence to ship the weapons across the border at Eagle Pass, where Vidaurri could receive them and where other shipments of arms headed for the governor's growing army were being crossed.[106] For the next several years, Santos helped Vidaurri import arms into northeastern Mexico, smuggling them across the river if necessary.[107] At other times, frequently with the aid of Basilio, Santos exerted considerable effort in assisting Vidaurri to recruit men in Texas, always skirting American neutrality laws.[108]

With the profits from his mercantile business and horse-trading, Santos began purchasing land in Laredo and in the brushlands of Webb and La Salle counties. By 1851, he had acquired two and one-fourth "sitios" of several thousand acres of land in Webb County alone.[109] In January 1852, he acquired 160 acres in La Salle County, four miles southwest of Fort Ewell along Los Olmos Creek, at a place called Charco Largo not far from the Laredo—San Antonio wagon road.[110] In 1855, he was able to purchase almost half of *porcion* fourteen from Feliciano Villarreal for $59.[111] In July 1856 he acquired part of porcion fifteen, nine miles upriver from Laredo, from an illiterate Leonicio Castillo for $50. The following year he acquired part of porcion sixteen from Castillo for $48.[112] Here on the Rio Grande, Santos built a small rock and adobe ranch house, hired vaqueros, and began to graze horses, cattle, and sheep. The ranch, however, was exposed and frequently targeted by Indian raids that swept through the era in the decade preceding the Civil War.

In April 1859, to escape the summer heat in Laredo, Santos took his family to San Antonio, as he had done for several years. From the Alamo City, he wrote Vidaurri saying he was willing to travel to Monterrey to assist the governor, should Vidaurri think it necessary. The political situation in Mexico was becoming tense: Vidaurri was becoming more and more critical of the Catholic clergymen, who were refusing out of "pure vengeance" to administer the sacraments to individuals they perceived to be too liberal and anticlerical. The clergy were "converting all political questions into religious ones," Vidaurri wrote, and "doing a thousand other condemnable things."[113] "What do I do in such a situation? Turn to extraordinary measures?" the governor asked. Vidaurri went as far as to say that the Catholic clergymen, especially the priests at Lampazos and Candela, were intransigent and that there was likely to be a "lake of blood," even that Mexico would be turned into a pile of "rubble" if the Catholic Church did not rescind some of its decrees. Vidaurri wanted Santos to consult with the bishop of Texas, Jean Marie Odin, in hopes of finding two "enlightened men of that happy country" who had "nothing to do with politics" and who would be willing to serve at Candela and Lampazos.[114] If Santos could assist, he would be doing his "motherland a great service," Vidaurri said. The governor realized that Santos would have to act "tactfully," but he was willing to commission him for such a mission. There is no evidence, however, that Santos ever contacted Bishop Odin, although the bishop was known to be concerned with activities on the border and in the interior of Mexico. Odin had even made a tour of the lower Rio Grande Valley in the summer of 1858.[115]

During the 1850s, as he struck out on his own, Santos's wealth slowly increased. Although he was enumerated as a common laborer and his real estate, along with that of his twenty-five-year-old wife, Agustina, was valued at only $600 in the 1850 census, he may have deliberately underestimated the value of his property, fearing taxation, as was common. Throughout the decade, Santos took time to write letters of introduction for leading Tejanos such as Ángel and Antonio Navarro, sons of José Antonio Navarro of Texas Revolution fame, who were traveling south to Monterrey on business.[116] When Vidaurri contemplated opening a new border crossing to increase revenues, Santos promised his assistance, telling the governor that he had political influence with "a lot of friends" in Texas, especially on the border.[117] Santos expanded his mercantile company by doing considerable business with the city of Laredo. He was also investing more and more in livestock. He acted as an intermediary between Governor Vidaurri and individuals in Texas who were purchasing large herds of horses and cattle in Nuevo León and Coahuila, and Vidaurri purchased large numbers of horses from Santos, who was said to have one of the best breeding herds in the area.

In the spring of 1854, Santos had obtained the government contract for the mail route past Los Ojuelos and through the brasada to Corpus Christi, as well as the twice-weekly route north across the Nueces River at Fort Ewell to San Antonio. Hiring drivers, buying horses and mules, obtaining forage, and providing water, not to mention station chiefs, on the three routes required much effort and many hours of bookkeeping.[118] In 1860 Santos was able to obtain a four-year mail contract for the twice-weekly 210-mile Laredo to Brownsville route, along with the weekly route upriver to Eagle Pass.

At the age of thirty-eight, Santos was enumerated in the 1860 census as a merchant with real estate worth only $500 but with merchandise and personal goods valued at $5,000. By the time of the Civil War, Santos had demonstrated, one observer remembered, such "great capacity" as an entrepreneur that he had become known on the border as "the merchant prince of the Rio Grande."[119]

Since Agustina was unable to have children, the couple adopted a two-year-old girl, also named Agustina, who was the daughter of Teodoro Mela and Refugia Chavez. Exactly why the couple gave up their daughter and Santos and Agustina decided to adopt her is unknown.[120] However, taking in orphan children, even if they were not relations, was a common practice on the frontier at the time. By 1860, the family included an adopted son, four-year-old Juan, in addition to eleven-year-old Agustina. Also listed in the Benavides home at the time was eighty-one-year-old Antonia Rios, probably a maid or relative, who was described as an "invalid."[121] By

1870 Agustina had married Lázaro Garza Ayala, army officer and future governor of Nuevo León, and had gone to live in Monterrey. Fourteen-year-old Juan was attending school in Laredo, and another adopted son, Santos, age seven, was "at home."[122] Yet another son, Eulalio, Santos's illegitimate child from Guerrero, was living with Agustina and her husband in Monterrey, where he was attending school.

Santos's two-story home on Flores Street, across from the treeless San Agustín Plaza and only a block from the riverbank, had become a beehive of activity. Here the invited as well as the uninvited frequently gathered. The house was covered by so many vines and adorned with so many roses and other flowers that visitors thought the residence looked more like a tropical hacienda than a house in dry south Texas. And by 1870, Santos's real estate was valued at $7,000.[123]

In late summer 1860, looking for horses to sell at a profit in San Antonio, Santos rode downriver to Mier, where he learned the "fatal news" of an "unfortunate event" that had resulted in the death of Governor Vidaurri's chief military supporter, Gen. Juan Nepomuceno Zuazua, at the village of San Gregorio, near Ramos Arizpe, Coahuila. Realizing Vidaurri's power was imperiled, Santos took four men and hurried ahead in the direction of Cerralvo before he learned that Vidaurri was still in power. Santos told Vidaurri that he had no "interest to be a soldier" but that he would do whatever was necessary to help the governor. In September, Santos rode as far south as San Carlos in the foothills of the Sierra Chiquita, southeast of Linares, before returning to Cerralvo. Again he wrote the governor, promising to join him if necessary.

Despite his decisive defeat by the Texas Rangers and the US Army at Rio Grande City on December 27, 1859, Juan Cortina had remained a serious threat to law and order in the lower valley and in Tamaulipas. In late August 1860, Cortina was seen near Rancho Mulato, near Burgos, and at the ranch of Francisco Gomez, where he was said to be rapidly rebuilding his army, possibly in an attempt to overthrow Governor Vidaurri. All the local commanders sympathized with the elusive Cheno, Santos told Vidaurri: "Everywhere bandits are rushing to join Cortina." Although the situation was dangerous, Santos assured Vidaurri that he was "aware of everything" that happened in Tamaulipas and that he would keep the governor advised.[124]

Cortina was later seen with as many as seventy men at La Vaquería. Several prominent landholders in the area were accused of giving aid to the revolutionary, and Santos speculated that bandits known to operate in the area were likely to join forces with Cortina. Santos, still looking for horses in the vicinity of Mier, was fearful for Vidaurri, but he was also in danger himself since he was on foot, having lost three of his horses, one of which was seized by soldiers when the animal was left grazing. He was hoping to purchase horses for himself and his servant, but none of the ranchers had any for sale, and he was forced to send a message to Mier for help. Santos told Vidaurri he was willing to "sacrifice anything," to marshal all his forces, in order to serve the governor "in any way possible."[125]

There were horses for sale in Laredo, but so many of them were stolen that Santos was reluctant to purchase them for resale. He was hoping Governor Vidaurri might be able to spare some from his large Mesa de Cartujanos. In October 1860, after finally being able to put together a large herd of horses, he and Cristóbal drove them to San Antonio, where some of the animals were sold. Santos advertised "200 Spanish mares, 100 horses, and two Spanish Jacks—all in good condition," in the *San Antonio Daily Ledger and Texan*, and the newspaper vouched for him, saying he "was a most respectable man" who could be "relied upon."[126] From the city of the Alamo, Santos headed to Austin with part of the herd, while Cristóbal, only twenty-one at the time, took other animals north for sale on the San Saba River.[127] The trip north proved to be financially lucrative for the two brothers, and they did not arrive back on the border for almost a month.

After returning to Laredo, Santos then headed north again, this time to Fredericksburg to escort his sister, María Andrea Leyendecker, back to the border for the winter. Always in delicate health, María Andrea enjoyed the Fredericksburg summers. But despite the freshness of the Texas Hill Coun-

This rare albumen print of Juan Nepomuceno Cortina was likely taken in Matamoros around 1864. At the beginning of the Civil War, Benavides and Cortina fought a bloody battle at Carrizo on May 22, 1861, and remained enemies for much of the war, although Benavides had no choice but to cooperate when Cortina rose to become Governor of Tamaulipas. Although the two men were from similar socioeconomic backgrounds, they went in opposite directions. Cortina became the defiant revolutionary, while Benavides did much to defend the political and economic status quo. *Jerry Thompson Collection.*

try and the hospitality of the Leyendecker family, she always missed her extended family back in Laredo and often yearned to return to the border.[128]

As of the second week of December 1860, Santos had not yet arrived back in Laredo from San Antonio, and friends and relatives began to worry. Death was always lurking in the shadows along the San Antonio road, and threats from bandits and Native Americans had again escalated. Santos had last been seen in Atascosa County, south of San Antonio, but then there had been no further news. It was as if he had disappeared off the face of the earth. Greatly alarmed, Eulalio took a small party and headed north to look for his brother. Then, a few days before Christmas, Santos magically appeared back on the border, with no explanation for his extended absence.

By the winter of 1861–1862, the issue of slavery had come to dominate much of the political discourse, even in the far western corner of the Southwest. Caught up in the controversy were the Tejanos, who were thought by many in South Texas to be actively involved in assisting runaway slaves to reach freedom in Mexico. It was widely believed that a mini Underground Railroad stretched south from the Guadalupe River through the heart of the brush country to the Rio Grande. Although much of what was reported about Tejanos and escaped slaves was more rumor than reality, in May 1858 a plot by Mexicans to assist runaway slaves was thwarted in Gonzales. Tejanos at Goliad and San Antonio were also accused of aiding runaway slaves.[129] Guadalupe County, just east of San Antonio, passed a resolution prohibiting "Mexican peons" from entering the county "because of their alleged sympathy with bonds-people."[130] In March 1860 the *Corpus Christi Ranchero* reported that Rodrigo Hinojosa, enumerated in the census as a "wild horse catcher," along with his son Juan, captured two runaway slaves and returned them to their owners. "Other Mexicans help slaves escape to Mexico," the newspaper went on to say.[131]

John S. Ford, who knew as much about the border as anyone, said that "Mexicans" were actively assisting runaway slaves and that as many as three thousand former slaves, once owned by men living in Texas, had settled in small towns and villages between the Rio Grande and the Sierra Madre.[132]

During the antebellum period, María de Jesús Carvajal appealed to American filibusters by saying that he would return runaway slaves to their owners in Texas. At the same time, many well-to-do Tejanos, such as the Navarro and Seguín families in San Antonio, supported the institution and owned slaves themselves. In fact, as many as fifty prominent Tejano families, mostly farmers and ranchers in the San Antonio area, were listed on either the 1850 or 1860 slave census in Bexar and Atascosa Counties, and elsewhere in Texas, as owning slaves.

No slaves lived in either Webb or Zapata County on the eve of the Civil War. The Benavides family, like most families in Texas, had no inclination toward abolition. Yet there is no evidence they ever aspired to own slaves. Through their political connections in Austin and their large landholdings, however, they tended to identify with the slaveholding planter elite in the state.

In their desperation to reach Mexico, runaway slaves frequently passed through the area around Laredo. Tejanos there and elsewhere on the border faced a moral dilemma. Should they capture the slaves and return them to their owners for a lucrative bounty, or should they help them find safe haven in Mexico? In 1858 two slaves owned by a man named William J. Porter were caught fleeing to Mexico and thrown in the Webb County jail. Porter sent his brother and two other men to retrieve the slaves, but they somehow became involved in a fracas in Nuevo Laredo and were killed. A week later, Porter himself arrived on the border with six heavily armed men. He met with the alcalde of Nuevo Laredo and demanded the murderers be arrested, but nothing was ever done.[133] In the meantime, David M. Level, a forty-five-year-old Virginia-born wheelwright living in Laredo, had somehow obtained possession of the slaves and returned them to Porter.

The most explosive incident involving runaway slaves in Laredo came several months later, on November 5, 1860. In a letter written to Henry and William Maltby's secessionist, pro-slavery *Corpus Christi Daily Ranchero*, a forty-one-year-old Irish-born clerk named Michael Lidwell, a political ally of Santos who was living in Laredo at the time, said that a black man claiming to be a "free Negro" had arrived at Laredo with two dun horses and persuaded the ferryman to allow him passage to Nuevo Laredo. After the news was quickly passed along to Santos that the man was probably a runaway slave, he gathered ten vigilantes armed with rifles and pistols and at eight that evening crossed to Nuevo Laredo. "In the face of the entire population of the place," Santos was said to have "seized the negro" and succeeded in "making good his retreat [with] his men to the boat."[134] The moment the party pushed off from the Mexican bank of the river, however, Mexican guards "opened a heavy fire upon them," severely wounding Fenis Mussett, a rabid secessionist and the customs collector from Carrizo. The rifle and pistol fire was returned "as warmly as the number of the party assailed could allow." Reaching the north bank of the river, the men dragged the wounded Mussett along with the runaway slave up the steep bank and scurried off to the safety of the town, where their captive was lodged in the city jail.

The *Ranchero* went out of its way to praise Santos for being "foremost in confronting danger in support of the laws and institutions of Texas." It was not the first time Santos had "distinguished himself in restoring runaway slaves to their owners," the *Ranchero* went on to say.[135] The newspaper also praised him for his refusal to "receive any recompense for his exertions." The writers hoped that Santos, through his actions, had gone a long way toward alleviating the widely held idea in Texas that people of "Mexican origin" were not loyal to the state. His daring actions had proven that citizens on the Rio Grande frontier were as committed as the most "rabid orator." In a few comments on November 17, 1860, the *Ranchero* again praised Santos for daringly crossing into Mexico to retrieve the runaway slave.[136]

Exactly how many slaves gained their freedom in Mexico is uncertain, but there is little doubt that thousands were successful in crossing the river. Although considerable economic incentive drove the capture and return of runaway slaves—rewards were as much as $300 in some cases—many less fortunate Tejanos, victims themselves of a social and economic system that viewed them as second-rate citizens, were thought to have identified with the plight of slaves and even assisted them in their long and dangerous trek. And at the same time that slaves were fleeing south across the border, peons, victims of a medieval, coercive labor-contract system dating back to the Spanish conquest, fled north from Mexico, hoping for a better life in Texas. During the Civil War, Santos and his men frequently pursued peons who were escaping from wealthy landowners and merchants in Tamaulipas and Nuevo Leon.[137]

Amid the heightened politics of the era, citizens of Laredo voted in the hotly contested gubernatorial election of 1860, which pitted Sam Houston against the incumbent, Mississippi-born Hardin Richard Runnels. In the race for governor in 1857, Runnels had been the only man to ever defeat Houston. The contest for governor in 1860 in the midst of the Cortina War was different, however. Runnels's mediocre record as governor, including his controversial attempt to put the Texas legislature on record as favoring the reopening of the African slave trade, combined with Houston's effectiveness as a campaigner and his promise to better defend the frontiers of the state, gave the hero of San Jacinto a victory by a vote of 36,227 to 27,500. The independent and pro-union Houston proved himself popular with Tejanos in San Antonio and on the border, and he carried Webb County by a vote of 110 to 90. In Zapata County, however, where a clique of pro-Southern office holders, merchants, and landowners controlled the ballot box, Runnels prevailed by a vote of 130 to 42.[138] Locally, Basilio, who had just finished a term as chief justice of Webb County, was elected to the House of Representatives, thus becoming one of only five Tejanos to serve in the state legislature during the nineteenth century. Santos was destined to be one of the five. Arriving in Austin, Basilio was appointed to the Committee on Public Lands and the Committee on Joint Indian Affairs. Unable to communicate effectively in English, Basilio chose his well-educated son-in-law, José María Rodríguez, as his interpreter.[139]

Back in Laredo by January 1861, Santos complained to Governor Vidaurri that a herd of horses Manuel Garza González and Juan Olivares had sold near Saltillo had actually been stolen from his ranch. Santos contemplated going to Saltillo to identify the animals, but with the growing violence on the border, he was fearful of traveling unless with a party of men. He had been in San Antonio, where he heard "loud rumblings of the separation of the South," and Basilio was in Austin, where the secession crisis was escalating.[140] Basilio had recently written Vidaurri from his ranch outside Laredo, saying that people were greatly worried that the candidate from the Republican Party, a man named Abraham Lincoln, who was not even on the ballot in Texas, was likely to win the election. If the tall prairie lawyer from Illinois did prevail, his victory was certain to "provoke without a doubt the question of slavery which is of the utmost importance and is very difficult to resolve." Learning that Vidaurri would be in Saltillo, Santos hurried south to see the governor, but when he arrived in the state capital, Vidaurri had already left for Monterrey. Back in Laredo, Santos wrote to Vidaurri that he was reluctant to make a second trip. "You know the problems one can run into when traveling alone in those parts," Santos told the governor.[141]

In March 1861 a party of forty Comanches swept down on Laredo. "The Indians are upon us," Cristóbal wrote his brother-in-law, Leyendecker. The towns and small villages upriver and downriver were virtually defenseless. Fourteen citizens from both sides of the border were killed, and a number of young boys and women were carried off as captives.[142] Santos, Refugio, and Cristóbal put together a small army of recruits, including twenty men from the small mud village of San Ignacio, nine from Guerrero, and eleven from Laredo. With Refugio as the guide and Santos as the leader, the men trailed the Comanches through the mesquite downriver in the direction of Carrizo.

Although the men from San Ignacio opted to return to their village, the three Benavides brothers led the remaining twenty men downriver in pursuit. Away from the river on the open prairie, at a place called Paraje del Gato, the brothers' posse succeeded in surrounding twenty-eight warriors, and a vicious fight ensued. One of the Laredoans, a seasoned veteran named Monico, shot one of the Comanches just as the man was hurling a hatchet at him. The Comanche was shot through the spine and was thought to be dead; he was later found unconscious but breathing and was promptly executed. Four of the Comanches lay dead when the remainder broke for safety, with the Benavides brothers and their men in pursuit. One of Santos's men was armed with a bow and arrow and shot a Comanche in the leg. "Little by little," Cristóbal told Leyendecker, "we caught up to the Indian and shot him full of arrows in his back, one in his eye, but the Indian stayed alive until he came up really close, so close that [we] shot him in the face with a rifle [and] blew him into pieces and he died."[143] Several of the Comanches who escaped were thought to have been badly wounded. One of Santos's men was killed, and three were wounded. Santos's defeat of the Comanches was heralded by newspapers throughout the state as a great victory.[144]

As the national debate over slavery intensified, however, attention on the border turned away from warring Comanches and Apaches. With the election of Abraham Lincoln in November 1860, mighty political winds swept from South Carolina across the Deep South to Texas. Secession fever grew, and Basilio brought ominous news from Austin: the nation was on the verge of a civil war. In Laredo, a most uncertain future loomed for Basilio and his nephews, especially for thirty-eight-year-old Santos.

CHAPTER III

SECESSION AND CIVIL WAR

"Good by my brother, I am a soldier."

—Cristóbal Benavides to John Z. Leyendecker, April 7, 1861

The secession crisis in the wake of the election of Abraham Lincoln in 1860 had an immediate and dramatic impact on Texas, even the small villages and towns on the Rio Grande such as Laredo. Far from the centers of power in the East, and even from Austin, Basilio Benavides wrote Governor Santiago Vidaurri to tell him that Texas was greatly agitated by the election of the rail-splitter from Illinois. The future did "not look too good," Basilio said. The South needed to be very careful with the North over the issue of slavery, which was "very difficult to resolve."[1]

At Rio Grande City on December 6, 1860, Starr County's leading citizens crowded into the county courthouse to debate the crucial question of secession. Led by John L. Haynes, a well-educated and assertive Virginia-born Unionist, several citizens rose to profess allegiance to Sam Houston and the Union. Arguing for secession, but not in favor of a Southern confederation, others spoke of somehow reviving the Lone Star Republic. At the conclusion of the meeting, a majority agreed to accept whatever action the state of Texas might take.

Upriver at the small village of Carrizo in Zapata County, Judge Isidro Vela called a meeting of the county's faithful. Gathering at the small two-story county courthouse on the village plaza a few days after Christmas, with a rare snow blanketing the landscape and a cold north wind sweeping down the valley, Judge Vela and the mercantile and ranching elite vigorously pressed for secession, while local customs collector and secessionist Fenis Mussett, apparently recovered from his wounds at Nuevo Laredo, spoke of "the felonious aggression of the Abolitionists of the North upon Southern institutions" and warned against submission to "Black Republican rule."[2]

Prominent citizens and public officials in places such as Laredo also gathered to pledge themselves to secession. In early January 1861, voters in Webb and Nueces Counties selected Philip Noland Luckett—a Virginia-born physician from Corpus Christi—and Henry A. Maltby—an Ohio-born secessionist, former mayor of Corpus Christi, and editor of the *Corpus Christi Ranchero*—to attend the state Secession Convention scheduled to convene in Austin on January 28. Although the population along the Rio Grande was overwhelmingly Hispanic, not a single Tejano was chosen for the 177-member state convention, despite the fact that José Ángel Navarro and Basilio Benavides were sitting members of the legislature. It was well-known that the majority of the Tejano population on the Rio Grande frontier was opposed to secession. John S. Ford admitted that the "Mexicans on both sides of the Rio Grande, as a general rule, looked upon the government of the United States as the most perfect of any in the world," and that they saw the actions of the "Confederates as an effort to break up the Union, and they were unfriendly."[3]

In Webb County, however, lived a "family of great influence who understood the questions upon which the South differed from the non-slaveholding states of the Union." This was the Benavides family. Ford later wrote that "the Benavides family broke ground in favor of secession" and "did the Confederacy an immense favor by declaring for her."[4] "They raised companies, fought Cortina and others, who made war upon the Confederate states," and frequently "crossed the Rio Grande, under orders, and visited upon the enemies of the Confederacy the vengeance their abortive invasions of our country had called for."[5] Ford was no doubt exaggerating both the affection that the Spanish-speaking population on the Rio Grande had for the Union and the degree to which the Benavides family supported secession, but he did not exaggerate this family's impact on the history of South Texas.

Santos and Basilio were like most Texans of their time. At first, they did not realize the severity of the crisis or that the country was tottering on the brink of disaster. On January 23, 1861, Santos told Governor Vidaurri that Texas was moving toward secession. Basilio was in Austin, and it was only a matter of time before the North and South parted ways and possibly even came to war.[6]

On February 1, 1861, before a packed and boisterous gallery of citizens in Austin, the Secession Convention voted 166 to 8 to present a secession ordinance to the people of Texas. Three weeks later, Texans voted 46,129 to 14,796 in favor of disunion. The secession ordinance was even more popular on the Rio Grande frontier than it was in other areas of the state, including the slave-holding and agricultural counties in East Texas. In the counties along the river from Laredo to the gulf—Webb, Zapata, Starr, Hidalgo, and Cameron—the ordinance was approved by a vote of 1,124 to 41.[7] In Webb and Zapata Counties, Santos would not have seen a single vote registered against secession, while downriver in Starr County, only two votes were cast in opposition. In fact, Webb County was one of only six counties in Texas where the secession vote was unanimous. Most of those who led the fight for secession on the border tended to be of the ranching and mercantile elite with close ties to the political establishment in Austin. Many others who voted for secession were economically and politically disadvantaged within the feudal patronage system of which Santos, along with the rest of the Benavides family, was an integral part.

At isolated military posts and settlements scattered across the vast southwestern frontier, including Fort McIntosh and Laredo, the winter of secession thawed into an angry spring. Increasingly heated debates came to characterize a discourse that had once been civil, and confusion and uncertainty became the order of the day. At the federal headquarters of the Department of Texas in San Antonio, seventy-one-year-old general David Emanuel Twiggs, who was known for his Southern proclivities, was in ill health, yet proud and protective of his command. On February 16, 1861, 250 zealous Texans waving the Lone Star flag swarmed into San Antonio's main plaza and occupied the rooftops and buildings housing Federal supplies and men. After ten days of tense negotiations, Twiggs was coerced into surrendering all federal property in the state. Although he was said to have wept like a child, the aging Georgian allegedly said, "If an old woman with a broomstick should come with full authority from the state of Texas to demand the public property, I would give it to her."[8]

On March 5, Basilio watched in awe as the Secession Convention, with little hesitation, declared Texas independent and voted to join the Confederate States of America. Basilio was still in Austin when, eleven days later, Unionist governor Sam Houston refused to take the oath of allegiance to the Confederate government and the lieutenant governor, New Orleans–born Edward Clark, was sworn in as governor. At a session of the district court in Brownsville, Santos's friend, Judge Edmund J. Davis, also refused to take the oath of allegiance to the Confederacy. Several months later, Basilio was selected to the Democratic State Convention that convened in Dallas on May 27, 1861, and although he arrived late, he was not the only one who was tardy. Only twenty-six counties were represented, and the convention deemed it "unwise and impolitic to make any formal nominations for governor or lieutenant governor." The convention was adjourned *sine die*.[9]

Only days after the vote to secede, the fifty-five-year-old Massachusetts-born Major Caleb Chase Sibley, a career army officer in the Third Infantry at sunbaked Fort McIntosh and a man Santos had come to know personally, received orders from department headquarters directing him to evacuate the post and turn over all federal property to authorities of the state. On March 12, following rather somber ceremonies on the parade ground at the desolate outpost just west of town, Santos watched as the Stars and Stripes were lowered and a friend and close political ally, twenty-three-year-old Irish rancher Charles Callaghan, took control. Although Callaghan had been charged with murder in July 1860, he was now designated as commissioner for the state. With twenty-five days' rations, the

Federals took up the 214-mile march for Fort Brown and Brazos Santiago.[10] If Sibley could not find transportation there, he contemplated crossing into Mexico and moving down the coast to Tampico, where he could locate a ship bound for northern waters. While he and his men were moving down the Rio Grande, however, a courier reached him with news that steamers were waiting at Indianola, and the bluecoats turned across the Wild Horse Desert for the Texas coast.

As was the case two years earlier, the departure of the Federal troops from Laredo had a devastating effect on the local economy. "The troops have left here lock stock and barrel and the consequence is that Laredo presents nearer than anything else a dismal and isolated grave yard," wrote Gardner W. Pierce, a forty-year-old, Vermont-born clerk. Once again the people suffered. Many of the poor in the community were without food and had no alternative but to "subsist upon prickly pear."[11]

No sooner had the bluecoats departed than Santos received authorization from the state of Texas to raise a company of as many as one hundred men for defense of the frontier. Charles Callaghan was named first lieutenant, Juan García was made second lieutenant, and Cristóbal would serve as sergeant. Writing from Laredo on April 7, 1861, Cristóbal wrote to his brother-in-law, John Z. Leyendecker, of enlisting in the army and described how his brother had received a commission as a captain. "Goodbye my brother, I am a soldier."[12]

At first, Santos was loosely attached to the Second Texas Mounted Rifles commanded by Col. John S. "Rip" Ford. Most of the regiment was engaged in occupying the forts along the San Antonio–El Paso road and in the southern half of New Mexico Territory, and there was little communication between Ford and Santos, who was essentially on his own. However, Ford did tell him that if the civil officials in Zapata County or any other county in the area should ask for assistance, he should comply with the request. "Your position is well chosen, and your company will, no doubt, do good service," Ford wrote in April 1861.[13]

The fighting that began the Civil War on the Rio Grande was rooted not in the issues of slavery and secession, but in the Cortina War that had swept over the lower Rio Grande Valley in 1859 and 1860. In September 1859, tired of the second-class status that characterized their lives, many Mexican Texans in the lower valley turned to a charismatic ranchero named Juan Nepomuceno Cortina, who led some seventy-five pistol-wielding raiders into the dusty streets of Brownsville. Shouting "Death to the Americans" and "Viva Mexico," Cortina and his men took possession of the town and killed six citizens, including the city jailer.[14] Although largely illiterate, Cortina issued a dramatic pronunciamiento demanding equality for Mexican Texans after retreating to his mother's ranch upriver from Brownsville. In the months that followed, he recruited a small army of five hundred Cortinistas from both sides of the border and twice decisively defeated the Brownsville militia and the Texas Rangers. At Rio Grande City on December 27, 1860, however, a combined force of Rangers and US regulars smashed Cortina, killing sixty of his men and driving his small army into Mexico.[15] Fueled by a burning resentment of the diminished status of the Mexican inhabitants of South Texas, Cortina and a few of his men remained active on the border for months.

Santos watched from Laredo as Cortina's appeal to the underprivileged villagers along the Rio Grande stretched as far as Zapata County, and Confederate authorities were sure that Cortina was poised to invade. He was moving upriver, it was said, recruiting soldiers as he went, and was intent on occupying Carrizo and even Nuevo Laredo, from which he would undoubtedly attack and plunder Laredo.[16]

Since its creation in 1856, Zapata County had been administered by a clique of merchants and large landowners headed by Henry Redmond, a crafty Englishman who had arrived on the border in 1839, shortly after Texas independence. Redmond acquired land, married into an influential local family, wisely made friends with the Benavides family in Laredo, and survived the bloody Federalist-Centralist wars that swept over the Rio Grande from 1839 to 1842. By 1861, he had developed a lucrative trading business in San Bartolo, or what some called Redmond's Ranch, just upriver from the small rock and adobe county seat of Carrizo. The rotund Redmond was instrumental in organizing the county that was named after his revolutionary friend from across the river in Guerrero, the mulatto hero of the Republic of the Rio Grande, Col. Antonio Zapata. Redmond became postmaster at Carrizo, justice of the peace, the first county judge, and, for a few years, collector of customs at San Bartolo.[17]

The political machine that ran the county included many of Santos's other friends. John D. Mussett, an articulate Arkansas lawyer, was now the acting deputy collector of customs at Carrizo, Pedro Díaz was the county sheriff, Trinidad Zampano was county clerk, Fernando Uribe was tax assessor and collector, and Agustín Díaz was district clerk. Another player in county politics and a friend and political ally of Santos was Blas María Uribe, a wealthy merchant and rancher who controlled the votes at the small mud village of San Ignacio, thirteen miles upriver from Carrizo.

The degree to which the *patrón* system controlled the county was indicated by the vote of 212 to 0 for secession. With the secession vote, however, came serious problems. Judge Vela made it known throughout the county that anyone who failed to vote in favor of secession would be fined fifty cents, a considerable amount of money for the poor who eked out a living in the small villages along the river.[18] When several individuals failed to show up at the polls, Vela ordered them arrested. What resulted was a full-fledged revolt that played right into the hands of Cortina.

On April 12, 1861, the day before the surrender of Fort Sumter in the harbor of Charleston, South Carolina, forty armed Tejanos and Mexicanos under the leadership of a thirty-nine-year-old ranchero named Antonio Ochoa seized control of the southern part of the county. Moreover, Ochoa and his followers, who took great pride in calling themselves Cortinistas, threatened to kill all the "Gringos" in the county and hang Sheriff Díaz.[19] Certain that Cortina was coming to their aid, Ochoa and his men were said to have been "marching about the county in armed bodies threatening the lives of Tom, Dick, and John Doe."[20] They "were not only attempting to prevent the county officers from taking the [Confederate] oath of office," but were "also threatening to forcibly take all public money."[21] Some feared that Ochoa would have enough men to seize the county seat of Carrizo. Eventually, the men were confronted by Judge Vela, owner of the large Rancho Clareño, who persuaded them to return to their homes. Although the dissidents backed down, they issued a pronunciamiento against the Confederacy and presented it to Judge Vela.

From his fortified ranch near San Bartolo, Redmond was in a state of panic. The insurrectionists demanded that their pronunciamiento be "forwarded to the U.S.," which Ochoa thought was "a few miles on the other side of Bexar," Redmond asserted. "[It is] hard to say how far their ignorance will lead them," Redmond went on to say.[22] From Fort Brown, Colonel Ford assured Redmond the troops at Laredo under Capt. Santos Benavides were more than capable of protecting him and the other Zapata County officials. Ochoa and his men were public enemies and their actions were treasonous, said Ford.[23]

The secessionist press in Texas followed Ford's lead in reporting that the insurrection in Zapata County had been inspired by ignorant Unionists. Ochoa and his men, it was reported, were in favor of "Old Abe, the rail splitter," and were demanding to communicate with federal authorities. With its ethnic and socioeconomic undercurrents, the threatened violence was, in reality, a reaction to Zapata County boss rule. Although Ochoa owned a small ranch near Clareño, most of his followers were poor vaqueros and *labradores* (farmers), many from Guerrero, across the river from Carrizo.[24] Some had ridden with Cortina during the Cortina War and were tired of the abuse and discrimination that had for some time been a part of the Texas political and social landscape.

To ensure peace in the county, Capt. Matthew Nolan, commanding a hastily organized Confederate company of twenty-two men, rode downriver from Santos's headquarters at Fort McIntosh. After a fifty-five-mile ride, Nolan bivouacked near Redmond's Ranch on the afternoon of April 14, 1861.[25] Although fatigued, the captain was determined to crush any resistance to state authority in the county. Judge Vela quickly issued warrants

A former bugler in the Second Dragoons, Maj. Matthew "Mat" Nolan had served as sheriff of Nueces County before the war and came to command Company G of the Second Texas Mounted Rifles. Nolan was responsible for the massacre at Rancho Clareño in Zapata County early in the war. Nolan was murdered in Corpus Christi in December 1864. Carte de visite by Louis De Planque. *Courtesy Brownsville Historical Association.*

Santos Benavides shortly after the Civil War. Neck beards had been popularized by men such as Henry David Thoreau, Horace Greeley, and John C. Calhoun. No photograph is known to exist of Colonel Benavides in uniform. *Jerry Thompson Collection.*

for the arrest of Ochoa and eighty of his men. Then Captain Nolan, Judge Vela, and Sheriff Díaz, whom the insurgents were still threatening to hang, marched for Rancho Clareño, where Ochoa was said to have his headquarters. Reaching the small river village before daylight on April 15, Nolan deployed his men around the ranch, and Sheriff Díaz ordered Ochoa's men, many of whom were still half asleep, to surrender. Most were in the process of doing so when one insurgent, according to Nolan, fired at Nolan's men, although one of the Confederate volunteers later confessed that not a single shot was fired by Ochoa or his men.[26] Nolan ordered an all-out attack on the ranch.

Outnumbered and caught off guard, Ochoa's men tried to surrender, but they never had a chance. Many were gunned down where they stood, while others were killed as they fled toward the river. Although Nolan later bragged that "nine Black Republicans" were killed in the skirmish, several of those were reported to have been noncombatants and were probably unarmed. Ochoa, the leader of the movement, was across the river in Guerrero at the time, but two of his lieutenants, Nepomuceno and Santiago Vela, were killed in the attack.[27] Looking into the incident twelve years later, a committee sent by the Mexican government to investigate problems on the border concluded that "inoffensive inhabitants were assassinated."[28]

Santos was camped with his men at Fort McIntosh when he received a letter from Colonel Ford saying the companies of Capt. Matthew Nolan and Capt. John Donelson were being withdrawn from the Laredo area and sent to the lower valley. Ford urged Santos to patrol the area between Fort McIntosh and old Ford Ewell on the Nueces River. More important, however, was the news that the long-anticipated Civil War had commenced. "The war has opened between the Confederate States and the government of Mr. Lincoln," Ford wrote briefly.[29]

In the days following the massacre at Rancho Clareño, unsubstantiated rumors rapidly spread along the Rio Grande: Cortina had formed an alliance with Federal authorities in the North, as well as Unionists in Texas, and he was preparing yet another attack on Texas.[30] Furnished with arms and

In this sketch by famed Texas artist Carl G. von Iwonski and published in *Harper's Weekly*, Tejanos can be seen "hauling wood, drawing water . . . smoking cigarritos . . . and drinking Pat's favorite," while camped on Los Moras Creek near Fort Clark at the beginning of the Civil War. *Harper's Weekly*, June 15, 1861.

horses paid for by the Unionists and hoping to reassert himself on the north bank, Cortina was again recruiting men.[31] Along with Teodoro Zamora, a leading lieutenant and the former county judge of Hidalgo County, as well as Antonio Ochoa, Cortina was reported to be marching on Carrizo to avenge the victims of the Clareño massacre. Fearing for his life, Judge Vela fled with his family to Redmond's Ranch. Although he received assurances from Mexican authorities across the river in Guerrero that they would do everything possible to apprehend Cortina and Ochoa, Vela was taking no chances. So popular was Cortina on the Rio Grande, even members of the Mexican army were deserting to join the wily revolutionary.[32] When Ford, commanding the isolated Confederate units on the vast Rio Grande frontier, received a plea for help from Redmond, he sent Santos downriver to assist the Zapata County officials. Santos hastily assembled his men on the plaza in Laredo, and they galloped off across Zacate Creek, bound for Redmond's Ranch. Pausing briefly at San Ignacio, Santos was told by several villagers who were thought to sympathize with Cortina that the revolutionary was already in possession of Carrizo and that if the captain cared for his life, he should immediately return to Laredo. Still, Santos pushed his men downriver, past Ramireño, and then to Redmond's Ranch, where the men were deployed around the small village.

Near Guerrero, Cortina was joyfully greeted by Ochoa and a number of Zapata County insurgents as a conquering hero. However, Cortina had no idea that the seemingly sympathetic alcalde of Guerrero, Juan G. Garza, was keeping Santos informed of his every move.[33] Garza went so far as to dispatch twenty-five men under José María Hinojosa to watch the main ford on the Rio Grande, just below Guerrero, in an attempt to impede Cortina's crossing. But after finding another crossing, Cortina splashed across the Rio Grande into Texas, and the next day, his advance guard skirmished with three of Santos's pickets below Carrizo. Reinforced by twenty men from Guerrero and a few men from Zapata County, including relatives of those killed at Rancho Clareño, Cortina's force was said to be growing hourly.[34]

By the morning of May 21, 1861, Cortina and seventy of his men had Santos completely surrounded at Redmond's Ranch. Cortina had sent waves of fear across Texas during the Cortina War in 1859, but he now sent two of his men under a flag of truce to the ranch in an attempt to persuade Santos to leave and let Redmond, Vela, Mussett, and their friends defend themselves. Influential citizens and friends from Guerrero crossed the river to tell Santos that Cortina's intention was to seek revenge only on Redmond and those responsible for the bloodshed at Rancho Clareño. Cortina was determined, they said, "to have Redmond's head before sundown."[35] But Santos stood firm and refused to forsake his friend. The two men had known and respected one another for over a decade, since the time Santos was serving as Webb County judge and Redmond as judge in Zapata County.

In the meantime, all sorts of rumors had reached the besieged Confederates. Cortina was reported to have between fifteen hundred and two thousand men under his command, and he was in control of both Roma and Rio Grande City. Two residents of Carrizo, Anselmo Flores and Pedro Reyna, attempted to persuade Santos to leave and let Redmond and his gringo friends defend themselves, but Santos had no doubt that Redmond's Ranch could be easily defended, especially the largest of the buildings, which was constructed solidly of stone and had been used before the war by the army. Moreover, enough water and food were available to last for several weeks. The men's morale was heightened by their possession of a six-pounder cannon along with an abundant supply of ammunition.

Several of Cortina's men were able to get within a few hundred yards of the ranch complex and fire a volley of shots at the defenders. Other Cortinistas could be seen on the small cactus-studded hills east of the ranch and across the river in Mexico. They did little more than ride around on their horses, however, a tactic Santos felt was being used to confuse his besieged Confederates. Santos, Mussett, Vela, and Redmond took turns gazing through a spyglass at the Cortinistas from Redmond's front porch.

Just as he had done when he seized Brownsville in 1859, Cortina cut all communications between Redmond's Ranch and the outside world, and through the night his men continued to fire indiscriminately into the ranch. One of Santos's couriers was captured on the river road from Carrizo to Roma, and another rider, Ángel Jiménez, was seized on the road leading upriver to Laredo. A third rider, mounted on Santos's horse, set off at a gallop and was able to get past Cortina's pickets and reach Laredo safely, however.[36] Within hours, thirty-six men under Capt. Refugio Benavides and Basilio Benavides, along with Lt. Charles Callaghan, were on their way to Carrizo, riding through the night to reach the besieged Confederates.

On the morning of May 22, 1861, after riding sixty-five miles in thirteen hours, the Laredo reinforcements ran into a party of Cortinistas near San Bartolo, and a skirmish ensued. Hearing the sounds of gunfire, Santos and his men saddled their horses and galloped out of Redmond's Ranch to join the fray. Cortina, too, heard the sounds of battle and pushed his men forward. In a running fight that began at 1:00 p.m. and lasted forty minutes, Santos and thirty-six of his men completely routed Cortina's raiders. A number of the Cortinistas appear to have been preoccupied with sacking the small two-story Zapata County courthouse and Mussett's store and were caught by surprise.[37] Seven of Cortina's men were killed in the initial charge, while several others were severely wounded. At the head of his men, Santos pursued the partisans to the river, where several more Cortinistas drowned while attempting to swim the Rio Grande to Mexico. With ten of his men, Cortina "gained the opposite side of the river in safety, and in ascending its banks, faced about, took an apparent disdainful view of his recent antagonist and master, uncovered, and with characteristic dignity, waved his hat, bidding them in the blandest tone . . . a courteous temporary adieu, informing them that he would give them another call in a few days."[38]

"Before attacking Cortina," Santos wrote in his official report, "I particularly ordered my men not to arrest any of the bandits, but to kill all that fell into their hands. Consequently I have no prisoners."[39] Eleven prisoners, some of whom were badly wounded, were shot by Santos.[40] Such had long been the fate of captured "bandits" on the Rio Grande frontier. Santos later admitted that he intended to exterminate the "whole band" and that his "prisoners were mostly dead men."[41] None of Santos's men were wounded or killed in the brief battle, although Lt. Juan García Soto and Pvt. Dario Areola lost their horses in the fight. Pvt. Ángel Jiménez, who had been captured by the Cortinistas the previous day, was liberated.

Only days after the battle at Carrizo, Santos gleefully carried the news of his defeat of Cortina north to San Antonio. When word reached Austin, accolades for the Laredo captain reverberated across the state. Ford promised to send enough Colt pistols to equip Santos's company as soon as possible, and although he did requisition the revolvers, Santos only received fifty old muskets that came by boat from Brownsville, along with some subsistence rations. In fact, many of the recruits in Texas were so desperate for weapons that the state legislature contemplated raising a regiment of Mexican Texans and arming them with lances.[42]

On May 29, 1861, Ford trumpeted Santos's defeat of Cortina in a proclamation entitled "Rout of Cortina," which repeated what Santos had said in his letter to Confederate headquarters in Houston on May 23.[43] Any defeat of the elusive Cortina was good news in Texas. "Thanks are due to Captain [Santos] Benavides and his men for their gallantry in expelling a foe from our territory," Ford wrote. "Thanks are also due to the Hon. Basilio Benavides, Refugio Benavides and the citizens of Webb County for their promptitude in going to the rescue of their fellow citizens of Zapata County, when threatened by imminent danger. They have shown themselves to be loyal to the government of the Confederate States under trying circumstances and deserve the commendation of every true friend of the South," he continued. Ford also sent a congratulatory letter to Santos: "Your judgement, ability, and gallantry in the affair receive encouragement from every quarter. I sincerely congratulate you upon your success. You and the people of Webb County have furnished indisputable evidence to the world of your devotion to the cause of Constitutional liberty."[44]

In Austin, Governor Edward Clark was equally felicitous. Prior to the battle at Carrizo, the governor appears to have had serious doubts as to the loyalty of the Benavides family, and he was overjoyed at the defeat of Cortina. "Whenever our enemies have appeared on our soil," the governor told the captain, "you and your brave men have been present and driven them back, with great honor to yourselves and the gratification of your state."[45] Clark even sent Santos an elegantly engraved pistol along with a congratulatory letter: "I am happy to believe in your hands it will always be used in the defense of your country and prove an instrument of terror and destruction to her enemies."[46] Governor Santiago Vidaurri also wrote from Monterrey to offer his congratulations.[47]

In November 1862, when Mayor Bartolo García found the Laredo city treasury $750 in debt, Santos offered to purchase several of the buildings at Fort McIntosh to help alleviate the deficit. At a special meeting, the city councilors agreed to auction the commissary building and, if the sale went well, then auction the remaining buildings. On December 11, Elentario Camacho purchased the commissary for $160, and the sale proceeded.[48] In

Santos Benavides's Civil War. *Map by Gary Zogby.*

all, several residences and buildings at the post were sold for $1,366.50 in Confederate money, which was more than enough to pay the public debt. Margarito Sanchez and Cristóbal Benavides purchased some of the larger buildings, while Santos was able to acquire two of the more neglected structures, one for $5 and another for $2. He also purchased the guardhouse for $80 and even a rock wall and an outdoor oven for $0.50, along with "some rocks forming a privy" for $3.50.[49]

As war engulfed the state, the number of runaway slaves seeking freedom in Mexico seemed to increase, as did the number of Texas Unionists fleeing persecution. Santos and his men were constantly engaged in an attempt to apprehend both. In July 1862, for example, Santos arrested two Unionists, Clug McKean and James R. Hord, and sent them to Confederate headquarters in Houston. The two men were part of the eighteen-man group led by Andrew Jackson Hamilton, a leading Texas Unionist, who had crossed the Rio Grande twenty miles below Laredo shortly before Santos and his men arrived on the scene.[50] At the same time, Mexican peons fleeing across the river in hopes of finding a better way of life in Texas also became common. In April 1861, Meliton Cardenas arrived in Laredo from Monterrey in pursuit of two of his servants. Santos gave Cardenas several soldiers to help in the search, but after three days the party returned to Laredo empty-handed.[51] Villagers on the border also skirmished with raiding bands of Native Americans, much as they did before the war. It was a time of confusion, violence, and great suffering.

On July 19, 1861, Santos received a short letter from Colonel Ford informing him that Gen. Earl Van Dorn wanted his company mustered into the service of the Confederacy as soon as possible. Van Dorn thought Santos "better qualified than any other to guard against forays from . . . disaffected neighbors."[52] Should Santos agree, Ford assured him that he and his men would be properly supplied.

By October 1861, with Cortina in retreat and the war in the East a thousand miles away, the six-month enlistments of the soldiers under Santos had expired, and several of the men were making plans to return to civilian life.

Confederate authorities in San Antonio and Houston, however, wanted the men to enlist in the regular Confederate Army for three years, or as long as the war lasted. When Capt. J. A. Settle had arrived at Fort McIntosh in early September 1861 to enlist the men into the Confederate Army, they had flatly refused. Santos told Gen. Earl Van Dorn, who was in command of the Department of Texas at the time, that the men would only agree to serve for one year and would possibly extend their enlistments for a few months but that they would not enlist for three years.[53]

A prominent graduate of the University of Copenhagen, a gifted linguist, jurist, and former militia captain from Corpus Christi, Charles Grimus Thorkeli de Løvenskiold was dispatched to the border by Governor Clark to report on the situation and try to persuade Santos and his men to enlist under the Stars and Bars. Traveling first to Brownsville in early October, Commissioner Løvenskiold learned that most of the men in the lower valley who were in state service had agreed to enlist in the Confederate Army and that at least two-thirds of the men's weapons had been either "lost or stolen." A close investigation revealed that some of the weapons had indeed been lost, but a number, including rifles and particularly pistols, had been traded for whiskey.[54]

Of greater concern to both Clark and Løvenskiold, however, was the status of Santos and his men at Laredo, as they continued to refuse to enlist for the duration of the war as other Confederate units were doing elsewhere in Texas. On October 24, 1861, Santos told Clark that he had asked Ford "to appoint some person" to muster his men "out of the service," but the colonel had refused.[55] Cognizant of the pervasive racism within Texas at the time, Santos was fearful that he and his men would be transferred away from Laredo or sent to fight in the East. Moreover, he could not understand why other companies in Ford's regiment had been allowed to enlist for only one year. Løvenskiold suspected that the insistence that Santos and his men enroll for the entirety of the war was, in some ways, a loyalty test. When the commissioner finally arrived at Laredo in late December 1861, Santos remained insistent that his men would not enlist for longer than twelve months.

Santos's company now had one hundred Hall carbines and an equal number of pistols, along with some wagons, mules, and a large amount of powder and ammunition. They also had a box of fifty muskets, and Løvenskiold had no doubt they were the best-equipped company on the border.[56] However, the new governor, Francis Richard Lubbock, was particularly fearful that the Laredo Tejanos might become hostile to the Confederacy because the men had not been paid since they first enlisted, and Løvenskiold was afraid they would refuse to give up their weapons. Many of Santos's men were poor, and their families were destitute. Some had been forced to sell off their goats and sheep for subsistence.

After Løvenskiold returned to Corpus Christi, with the status of the soldiers still in limbo, Santos sent 1st Lt. Charles Callaghan to meet with the commissioner. Arriving on the coast, Callaghan bluntly told Løvenskiold that if the Laredo Tejanos, who were out scouting for Native Americans most of the time, were not mustered out soon, they would have no alternative but to disband their own company. "I had better be on hand to muster them out properly before they disband themselves, or otherwise the officers could not guarantee the security of the arms and public property," Løvenskiold bluntly told Governor Lubbock.[57] Speaking for Santos, Callaghan told Løvenskiold that Santos had been able to persuade his men to enlist in the Confederate Army but for only one year.[58] Governor Lubbock was greatly concerned. Reporting the news from Texas, the *New York Times* delightfully quoted John D. Mussett, the deputy collector of customs at Carrizo, as saying that if Santos and his men did not reenlist, "the entire frontier from Ringgold Barracks to Eagle Pass would be exposed."[59]

In December, Løvenskiold reminded Governor Lubbock that Santos and his men had "done the state good service" and were "more effective than any of the other mounted companies on the frontier." "[They had] kept that section clear of Indians, and prevented, and are preventing, a second 'Cortina' War by lawless Mexicans." Such a company was badly needed at Laredo, the commissioner argued: "If the [Santos] Benavides company is not

The Virginia-born Gen. James Slaughter, whom Benavides had known from the time Slaughter was a young officer in the artillery supervising the building of the large star earthen fortification at Fort McIntosh. After resigning his commission in 1861, Slaughter rose in Confederate ranks to become a brigadier-general and Gen. Albert Sidney Johnston's assistant inspector general at the Battle of Shiloh. After 1863, Slaughter was transferred to Galveston where he commanded the eastern subdistrict of Texas. In Brownsville, he tried in vain to mediate the growing conflict between Ford and Benavides. After General Smith surrendered the Trans-Mississippi Department in June 1865, Slaughter held on to command in Brownsville, trying to cross as much cotton into Mexico as possible. Although arrested on embezzlement charges by Colonel Ford, Slaughter rode upriver to join Benavides at Ringgold Barracks and continued to cross cotton into Mexico, before he finally fled into exile. Slaughter eventually returned to live in New Orleans but died of pneumonia while visiting Mexico City in 1901. *Courtesy Library of Congress.*

mustered into the service of the C. S. now, they will of course disband, and it will be impracticable hereafter to get any Mexican citizen to enlist or form another company, while the state, as well as the Confederate Government, will be blamed and rendered unpopular about it." The Tejanos were certain to "attribute their non-acceptance to prejudice against their nationality."[60]

In comparison to other troops Løvenskiold had inspected in Texas, who were "void of discipline, self-esteem, or esprit de corps," the soldiers from Laredo clearly stood out, and Santos was to be praised for his "high abilities" and his discipline. In nine months only four men had deserted, and only two weapons had been lost. "History and posterity may bear witness to your deeds of valor and patriotism in the Southern cause," Løvenskiold told Santos. It was "false slander . . . that because citizens of Mexican origin you neither could be trusted as far nor fight as well or as valiantly as those of your fellow citizens who have only Anglo-Saxon blood coursing through their veins," the commissioner told him.[61]

By late 1861 Captain Santos Benavides's legacy had largely been assured. There was little question as to his leadership and his place in border history. But what Løvenskiold was telling Santos and what he was reporting to Governor Lubbock in Austin were somewhat contradictory. "A very strong under-current is running among the Mexican population on both sides of the river, against the Confederacy," Løvenskiold told the governor. Disloyalty to the Confederacy was being promoted in Laredo by a "few northern born Americans," whom the commissioner referred to as "secret enemies to the south."[62] What had aroused Løvenskiold's sensitivities was a meeting in Laredo, attended by soldiers and civilians and arranged by Gardner W. Pierce and Santos's brother Refugio, for the purpose of dissuading Santos's Tejanos from enlisting in the Confederacy. Pierce, in particular, was a strong Unionist. "Do you suppose for one moment I would march musket & ball ready in hand against my father, mother, brothers & sisters? No, no, no," the Illinois-born Pierce told John Z. Leyendecker. According to Løvenskiold, the anti-Confederate instigators had spread the word that the Southern secession was little more than a pronunciamiento by Jefferson Davis and

Gen. Edmund Kirby Smith, West Point class of 1845, joined the Confederate Army only to be wounded at First Bull Run. Smith came to command the vast Trans-Mississippi Department in January 1863, and he worked to assure Benavides's loyalty and keep the cotton roads open to the border. Smith offered to make Benavides a brigadier general if Santos could raise a regiment. When serious problems developed between Benavides and Ford, Smith threatened a court-of-inquiry. The Rebels west of the Mississippi held out until Smith formally surrendered at Galveston on June 2, 1865. Hoping to avoid arrest for treason, Smith fled to Mexico after the war. *Courtesy Library of Congress.*

that the North, because of its population and industrial base, was certain to prevail. Pierce and others feared that anyone implicated in the rebellion and "found with arms in his hands [would] be hung and his property confiscated."[63] Løvenskiold had insisted that Refugio Benavides and the other traitors be thrown in the guardhouse on the plaza and the crowd dispersed. Santos, of course, would never have had his brother arrested.

In desperation, Løvenskiold turned to Charles Russell, who represented Webb County in the state legislature. In turn, Russell asked Governor Clark to intervene with Gen. Paul O. Hébert, commander of the Department of Texas, to allow the Laredo soldiers to enlist for one year rather than the duration of the war. By the second week of December, Løvenskiold was in Laredo, where he met with Santos personally. The Dane also approached the Webb County commissioners with the idea of releasing some $300 in school funds for Santos's men. When the commissioners refused, Løvenskiold asked that each soldier be given $30 from the school fund and assured them that the state would reimburse the county. Still the commissioners refused. In all, Løvenskiold spent several weeks in Laredo, fearful that if Santos's border Tejanos failed to muster into the Confederate Army, it "would have a most injurious effect on the whole Rio Grande Country."[64]

Finally, Governor Lubbock wrote Santos with news that General Hébert had agreed to the one-year enlistment for his men, although the governor told the general that he was making an "unjust distinction" and that Santos was "crucial." "[He] has done great service in keeping Indians and Mexican Marauders off our soil," Lubbock told Hébert. Santos would also keep the "Lincolnites off."[65]

Three days after Christmas, Santos wrote the governor: "in the name of the people of this section of the country for the interest you have taken in the company."[66] He went on to say that he had effectively policed the middle border. Since the formation of his company, those depredating within one hundred miles of Laredo had been severely punished. The war, however, had led to an increase in banditry and despite Santos's vigilance, raids by Native Americans continued. They knew the white men were at war with one another, and the settlements on the Rio Grande were now more vulnerable. Only weeks after Santos wrote the governor, two men were killed a short distance from town.[67] José María Rodríguez, Basilio's son-in-law, would testify years later that in 1862 alone Native Americans, thought to be Mescalero Apaches and Kickapoos, raided the Laredo area eight times, stealing cattle and horses.[68]

On January 1, 1862, Løvenskiold mustered in Santos's men on the plaza in Laredo while at the same time providing a glowing tribute to Santos's Tejanos: "[You have] rendered the state and country much efficient and important service in crushing out the rebellion in Zapata County, in expelling the outlaw Cortina and his followers, and in giving ample security to the lives and properties of your fellow citizens." Moreover, he told Santos, "[you have] upheld the laws of our common country, supported and sustained its officers and government . . . making subordination and obedience your watch word. Not a single complaint has been preferred or raised against you for any usurpation of power, and violation of law and trespass on private rights, or any misconduct." "I have passed several weeks amidst your company, and sobriety, good behavior, and excellent discipline characterize them at all times and in all places," the Danish-born inspector concluded.[69] Years later, a chronicle of the great men in Texas history would say that "perhaps a more gallant set of men than the one hundred enlisted by Captain Benavides never mounted a horse or fought under a more gallant commander."[70]

Thirty-two men who had been in Santos's original company refused to reenlist, but within two weeks Santos had eighty men. In April, Refugio Benavides mustered in a company of his own at Ringgold Barracks. With the exception of 1st Lt. Gardner W. Pierce, whom Løvenskiold had accused of treason, all eighty-five men in the company were Tejanos.[71] At the time, Santos's company was attached to Col. Philip Noland Luckett's Third Texas Infantry. The Virginia-born Luckett was appointed to the United States Military Academy at West Point but had failed to graduate and instead studied medicine and moved to Corpus Christi in 1847. Luckett had served with John Ford's Texas Rangers in the Laredo area before the war, and Santos met him then for the first time. In 1861 Luckett was selected to represent Nueces and Webb counties in the Texas Secession Convention and was part of the Committee of Public Safety that coerced Gen. David E. Twiggs into surrendering the Department of Texas.[72]

Santos's loyalty to the Southern cause was critical to the security of the Texas-Mexico border. Had Santos and that element of the Tejano population he represented refused to join the Confederacy, remained neutral, or joined the Federals, as some feared they might do, the entire Rio Grande flank of the Confederacy would have been dangerously exposed.[73] Astute secessionists in Austin, including Governor Lubbock and others, were quick to realize Santos's crucial role on the middle border, and they took every opportunity to play to his ego and pander to his vanity.

After the fight with Cortina in the spring of 1861, Santos had left brother Cristóbal with a few men at Carrizo while he moved his small command to Rancho Clareño.[74] From the Mexican bank of the river, Cortina's men continued to take potshots at Santos's, and along with this reminder of Cortina's occupation of Brownsville and Rio Grande City in 1859 came the great fear that Cortina would cross the river to "rob and murder" and "burn the towns on the Rio Grande." Roma and Rio Grande City were thought to be particularly vulnerable, and the town leaders there hastened to organize local militias.[75] Rumors persisted that Cortina was in camp near Mier with as many as two hundred men, continuing to boast that he held a commission from both Benito Juárez and Abraham Lincoln. Some even thought that Cortina had met José María de Jesús Carvajal, best known on the frontier for his siege of Matamoros in 1851 during the Merchants' War, and that the two warriors and connivers had agreed to combine their forces.[76] Only one thing was certain—the Rio Grande frontier had not heard the last of either Juan Nepomuceno Cortina or José María de Jesús Carvajal.

Shortly after the fighting at Carrizo, Santos had written Governor Vidaurri with news of his defeat of "the bandit Cortina and 70 of his thieves." The captain said he and his men were active against the Indians and he was hoping to meet with Gen. Guadalupe García of Tamaulipas in Guerrero "to resolve the difficult issues that are detrimental to both sides of the border."[77] Santos wanted permission to cross the border in pursuit of hostile Indians or Cortina's revolutionaries, both of whom were contributing to the turmoil on the river. He was sure no one would complain if he crossed into Mexico, and should he do so, he promised to immediately notify local authorities.

Santos was in command of a vast area of South Texas and the border stretching north from Laredo to the Nueces River, upriver as far as Eagle Pass, and downriver beyond Carrizo. "I know you will do everything the right way," Governor Vidaurri told Santos, though he was reluctant to allow forces from Texas into Mexico. However, he did join forces with Santos to restore peace to the river by issuing orders for Cortina's arrest, and he thanked Santos for the news that revolutionaries were continuing to plot against him in Tamaulipas. "I would like to know who is so barbaric and senseless to dare complain about me; it is implausible," a vain Vidaurri wrote.[78] The governor was particularly concerned with a band of robbers operating in Coahuila, south of Eagle Pass.

In late May, hearing of the fighting in Zapata County, Gen. Guadalupe García, who was in command of the Mexican forces on the Tamaulipas frontier, had crossed the river to meet with Colonel Ford at Fort Brown. The general offered, as Governor Vidaurri had done, to cooperate with Santos in arresting Cortina, Ochoa, and their followers.[79] In late June, General García wrote Santos to personally compliment him on his defeat of Cortina. "I am not blind to the good services you have lent me," García said. The general said he was doing everything in his power to prevent the "raids that at every chance Cortina and his men engage[d] in." He was comfortable with Santos crossing the Rio Grande while in pursuit of Cortina or his revolutionaries, but he asked for time to allow Mexican forces to apprehend Cortina first. García was sure he could catch the wily Cortina, who was thought to be moving against Reynosa. The general promised to send cavalry to Guerrero and station more men in Reynosa. He promised to open a "formal campaign" against Cortina and coordinate his efforts with those of Governor Vidaurri.[80] García would meet with Santos in Guerrero as soon as possible.

Colonel Ford, on the other hand, was reluctant to allow Santos to cross the river, fearful that the captain would be ambushed by Cortinistas thirsting for revenge for the Rancho Clareño massacre, as well as their bloody defeat at Carrizo. If Santos was defeated and killed in Mexico, Ford vowed to take "bloody revenge." "[But] that would not bring your gallant men back. We need you and them. Don't let them get the advantage of you," the Confederate colonel told Santos.[81] If Santos did cross the Rio Grande, he was to "go as a friend of Mexico" and "avoid molesting peaceable citizens."[82]

In reality, Ford did not respect or trust General García. Although García promised to cooperate with Santos in policing the border, the general was wary of any relationship with Confederates in Texas. To complicate matters, Santos did not trust García either, and he did not like taking orders from Ford. But everyone on the border realized the explosiveness of the situation and the international implications of Santos entering Mexico.

In early July 1861, Santos and several of his men left Carrizo for Brownsville to confer with Confederate authorities and arrange for weapons, supplies, and pay. Arriving in the lower valley, Santos ran into Ignacio Comonfort, former president of Mexico who had been in exile in the United States after resigning in 1858. Comonfort had in his possession a letter from Governor Vidaurri praising Santos as brave and trustworthy and recommending that the former president ask Santos for an escort to Laredo. After considerable discussion, Santos agreed to assign Comonfort twenty men who would guard him all the way to Lampazos.[83] When Ford learned of the agreement, he warned Santos "to have nothing to do with Mexican revolutions."[84] The defiantly independent Santos paid Ford little heed.

Thought by some to be a bureaucrat of minor importance, Comonfort was in reality a major player in Mexican politics. He had helped write the Plan de Ayutla, which set forth a long list of grievances against Antonio López de Santa Anna. When the dictator was forced into exile in 1855, Comonfort was made minister of war under the liberal, provisional presidency of Juan Álvarez. When Álvarez resigned a few months later, Comonfort was thrust into the presidency. Trying to maintain a difficult coalition, Comonfort sought to placate the dissidents by appointing several conservatives to his cabinet. He struggled to find a middle ground between the liberals and the conservatives and wound up alienating both. Comonfort did help usher in the Constitution of 1857, which abolished many of the privileges and abuses of the Catholic Church, but a reactionary junta of generals attempted to nullify the constitution and abolish the liberal Reform Laws by staging a coup d'état with the Plan de Tacubaya. After wavering again and finally siding with the generals, Comonfort was forced to resign in January 1858, and he was replaced by Benito Juárez, a liberal, anti-clerical Zapotec Indian from Oaxaca. As Comonfort watched from exile in the United States, Mexico was plunged headlong into civil war.[85]

Comonfort tried to cross the Rio Grande at Matamoros in hopes of going on by stage to Monterrey to join Governor Vidaurri, a fellow Mason, but he was met with anger and threats, and he returned to Brownsville. Still hoping to cross into Mexico, Comonfort rode upriver with Santos only to watch a heavily armed party on the opposite bank shadow his every move. Not far from Rio Grande City, the two were joined by men from Santos's company who had ridden downriver from Carrizo.[86] Santos carried provisions for his men in several wagons, but he did not have their pay or the weapons he had been promised. After a long and fatiguing ride, the party arrived safely at Laredo on July 13, 1861, where a formal letter from Vidaurri awaited Comonfort, inviting him to Monterrey. Comonfort responded by thanking the governor for his assistance, especially the letter of introduction to Santos that had made possible his safe passage to Laredo. During their long journey upriver, Comonfort told the governor, he found in Santos a "complete man" whose friendship "it would be favorable to cultivate."[87]

After more than a week in Laredo, and meeting with hostility from authorities in Nuevo Laredo, Santos and Comonfort made plans to cross the river on the night of July 21, 1861, at Rancho La Pita, with a wagon carrying provisions and four trusted men. They would cross at sunset and continue until midnight, when they would make camp in Nuevo León and rest before proceeding on to the Rio Salado and Lampazos. As they were preparing to cross the Rio Grande, Santos learned from his spies in Nuevo Laredo that authorities in Tamaulipas were determined to arrest the former president and that several parties were carefully patrolling the border. Santos instead led Comonfort upriver to Eagle Pass, where he could cross safely into Coahuila at Piedras Negras and where the former president was warmly welcomed. From Piedras Negras, Santos and Comonfort rode 120 miles south to Lampazos, where they found Vidaurri anxiously awaiting them at his residence.

Hearing of Comonfort's safe return to Mexico, Juárez was furious and immediately ordered Governor Vidaurri to arrest the former president and send him to Mexico City. Vidaurri responded with a long list of reasons why Comonfort should remain in Nuevo León. In defiance of the federal government, the caudillo even named Comonfort head of the Nuevo León militia.[88] It was yet another example of the strained relationship between Juárez and Vidaurri that at times neared the breaking point.

After four weeks and over seven hundred miles in the saddle, Santos arrived back in Laredo in late July, where he promptly purchased a carriage for 350 pesos.[89] Santos had been in Laredo for only a few days when Dr. Juan Ortiz arrived from downriver with news that Cortina was on the march again. The insurgent was near Mier with as many as two hundred Cortinistas, slowly moving upriver and recruiting men as he went.[90] General Guadalupe García had sent a company of soldiers from Matamoros to arrest Cortina, but in response Cortina showed them a commission from both Juárez and Lincoln authorizing him to recruit men. Santos had no doubt the papers were forged, and he started immediately for Carrizo with fifty men. By sending a few men into Mexico as spies, Santos could easily learn Cortina's whereabouts and intentions, and he was determined to give Cortina battle once again.

By 1862, affairs on the Rio Grande were becoming terribly convoluted. A serious rift developed between Santos and Vidaurri when the governor heard that the captain was supporting José María de Jesús Carvajal, who was on the river recruiting yet another band of filibusters with the inten-

José María de Jesús Carvajal was one of the most fascinating individuals on the Texas-Mexico border for much of the 1850s and 1860s. Although Benavides broke up one of Carvajal's attempts to invade Mexico in May 1862, the powerful governor of Nuevo León and Coahuila, Santiago Vidaurri, mistrusted Benavides's relationship with Carvajal. Carte de visite by Mathew Brady. *Courtesy Lew Wallace Collection, Indiana Historical Society.*

tion of crossing into Mexico. Carvajal announced his support of Jesús de la Serna, who was challenging Gen. García over the governorship of Tamaulipas, and when Serna was expelled, the American-born Carvajal laid siege to Matamoros with as many as a thousand men. Colonel Ford, commanding the Confederates on the opposite bank of the river, was forced into a difficult and delicate situation. Professing neutrality in the struggle for power in Tamaulipas, Confederate authorities seized two pieces of artillery and all of Carvajal's small arms. But Ford had been a filibustering colleague of Carvajal in 1851, and he returned the weapons to his old friend. Supplied with even more weapons by the companies of Richard King, Mifflin Kenedy, and Charles Stillman, Carvajal crossed the river again and attacked several towns before being forced to retreat. Vidaurri, whom Juárez had placed in command of the military in Tamaulipas, was particularly incensed and demanded the right to cross the river to attack Carvajal, just as Ford's Texas Rangers and the US Army had done in 1860 when trying to apprehend or kill Cortina.

Governor Vidaurri strongly suspected that Santos was somehow involved in supporting Carvajal. The governor lectured Santos on how they had always been good friends and how he had always held Santos in "high esteem." The governor could not understand how Santos could support someone who had caused so much suffering.[91] Carvajal was in a position to bring great "displeasure and evil for both countries," Vidaurri told another Tejano, Ángel Navarro.[92] Santos's only defense was to say that the governor was badly misinformed. He said he had never supported Carvajal in the past and had no intention of doing so in the present; they were enemies as a consequence of Carvajal being an enemy of Vidaurri. "Your enemies are made my enemies," Santos concluded. "Your friend would not sell himself at any price."[93]

Still, Vidaurri reminded Santos that he was now the military commander in Tamaulipas. Surely Santos knew that Carvajal was challenging Vidaurri for power and in defiance of the central government. For months, Santos continued to deny any collusion with Carvajal, and he promised

To avoid the Union blockade during the Civil War, long lines of cotton-filled wagons arrived on the border from as far away as Louisiana and Arkansas. Border communities such as Brownsville, Rio Grande City, Laredo, and Eagle Pass experienced unprecedented economic activity. For decades, many in the Texas-Mexico borderlands would remember the years from 1861 to 1865 as the "Cotton Times." Carte de visite. *Jerry Thompson Collection.*

Vidaurri he would be a "sentinel in everything" that interested the governor.[94] Vidaurri may have falsely assumed that because Ford had befriended Carvajal, so, too, had Santos. But the historical record gives no hint that Santos was involved in Ford's decision to allow Carvajal use of the north bank of the river to attack the liberal forces in Matamoros. Because Santos was to pursue "bandits" into Mexico, Vidaurri asked for the right to pursue Carvajal into Texas. Ford diplomatically refused this request, however.[95]

In the eyes of many liberals in Mexico, Confederate authorities in Texas were in clear violation of the Confederacy's publically professed policy of neutrality. During the Carvajal affair, Governor Vidaurri had gone over Colonel Ford's head to Governor Lubbock in Austin, demanding that Carvajal be arrested and extradited. When Confederate authorities refused, Vidaurri responded by doubling the tax on cotton crossing into Mexico, saying that he needed the money to bolster his defenses against Carvajal.[96]

With the French invasion, the political and military climate in Mexico changed overnight. Throughout his friendship with Vidaurri, Santos had frequently offered to assist the governor. Abruptly, in February 1862, Vidaurri wrote to say the "republic had been invaded by foreigners," and he was hoping Santos and his men could ride south to assist him. Vidaurri was fearful that Carvajal, who had been a thorn in his side for several years, was again threatening the Mexican Republic. Santos's continued support of Carvajal was, the governor said, causing great harm.[97] On February 7, 1862, Santos wrote to remind the governor once again that he had never supported Carvajal and that Vidaurri was misinformed. Because he was a Vidaurri partisan, he had always been a bitter enemy of Carvajal, Santos said. Santos was willing to die with Vidaurri on the battlefield, he said, and he even offered his "small fortune" for the cause of the republic. There was only one problem: just the previous month he and his one-hundred-man company had enlisted in the Confederate Army. Any union with Vidaurri on Mexican soil would be impossible. Nevertheless, Santos would aid in the struggle against the Imperialistas in every way possible. "It is impossible for me to leave the country under the present circumstances without dishonoring the name of our race. I am proud of being Mexican and of that proving to the whole world that Mexicans are faithful where ever they are found, and that they are worth as much as the best men of any other nation," Santos concluded.[98] Ultimately, Vidaurri understood Santos's competing binational loyalties, and the bond between the two, although strained by Carvajal, remained as strong as ever. To Vidaurri, Santos was a "true and sincere friend, a man of honor, and a commendable patriot."[99]

Eventually realizing he ran the risk of being arrested in Texas and extradited to Tamaulipas or Nuevo León, where Vidaurri was certain to have him executed, Carvajal took flight. A man of many colors, Carvajal wound up with the liberals in central Mexico during their continuing struggle with Mexican conservatives and the French imperialists of Napoleon III. On April 24, 1862, Santos's friend and former ally, Gen. Hamilton P. Bee, took command of the Sub-District of the Rio Grande, and Colonel Ford, largely because of his mishandling of the Carvajal affair, was relegated to a desk job in Austin.[100]

For the Benavides family, the Civil War abounded with economic opportunities. Besides being an officer with exhausting responsibilities, Refugio Benavides was named the local postmaster, and Santos and Cristóbal were given contracts to carry the mail to San Antonio, Brownsville, and Corpus Christi. Basilio Benavides brought corn from Mexico to sell to the Confederates, as did Santos's younger brother, Eulalio. Throughout 1862, Santos imported and sold thousands of pounds of corn to feed the horses of his men. Cristóbal also had a lucrative contract to supply the Confederates on the border with wood. On at least one occasion, Eulalio was contracted to sell beef to his brother for five cents per pound. Santos also sold beef at the same price, as well as items from his store, such as brooms, cups, and saucers. In April 1863, Teresa Benavides even rented a house on the main plaza to Santos, which he could use as his headquarters for fifteen dollars a month.[101]

Even as his family was thriving, Santos remained a man with complicated and conflicted transnational loyalties. Arriving in San Antonio on March 28, 1862, to confer with General Bee and Confederate authorities, he learned that Carvajal, who was said to be back in Mexico, was interested in obtaining a commission to raise a regiment of troops for the Confederacy. Bee was fearful that if Carvajal was granted such authority and did raise a regiment, he would use the soldiers not to defend the border but to invade Mexico, as he had done in the past. Such an invasion under the rebel flag would be diplomatically catastrophic and might well bring on a war. Bee wanted Vidaurri's opinion on the subject and asked Santos to contact the governor without delay. In response, Santos sent a courier rushing south. "I would like to know your feelings about this. Do you think this would be harmful to Mexico or not," Santos queried. Again, Santos assured Vidaurri of his loyalty. "I am a Vidaurrista," he proudly proclaimed.

The captain was given a fifteen-day leave to visit with Governor Vidaurri at Monterrey, though he did not get away until the end of April, and Confederate authorities on the border continued to worry about Carvajal and other filibusters who were violating the neutrality laws and dragging Texas and the Confederacy into the bloody war in Mexico. At the same time, many people still feared that Cortinistas gathering on the south bank of the river would sack towns and ranches on the Texas side of the Rio Grande. Santos asked Vidaurri to keep him informed: "[Send] timely news of when you think something like this could happen."[102]

On April 7, 1862, Vidaurri responded to Santos's "gracious letter," saying that under no circumstances should Carvajal be allowed to raise a regiment in Texas. Carvajal was a "sworn enemy of Mexico," and his only objective was to damage the country. Surely Confederate authorities in Texas could see this. The governor wanted Santos or someone in Texas to arrest Carvajal and his followers and turn them over to authorities in Mexico, where they could be placed on trial for the "innumerable and scandalous crimes they have committed . . . against morality and public order."[103] Carvajal, the governor warned, was in a position to cause "immense damage," and destroy the relations between "our states."

By the late spring of 1862, Santos's seventy-six-man company, along with the seventy-nine men in brother Refugio's company, had been assigned to the Sub-District of the Rio Grande. Besides the ten companies of Col. P. N. Luckett's Third Texas Infantry that were stationed at Ringgold Barracks and Fort Brown, Refugio's and Santos's Tejanos were the only soldiers on the river.[104] Santos and Confederate authorities in Texas were satisfied that Vidaurri had issued orders protecting the frontier from the mouth of the river to Piedras Negras, but the land was so vast and the border so long that ten times the number of soldiers Vidaurri and the Confederates had there could not have policed the whole area.

In early May 1862, Santos rode to "Carvajal's Ranch," where he found close to two hundred men milling around, most of them armed. He was able to peacefully "dissolve" the small army, whose members dispersed in different directions, most of them crossing into Mexico. Santos assured Vidaurri, "[My actions] mirror greatly with your wishes." Santos had information he did not "trust to write in ink," but after a visit to Confederate headquarters in San Antonio, he promised to travel south to see Vidaurri in person.[105]

In the meantime, Santos asked for favors for two unnamed friends who were hoping to cross 850 bales of cotton into Mexico without customs duties or fees being imposed. Henry Redmond was also interested in exporting four hundred bales of cotton to Mexico, and he asked Santos to intervene with Vidaurri on his behalf. Redmond further asked if he could deposit as many as two thousand bales of cotton in Nuevo Laredo and not pay duties until the cotton was taken into the interior. Deferring to the central government's strict regulations on customs duties, Vidaurri responded that he would not be able to alter the rules for Redmond or Santos's other friends.[106] Although Vidaurri congratulated Santos for disbanding Carvajal's "gang of criminals," the governor was still hoping the elusive Carvajal could be apprehended and turned over to authorities in Mexico. He was, however, reassured by Santos's actions that someday there would be "tranquility on the border."[107]

Back in San Antonio in the heat of late July, Santos found everything "good and peaceful" and the news from the war "very favorable," as reported in the Southern press, although in reality, the South was on the defensive. Forts Henry and Donelson on the Tennessee and Cumberland Rivers had surrendered; Nashville had been evacuated; and Gen. Albert Sidney Johnston, in command of Confederate forces in the West, had been turned back on April 6–7, 1862, in the horrific Battle of Shiloh on the banks of the Tennessee River. The general himself lay dead. Four hundred miles to the west, Confederates had been defeated at Pea Ridge in northern Arkansas. In distant New Mexico Territory, at the southern tip of the towering Sangre de Cristo Mountains, Gen. Henry Hopkins Sibley's once-proud band of Texas farm boys, determined to create a Southern empire in the desert Southwest, had been turned back at Glorieta Pass and were in pitiful retreat. Even more striking was the fact that on April 29, 1862, Union sailors and marines had taken possession of New Orleans, the largest port in the South. Only from the East, where Gen. Robert E. Lee had assumed command of the Army of Northern Virginia, came good news. After a series of battles that sent shockwaves across the heartland, Gen. George McClellan's blue-clad Army of the Potomac had been driven from the gates of Richmond. Back on the border, Santos forwarded several newspapers to Governor Vidaurri in Monterrey.[108] Although Santos was never comfortable speaking English himself, he could read and comprehend the language.

In late October 1862, Santos told Governor Vidaurri he no longer had any hope of a short war that seemed "prolonged more and more every day."[109] Moreover, Santos was still having to deal with hostile bands of Native Americans, who offered a more immediate threat to the town than distant armies in blue. Soon, however, the full effects of the war that had once seemed so far away were coming to be felt even in the "dark corner of the Confederacy," as it came to be called.

What little food supply the citizens of Laredo possessed grew short; the situation became desperate, and the people began to go hungry. On October 14, 1862, Santos wrote Governor Vidaurri from his headquarters at Laredo saying the town of three thousand people was in "very short supply of provisions."[110] Citizens were subsisting on meat, of which there was an adequate supply, but Santos was still hoping the governor could provide assistance, especially with the essential commodities of corn, flour, and beans. So desperate was the situation that Santos was preparing to send his family to Monterrey or one of the towns in Nuevo León or Coahuila where food supplies were more substantial.[111] Vidaurri responded by saying he would do all in his power to assist the people of Laredo, and by December wagonloads of beans, corn, and flour were beginning to arrive in the community. He also offered his spacious home in Lampazos should Santos remain determined to send his family away.

On behalf of the entire population of the town, Santos wrote to thank Vidaurri for his assistance.[112] Several months later, Santos sent the governor a purebred "American horse," a thoroughbred that Santos had purchased from a stable in San Antonio. It is uncertain whether the horse was request-

A busy market scene with water carriers and ox carts was photographed in Brownsville in 1864. *Courtesy UT Institute of Texan Cultures at San Antonio.*

ed by the governor or was presented as a gift to Vidaurri for his friendship and his assistance in providing the town with food.[113] What is clear, however, is that in a time of great crisis and human want, Santos and his Tejanos looked more to Mexico than to their native Texas for assistance.

Although Governor Vidaurri had offered his home in Lampazos to Santos's family, Santos thought it best to send them on to Monterrey, where his daughter, Agustina, could continue her education. She had been attending school in San Antonio, but Santos was upset when she returned home ill and having forgotten how to write Spanish.[114] Vidaurri wrote recommending the convent in Monterrey, saying that his daughter Rosita had attended school there and the cost was only fifteen pesos a month. Young women in the school were properly instructed in religion, reading, writing, grammar, embroidery, geography, drawing, music, and Castilian Spanish, although no instruction in the piano was available, as Santos had hoped. Each student was expected to furnish her own bed, eating utensils, and clothes.[115] Santos responded by thanking the governor for the information and wishing him great "success over the French invaders."[116]

By Christmas 1862, Santos was back in San Antonio to confer with Confederate authorities. A month later he complained to Vidaurri from Laredo of the situation in Tamaulipas, which was becoming "more complicated as the days go by." Banditry was out of control, and the authorities at Camargo, Reynosa, and Matamoros were indifferent. Santos thought that the new governor, Albino López, had been sincere in his attempts to suppress the lawlessness, but his efforts were of little avail. Santos's influence on Governor Vidaurri is evident in the fact that the governor quickly sent letters to Governor López and General Bee asking that they do all in their power to control the lawlessness on the Rio Grande.[117] In mid-August 1863, during the heat of the brutal South Texas summer, Santos wrote Vidaurri again to complain of the robbery along the river and reiterate the necessity that they cooperate to do "everything possible to get rid of the bandits" who had caused them "so much harm."[118] The more the outlaws went unpunished the bolder they became. Moreover, Native Americans were still a threat, and villagers lived in constant fear.[119]

At Laredo and Carrizo, Santos never faced the levels of desertion that Colonel Bee did at Fort Brown and Ringgold Barracks and in the lower valley. From Brownsville in late February 1863, Bee had complained to Governor López that scores of his men, fifteen in the last three days, had fled across the shallow waters of the Rio Grande to Matamoros, where Leonard Pierce Jr., the American consul, offered the men a gleeful welcome, fed and clothed them, administered an oath of allegiance, and sent them to New Orleans, where they were enlisting in the Union Army. "I confess that my position is annoying," Bee wrote, and "I must either take my men back by force or submit to the mortification of seeing my command demoralized."[120] Bee hoped the Mexican authorities would agree not to transport the deserters to any foreign port and keep them at least ninety miles from the border.

From the beginning of the war, Texas refugees who were being oppressed for their beliefs had poured across the border into Matamoros, where Pierce gave them refuge. Originally from Eastport, Maine, the fiery thirty-four-year-old American consul had spent one year in Chihuahua, where he had learned to speak Spanish, before moving to Texas in 1857.[121] For almost two years after moving to Matamoros, Pierce had opened the consulate door to hundreds of refugees. Many arrived destitute, with little more than the clothes on their backs.[122] Probably the best-known Texas refugee to show up in Mexico was former congressman Alexander J. Hamilton, who arrived in Matamoros with fifteen men on July 29, 1862, after a frightful escape from Austin.[123]

To avoid Santos and his Confederates, some of the refugees were forced to cross the Rio Grande far upstream, at its confluence with the Devil's River. Many were Germans from the Texas Hill Country, some of whom had managed to escape the infamous Nueces massacre on the west prong of the Nueces River on August 10, 1862, when Confederates ambushed sixty-five German Texans on their way to Mexico. A Texas newspaper dubbed it "The Battle with the Traitors."[124] One refugee who later joined the Union Army, Prussia-born William Huster, recalled "traveling the dreary road to the Rio Grande" when a seven-hour firefight erupted with a superior force of Confederates four hundred miles from the mouth of the river. After losing seven of his brave companions, "perfectly destitute" and "without clothes or money," the thirty-nine-year-old Huster managed to make his way to Matamoros to find refuge with Pierce at the American consulate.[125] At one Confederate camp on the Rio Grande, a skull belonging to a German refugee killed while trying to cross the river was hung from the top of a commissary hut as a trophy of war. One twenty-year veteran of the Old Army arrived in Matamoros recalling how he had been "hunted like a wild buffalo" in Texas.[126]

When Pierce's successor, Emanuel D. Etchison, a dry goods merchant from Maryland, arrived in Matamoros, he, too, faced the problem of caring for hundreds of Texas refugees, both those fleeing conscription and the growing numbers of deserters from the Confederate Army. The fugitives, old and young, arrived "destitute, forlorn, hungry and naked, sick and emaciated." Many had been forced to beg in Mexico, and once in Matamoros, they stood out by their "nakedness, their pale faces & haggard looks, their sunken and glaring eyes."[127]

In her letters to her family in Laredo, written from Fredericksburg in the Texas Hill Country, Andrea Leyendecker also felt the great fear shared by many Texas Unionists. The frail and frequently sick Andrea worried incessantly that her merchant husband John would somehow die in the violence, simply because he was of German descent. "The volunteers have killed many men here who still favor the Union," she wrote.[128] As early as July 1861, Andrea had heard the rumor that the "South was against all German people" and that Confederate forces had killed "500 Germans because the greater number of them [were] supporters of the North."[129] In reality, more German Texans enlisted in the Confederate Army during the Civil War than in the Union Army, but this fact made little difference to rebel authorities in Texas, who possessed an almost paranoid fear of German dissidents and freethinkers in the Hill Country. Andrea dreamed of weeping uncontrollably when her husband was sent off to war; little did she know

Bales of cotton and a cotton press at Piedras Negras, Coahuila, opposite Eagle Pass, can be seen during the Civil War in a sketch by C. E. H. Bonwill. The shanty of "Los Amigos del Erayo [Bravo]" can be seen on the far right. The powerful governor of the states of Coahuila and Nuevo Leon, Santiago Vidaurri, was dependent on the large revenues from the customs duties levied at Piedras Negras. *Frank Leslie's Illustrated Newspaper*, September 3, 1864.

that in a short time her dreams would become reality. Her husband John would soon be wearing the uniform of the Confederacy.[130]

Jacob Leyendecker, John's twenty-seven-year-old younger brother, also marched off to New Mexico Territory with the Sibley Brigade as a private in the Fifth Texas Mounted Volunteers. After the disaster at Apache Canyon in northern New Mexico Territory in March 1862, when Confederate supplies went up in flames during the Battle of Glorieta, the Texans were forced into a long retreat, and Jacob fell ill and was taken prisoner. The news of his capture was slow to reach Fredericksburg, and for many months his family feared that he was dead. Although a large number of the Sibley Brigade who were taken prisoner in New Mexico were paroled and returned to Texas, Jacob was among those sent east along the Santa Fe Trail to Fort Riley, Kansas, and then to Fort Leavenworth, before being interred at Camp Douglas, Illinois. Leyendecker and his Confederate colleagues were exchanged at Vicksburg, Mississippi, on September 22, 1862, and he returned home to his family in Fredericksburg.[131]

Throughout 1862 and 1863, violence continued to spill across the Rio Grande, causing confusion and threatening diplomatic relations, and Confederate authorities struggled continuously to tighten their control of the border. Ultimately, Santos issued orders specifying that anyone crossing into Texas from Mexico must carry a passport from the town where they lived. Travelers were also required to have proper papers for any livestock being crossed into Texas; otherwise, the animals would be confiscated. Santos asked Governor Vidaurri to publish the regulations in *La Gaceta de Monterrey* and the *Boletín Oficial*, the official newspapers of the Vidaurri government.[132] In the fall of 1863, orders would be issued to endorse Santos's attempt to regulate the passage of cattle across the Rio Grande: anyone crossing cattle into Mexico would need papers indicating that people in the towns where the cattle were being driven were going to eat them. "Tamaulipas does not have the right to take out more than what can be consumed," Santos told Vidaurri.[133]

In April 1862, a large party of Mexican refugees, or Rojos, as they were called, had infuriated Governor Vidaurri by crossing the river into Coahuila, sacking the village of Guerrero, and burning a large part of Piedras Negras, opposite Eagle Pass. "I cannot suffer that these villains are shamefully insulting Mexico," the governor wrote. "If another similar act is repeated," he warned, "I will have no choice but to take action against Texas."[134] If Confederate authorities did not stop such raids, their failure to act would strongly indicate that they were not only harboring criminals who were protected by a "ditch," but were aiding and abetting them. A break in diplomatic relations seemed the only recourse, and as far as the governor was concerned, treaties between Mexico and the United States did not apply to the relationship between Mexico and the Confederacy. Santos should do everything in his power to stop such raids. With so few men and the border so extensive, however, there was little he could do.

A week after Vidaurri issued his warning, Santos informed the governor that "known criminals dangerous to both sides" were gathering at Rancho de San José, opposite San Ignacio, with the intention of invading Texas. Santos urged Vidaurri to send a small force to "go after them," and again he offered his assistance in maintaining law and order on the river. At the same time, Santos asked for the latest news of the war with the French imperialists and assured Vidaurri that he was keeping an eye on Carvajal. Vidaurri sent a dispatch to Santos promising "quick action to destroy" the outlaws. Santos replied promptly, recommending that if Vidaurri would send twenty to thirty men from Nuevo Laredo, the bandits at Rancho de San José could be dispersed or captured. Although he was patrolling a large stretch of the border, Santos was sure that if the robbers crossed the river he could easily disarm them and deliver their arms to Vidaurri. "I will not permit anything that could bother you," Santos promised.[135]

Santos continued to worry about the raiders who were using the south bank of the river as a haven from which to strike into Texas and steal livestock. In command of the river from Eagle Pass to Rancho Clareño, Santos promised Vidaurri he would do all in his power to stop the banditry. But the border incursions continued to intensify. In fact, raids into Texas by insurrectionists operating out of Mexico came close to paralyzing Confederate operations on the border. Troops vital to Confederate fortunes elsewhere had to be assigned to the Rio Grande.

Beginning in 1862, Union agents operating out of Matamoros, called *enganchados*, had commenced recruiting Tejanos and Mexicanos.[136] One Cortinista who came under Union influence was thirty-two-year-old Octaviano Zapata, who owned a small ranch near Rancho Clareño in Zapata County. A close ally of Cortina, Zapata had escaped the Clareño massacre in April 1861 and, along with his wife and three children, taken refuge in Guerrero. Burning with a desire to strike back at his enemies in Texas, Zapata was able to recruit between sixty and eighty men in and around Guerrero. Potential recruits were offered as much as one hundred pesos in gold and promised fifty acres of land in Texas for single men and 150 acres for married men. Such monetary enticements were very appealing to many of the poor and landless who lived along the river.

In early December 1862, Zapata's raiders crossed the river near Roma, some eighteen miles above Ringgold Barracks, and attacked a Confederate supply train. Three weeks later, on December 26, another train of three wagons en route from Fort Brown to Ringgold Barracks and escorted by five soldiers was attacked by Zapata's raiders at Rancho Soledad near Las Cuevas, fifteen miles below Ringgold Barracks.[137] The Confederates were caught completely by surprise and made no attempt to resist, except for one soldier who opened fire on the raiders with his revolver, killing two of Zapata's men. The Zapatistas killed all the teamsters except one man, who escaped to Ringgold Barracks. All the wagons were taken to the riverbank, ransacked, and the goods carried into Mexico.[138] In retaliation for the wagon raid, a company of Confederates from Ringgold Barracks rode to Rancho Soledad, where "strong circumstantial evidence" indicated that many of the Tejano families living in the vicinity were involved in the raid. As a result, the soldiers burned sixteen jacales in the village and rode triumphantly back to Ringgold Barracks.

On the same day as the Rancho Soledad raid, another party of two hundred Mexicans under Zapata crossed into Zapata County, rode to the ranch of sixty-two-year-old Isidro Vela at Rancho Clareño, seized the judge, and hanged him from a mesquite tree. Before crossing back into Mexico, the raiders "posted a placard on the body warning they would kill any person who dared to take the body down for burial."[139] Hearing of the hanging, Gen. Hamilton P. Bee, only recently appointed commander of Confederate forces on the Rio Grande, complained bitterly to Governor López that Zapata's raiders had killed an "estimable patriot and citizen." Particularly irksome to Bee was the fact that the raiders crossed into Zapata County carrying a "Yankee flag," which had "no right on the soil of Texas."[140] Bee demanded that Zapata, whom he claimed was attached to the First Texas Cavalry, be apprehended and sent to Brownsville for trial. In response to Bee's constant complaints, Governor López agreed to order Zapata's arrest and to intercept any shipments of arms. López admitted that Zapata had been coming and going from Bagdad in Tamaulipas. At the same time, the governor agreed to arrest two of Zapata's associates, thirty-year-old Cesario Falcon and thirty-nine-year-old William Huster, and try them under the laws of the Republic of Mexico.[141]

Governor Vidaurri, too, wanted Zapata captured, and he promised to use his influence with the authorities in Tamaulipas. The governor also warned Santos that thirty to forty "bandits" under the leadership of Andres Valenzuela were operating upriver from Eagle Pass and that they were likely to cross into Texas. They had already committed a number of robberies and "other excesses" in several towns in Coahuila. If Zapata or Valenzuela was apprehended, Vidaurri wanted them turned over to him at Lampazos or at Piedras Negras.[142] Santos was successful in capturing one of Zapata's associates, Perez Villarreal, but Zapata himself remained elusive.

One of Zapata's zealous recruits, Guillermo Vino, had been successful in running off several herds of cattle from the Texas side of the river, as well as thirty-two horses from a Confederate company under Capt. Refugio Benavides that was camped near Roma.[143] Demanding that the alcalde of

Mier assist in capturing the raiders, Refugio crossed into Mexico with fifty-four of his Laredo Confederates. He was able to track about 150 of the Zapatistas southeast to Mesquital Lealeño, downriver from Guerrero, where they were found encamped in a large corral. In the fight that ensued on December 29, 1862, much of it hand to hand, eighteen of the Zapatistas were killed, fourteen wounded, and several taken captive. Zapata, however, was able to escape into the dense chaparral with most of his men. The Confederates seized fifty-eight horses and fifty-four old saddles, along with documents implicating the enganchados and their recruits in the raid on Rancho Clareño. The captives taken in the fray were reported to have "escaped,"[144] but in reality they were probably executed, as had been the case following Cortina's defeat at Carrizo in May 1861. In the two-hour fight, two of Refugio's men were wounded, and twenty-five horses were lost. After torching several small jacales, including that of Jesús Vidal, the Confederates crossed the river back into Texas.

In the fighting on the border, Capt. Refugio Benavides proved to be "one of the most discreet and steady fighters." The same was true of Capt. Cristóbal Benavides, who, like his two older brothers, "was always ready to charge any force of Yankees . . . regardless of numbers." The three brothers, according to Colonel Ford, "gave the Confederate cause a popularity on the lower Rio Grande which enabled its defenders and advocated to maintain a hold upon a large extent of territory" that might otherwise have been lost.[145]

Santos remained confident that Mexican authorities could stop the depredations along the river and continued to do everything in his power to police the north bank. In January 1863, a squad of Santos's men daringly crossed into Mexico and recovered a herd of horses that had been stolen on the Nueces River. Early the same year, four bandits who were accused of stealing cattle in Texas had been arrested and sent to Matamoros under a heavy guard. A few months before, Santos had caught one cattle thief who was known to have murdered a man and brought him into Laredo. "I hung him in the plaza," Santos bluntly told Col. Philip N. Luckett.[146] Exactly how many men Santos hung during the Civil War is uncertain, although the historical record hints that it was more than just a few. When he heard rumors that three assassins were passing through the area, Santos told his brother-in-law, Leyendecker, to keep a sharp lookout for anyone looking suspicious. "If by good fortune you should get hold of either one of the three murderers . . . you will hang them immediately." In fact, Santos went on to say, "should you at any time take prisoner any thief or murderer, no matter of what nation, hang him."[147]

Sometime in early 1863, the enganchado Octaviano Zapata went to New Orleans at the invitation of Union officials, where he was given a shipment of arms. By March, he was taking them back to Bagdad on the steamer *Honduras*. Fearful of continued raids into Texas, General Bee demanded that Governor López confiscate the arms and arrest Zapata. Although López assured Bee that he would do everything possible to comply, within weeks Zapata was in camp near Guerrero saying he had been given the rank of colonel by Union authorities. Moreover, Zapata had been promised money, uniforms, and other rewards, in addition to arms, to help end the "Confederate War."[148] "¡Que Viva la Unión!" became Zapata's battle cry as he made additional raids into Texas. Mexican authorities managed to arrest Zapata and send him to Matamoros, but he was only held for a short time. The "outlaw Zapata is again at liberty," Bee protested, "notwithstanding the many crimes and outrages he has committed against the peace and safety on both sides of the river." Since Zapata was thought to be a citizen of Texas, Bee asked that he be extradited to stand trial in the Lone Star State. Bee argued that Zapata continued to conspire with Leonard Pierce, the American consul in Matamoros, to recruit men with the intended purpose of raiding into Texas. At Mier, Zapata was blamed for the assassination of Col. Jesús García Ramirez of the Mexican National Guard, who was a close friend of Santos.[149] In late August 1863, Mexican troops were ambushed and routed by Zapata on the road between Guerrero and Mier. Governor Vidaurri was so upset he wrote Santos to again propose the two "join forces" and do all they could "to get rid of the bandits that cause many evils." Santos knew,

Vidaurri said, that Rancho de San Ignacio had "always been a place where criminals get together."[150]

Another potentially explosive international incident occurred at Los Dos Laredos on March 10, 1863, this time involving Santos. Only hours before marching downriver to Carrizo, Santos allowed two of his men to cross the Rio Grande to visit friends and relatives in Nuevo Laredo. The soldiers were told by the alcalde in Nuevo Laredo "that if they wished to pass about the town, they must leave their pistols which they had in their belts with him until they were ready to return."[151] What caused the confrontation that followed is uncertain, but twenty-seven-year-old private Encarnación García, a laborer by profession, was mortally wounded. Carried back to Laredo on the ferry, García died within hours.[152] According to Santos, Private García, along with a second unnamed soldier, was in the process of complying with the request to disarm when they were fired on by the Nuevo Laredo police. The Mexican version of the incident alleged that the two men had "committed some disturbances" and that the police were attempting to arrest the pair when the Confederates drew their pistols and a gunfight erupted.[153]

Whatever the truth, news of the gun battle and García's injury took only minutes to reach Santos in Laredo. With several of his men, Santos commandeered the ferry and hurried to the office of the alcalde to ascertain the facts of the case.[154] While the meeting was underway, news of García's death spread among the Confederate Tejanos on the north bank. Moments later, forty of Santos's men had swum their horses across the river to revenge the death of their comrade. However, Santos met the angry men at the riverbank and asked them not to enter Nuevo Laredo until he had completed his consultation with the alcalde.

In blunt language, Santos demanded that the alcalde arrest those responsible for the death of García.[155] The alcalde replied that he did not have sufficient forces to make such an arrest, to which Santos responded that he was more than able to make the arrests, but by the time the alcalde agreed, Santos reported, the "assassins had all fled."[156] For several hours, Santos and his men searched the town and surrounding countryside, but the men could not be found. With little alternative, the alcalde agreed the hunt could continue, but after three days of frantic searching, Santos was forced to admit he had no "clue of the direction they had taken."[157]

In crossing with his men to Nuevo Laredo, Santos came close to creating an embarrassing situation, and when the news reached Matamoros, Governor López was furious. The event was yet another example of rambunctious and out-of-control Confederates trampling on the soil of Mexico, of the constant insults to the civil and military authorities of Tamaulipas. To López, the Nuevo Laredo incident was among "the most serious crimes against international law" and certain to "produce bitter feelings." López warned General Bee that the events in Laredo deserved "particular attention" and, if repeated, would produce "direful results."[158] In an apologetic mood and playing for time, Bee promised López he would investigate the incident as soon as he had Santos's official report.

Once General Bee, a close friend of the Benavides family ever since he had established himself as a merchant in Laredo, had read Santos's official report, he forwarded it to Governor López. "From my long acquaintance with Captain Benavides and high appreciation of him as a man of prudence and discretion," Bee wrote, "I am satisfied that the authorities on both sides of the line may equally confide in him as not likely to do any act to compromise the relation which should exist."[159] A year later, when Juan Cortina arrived in Nuevo Laredo with a small band of men, officials there still bitterly recalled how Santos and his men were in the habit of crossing the river and "mocking the authorities and doing whatever they wanted."[160] Cortina issued orders requiring anyone crossing from the Texas bank of the river to have proper papers and be disarmed.

One of the most notorious characters to arrive in Laredo during the Civil War was nineteen-year-old Benjamin Thompson. The English-born Thompson had enlisted in Lt. Col. John R. Baylor's Second Texas Mounted Rifles in the early summer of 1861. During a drunken New Year's Eve celebration at Fort Clark, Thompson seriously wounded a corporal.[161] Later in the war, after being discharged, Thompson and his brother Billy allegedly arrived in Laredo, where they organized a game of monte at a saloon that was owned by Dick Miller at Nuevo Laredo. Thompson won twenty-one Colt revolvers, valued at twenty dollars each, in addition to seven Remington pistols and three self-cocking pistols. The next night, after Santos's men had been paid, he claimed to have won $1,900, but when he attempted to close the game, the players started to scuffle, men drew their weapons, and Thompson shot and killed Lt. Martin Gonzales and Sgt. Miguel Zertuche. Thompson and his brother supposedly fled across the river to Laredo and then north through the brush country. No official record substantiates the incident, however.[162] Considering the commotion that was created when Pvt. Encarnación García was killed in Nuevo Laredo, Santos almost certainly would have reported the deaths of two of his men officially, or at least noted their demise in a muster roll. This suggests that much of what Thompson recalled was likely to have been imaginary.[163]

While in camp at Carrizo on the morning of April 12, 1863, Santos received notice that a party of cattle thieves had driven a large herd of animals across the river several miles downriver. He immediately dispatched a note to the military commander at Guerrero, saying he was taking up the trail of the thieves. With thirty men, Santos crossed the river and followed the trail of the animals upriver in the direction of Guerrero. Reaching the Rio Salado, just below Guerrero, he sent a second note into Guerrero asking Mexican authorities to assist him in the apprehension of the rustlers. The comandante there bluntly responded by telling Santos that he was in violation of international law and must return to the north bank of the river immediately.

Neither intimidated nor deterred, Santos rode directly to Guerrero, where he met with both the alcalde and comandante. The alcalde told Santos that in consideration of the agreement existing between Tamaulipas and Confederate authorities in Texas, he would do all in his power to apprehend the thieves. The military commander, however, angrily responded that he was under no such obligations and that he would only obey orders from Governor López. Moreover, he had enough men to drive Santos back into

Texas, if necessary. Santos had no doubt that the military commander was a liar; that he was working closely with the cattle thieves, especially José María Fernandez; and that the two had frequently been together in Guerrero. Furthermore, Santos blamed the military commander for informing Governor López of his "attack on Nuevo Laredo." He did not doubt that the comandante was "protecting all the thieves and assassins" along the river.[164] Santos threatened to invade the town, but after several hours he backed away and rode back to Carrizo with his men.

Not wanting to provoke another international incident by seizing Guerrero, Santos concluded that the only way to get rid of the bandits being harbored in the towns on the Mexican bank of the river was to "force the people to drive the thieves out." Santos knew that a large part of the Guerrero populace survived by maintaining their herds of cattle and property on the north bank of the river. "I propose to put them entirely at the mercy of the banditti they are harboring," Santos wrote headquarters, by issuing an order prohibiting "them to have arms on this side of the Rio Grande."[165] Within days, a number of leading ranchers from Guerrero were calling on Santos, saying they were afraid to go to their ranches without arms and if they lost their herds, they and their families would go hungry. As soon as officials in Guerrero quit harboring the thieves, Santos told the townsmen, he would he rescind the order. Not long after, most of the thieves had left Guerrero.

Hearing that Santos had crossed into Mexico yet again, Governor López immediately wrote General Bee to complain, asserting that what Santos had done was not in "conformity with the ratified agreement," that only in "cases of absolute necessity" were Confederate troops to cross the river. No "absolute necessity existed," López wrote, in Santos's trailing a band of cattle thieves. Santos's invasion of Nuevo Laredo, and his crossing at Guerrero, had caused a "deep distrust against him," López went on to say. Moreover, through his actions Santos had "created the utmost want of confidence in the towns."[166]

After receiving Governor López's complaints and Santos's report from

Virginia-born Gen. John Bankhead Magruder was known as "Prince John" to his friends because of his lavish life style and predilection for the dramatic. Magruder, who spoke with a lisp and who had lost an arm in Mexico, is perhaps best remembered today for his delaying tactics and elaborate ruses during the 1862 Peninsula Campaign that deceived Gen. George B. McClellan into believing the Confederate defenders at Yorktown were much larger than they actually were. Performing poorly and drinking excessively during the Seven Days Battles, the eccentric Magruder was exiled to the Trans-Mississippi by Gen. Robert E. Lee. Magruder commanded forces that recaptured Galveston on January 1, 1863, and he commanded the District of Texas, New Mexico, and Arizona in the last months of the Civil War. Said to have been the wittiest man in the "old army," Magruder fled to Mexico after the war where he entered the service of Emperor Maximilian. *Courtesy Library of Congress.*

Carrizo, General Bee rushed a lengthy letter across the river to the governor in Matamoros. Operating under the theory that the best defense was a good offense, Bee told López that it was a well-known fact that a number of cattle thieves had their headquarters in Guerrero, in particular Octaviano Zapata. Bee wanted the stolen cattle returned to Texas and said that both cattle and horses were stolen in Texas and driven into Mexico with "lamentable frequency."[167] He did, however, promise López that he would order Santos not to cross the river again.

Although preoccupied with events elsewhere, diplomats in Mexico City, as well as in Richmond and Washington, DC, were forced to devote more and more of their attention to the growing uneasiness on the Rio Grande. On May 2, 1863, because of his "gallant conduct" in defense of the frontier, Santos was promoted to major by Gen. John B. Magruder, commanding the districts of Texas, New Mexico, and Arizona. Six months later, he was made a colonel.[168]

Late on the evening of September 1, 1863, in a strange reversal of events, Santos was in camp at Carrizo when he received an urgent dispatch from the Guerrero alcalde, saying a detachment of Mexican troops had been attacked and routed by a large party of outlaws led by Zapata. With most of Capt. Cristóbal Benavides's Company H and Capt. Thomas Rabb's Company I, seventy-nine men in all, Santos rode immediately downriver to Rancho Clareño, splashed across the Rio Grande into Mexico, found where Zapata had ambushed the Mexican troops, and followed his trail downriver in the direction of Mier. Early the next morning, Santos's scouts located Zapata's camp near a mesquite thicket in the bottom of a ravine near the river, and with little hesitation, Santos ordered an all-out attack. "I directed the non-commissioned officers of Company H to select the leaders of the banditti, all of whom were known to them, and without delay attack the scoundrels," Santos wrote. The high banks of the ravine forced Santos's men to enter in single file. In the furious fighting that followed, much of it hand to hand, blood flowed freely. Zapata, who claimed the rank of colonel in the Union Army, and his lieutenants, Manuel Villarreal, Guillermo Vino, and Monico

Salinas, were all killed.[169] Although ten of Zapata's men died in the furious fight, none of Santos's men were killed or wounded. Fourth Corp. Natividad Herrera, twenty-five years old, was said to have killed Zapata with the butt of a rifle while the outlaw blazed away at the corporal with his pistol. First Lt. R. F. Haskins also distinguished himself, Santos said. "Should E. J. Davis ever invade the Rio Grande with his regiment of refugees and outlaws, he will miss his friend Zapata who had the power to do us great injury," wrote General Bee.[170]

Among Zapata's personal effects, Santos found copies of two letters Zapata had written to Antonio Pérez, a prominent citizen of Guerrero, appealing for support. Zapata said he had been "overwhelmed by the Confederates" and forced to attach himself to the army of the American Union. Moreover, he had been commissioned a colonel with orders to take control of the American bank of the river. Zapata hoped Pérez would join him in a "very just and sacred cause."[171] At the conclusion of the war, Zapata and his men would be given land and money in Texas.[172] Santos had little doubt the letters implicated Union authorities, especially Leonard Pierce, in the recruitment of Mexicans into the Union Army.[173]

Only days before being forced out of the lower valley by Federal forces advancing from Brazos Santiago, General Bee was excited that Santos had killed the notorious outlaw Zapata. Zapata was an "emissary of the Lincoln Government," Bee remembered, and had, for so long, been a terror on the frontier, having once crossed the Rio Grande carrying the flag of the United States. Bee wrote army headquarters in Houston, praising Santos for his "untiring energy and patriotism." Bee also pointed out that Capt. Cristóbal Benavides and Capt. Refugio Benavides, along with their men, had given their "unyielding support" to the Confederacy. Moreover, they were "all Mexicans," Bee pointed out.[174]

The Texas state legislature, always anxious to praise the Benavides brothers and assure the loyalty of the Tejano population they represented, had passed a joint resolution on March 6, 1863, lauding the brothers, particularly Santos and Refugio, for their "vigilance, energy, and gallantry displayed . . . in pursuing and chastising the banditti infesting the Rio Grande frontier."[175] Copies of the resolution were sent to General Magruder and other Confederate officers in Texas. When Magruder received a copy of the resolution, he asked that it be read before every assembled regiment, battalion, and unattached company in his district.[176]

As a colonel in the Confederate Army, Santos was at the height of his military career. Throughout most of 1863 he was in command of the "Line of the Rio Grande," a vast area stretching from the lower valley to the twisting canyon lands above Eagle Pass.[177] He would long be remembered as the highest-ranking Tejano in the rebel army and one of the most respected military leaders in Texas.

To the north and east, among the gentle hills and farmlands of southern Pennsylvania, in some of the fiercest fighting of the war, Gen. Robert E. Lee's once magnificent and seemingly invincible Army of Northern Virginia had been badly bloodied, leaving thousands of dead and wounded at Gettysburg. Lee had fallen back across the Potomac River beyond the Blue Ridge Mountains. To the west, on the Mississippi River, the once proud rebel garrison at Vicksburg, Mississippi, the Gibraltar of the Confederacy, fell on July 4, 1863. Downriver at Port Hudson, Louisiana, after the last Union campaign to liberate the Mississippi River, the South capitulated yet again. On the border, an army in blue chased General Bee out of Brownsville and occupied the lower valley. Upriver, Col. Santos Benavides stood alone with only a few hundred men. With the arrival of the Union Army on the Rio Grande frontier, the clouds of war were darkening and the tide was turning for Santos, his brothers, and the defiant Confederacy.

CHAPTER IV

COTTON AND BLOOD

"At Laredo the faithful Benavides kept watch and ward!"

—Gen. Hamilton P. Bee, *Laredo Daily Times*, September 26, 1884

On February 1, 1862, one of Santos's scouts galloped into San Agustín Plaza with news that a large wagon train was approaching Laredo on the San Antonio Road. Fifty mule-drawn wagons, all bulging with cotton bales, stretched for more than a mile. As the cotton was unloaded, Santos realized a new era was beginning, one that would dramatically alter the economic livelihood of communities all along the border. He knew the cotton trade would profoundly influence not just Laredo and South Texas, but also Tamaulipas and even Nuevo León and Coahuila. This white fiber—the backbone of the Southern economy and the result of endless African American toil and suffering, sweat, and blood—was bound for Mexican textile mills and foreign ports such as Havana, Liverpool, and Dublin, as well as Philadelphia, Boston, Providence, and New York. By June 1864, as many as 250 to 300 bales of cotton were arriving daily at Laredo.[1] To many citizens of Laredo and the borderlands, the years from 1861 to 1865 would be remembered not as the Civil War period but as the "Cotton Times."

Early in the war, when some European countries seemed hesitant to recognize the infant Confederacy, Jefferson Davis and his cabinet urged that cotton be withheld from the world market in hopes of forcing recognition or even naval intervention, especially by Great Britain and France. Realizing, however, that trade with Mexico would allow them to exchange Texas

This image of four Laredo Confederates, Capt. Refugio Benavides, Lt. Atanacio Vidaurri, Capt. Cristóbal Benavides, and Capt. John Z. Leyendecker, was likely taken in Brownsville in 1864 or early 1865, probably by Louis de Planque. *Courtesy of Ursuline Sisters.*

cotton for badly needed war supplies, Confederate authorities exempted those shipments.[2] As the only Southern state with a foreign border, Texas had a way around the Union blockade. This presented unique economic opportunities for the state. Most Texas cotton planters preferred the long and arduous overland wagon trip to the Rio Grande to the dangers of running the blockade. Moreover, as the price of cotton increased from sixteen cents per pound in August 1862 to eighty cents in November 1863, trade in cotton became a lucrative business. As the trade grew, however, corruption abounded, and the Confederate government and its military were forced to take charge.

What started as a trickle swelled into a river that made fortunes for both Texans and Mexicans, men such as Richard King, Mifflin Kenedy, and Patricio Milmo. Mexico got the cotton, and Texas received badly needed war materials. Enfield rifles, ammunition, percussion caps, as well as powder, lead, coffee, blankets, shoes, sugar, rope, and cotton goods of all kinds—in fact, everything imaginable that could be used by the Confederate Army—were brought into Texas from Mexico. The degree of the trade across the border was exemplified in November 1862, when the American consul in Monterrey, M. M. Kimmey, casually reported to Washington that rebel agents had requisitioned six hundred thousand blankets.[3] So extensive was the trade, that it became an integral part of the economic health and vitality of the Confederate trans-Mississippi, especially after the fall of Vicksburg and Port Hudson, when the region became isolated from the rebel government in Richmond.

Leading a nomadic existence while carrying Louisiana cotton to Mexico, Kentucky-born Eliza Moore Chinn McHatton Ripley remembered "hundreds of huge Chihuahua wagons . . . parked with military precision" outside San Antonio, "waiting their turn to enter the grand plaza, deliver their packages of goods and load with cotton."[4] John Warren Hunter, who as a fifteen-year-old teamster helped haul cotton to the border, recalled seeing "a never-ending stream of cotton pouring into Brownsville."[5] Across the river in Matamoros, Hunter remembered "ox trains, mule trains, and trains of Mexican carts, all laden with cotton coming from almost every town in Texas."[6] To the young man, Brownsville was "the greatest shipping point in the South," and Matamoros had become "a great commercial center [with] cotton and other commodities . . . pouring into her warehouses."[7] Matamoros was, the diehard Yankee and American consul Leonard Pierce Jr. wrote, "the great thoroughfare to the Southern States."[8] On the Rio Grande, cotton was "exchanged for English, French, Prussian and perhaps Harpers Ferry Rifles; here the convict gray clothing of England and France found a ready market in exchange for the cotton of Messrs. King & Kennedy [*sic*] & Co. and here the Jew and Gentile, Gog and Magog, found their first oasis from the cotton fields of Texas, on their way to Mecca (Liverpool)," a Texas Unionist wrote.[9]

At Brownsville, the cotton was frequently placed in small shallow-draft paddle steamers operated by the company of King, Kenedy, and Stillman and taken sixty-five miles down the narrow, twisting Rio Grande to its mouth at Bagdad. There, many of the steamers, operating as lighters, hauled the cotton to the larger seagoing vessels anchored in the choppy waters of the gulf, two to four miles offshore.[10] In early 1863, Lt. Col. Arthur James Lyon Fremantle of the British Coldstream Guards, while on a three-month tour of the Confederacy, said that Bagdad consisted of little more than "a few miserable wooden shanties."[11] Later in the war, when the majority of the cotton was crossed by ferry to Matamoros and taken in wagons to Bagdad, where as many as 150 vessels from all over the world waited to take it on and discharge their cargoes, the town had evolved from a small fishing village to a bustling port of fifteen thousand citizens.[12] However, the wind-swept community consisted of "dirty looking buildings" where "blockade runners, desperadoes, the vile of both sexes, adventurers, the Mexican and the rebel" gathered and where "numberless groggeries and houses of worse fame," that is, "vice in its lowest form," "held high carnival."[13] The *Daily Ranchero* of Matamoros referred to Bagdad as a "sand hole on the gulf," while a correspondent for the *New York Herald* found the town to be "a dirty, filthy place" with streets "covered with slime and mud puddles."[14] The *Herald* reporter wondered how "anyone [could] live there at all."[15]

On both sides of the border, corruption was rampant and reached the highest levels of the government and military. When the English blockade runner SS *Rob Roy* reached Bagdad in 1863, William Watson found the Mexican customs officials hurrying to extract as much money as possible from various duties and charges. "Everyone competed to grab what he could and many schemes there were to make money out of the crisis," Watson wrote.[16]

Although many of the cotton firms operating on the Rio Grande were owned by either English or German entrepreneurs, the most influential of the cotton traders was the Mexican firm of Milmo and Company out of Monterrey. This company was headed by Patricio Milmo, the influential son-in-law of Governor Santiago Vidaurri, who led the progressive, popular, politically autonomous government of Nuevo León and Coahuila. Patricio Milmo O'Dowd came to Mexico in 1845 and sixteen years later married the governor's daughter, Prudencia. The most important private merchant on the border and the wealthiest man in South Texas, however, was José San Román. With offices in both Brownsville and Matamoros, as well as flocks of busy clerks, Román was a quiet, politically influential, and self-made man, a bachelor and native of Bilbao, Spain.[17]

As Lincoln's blockade of the South tightened, cotton producers, traders, and teamsters, almost all of them strangers, crowded into the border towns. On the Mexican bank of the river, thousands of teamsters patiently waited with their carts to transport cotton to Matamoros or Bagdad. Although turbulent Mexican politics and the Union Rio Grande expedition at times interrupted and curtailed the flow of cotton, by late 1863 more than 150,000 bales had crossed from Brownsville to Matamoros. By the end of the war, 320,000 bales had been sent across the Rio Grande.[18] At the same time, both the cotton trade and the devalued Confederate currency served to inflate labor costs and the price of commodities. At Laredo in July 1864, the Cotton Office complained that laborers were asking anywhere from $3.00 to $6.00 per day and that board had increased to as much as $2.50 to $3.00 per day, costs unheard of before the war.[19]

Two main routes were used by teamsters taking cotton to the border. Much of the cotton from Central and East Texas came through Alleyton, the bustling railroad terminus on the lower Colorado River, west of Houston. From here rattling wagons and creaking ox carts carried the cotton slowly across the coastal prairie to King Ranch, a major staging and refitting hub on the cotton road, prior to the final 124-mile push across the burning sands of the Wild Horse Desert to Brownsville and the river.

A second route from Central Texas took cotton to San Antonio and then to King Ranch. From San Antonio, cotton was also taken south across the Nueces River to Rio Grande City or Laredo, or west and then south through the semiarid brush country to Eagle Pass, where the precious commodity was hauled down the south bank of the river to Matamoros.

This carte de visite of Capt. Cristóbal Benavides was taken late in the war, most likely in Brownsville by Louis de Planque. *Courtesy of Martin Callahan.*

From King and Kenedy's warehouse at Rio Grande City, cotton was hauled downriver by steamer to Bagdad.

Some of the cotton was carried south from Eagle Pass and Laredo to Monterrey, after which it was hauled hundreds of miles across deserts and mountains to textile mills in Querétaro, Durango and Guadalajara.[20] Each year three thousand to four thousand bales were transported to mills in Coahuila and Nuevo León alone. As the cotton trade expanded, the military in Texas used the opportunity to import vast amounts of tin, lead, copper, iron, nitrate of potash, quicksilver, sulfur, saltpeter, powder, and percussion caps, as well as blankets, shoes, and coffee.[21]

Despite the booming economy on the border, the flow of cotton across the Rio Grande, combined with the chaotic political atmosphere of Mexico, often produced a combustible state of affairs. Following the Union occupation of the lower valley in late 1863, the vast majority of cotton and war materials had to be crossed upriver at Laredo or Eagle Pass.

To bring some sense of order to the lucrative trade, the government in Richmond established a Texas Cotton Bureau, operating under the Confederate Cotton Bureau, to regulate the flow of cotton into Mexico, but from the beginning it was riddled with systemic corruption. The corruption was on such a grand scale that Texas newspapers railed against the bureau and demanded that it be reformed. Leading military figures such as General Bee and even General Magruder were alleged to be involved in the wide-scale improprieties. Moreover, the Texas Cotton Bureau claimed anywhere from 25 to 100 percent of the cotton crop.[22] But because Gen. Edmund Kirby Smith, commanding the Confederate trans-Mississippi, hoped to exchange Confederate cotton for badly needed war materials, he authorized agents in Mexico to negotiate the sale.

Much of the Confederate cotton from East Texas and from as far away as Louisiana and Arkansas was carried by Mexican teamsters, and when aggressive conscription officers began drafting the carters for the army, they pleaded that they were citizens of Mexico. Even men who had lived in Texas for decades claimed they were Mexicano, not Tejano, and many were greatly concerned that the trade would be seriously curtailed or even brought to a halt. Their livelihoods endangered, afraid they might be drafted to fight in the East, far from their families and homes, teamsters developed alternate routes to avoid San Antonio and King Ranch.[23] At Rio Grande City, it was said the Confederate conscription officer was "playing the very devil." As far as thirty miles from the border, teamsters were abandoning their wagons loaded with cotton and fleeing on foot into the chaparral.[24] Both Gen. Edmund Kirby Smith, overseeing the trans-Mississippi, and Gen. John Bankhead Magruder, commanding the districts of Texas, New Mexico, and Arizona, responded to the crisis by issuing orders prohibiting Mexicans from being drafted into the army. Enrolling officers were not to interfere with the teamsters, and Maj. Charles Russell, agent of the Cotton Bureau, was to give them special passports.[25] But even conscripts who were assigned as teamsters began deserting, which forced Colonel Ford to issue orders threatening severe punishment. "Any teamster who shall persuade, entice, or hire a conscript teamster to quit the service for which he has been detailed [will be arrested]."[26]

In March 1863, trouble developed along the route running through King Ranch when Confederates killed several Mexican herders in the vicinity of the ranch. Fearing a repetition of the violent racial intolerance that characterized the infamous "Cart War", which had paralyzed commerce between San Antonio and Indianola in 1857, General Bee issued orders for the apprehension of individuals responsible for the crimes. Under guard, the perpetrators were to be taken to Corpus Christi for trial.[27] Although the killings stopped, no one seems to have ever been arrested or brought to trial. Problems and violence along the cotton routes forced Confederate authorities to allocate precious human resources to South Texas when these were vital to rebel fortunes elsewhere.

The Union occupation of the lower Rio Grande Valley in late 1863 never seriously curtailed the torrent of cotton flowing into Mexico, nor the flow of war materials into Texas. With Laredo and Eagle Pass open to the rush of Confederate cotton, the length of the new cotton road was extended by as much as three hundred miles and the cost escalated by 50 percent. The route from San Antonio to Eagle Pass was much longer than the trail stretching south from San Antonio to Laredo, but it had less sand and more water, and it was the preferred route, although Union guerrillas operating out of Mexico frequently lurked in the brasada, waiting to pounce. As the trade shifted upriver, General Magruder put considerable trust in Santos and agreed that cotton could "be crossed at such points as Col. Benavides may suggest."[28] But controversy developed in March 1864, when Santos began seizing cotton and selling it to pay his men, who had not been paid in six months and whose families were suffering. Santos told Governor Vidaurri he was only taking "government cotton, not private cotton."[29] The Cotton Bureau, which was struggling to bring some semblance of order to the profitable trade, was highly critical of Santos but could do little.[30] In January 1864, while camped at San Ignacio, Santos wrote General Magruder asking that he be given specie for the "support of his command." Magruder agreed, and within days a wagon train of cotton at Gonzales was sent to the border to be turned over to the quartermaster of Benavides's Regiment.[31]

On May 21, 1864, in hopes of more efficiently procuring war materials in Mexico, the Confederate Senate established the Bureau of Foreign Supplies, which was charged with establishing cotton depots and purchasing cotton for export. But General Smith was not willing to relinquish control over the cotton trade, and he continued to impress one-half of all the cotton in the trans-Mississippi throughout the summer of 1864.[32]

Although war materials flowed into the Confederacy from Mexico, some munitions were purchased in Texas and crossed back into Mexico. In February 1862, for example, Santos had sent a special messenger to Lampazos to inform Governor Vidaurri that a party of seven men had arrived in Nuevo Laredo from Camargo with the expressed intention of using silver to purchase as much ammunition as possible in Laredo. Speculating that the party was sent by Carvajal, Santos issued orders prohibiting arms and ammunition sales in the area under his command. Thwarted by Santos's hastily conceived restraints, the men retreated downriver, but not before saying they would get revenge for the rude treatment they had received. "Your enemies send me thousands and thousands of curses and also promise vengeance against me," Santos told Vidaurri, but "I don't pay attention."[33]

At the same time, the governor urged Santos not to "ignore the conflict that is found in the Mexican Republic." Vidaurri remained hopeful that Santos would somehow find a way to join him, but he realized how conflicted Santos was by the war on the border. Santos was a man with a dual allegiance—someone intensely proud of his Mexican heritage who was loyally serving in the Confederate Army. But even in the rebel army, Santos could help his friends "to defend the Mexican nationality," Vidaurri told him.[34]

The lives of Santos and his men were soon changed dramatically by the sound of Union bugles echoing from the Gulf of Mexico. After escaping Texas, Unionists Edmund J. Davis and John L. Haynes went to Washington, where they told President Lincoln that the presence of the Union Army in Texas would encourage large numbers of Texas Unionists to join the Federal ranks. Moreover, from a base on the Rio Grande, Mexican Texans, many with deep-rooted and legitimate grudges against authorities in Texas, could be recruited for the Union cause.[35] Both Davis and Haynes were politically ambitious and opportunistic, and few understood the Mexican population of South Texas as they did. Safely in Washington, Davis and Haynes helped persuade the president to send an army to the border to, in Lincoln's words, "reinaugurate the National Authority on the Rio Grande first, and probably the Nueces also."[36] In the months that followed, Lincoln's action was widely reported in both Northern and Southern newspapers.

In twenty-six ships, the men of the Texas Union Expedition, under the command of Gen. Nathaniel P. Banks, sailed from a cold, gray New Orleans dawn and into a frightening storm off Aransas Pass. On November 2, 1863, at precisely noon, the seasick Federals "gave three hearty cheers . . . by the waving of hats and handkerchiefs," and after stumbling through the surf and sand at Brazos Santiago, they planted the Stars and Stripes on the island.[37] "The flag of the Union floats over Texas today," Banks proudly told

Lincoln.[38] For two days, the men in blue continued to wade ashore, many of them holding their rifles over their heads and away from the boiling surf of the Gulf.

The Texas Union Expedition was composed mostly of zealous young men from the Midwest, soldiers from Illinois, Indiana, Iowa, Missouri, and Wisconsin. But the expedition also included men from New England and two regiments of the Corps d'Afrique, as well as the First Texas Cavalry under the command of Santos's former friend and political ally Edmund J. Davis, now decked out in the uniform of a Union colonel. The Federals would remember Brazos Island as a barren and inhospitable place of "sand and sand hills . . . in every direction," and they were anxious to get to Brownsville.[39]

Three days after landing on Brazos Island, the advance column crossed the narrow straits of Boca Chica and began marching for the Rio Grande. In all, 6,998 bluecoats came to the border. They came to stanch the flow of cotton into Mexico and the flow of supplies and profits into Texas. The highest echelons of Union command talked of pushing up the Rio Grande, past Laredo and Eagle Pass, into the vast expanses of the Chihuahuan Desert to link up with Gen. James Henry Carleton's California Column in the trans-Pecos and thus control the entire 889-mile Texas-Mexico border. Col. John S. "Rip" Ford thought the Federals would probably try to occupy the entire Rio Grande frontier and that Laredo would have to be sacrificed. But he was determined to hold Eagle Pass—to keep at least one cotton road open. "I shall do everything in my power to prevent a junction of his forces and to beat him," Ford told Confederate headquarters in Houston.[40]

Lincoln also had other reasons for sending an army to Texas. He had no doubt the French imperialists in Mexico were in glaring violation of the basic tenants of the Monroe Doctrine. But with the war still raging not far from Washington, he was reluctant to involve the nation in a war with Napoleon III. However, the president could at least show his displeasure with the Mexican empire by waving the Stars and Stripes at the French.

Lincoln was also hoping, as was suggested, that a Federal army in Texas could provide a safe haven for the large number of Unionists who were being persecuted and who were fleeing the state in droves.

Arriving with the Union Army was another former acquaintance of Santos from Rio Grande City. John L. Haynes had represented Starr County in the Texas House of Representatives at the same time that Basilio served there. Although Davis escaped Texas with his family, Haynes was forced to leave his wife and four children behind.[41] "I left Texas," Haynes confessed, "from a sense of duty to my country, to my conscience and I wish to do my whole duty in the restoration of the authority of the nation."[42]

At Confederate headquarters at Fort Brown, General Bee had been concerned for some time that Davis and Haynes, along with Leonard Pierce, were plotting to have Juan Cortina attack Brownsville while the Federals were advancing from the coast. Knowing that Cortina was bitterly opposed to the Confederates, Haynes had been in contact with the Mexican insurrectionist to inform him that a Union invasion of Texas was imminent.[43] As early as June 1863, Bee had sent a spy to New York City to ascertain "the intentions of the Federal Government in regard to Texas."[44] A second spy found employment on a ship making the Bagdad–New York City run and was to gather as much information as possible. By August, Bee was convinced the invasion would be under way once the "Sickly Season" had passed.

Yet, when the invasion did come, Bee was poorly prepared. By August 1863, he was forced to move a large part of his command out of Fort Brown to avoid the summer illnesses that had plagued the post for years. Still, as much as one-third of the rebel army in Brownsville was reported to be sick.[45] At one time, every single officer in Brownsville, except for Bee, was ill. "The panic amongst the troops renders it impossible to keep them here, for at dress parade on yesterday there were but two officers out of four companies, the rest being sick or on duty," Bee wrote on August 15, 1863.[46] Another problem was that conscripts assigned to the Rio Grande often deserted as soon as they arrived. Bee had been furnished with twenty-five new wagons and over two hundred wild mules, but he had no one to break the animals. To complicate matters, merchants were refusing to accept Confederate currency, and teamsters could not be found, nor anyone even to harness the mules. With his small, sickly army, Bee thought it senseless to remain on the Rio Grande. "My force is too small to make any successful defense and I do not aspire to lead a retreat," he wrote.[47] But when the invasion came, Bee was still in Brownsville, and there was little he could do.

With the news that Union forces were landing on Brazos Island, Bee sent Capt. Henry T. Davis and nineteen men to Point Isabel to spy on the Yankees. Davis climbed the lighthouse from which he had a clear view across the murky waters of the Laguna Madre and Brazos Santiago Pass. With a spyglass, he watched for hours as hundreds of Federals disembarked from vessels large and small. Through the haze, Davis counted six regimental flags and twenty-six vessels, both sail and steam, as well as several artillery batteries.[48] "The enemy are in force. Brazos Island is covered with tents," Bee wrote in a frenzy.[49]

The impending arrival of the Union Army on the Rio Grande set off a chain of events. One was the mutiny of the unpredictable captain Adrián J. Vidal, Mifflin Kenedy's impetuous stepson, who had been given command of a cavalry company at the mouth of the river. Unbeknownst to the Confederate command in Brownsville, Vidal had fallen under the influence of the charismatic and always conniving Cortina. Vidal may have also been in touch with the commander of the Union ships blockading the mouth of the Rio Grande. On the evening of October 28, just as darkness engulfed General Bee's headquarters at Fort Brown and only days before the Federals began wading ashore at Brazos Santiago, rumors reached Brownsville that Vidal and his entire company had mutinied and, with the help of Texas Unionists from Matamoros, were planning to attack Brownsville during the night. With the "garrison and citizens thrown into a panic," Bee called a council of war. At the same time, he issued orders recalling three companies of Col. James Duff's Thirty-third Texas Cavalry that had been ordered to Houston only days earlier and who were thought to be encamped on the

Palo Alto prairie. Fearing that Vidal was intent on sacking Brownsville, Bee organized and hastily armed a militia company for a six-month tour of duty.[50]

General Bee was also fearful that he would be attacked by either Cortina, Unionists from across the river, or both. His men pulled a twenty-four-pounder cannon and an eight-inch siege howitzer into position to guard the arsenal and the Fort Brown garrison. Bee's more dependable regulars were placed on the outskirts of the town and remained on alert throughout the night. But Vidal's attack never materialized. Crying "Muerte a los Americanos," the Vidalistas passed within a mile of Brownsville at about 3:00 a.m. on October 29 and continued along the river road for nine miles, plundering several ranches and killing at least ten unoffending citizens.[51] In Mexico, Vidal joined Cortina, only to be captured by the French while hiding on a steamboat at Camargo, charged as a spy, and executed.[52]

With the Union Army advancing on Brownsville, General Bee contemplated taking what cotton he could and fleeing upriver to Rio Grande City to join Santos. Pressing every wagon and many of the horses in Brownsville into the service of the Confederacy, Bee was eventually able to assemble forty-five wagons and load them with military equipment and cotton. He finally concluded that it would be impractical due to the "narrow and tortuous road" to advance through the dense chaparral along the river. Instead, he would take his small force east from Brownsville to slow the Union advance and give the slow-moving wagon train time to move north across the Palo Alto prairie to the Arroyo Colorado. "I received no assistance from the citizens of Brownsville," Bee complained, and on the morning of November 3, the militia company dissolved and disappeared.[53] A number of his men walked away and crossed the river to Matamoros.

Before departing Brownsville, Bee ordered Fort Brown fired. As many as two hundred bales of cotton that could not be ferried or floated across the river were also burned. Unfortunately, the flames spread from the fort to the town, and within minutes an entire block of buildings along Levee Street in front of the ferry was ablaze.[54] Unsurprisingly, the frightened townspeople

With the Union Army approaching Brownsville in November 1863, an "English Artist" made this sketch for *Harper's Weekly* of panic-stricken cotton traders and businessmen rushing goods across the Rio Grande. *Harper's Weekly*, February 13, 1864.

were more intent on stopping the spread of the fire than assisting the Confederates' escape with their munitions and cotton. Considerable plundering by townsmen and soldiers alike also added to the confusion, and the loss of so much private property caused great animosity toward Bee and the rebels. In the midst of the chaos, eight thousand pounds of powder at Fort Brown exploded, breaking windows, destroying commissary stores, and further terrorizing the helpless citizens. Finally, at midnight on November 3, 1863, General Bee and his small command bid a fatigued and drunken adieu to Brownsville. More than four hundred Unionists lined the south bank of the river to hiss and curse at the panic-stricken Confederates. "Peril was around me on all sides," Bee wrote.[55] The South Carolina–born general headed north with a ten-man escort and a wagon train of cotton, said to be worth $1 million, through the chaparral for the Arroyo Colorado and King Ranch. However, many of the heavily loaded wagons accompanying Bee were unable to cross the ever-moving sands of the Wild Horse Desert, and much of the cotton had to be thrown out of the wagons and burned.

Reaching King Ranch on the Santa Gertrudis six exhausting days after leaving the border, General Bee wrote Santos saying he had directed several of the cotton trains that were at or near King Ranch to Laredo. Santos was to see that the cotton was safely passed into Mexico. Cristóbal and Refugio with their companies were to guard the roads leading to Laredo. Santos, who was now in command on the Rio Grande, was to recruit additional men, if possible, and undertake a guerrilla war against the invading Yankees. The two men had discussed such a contingency on more than one occasion, and Santos was agreeable. "The whole country looks to you and your gallant, faithful men," Bee wrote. The general asked for one thousand cavalrymen to operate on the Rio Grande, and he promised to join Santos on the river as soon as possible. "[Together] we will sweep from the earth the traitors who have disgraced us," Bee promised.[56]

Santos was uncertain where to establish his headquarters, but he was sure that with reinforcements he could hold the Federals in the lower valley. Reaching Corpus Christi and still grasping for straws, Bee issued orders for all Confederate deserters on the Rio Grande to join Santos at Laredo.[57] Few, if any, responded.

As General Bee was fleeing north, Charles Russell, the Confederate quartermaster at Fort Brown, hurried across the river to Matamoros. Russell hoped to secure Confederate supplies in the city and redirect others that had yet to arrive. But as crowds marched through the streets chanting "Death to the Confederacy," Russell began to fear for his life and rushed to find refuge with King and Kenedy. The two steamboat entrepreneurs provided the quartermaster with a carriage, and he fled Matamoros in the early morning darkness and hurried to Monterrey, where he knew he would be safe with Governor Vidaurri and Milmo. Before leaving Matamoros, Russell sent a special express to Santos. It was critical that a lifeline to Mexico remain open at either Laredo or Eagle Pass, Russell said. Santos was to "concentrate his forces at some point below Roma" and halt any Federal advance until all the cotton at Laredo and Eagle Pass could be safely crossed into Mexico. With as many as three hundred men, the Confederates hoped, Santos could not only stop the Federals but force them back into the lower valley.[58]

In the strangest turn of events since the fighting at Carrizo in the early months of the war, Santos was reported to have made an agreement with Cortina to protect the Confederate cotton crossing the border at Laredo. The unpredictable Cortina had seized power in Matamoros and proclaimed himself governor of Tamaulipas. Hearing the news, General Magruder wrote Cortina a brief note congratulating him on his "willingness to cooperate with Confederate authorities." Even Gov. Pendleton Murrah seemed excited over the alleged agreement.[59] No sound evidence exists, however, for any such agreement, and Magruder may have been misinformed. Cotton continued to flow across the river at Eagle Pass, as well as at Laredo. In fact, the Union occupation of the lower Rio Grande Valley did little to stop the quantity of cotton crossing the border. "The occupation of Brownsville has no effect in stopping the trade," M. M. Kimmey, the US vice consul in Monterrey, told Secretary of State William H. Seward. Kimmey also watched from Monterrey as Confederate traders continued to send "enormous quantities of goods to Texas through Eagle Pass and Laredo."[60]

Unable to prevent the Union invasion of the lower valley, General Bee was forced to defer to Santos in matters on the border. Both Bee and Gen. James Slaughter recommended Santos be promoted to brigadier general and placed in command of what remained of Confederate forces on the river. Santos, Bee and Slaughter argued, was the only one on the river who was capable of rallying "the population to [the Confederates'] assistance."[61] Due to his "strong personal influence," Santos could easily create "a guerrilla force" and turn "a quasi-hostile population into most valuable auxiliaries."[62] The idea of making Santos a brigadier general went over well at Confederate headquarters in Houston and in Shreveport. "In consideration of your gallant and distinguished services, recently called to the attention of the Lieut. General Comd'g by Brig. Genl's Bee & Slaughter, you are hereby authorized to raise a regiment of Partisan Rangers in Western Texas, from any men, whether within conscript age or not, not now in service, which regiment you will be appointed to command," Gen. Edmund Kirby Smith told Santos in early November 1863.[63] Both Smith and Magruder wanted to assure Santos's loyalty and keep the cotton road open. Considering the rapidly declining state of affairs on the border, Santos realized he would have difficulty raising a regiment, but he badly wanted to be a general and was willing to recruit as many men as possible.

In the weeks after the Union occupation of Brownsville, the situation at Ringgold Barracks and Rio Grande City, where Santos had temporarily set up his headquarters, became eerily similar to the one in Brownsville. Hearing that the Union Army was on the coast and moving inland, two companies dissolved in the night and fled across the river to Camargo. Santos, however, called his Tejanos together and bluntly told the men that a large Federal army was on the coast and that if any of them did not want to fight, he would issue discharges and extend his sincere thanks for their valuable services.[64] "The answer was," General Bee would write, a resounding "'*Viva la Confederacion!*' '*Viva Major Benavides!*' Not a man left him."

Santos told Bee that if necessary he would launch "a guerrilla war to the last." "This has given me great satisfaction, and does not surprise me," Bee wrote from his camp near King Ranch. When he learned that Santos was willing to defend the border to the end, Bee realized it was likely to remain open for some time, and he issued orders diverting as many cotton trains as possible to Laredo. Although these were the most difficult of times on the Rio Grande, Santos was, Bee wrote, "a gallant, influential leader," someone who was determined to defend to the death what had become the darkest and loneliest corner of the besieged Confederacy.[65]

Although the Federals would most likely seize Laredo, the Confederates hoped Santos could keep open the road to Eagle Pass. Since Davis and Haynes were successfully recruiting large numbers of Tejanos and Mexicanos in the lower valley, Magruder speculated they would also be attacking wagon trains on the San Antonio–Eagle Pass road.[66] In January 1864, one of Santos's spies in the lower valley brought him a document signed by

Antonio Abad Días, whom Haynes had recruited as a captain for the Union Army. Encouraged by Haynes, Días was attempting to recruit men in Mexico, saying the Federals were offering a bounty of one hundred pesos to all recruits, twenty-five to be given upon enlistment and seventy-five at the end of the war. The men would be given an overcoat, a jacket, pants, a shirt, underwear, shoes, socks, a hat, and provisions of all kinds. The men would be given weapons, but men who were likely to desert were not wanted.[67]

To keep Santos active and loyal, Magruder promised to send him 1,250 bales of Confederate cotton to help pay his men whose families were in a "starving condition."[68] Another 250 bales of Confederate cotton in Monterrey would also be credited to Santos. The cotton was worth $150,000, Magruder guessed, and with the money Santos could not only pay his men, but procure badly needed arms from Union deserters and anyone else on the border who possessed a weapon and was willing to sell it. With such support, Santos could turn back any Union advance.[69] The money from another five hundred bales that was sold in Monterrey could also be used to pay Santos's men. And another one thousand bales were to be set aside "to his credit for the support of his army and himself," Magruder wrote.[70] The general would do anything to keep Santos loyal. In March 1864, Magruder ordered cotton from the small Confederate depot at Banquete, which had become obsolete as a result of the Union occupation of the lower valley, be sent to Santos at Laredo for sale in Mexico.[71] Santos was to use "such inducements as would probably bring to his standard the whole of the border population."[72] Keeping the colonel from Laredo in the rebel fold was "the only plan by which the cotton trade to Mexico [could] be protected," the general was forced to conclude.[73] By late 1863, except for the small Confederate garrison at Fort Duncan, Santos's Tejanos were all that remained of the once-proud Confederate Army on the Rio Grande.

Maj. Charles Russell arrived in Laredo in late November 1863 with funds to pay the freight on Confederate cotton that was being sent across the river. Despite the frontier being "wholly unprotected," Governor Vidaurri had given him an escort at Monterrey and a loan of $100,000. Santos was still below Carrizo with only 150 men and was providing "fine service," Russell wrote. "He swears he will protect the Rio Grande, and in view of the importance of this trade I hope he will be re-enforced," the commissioner continued.[74]

Only weeks after the arrival of the Union Army in Brownsville, Colonel Davis and more than fifteen hundred men, many of them from the First Texas Cavalry, were already in the field. The Texas cavalry, reinforced by infantry from the captured steamer *Mustang*, forced Santos out of Ringgold Barracks, and an advance guard of two hundred men under Colonel Haynes pushed as far upriver as Roma.[75] Learning the Federals were nearing Rio Grande City, and perhaps fearing he might be out-flanked, Santos and twenty men fled across the river to the safety of Camargo, but not before the colonel was able to send some twenty-five hundred bales of cotton across the river. Davis arrived to find only eight bales of cotton on the wharf.

When Union general N. J. T. Dana received the news that the Federals were in possession of Ringgold Barracks and Rio Grande City and that Santos had fled across the river, he sent a dispatch to Pierce at the American consulate in Matamoros. "Now, is he a Mexican or a Texan?" Dana asked. "I am not disposed to play hide and seek with such cut-throats as he is. If he is a Texan, I shall demand him, as a renegade, for punishment. If he is a Mexican, it must be looked to that he answers properly to the Mexican authorities for his outrages against our laws."[76] Dana may have been confused and probably saw Santos as just another Mexican bandit or revolutionary. He appears not to have understood exactly who Santos was, his rank in the Confederate Army, or the transnational complexities of the war on the Rio Grande. In reality, Santos was both a Texan and a Mexican, someone who lived in Texas, but who valued his Mexican ancestry and maintained political alliances in Mexico.

Realizing how valuable Santos was to their success on the Rio Grande, Davis and Haynes tried to lure Santos and his two brothers into the Union ranks. It was rumored at the time that Davis was authorized to offer Santos a commission as a brigadier general if he would break with the Confederacy.

Davis allegedly rode upriver along the Mexican bank, probably with the tacit approval of Cortina, to Nuevo Laredo, where he sent a messenger across to ask for a meeting with his former friend and political ally. Santos agreed to talk, but he was so unpopular in Nuevo Laredo that he was reluctant to cross the river and asked instead that the meeting be held at his home in Laredo.[77] There is no evidence, however, that the two men met until after the war. Davis was certain to have remembered his near death at the hands of Confederate ruffians when they seized him near the mouth of the river a few months earlier and almost hanged him.[78]

From their base at Brownsville, the men of the Union reconnaissance struck hundreds of miles into the interior. A Union patrol destroyed the salt works at El Sal del Rey, and by December 1863 raiders in blue crossed the Wild Horse Desert. From a forward camp at Las Ánimas, Capt. James Speed led seventy cavalrymen, about one-half of them recently recruited Tejanos and Mexicanos, in a raid on King Ranch. Since the beginning of the war, the ranch served as a major way station on the cotton road, a place where weary teamsters found water, food, and rest. For many of the Tejanos, King Ranch became symbolic of the arrogance and elitism of the rapidly consolidating ranching empires in South Texas, and because Richard King was a loyal Confederate, the ranch became a target. Many former Cortinistas now in the Union Army hoped not only to destroy the ranch but to kill King and Kenedy, if possible. Two days before Christmas 1863, Captain Speed and his raiders struck the ranch, killing Francisco Alvarado, one of King's vaqueros; driving off horses and mules; plundering the ranch house; and smashing King's furniture before retreating to Las Ánimas.[79]

In the area south of the Nueces River, it was the Union Army, rather than Santos, who unleashed a vicious guerrilla war. Two of the most active Tejano guerrillas were Cecilio Valerio and his son Juan. Loosely attached to the Union Army, the senior Valerio was reported by Colonel Ford to be "an active officer; well acquainted with the country; brave and vigilant."[80] The Valerios, along with other Tejanos and Mexicanos, were active in raiding the ranches in the Nueces Strip and delivering large herds of cattle to the

Union Army on the border.[81] In fact, the well-orchestrated and wide-scale cattle raids that plagued the region for two decades after the war had their origins in the Civil War. Cecilio Valerio, whom legend holds was not only in contact with Union authorities in Brownsville but the Union Navy off Padre Island, was said to have been paid in gold by the Federals.

While camped with 126 of his guerrillas at a watering hole called Los Patricios in what is today Jim Wells County, Valerio was attacked by Confederates under Capt. Mat Nolan early on the morning of March 13, 1864.[82] With their Burnside carbines, revolvers, and sabers, Valerio and his men took up arms in a dense mesquital and, according to Nolan, fought "most gallantly and could only be repulsed after a desperate fight and at the cost of much blood and property." In the brief but vicious fight, three Confederates and five guerrillas were killed. Nolan and his men found several pools of blood near the mesquital, indicating that some of the guerrillas had been seriously wounded. Valerio left behind thirty-one horses, 107 blankets, six Colt revolvers, five Burnside carbines, and twenty-five sabers. Unfortunately, no written report from the Union side of the bloody encounter has been found.[83]

With the Union Army in control of Rio Grande City and Federal guerrillas striking as far north as the Nueces, Santos could clearly see the turning of the tide. Yet he remained defiant and combative. On December 3, he drafted a letter addressed to the "People of the Frontier," which was published in several Texas newspapers. The Federals had taken Roma and pushed upriver as far as Carrizo. Laredo was certain to be attacked, and the people were greatly alarmed. In his letter Santos reported that Union officers had "armed all the Mexican thieves on both sides of the Rio Grande." He was particularly miffed that Adrián J. Vidal, the reckless stepson of Mifflin Kenedy who had raised a company of soldiers for the Confederacy early in the war, had gone over to the Yankees. Vidal became a "Mexican traitor" who had been sent to "murder and rob all Americans." The "excesses which those thieves have already committed are most horrible," Santos went on to say. Reflecting the racist inclinations of most Anglo Texans and the Texas press at the time, Santos asserted that the main force of the enemy consisted of "niggers, renegades, and Mexican banditti."[84]

Santos admitted he had only 150 reliable men with which to defend Laredo, but with two hundred recruits he was sure he could drive the enemy back to their breastworks outside Brownsville. "I appeal to every man on the frontier, old and young, to come to the protection of his country. If you stay at home and my small force [is] unable to check the advances of the enemy, you will either be murdered by the banditti, or be ruled over by niggers and renegades," he wrote, parroting what Ford and others were saying. Santos was hoping unattached companies could rendezvous at old Fort Ewell on the Nueces River. If the men could bring their horses and weapons, Santos could furnish them with ammunitions and rations. Under his authority, men could join independent companies and serve for a little as one month or as many as six. Moreover, anyone who joined his command would be exempt from conscription. Once the Federals were defeated, Santos would guarantee the men's safe return to their homes.[85]

Although determined to defend Laredo, Santos feared it was only a matter of time before Union bayonets would be in San Agustín Plaza, and everything he had struggled to build over two decades would be lost. In early December 1863, when the news reached Laredo that the Federals were disembarking on the coast, he gathered his immediate family, including his sisters and an unnamed brother-in-law, and sent them to Monterrey by way of Presidio del Rio Grande (Piedras Negras), asking Governor Vidaurri to look to their safety and welfare. Agustina had in her possession more than enough money for the trip and their extended stay. Santos also arranged with Patricio Milmo to provide credit to the family, if necessary. "I shortly await having a fight with the enemy" and hope that "god lets me have a good fight," Santos told Vidaurri.[86]

By Christmas 1863, Santos wrote Vidaurri from Laredo: "The enemy will reach this city, since there is not a force close enough to repel them." Santos had little doubt that all his property, including his recently completed two-story home on the west side of the plaza, would be seized and perhaps destroyed. Besides the main house, Santos also owned several vacant lots, an adobe house with a straw roof, and a nearby rock corral. To save his home, Santos entered into a most ingenious scheme with Vidaurri by which he would draw up an agreement to sell the house to the governor. The contract would be backdated to July 1862, when Santos had visited Vidaurri in Monterrey. Trusting the governor, Santos had no doubts that after the war the property would be returned to him. "You know how to make these documents," Santos told the governor. Vidaurri could even rent the house, which had been vacant since Agustina left for Monterrey. "Everything could easily be arranged, leaving only you and I to know the rest," Santos confided.[87] Although Vidaurri agreed to the idea, he asked Santos to obtain the signatures of witnesses to the scheme. However, such affidavits and contract were probably never completed. Well into 1864, the Civil War continued to rage across the South Texas landscape. At Laredo, Col. Santos Benavides and his gallant band of Tejanos awaited the arrival of Union bayonets.

CHAPTER V

FORSAKEN CORNER OF THE CONFEDERACY

"I have to fight to the last; though hardly able to stand, I shall die fighting."

—Santos Benavides, March 19, 1864

When Gen. John B. Magruder replaced Gen. Paul Octave Hébert in command of the District of Texas, New Mexico, and Arizona, he renewed Confederate efforts to reoccupy the lower Rio Grande Valley. The man given the job of driving the Federals from the Rio Grande was none other than Col. John S. "Rip" Ford, who knew as much about the geography and people of the region as anyone. On December 22, 1863, General Magruder wrote the black-bearded, white-haired Ford to suggest that he recruit and assume command of a cavalry force sufficient to reoccupy the Rio Grande frontier. Relieved of his conscription duties in Austin, Ford set up headquarters at San Antonio and began to assemble a small army. "These were the days when strong passions ruled," Ford would write.[1] At Magruder's suggestion, Ford was to give every indication that he intended to occupy Indianola and the central Texas coast, but upon leaving San Antonio, he was to march for the Mexican border. "You will not let a soul know of your intended movements," Magruder wrote. "By making a sudden and rapid movement, you may be able to create a panic among the enemy."[2]

In late December 1863, as Ford was building his small army in San Antonio, he became concerned that Santos would make a forward movement and alarm the Federals in the lower valley. "You will only attack parties of the enemy coming near your lines," Ford told him. The Federals were to "believe that no forward movement is intended in the direction of the lower Rio Grande." Moreover, Santos was to make every effort to leave the impression with citizens and military on the south bank that the troops being assembled at San Antonio would operate against Indians. "Keep out scouts," Ford urged, and "keep yourself informed of the movements of the enemy."[3]

Ford was also concerned that before he could go on the offensive in the lower valley, he would be hit by a Federal advance from the Trans-Pecos. "Should the enemy advance from El Paso our whole available force will be thrown upon Fort Clark," Ford wrote Santos at Eagle Pass. Although Ford thought it unlikely that Federals could advance all the way from El Paso, he made plans to defend Dead Mans Pass, a remote and perilous canyon on the San Antonio–El Paso road, west of San Felipe Springs and just east of the Devils River. Here, he thought, would be an ideal place for the Confederates to make a stand.[4]

Back in New Orleans, Gen. Nathaniel P. Banks, the commander of Union forces in Texas, wanted to "keep a close watch upon [the Rio Grande] as far north as possible" and establish contact with General Carleton in the Trans-Pecos.[5] With news that the California Column had arrived in southern New Mexico and was in possession of Texas as far east as Fort Davis, even sending scouts to Horsehead Crossing on the Pecos River, General Banks wrote General Carleton proposing that their two armies link up to seal the entire 804-mile Texas-Mexico border and cut the flow of cotton into Mexico. Perhaps the two armies could even meet in San Antonio. However, Gen. Napoleon Jackson Tecumseh Dana, commanding the Department of the Gulf, realized that to occupy the "immense line of the frontier of the Rio Grande" would "require an expenditure of force and resources" that seemed to him "unjustifiable."[6]

In such a vast land, communication between the two armies was difficult at best. In late 1863, General Banks dispatched a courier with a message for General Carleton. The messenger was to make contact with T. P. McManus, a Union guerrilla operating in the Eagle Pass area, and then proceed west to find Carleton or his advance guard somewhere in the Trans-Pecos.

John S. "Rip" Ford. During much of the Civil War, Santos Benavides was subordinate to Ford. With the creation of Ford's Cavalry of the West as Benavides struggled to raise a regiment of his own, a feud developed between the two men over recruiting that greatly hindered Confederate command on the Rio Grande. Ford's request that Benavides be court-martialed on an array of charges was never approved, largely because of Benavides's political influence on the border. When Ford sat down to write his memoirs late in life and he asked Benavides for specifics on his defense of Laredo in March 1864, Santos refused to respond. *Courtesy Lawrence T. Jones III Collection, DeGolyer Library, SMU.*

The horseman, however, was overtaken and attacked forty-five miles northwest of Eagle Pass near San Felipe Springs, where he was badly wounded by four of Santos's "Mexicans," who were hired by "Christ killing Jew cotton speculators," McManus asserted.[7] A second letter did get through by way of Monterrey, Parras, and Chihuahua, and in early December 1863 was carried north across the desert to El Paso and then to General Carleton at Mesilla.[8] With the encouragement of Myndert M. Kimmey, the American vice-consul at Monterrey, Carleton thought seriously of sending a small force to seize or destroy the cotton at Eagle Pass, where as many as 250 Texas Unionists who had congregated in Monterrey could join the Federals.

Chief of Staff Henry W. Halleck realized that logistics prohibited the Union Army from advancing very far into the vast and inhospitable Trans-Pecos, but he urged General Carleton to launch a "demonstration . . . on the upper Rio Grande which would at least embarrass the rebels in that quarter."[9] Carleton also knew that pushing any sizeable force across the vast expanses of the treacherous Trans-Pecos would be a logistical nightmare even worse than what he experienced in crossing the Sonoran Desert from California in 1862. And to do so would further agitate the Mescalero Apaches, who had proved such formidable enemies of the Texans in 1861 and 1862. Besides, his twenty-six-hundred-man California Column was thinly spread out over far West Texas and New Mexico, and already preoccupied with campaigns against the Mescaleros and Mimbres Apaches as well as the Navajos. Carleton was able to send only small patrols into the Trans-Pecos, one as far east as Fort Lancaster. Moreover, thanks to the disinformation being disseminated by Henry Skillman—the capable, hard-riding, heavy-drinking Confederate spy and courier who operated freely in the Trans-Pecos before the Federals killed him at Spencer's Ranch near Presidio in April 1864—Carleton had come to fear a sizeable Confederate advance from Texas, and he was in a defensive mode.[10]

One serious problem facing the Confederate Army in South Texas was the "Milmo difficulty." On December 11, 1863, Patricio Milmo, the son-in-law of Governor Vidaurri and the largest cotton trader in Mexico, seized seven trunks containing $16 million in Confederate notes, claiming he was owed a half million pounds of cotton. The trunks were in the care of Clarence C. Thayer, the Confederate treasury agent, who had arrived in Matamoros on November 6, 1863, to deliver the funds to San Antonio, thus relieving the money shortage in the Trans-Mississippi Department and helping to restore confidence in the Richmond government. Maj. Charles Russell, the Confederate quartermaster in Brownsville, persuaded Thayer to place the funds with the reputable Milmo and Company, who would transport them to Monterrey and then to Piedras Negras, where they could be crossed to Eagle Pass and taken to San Antonio. Milmo, who had a number of grievances against the Confederates, not only seized the Confederate funds but all the cotton at Piedras Negras and refused to release the funds until the debt was paid in full.[11]

During a series of meetings, Vidaurri failed to persuade his son-in-law to release the funds. The governor was fearful that Confederate authorities in Texas would retaliate, and he wrote Santos, pledging not to embargo any cotton. He was not complicit in the actions of his son-in-law, but he did everything possible to protect Milmo's interests, giving preference to his cotton and even asking Santos to treat Milmo as if he were family.[12]

Just as Vidaurri had feared, Gen. Edmund Kirby Smith, commanding the Confederate Trans-Mississippi Department and acting along with the Confederate State Department, issued orders halting the shipment of cotton and other goods to Mexico on January 12, 1864.[13] At the same time, all Mexican assets in Texas were frozen until the dispute with Milmo could be resolved. Wagon trains loaded with cotton arrived at Laredo and Eagle Pass only to be prohibited from crossing the river. Cotton piled up to such an extent that by March 1864, five thousand bales were stacked in San Agustín Plaza at Laredo and an equal amount at Eagle Pass. The $40,000 to $50,000 revenue that Vidaurri received monthly from the Piedras Negras customhouse was reduced to a pittance. Realizing the gravity of the situation, General Smith sent a three-man delegation of Col. Thomas F. McKinney, Judge Thomas J. Devine, and Capt. Felix Ducatet scurrying south to meet with Vidaurri. The commissioners assured the governor the debt owed Milmo would be paid, but they wanted Vidaurri to assure the release of the Confederate funds. When Milmo was guaranteed that he and his partner, Evaristo Madero, would receive twenty-two hundred bales of Confederate cotton, he agreed to the proposition.[14]

Not trusting Vidaurri and Milmo, General Magruder told Santos on March 2, 1864, to redirect all the cotton heading into Mexico by way of Eagle Pass to Laredo, where it could be sent into Tamaulipas instead of Coahuila. Santos was to meet immediately with the governor of Tamaulipas and make arrangements. Confederates on the border were to make every effort in the future to avoid another Milmo debacle. "Rely on your known intelligence to arrange this important business," Magruder told Santos.[15] But at Laredo, serious problems developed with the Cotton Bureau.

Cotton was frequently smuggled across the river at night both above and below Laredo, and perhaps few agents were as corrupt as Kentucky-born C. W. Thompson. Santos accused Thompson of crossing cotton illegally and accumulating $2,000 in bribes. On the night of April 3, 1863, Santos learned that Thompson fled Laredo with $7,000 in treasury funds. He was last seen riding rapidly downriver, presumably to cross at Carrizo or Rio Grande City and find refuge with Leonard Pierce, the US consul at Matamoros, but a squad of Santos's cavalry was able to apprehend him a few miles outside of Laredo. Santos urged Magruder to make an example of Thompson. "The abstraction of government money by agents of the government," Santos wrote, "[has become] so frequent, that government agents are now looked upon as little better than highway robbers." Citizens of Laredo were demanding to know "why a wholesale robber should escape," while he who stole a cow or horse met "with the just punishment of death."[16] On June 5, 1864, Santos would issue special orders halting the flow of cotton across the Rio Grande.[17] Despite his complaints to army headquarters, the corruption at Laredo continued to such a degree that the inland port was officially closed in August 1864.

In early 1864, the war was going badly for the Confederacy, morale in

Texas plummeted, and desertions escalated. Colonel Ford was fearful that if something was not done to improve army morale, he would "have a mob instead of an army."[18] In South Texas, hundreds of once-zealous rebels were seeking haven in Mexico. One such individual was a friend of Santos, José Ángel Navarro III, the Harvard Law School-educated son of José Antonio Navarro of Texas Revolution fame. José Ángel was also the brother of Capt. Sixto Navarro, a captain in the Eighth Texas Infantry who later served in Santos's regiment. In November 1863, José Ángel Navarro learned in San Antonio that court-martial charges were being prepared against him, and he fled to Mexico. Arriving in San Fernando de Rosas on November 31, Navarro wrote Governor Vidaurri, saying that he had been treated with "injustice" in Texas. "We of Mexican extraction do not enjoy the same privileges [as Anglos]," Navarro wrote.[19] Vidaurri responded by saying it gave him "much pleasure" that Navarro would be coming to live among them.[20] José Ángel Navarro had ably served with Basilio Benavides in the state legislature and in 1860, at the behest of Governor Sam Houston, was appointed as a commissioner to investigate the causes of the Cortina War.[21] Navarro had long resented the deep-rooted discrimination in Texas against Tejanos, and he had fought against the blatant nativism in the legislature. "I'd prefer living there with those that I can naturally get along with better," Navarro told Vidaurri.[22]

In early February 1864, the *San Antonio Herald* reported all was quiet "all along the Rio Grande." Santos was in command of three hundred men at Laredo, and "no enemy was near." "[Santos] Benavides deserves the thanks of every true man of the state for his faithful and efficient services," the newspaper went on to say.[23] Yet Santos continued to worry that Laredo would be attacked and sacked. Even the weather seemed to be conspiring against the Confederacy. The winter of 1863–1864 was the driest and coldest Santos could remember. The area south of the Nueces River was gripped by a terrible drought that dried up watering holes, turned cattle into skeletons, and seriously curtailed military operations. The South Texas landscape was bleak almost beyond description. "You cannot imagine how desolate, barren, and desert like this country is; not a spear of grass, nor a green shrub . . . nothing but moving clouds of sand to be seen on these once green prairies," a rebel officer recalled. "Around water holes . . . could be seen hundreds of domestic animals, dead, their flesh seemingly dried upon their bones," Ford wrote.[24] Even the Nueces River was dry for miles.

The arrival of long casualty lists from battles east of the Mississippi underscored the fact that the Confederacy was now on the defensive. This did not help army morale in Texas. Confederate confidence in the East had remained high, but by early 1864, with the steady advance of Union forces, the spirits of Southerners began to falter. The struggle of Texas and the Confederacy caused tensions between Santos and Ford to escalate. Santos shared Navarro's feelings about the discrimination against Tejanos in Texas. Under orders to make every effort to cooperate with Ford, Santos did his best to suppress his feelings. Setting aside his envy and much of his pride, he rode north to meet with Ford in San Antonio to coordinate their efforts to drive the Yankees out of the lower valley.

Weeks earlier, Santos learned from his scouts in the lower valley that a Union expedition consisting of fifteen hundred cavalrymen, including "300 Mexicans and 200 Negroes," had left Fort Brown on January 18, 1864. "I suspect that they may have gone in the direction of Corpus Christi or San Antonio," Santos wrote.[25] On January 29, 1864, Santos assured Ford that he was making every effort to watch any "forward movement of the enemy." Scouts he had sent downriver would return in a few days.[26] If the Federals did move upriver from Rio Grande City, all the cotton stockpiled in San Agustín Plaza waiting to be ferried to Nuevo Laredo would be transported to Eagle Pass, and any wagon trains on the road from San Antonio to Laredo would be diverted upriver.[27]

In February 1864, to make sure he was not caught off guard, Santos sent thirty-year-old lieutenant Martin Gonzales and twenty-five men two hundred miles deep into the lower valley, all the way to the outskirts of Brownsville, but the lieutenant could detect no forward movement of the Federals. A few weeks later, however, Confederate partisan George Pfeiffer wrote Santos from Matamoros that a Union force under Col. John L. Haynes had left Brownsville the second week of February. Pfeiffer was sure the small army was going to Corpus Christi, but he had also heard rumors that a second Federal force would be striking north to the Nueces River before pushing west to the Rio Grande with intentions of destroying the cotton that by then had "accumulated in large quantities at Eagle Pass."[28]

Santos was sure that if the Federals did move out of the lower valley they would attack either Corpus Christi or Eagle Pass, not Laredo. Ford urged Santos to get behind the Federals and join with Capt. Mat Nolan's small force on the lower Nueces River. If Santos determined that the Federals were moving parallel to the coast, Ford wanted him to follow "close upon his heels, harassing him day and night." As he did so, Santos should communicate with Nolan by express. "Make everything he gains cost him blood," Ford wrote. Santos and Nolan were to "call upon the people in the name of patriotism, of liberty, and all that is dear to man, to shoulder their arms & defend their homes & property, their wives and their little ones against the brutal assaults of an enemy who respects neither age, sex or condition, who plunder alike the homestead, the halls of legislature and the temples dedicated to the worship of Almighty God."[29] If the Federals marched in the direction of Eagle Pass, Santos could still join with Nolan and attack the enemy and "drive him into the mountains." If Santos was unable to repulse the Federals, he was to "retire before him disputing every point affording facilities for defense." Santos was to "annoy the enemy in every possible way." Should the Federals move west instead of north, Santos could also join with the small rebel force at Eagle Pass under Captain George H. Giddings and "hold that point at all hazards."[30] If all else failed, the cotton on the Texas bank of the river was to be burned rather than fall into the hands of the Yankees.

A short time after Santos arrived in San Antonio to meet with Ford, an express rider hurried into town with news that Eagle Pass was about to be attacked by Confederate deserters on the west bank of the Rio Grande. Early on the morning of February 8, Santos hurriedly left San Antonio on horseback with a small escort. Arriving at Fort Duncan five days later, he determined that the "Renegades" on the opposite bank, all of whom were well armed, were indeed planning to attack the town in hopes of burning or carrying off the large quantity of cotton stored there. If the cotton could be hurriedly crossed, Santos speculated, the renegades would likely drift away. With the assistance of the Piedras Negras comandante, Santos was not only able to cross much of the cotton but to compile a list of the names of the deserters.

While on the road, Santos was making every effort to keep an eye on Union forces in the lower valley. Capt. Refugio Benavides, who was spying on the Federals there, reported that as of January 18 they had made no forward movement. Despite what Refugio and other scouts were saying, Santos kept hearing rumors that the Federals were preparing to move, and as soon as Refugio arrived back in Laredo, he sent a spy to Brownsville, hoping he would soon report back to Laredo.[31] In mid-February, while he was still at Fort Duncan, Santos received from Refugio an express saying the bluecoats were only venturing out of Brownsville to procure grass and water for their animals.[32] All Refugio's scouts could find on the Rio Grande below Laredo were small bands of desperate and disillusioned Confederates, many from the interior of the state, who were deserting into Mexico.

Late on the night of February 25, however, Santos received a second express from his older brother saying that his spies had brought news into Laredo: one hundred infantrymen on steamers and four hundred cavalrymen, "mostly Yankees," left Fort Brown. Refugio thought the Yankees were headed for Corpus Christi, but he was not sure.[33] Within hours, Santos dispatched a rider downriver with orders to send scouts out from Laredo in every direction.

Santos returned to Laredo so exhausted from so much time in the saddle that for days he was unable to get out of his bed. At his home on the plaza, Santos listened to scouting reports and remained certain that any Federal advance on the town could be detected well in advance. Besides hearing that much of the Federal cavalry force had left the lower valley, des-

In this greatly exaggerated drawing made in 1851, a small pack train and wagons can be seen crossing the mouth of Zacate Creek before entering Laredo. Not far from the banks of the creek, on the eastern outskirts of the town, Col. Santos Benavides gallantly turned back a Union attack on March 19, 1864. Unknown artist. Engraving by Louderman & Hoffman. *Emory,* Report of the United States and Mexican Boundary Survey (1857–1859). *Courtesy of the Center for American History, University of Texas at Austin.*

tined for Corpus Christi or San Antonio, he also heard rumors that a Union force was intent on advancing upriver against Laredo before striking Eagle Pass. As Santos continued his recuperation, cotton continued to pour into the town, and much of it was stockpiled in San Agustín Plaza, where it was to be transported across the river on the town's only ferry.

On March 14, 1864, Santos wrote General Slaughter in Houston to say that the route between Laredo and San Antonio was "entirely safe." He was hoping he would be granted "discretionary powers" that would greatly expedite the shipping of cotton into Tamaulipas. Although he remained ill, Santos promised to visit the governor of Tamaulipas in person to negotiate the "safe introduction of cotton" and discuss other matters that would "keep this frontier more peaceable."[34] He concluded by assuring General Slaughter that he had seen no sign that any of the sizeable force of "Yankees at Brownsville" had advanced out of the lower valley.

When he arrived in Laredo on March 17, Thomas B. Dwyer, an Irish-born businessman and former Unionist who was in town on cotton business, had written Ford to describe Santos's condition. Santos had "been in the field constantly—without a tent, or bed, & often without blankets—without any food often for hours—long intervals without water & almost all the time riding rapidly through the country," Dwyer reported.[35] Dwyer thought it "most cruel" to leave Santos in command "in his present state of health." He thought a competent officer needed to take command until Santos could recover.

Several days later, on the afternoon of March 19, 1864, the former mayor and chief justice of Webb County came racing his horse into San Agustín Plaza.[36] Cayetano de la Garza said he saw a large blue-coated cavalry force approaching the town in a cloud of dust from downriver. At first Santos was skeptical, thinking that Garza had somehow seen a herd of cattle or a slow-moving wagon train. Colonel Ford had a large force bound for the border, but Santos knew they were more than a week away. There was no way a large enemy force could have gotten by Santos's pickets at Carrizo and his scouts in the valley, but Garza insisted the community was in eminent danger, and this well-to-do rancher and relative of the colonel would come to be known as the "Paul Revere of Laredo." Rising from his sick bed, Santos knew the moment he had feared and dreaded for months was at hand, and he sounded the alarm as soldiers and civilians grabbed their weapons and ran through the streets and across the sunbaked plaza.

With cotton continuing to flow across the Rio Grande at Laredo and Eagle Pass, Union authorities had decided to send a small expedition upriver to seize the five thousand bales known to be in San Agustín Plaza, which were guarded by fewer than one hundred men. The two-hundred-man Laredo expedition, about half of which was from the Tejano Second Texas, was led by Maj. Alfred E. Holt, a close friend of Col. Edmund J. Davis. Guided by men who knew the area well, the Federals had moved along the Mexican bank of the Rio Grande for some distance before recrossing into Texas, and then advanced along trails through the chaparral away from the river. They were clearly advancing on the town. Santos sent a rider racing to recall one hundred men from a grazing camp twenty-five miles north of town on the San Antonio road. In all, Santos had forty-two men from Cristóbal's Company A and Refugio's Company I, along with thirty men from Capt. George Chapman's Company C, which had arrived in Laredo only days earlier. Several citizens also volunteered and were deployed as sharpshooters on top of the adobe buildings on the east side of the plaza.

Although the Union cavalry was thought to outnumber his small command by ten to one, Santos was determined to stand and fight. "This would not have happened," he said, "had I not been confined to bed for some days. I would have known all about their advance and would have gone below and attacked them. As it is I have to fight to the last; though hardly able to stand, I shall die fighting. I won't retreat, no matter what force the Yankees have—I know I can depend on my boys." Santos then gave specific orders to his brother Cristóbal: "There are five thousand bales of cotton in the plaza. It belongs to the Confederacy. If the day goes against us, fire it. Be sure to do the work properly so that not a bale of it shall fall into the hands of the Yankees. Then you will set my new house on fire, so that nothing of mine shall pass to the enemy. Let their victory be a barren one."[37]

Santos sent a small cavalry squad to harass the Federals while citizens rushed about, using cotton bales to barricade the streets leading into San Agustín Plaza. With what weapons they could gather, men, women, and boys lined the flat rooftops of the rock and adobe buildings. As the Federals steadily advanced under the hot afternoon sun, determined to seize or destroy the cotton in the plaza, the ailing colonel rode out to meet them. Still fatigued and unsteady in the saddle, Santos took his men to a large rock corral not far from Zacate Creek and the Rio Grande, close to the wagon road to Carrizo, which wound across the steep banks of the small, rocky waterway. Here, Santos calculated, his men would have the best cover and clearest field of fire. A small reserve remained in the town for one last defense should Santos be forced to retreat. As a ruse, the colonel sent twenty-three-year-old third sergeant Darío Gonzales, bugle in hand, racing up and down Zacate Creek to blow his horn at every opportunity. Santos hoped to give the impression that far more men were preparing to defend the town than were actually present.

Armed with "Burnside carbines, revolvers, and sabers," the advancing Federals, commanded by Major Holt, numbered little more than two hundred men. As they approached Laredo, the Union cavalry dismounted, formed into groups of forty, and attacked. Three times the Federals advanced, and three times, under withering fire, they were repulsed by Santos's Confederates.[38] For three hours, "Benavides and his men fought with the coolest bravery," an eyewitness reported. Juan Ibarra, a civilian, as well as J. S. Swope, a major in the militia, were praised by Santos for their great heroism. The Kentucky-born Swope rode a "magnificent sorrel" and charged into the Federal ranks, wildly emptying his pistol before his horse was hit three times and killed. Not to be outdone, Ibarra charged to within thirty yards of the Federals and exchanged shots with the bluecoats until his horse, too, was shot down.[39] The sound of pistol and musket fire echoed up and down the rocky defiles of Zacate Creek and across the Rio Grande to Nuevo Laredo and beyond. The bluecoats were eventually "repulsed by the vigorous fire" of his "gallant men," Santos reported.[40]

The Federal cotton raid on Laredo was a disaster. Although Union officers left no written record of their attack on Laredo, it is evident that they simply gave up and retreated back into the chaparral after three assaults, carrying their wounded as they went. As the sniping slackened at about eight that night and darkness crept over the town, the Federals went into a makeshift camp a mile to the east, along the small hills just east of Chacon Creek. Colonel Santos Benavides's gallant defense of Laredo was perhaps his crowning achievement. His defiant fearlessness would long be remembered in the history of the town and the borderlands.

At seven in the evening, Santos dictated a two-page account of the Federal attack and sent a courier to find Colonel Ford, thought to be somewhere on the Nueces River. Dwyer also wrote Ford: "For God's sake, hurry up. and we shall be soon all right."[41] Santos had just received word from spies that Laredo was to be attacked again, this time by three hundred infantrymen with two pieces of artillery. Although desperately short of ammunition and realizing he would be helpless against the artillery, Santos planned to attack the Federals before they could lay siege to the town.[42]

Darkness brought little solace to the civilians and soldiers defending the town. Everyone remained vigilant, certain that sunrise would bring yet another attack. The eerie stillness was broken at two o'clock in the morning, when pickets north of town reported a sizeable cavalry force advancing at a gallop. In the blackness, Santos's men grabbed their weapons and quickly prepared for a defiant last stand. "A general rejoicing took place among our little force," the colonel wrote, when a lone horseman was followed by Confederate reinforcements from the grazing camp north of town. Bugles sounded, and soldiers and citizens shouted with joy. The small bell atop San Agustín Church pealed the good news into the early morning darkness. Undoubtedly, the ringing could also be heard in the Union camp near the banks of Chacon Creek, east of town.

In the night, Santos had also sent a courier on the lengthy ride to Eagle Pass to urge Capt. George H. Giddings to make the 108-mile march downriver to join him "as soon as possible." If Santos was not reinforced, he would be forced to evacuate the town and retreat upriver, where he would join Giddings in a spirited defense of Eagle Pass. At the same time, Santos was hoping Ford could reach the Rio Grande at Rancho Clareño or a spot upriver near Carrizo and gain the Union rear.

As daylight broke over the brasada, Santos sent Refugio with sixty men to locate the enemy soldiers and determine if they were still intent on attacking the town. Capt. Refugio Benavides rode out past the bullet-riddled corral along Zacate Creek, where his men spotted a number of bloody trails along the rocky creek bed. A grisly trail of blood-soaked rags led into the tall grass and scrubby mesquite toward the Union camp, which had been abandoned. Discarded clothing and bayonets lay everywhere on the dry earth, and it was evident the Federals had rested and regrouped and then begun a hasty withdrawal, probably upon hearing the noisy arrival of rebel reinforcements. Five valuable horses, all branded "US," had been left behind. On their long and dusty retreat to Ringgold Barracks and Brownsville, several soldiers from the Second Texas Cavalry deserted into Mexico.[43] For the remainder of the war the Federals would never again advance as far upriver as Laredo.

Colonel Ford had been in camp near Banquete when an excited courier galloped up with the news that Laredo was attacked. After forwarding Santos's dispatch to General Magruder in Houston, Ford sent messengers to all his troops in the field with orders to "hurry up" for the border. At first Ford feared the Federals, perhaps numbering as many as one thousand men, would make a "dash upon San Antonio." But when he detected no movement in that direction, he decided Santos must be reinforced as rapidly as possible. "I desire to take the Yanke[e]s in the rear," Ford told one of his regimental commanders, Lt. Col. Daniel Showalter, and added that he would march for the border immediately. "Hasten up. There is not a moment to be lost. Order all to the front."[44] At the same time, Ford wrote Capt. John Littleton, who was with his company at the village of Helena, seventy miles southeast of San Antonio, to tell him to march for the Rio Grande, as well: "Move at once with all the men you can [and] capture their trains & defeat them."[45] Learning that the bluecoats had used the south bank of the Rio Grande in their advance on Laredo, Ford wrote Magruder that he might be forced to fight the "Mexicans as well as Yanke[e]s."[46]

When a second express brought news that the Federals who attacked Laredo were in retreat, Colonel Ford promised to strike them before they reached Brownsville. From his camp on San Fernando Creek, south of the Nueces River, twelve days after the cotton raid on Laredo, Ford wrote Santos a congratulatory letter: "[You have] added to the reputation you and your command had already acquired."[47] Ford also praised Santos to Magruder, saying to the general that Santos had met and turned back the "enemy in a very gallant manner." Ford recommended the general issue a special order congratulating Santos and also mention the gallantry of Juan Ibarra and J. S. Swope.[48]

On the third day after the battle, a report reached Santos that a large Federal force was again approaching the eastern outskirts of the border town. Santos, "being very much exhausted . . . again got into his saddle and galloped out at the head of a body of his men determined to fight." The colonel was so weak that he tumbled from his horse, hit his head on the ground, and likely suffered a concussion. As he was carried to his home on the plaza, his family feared for his life. "The side of his head pains him considerably," Dwyer told Colonel Ford.[49] Santos's nervous energy had at last played out, and according to W. W. Camp, the regimental surgeon, he was so exhausted as to be unfit for duty. Confined to his bed with "fatigue and exposure," Santos was only to rise "at the hazard of his life." He was so sick and affairs on the border were so "unsettled" that Camp told Ford he thought Santos "should be relieved from duty."[50] When Colonel Ford, who was continuing his push for the border, heard of Santos's precarious condition, he urged him to allow some "officer in rank . . . to take charge of the troops." Ford promised to be on the river soon, at which time he would relieve the Laredo colonel himself. As Ford should have suspected, however, Santos was not about to be relieved, despite the delicate condition of his health. Ford in the meantime promised to attach Capt. Pablo B. Alderete's company to Santos's regiment.[51]

Colonel Ford was cautious about taking his army into the area south of the Nueces River because of the drought conditions, and he was still in camp on San Fernando Creek on April 7, 1864, when he wrote Santos to say that he was at last prepared to march for the border as soon as he received a supply of forage. Ford was sure his men could carry enough water for themselves, but he was concerned about their horses. Ford hoped Santos could establish a supply depot thirty-five miles east of Laredo at Los Ojuelos, one of the few natural springs in the area, or perhaps farther south at Rancho Randado, closer to Rio Grande City, where several wells had been dug.

That same month, Colonel Ford wrote Santos again to say he was "much pleased at [Santos's] activity and efficiency."[52] Santos responded with his plans to push his small army east to Los Ojuelos. His scouts were reporting that the Federals "were in full retreat, marching day and night," including the five hundred Federals and two pieces of artillery that were at Ringgold Barracks. Santos no longer feared that Laredo would be attacked, but wrote to Ford that "I will be always ready to join you with my command at a moment's notice to meet the enemy."[53]

Although the Union Army never again advanced as far upriver as Laredo, Federals in Brownsville helped orchestrate considerable chaos at the small rebel river outpost of Eagle Pass. A Unionist named T. P. McManus had been sent to Piedras Negras, opposite Eagle Pass, to recruit men for the First Texas Cavalry and to "operate against the Rebel trains on the San Antonio-Eagle Pass route."[54] In the process, McManus was to gather as much information as possible on military operations and events in the interior of Texas, a task he accepted with determination and dedication. "To prevent me from sending you an express," McManus wrote General Dana, "every mesquite in the state would have to be garrisoned with rebel bayonets."[55] Much of the information McManus was able to relay to Brownsville came from "reliable gentlemen" in San Antonio, Austin, and Houston. From his guerrilla base in Mexico, McManus was able to recruit several Unionists, some of whom had barely made it out of Texas alive, and send them to Brownsville. McManus also hoped to make contact with Gen. James Carleton, who had arrived in southern New Mexico on the heels of a Confederate retreat from the territory. It was thought that a Federal force from New Mexico could move along the San Antonio–El Paso road to link up with Col. John L. Haynes, who might be on the Nueces River with units of his Second Texas Cavalry.

On April 3, 1864, the Union guerrillas robbed the San Antonio–Eagle Pass stage not far from the border, stole the horses, and fled back into Mexico. On several other occasions McManus was able to seize wagon trains along the route, burn their cotton, and take their horses and mules. Many of the citizens living along the route west of San Antonio were said to be in sympathy with the Union guerrillas and bitterly hostile to the Confederacy.[56] Union officials at Brownsville were even hopeful guerrillas could penetrate as far as Fort Inge at Uvalde and prevent the "killing of Union men on their way out."[57] During the first week of April, Confederate Capt. J. B. Weyman, who had taken command of Fort Duncan, reported chasing various bands of Union guerrillas into Mexico. Weyman complained that Francisco García, comandante at Piedras Negras, had promised to apprehend the raiders but would "not deliver the thieves up." Weyman was convinced that McManus held a "Yankee commission to burn, murder, and destroy . . . the people and ranches of Western Texas."[58]

Two months later, on June 17, 1864, forty Union guerrillas led by McManus brazenly crossed the Rio Grande five miles above Eagle Pass and raised the Stars and Stripes on the north bank of the river. Fearing an attack on Eagle Pass, Capt. James A. Ware, the new post commander, put his thirty-four-man garrison on alert and called out a local militia company. He placed guards at the post hospital, the customhouse, the quartermaster's storehouse, and several businesses. Fifteen men were sent to patrol the area to determine McManus's whereabouts. Shortly after noon, just as the Confederates and townsmen had finished barricading the streets of the small river town with cotton bales, McManus's guerrillas struck. Spurring their horses past the barricades, they captured Captain Ware and several of his men, although a small force of Confederates made a stand at the post hospital near the river. After releasing their prisoners and carrying off the firearms they had seized, McManus and his men retreated back into Mexico.[59]

Champion of the Union guerrillas operating on the middle Rio Grande, McManus was able to create so many problems at and near Eagle Pass that General Magruder was forced to temporarily change the route of the cotton being sent into Mexico to the San Antonio–Laredo road, along which Santos held sway. But despite McManus's determination, Union guerrillas never seriously curtailed the stream of cotton flowing into Mexico, nor the flow of war materials into Texas. With Laredo and Eagle Pass opened to the rush of Confederate cotton, however, the length of the new cotton road was extended by as much as two hundred miles, and the cost escalated by 50 percent. The recapture of the lower valley thus became a major Confederate objective.

As Santos advanced into the lower valley, Colonel Ford wanted him to transport a large quantity of flour from Laredo to a point near Sal del Rey. Ford also wanted him to hire as many as twenty vaqueros to gather beef cattle, horses, and mules. If he could not find sufficient grass to support the animals, he was to slaughter up to 60,000 pounds of beef and dry the meat into jerky.[60] Santos was to prevent any cattle, hogs, sheep, subsistence stores, or property of any kind from being taken into Mexico, and if he caught individuals taking animals across the river, he was to seize the animals.[61] Hogs were to be slaughtered, the meat salted and made into bacon. In addition, the colonel was to organize any conscripts in Laredo and muster them for the war. From old Fort Merrill on the Nueces River, Ford would move to San Diego and then to a point near Sal del Rey. He did not want to approach the Rio Grande for fear the Mexicans on the south bank would "telegraph" his movements to the enemy. Secrecy and celerity were the keys to success.[62] To assure that he would not be surprised, Santos was to keep scouts out in the direction of the lower valley. Writing five days after receiving Ford's orders, Santos assured Ford that he was in the process of putting all of his instructions into force all "along the line."

At the beginning of that year, Santos had written to Colonel Ford and promised to "strictly obey" any orders. But almost from the beginning of the war, Ford had a difficult time dealing with Santos's independence and the Laredo colonel's reluctance to cooperate. Even before he left San Antonio with his expeditionary force, Ford had written to Santos reminding him of General Magruder's previously issued orders placing Santos under Ford's command, a copy of which Ford had sent to Santos.[63] Santos was no longer under the command of Col. James Duff, and he was not to obey any orders from Duff. Ford had even sent Santos a letter he had received from Duff in which Duff acknowledged that Santos was henceforth to answer to Ford.

As he prepared to move from San Antonio in early 1864, Colonel Ford had once again urged Santos to keep scouts out in the direction of the lower valley and as far east as the village of La Garita, thirty-five miles northwest of Corpus Christi, not far from the banks of the Nueces River. Two Tejanos, Casiano Cervantes and Tómas Vasquez, were known to be carrying dispatches between Corpus Christi and Brownsville, and Ford wanted them apprehended.[64] A large advance guard should be stationed at Los Ojuelos, and Santos was to be ready to join Ford "at a moment's warning."

One of the major obstacles facing Ford's Cavalry of the West was the severe drought that had plagued South Texas and particularly the lower Rio Grande Valley for four years. So bad was the situation in South Texas that Ford attempted, without success, to acquire several camels, part of a herd that had once been stationed at Camp Verde during the 1850s. Not sure of what he would find south of the Nueces, Ford contemplated subsisting his army on jerky.[65]

South of San Antonio, Ford was surprised to see large amounts of cotton that were secreted in the brush country, and he was angered to see evidence along the lower Nueces of the trade that had developed with the Federals in Brownsville. "Men who furnish the Yankees are aiding and abetting the enemies of our country," he wrote, "and are committing treason."[66] Learning that a Union force had left Brownsville for either Corpus Christi, Laredo, or Eagle Pass, Ford ordered Capt. Mat Nolan, who had been a bugler in Ford's company of rangers in the 1850s and who was already in camp on the Nueces River, to make contact with Colonel Benavides at Laredo. If necessary, the two could combine their forces in the vicinity of old Fort Ewell and, if the enemy should move in the direction of the upper Rio Grande, "hang upon his rear and harass him day and night—beating up the pickets, capturing his trains, stampeding his animals and allow him no rest."[67]

Striking down the Nueces River and following what remained of the meandering stream downriver to San Fernando Creek, an isolated Confederate outpost west of Corpus Christi and south of the Nueces, Ford was able to link up with Captain Nolan. Nolan informed Ford of his vicious and bloody fight with Cecilio Valerio in the brush country. In camp at San

Fernando, Ford sent out scouts, but they could find no Federals north of the Wild Horse Desert. He did learn from Santos at Laredo that some five hundred Federals with two cannon were at Ringgold Barracks.[68] Moving on to the King Ranch on Santa Gertrudis Creek, Ford received news from Santos of the Union attack on Laredo.

Leaving Major Nolan to help guard the Brownsville–Corpus Christi road south of King Ranch, Ford struck out for Los Ojuelos, some forty miles east of Laredo, where he hoped to link up with Santos and Giddings, who was thought to be moving downriver from Fort Duncan. Ford was pushing through the drought-ridden landscape when, on the night of April 14, the heavens opened up and a life-giving rain began to fall on the dry land. Within days new grass began to spring up, giving new life to the landscape and providing badly needed food for the horses and mules of the Confederate command.[69] Ford continued past Los Ojuelos toward Laredo, where he arrived three days later and was greeted by Santos. Ford was surprised to find Governor Vidaurri at Santos's home on the plaza. Santos had written Confederate headquarters in Houston to say that Vidaurri had arrived at Laredo on March 25 accompanied by a party of "faithful friends and are at the moment my guests." Santos was sure that everyone at Confederate headquarters would agree that Vidaurri "merits all . . . sympathy."[70] Not long after he reached Laredo, the governor hurried on to Houston, where General Magruder welcomed him to one of the city's finest hotels.

The tumultuous and chaotic situation in Mexico continued to require considerable attention from Santos and the other Confederates on the border. The American Civil War coincided with a crucial time in Mexican history, and events on the Rio Grande were dramatically impacted by events in the Mexican interior, particularly the flight of President Juárez and his liberal Republican government from Mexico City. After a siege of almost two months, the French army under Gen. Elie Frédéric Forey captured Puebla on May 16, 1863, and less than a month later, the Imperialistas triumphantly marched into the capital.[71] As Santos watched from afar, Gen. Tomás Mejía drove Juárez and his ragtag army from San Luis Potosí in December 1863, and it appeared as if both Tampico and Matamoros would fall to the forces of the empire. Nothing, it seemed, could stop the French. In Monterrey, Governor Vidaurri, the "Lion of the North," began to sway in the wind. To assure his allegiance, Juárez named him comandante of Tamaulipas. But even after Juárez arrived in Saltillo in January 1864, Vidaurri continued to vacillate. The governor was fearful that Juárez would demand the customs receipts from Piedras Negras, where Texas cotton diverted from the lower valley continued to flow into Mexico.[72] Late in February 1864, alarming news reached Laredo from Monterrey.

Although the fiercely independent governor Vidaurri warned Juárez to stay away, the president entered Monterrey on February 12, 1864, with his small army. Vidaurri was nowhere to be seen, having barricaded himself in the Ciudadela, a fortress within the city. When the president finally did make contact, the two men conducted a heated exchange during which the caudillo's son drew a pistol and threatened Juárez.[73] As the beleaguered president fled through the streets in his carriage, Vidaurri declared himself in open revolt and pronounced against the government. Reaching Saltillo, Juárez struck back by issuing a decree separating Coahuila from Nuevo León and declaring Vidaurri to be in open rebellion. At the same time, Cuban-born José Quintero, the able Confederate agent in Monterrey, learned that Vidaurri was willing to sell large quantities of munitions he had stockpiled in Monterrey at "reasonable rates." General Magruder directed Santos to "write or send someone to Monterrey" to make arrangements for purchasing the war materials and instructed him to keep the entire mission secret and not "breathe a word of it to anyone." Once the arms were safely on the north bank of the Rio Grande at Eagle Pass, they would be paid for by the Cotton Bureau in silver.[74]

With a sizeable liberal army advancing on Monterrey, however, Governor Vidaurri fled with some of his troops and a bodyguard for Lampazos and then Laredo, where he knew he could find refuge with Santos. He had hoped to deliver badly needed war materials consisting of "eighteen pieces of light artillery, a large quantity of ammunition, a number of Sharp's carbines, and 15 million percussion caps" to Santos.[75] But Vidaurri told Santos that the "celerity of his march and the miserable state of the country obliged him to abandon the pieces wherever the mules gave out."[76]

Halfway between Monterrey and the border, on a barren plain near the foothills of the Sierra Madre at Villa Aldama, Vidaurri's army was overtaken and crushed by sixteen hundred liberals.[77] When many of Vidaurri's defeated *norteños* went over to the liberals and swore allegiance to Juárez, the governor, with a small "party of faithful friends," as well as the state archives and treasury, raced on to the Rio Grande and the safety of Laredo and his long-time friend and confidant.[78] Before his army had been overtaken, however, the governor had secreted most of the war materials in the homes of friends and political allies. No sooner had Vidaurri arrived on the border than Santos dispatched Nicolás Sanchez, a relative and frequent courier between Laredo and Monterrey, to Villa Aldama with letters from Vidaurri to the parties who had helped hide the armaments.[79] The Juaristas, however, had found the war materials, and when Sanchez attempted to procure the supplies, he was arrested and almost executed.

Meanwhile, Colonel Ford and Santos learned that Federal authorities had secretly sent a delegation to Monterrey to discuss with Juárez their using the south bank of the river to attack Laredo and Eagle Pass. Col. John L. Haynes was said to be a member of the delegation.[80] Ford and Santos agreed that such a movement against Laredo or the upper Rio Grande from Mexican soil "would be tantamount to a declaration of war by the Juárez government" on the Confederate States of America. If such a plan ever reached fruition, Ford was willing to place his small army "side by side with the French."[81] "Would I not be justifiable in crossing the Rio Grande to meet the enemy?" Ford asked General Magruder.[82] Unbeknownst to the Confederates was the fact that Juárez had refused the Federal request, arguing that "Mexico was too small and weak a nation to wage war against either the United States or the Confederate States."[83]

By early April, Juárez had set up his government in Monterrey, but he was forced to flee when the army of the empire, supported by French money and prestige as well as by the Catholic Church, marched on the city in August. Riding in an old carriage with a small escort, Juárez disappeared into the deserts of northern Mexico before reappearing at El Paso del Norte. With the governors of Chihuahua and Sonora wavering as Vidaurri had done, the liberal cause was all but dead. Ferdinand Maximilian Joseph and Marie Charlotte Amélie Augustine Victoire Clémentine Léopoldine paraded into Mexico City to assume the throne, and a new era dawned on the Rio Grande.

Vidaurri was safe in Texas, but Santos continued to worry about Ignacio Comonfort. After Santos had helped the former president return to Mexico, Comonfort had convinced Juárez to name him general-in-chief of the army that was being organized to resist the French. On November 13, 1863, near San Juan de la Vega, on the road from Querétaro to San Luis Potosí, Comonfort was mortally wounded by a band of guerrillas and died while seeking medical attention.

In April of 1864, Santos's small command was in such desperate need of ammunition and provisions and without means of acquiring them that General Magruder ordered several wagons of Confederate cotton from the depot at Banquete delivered to Santos in Laredo.[84] But in early May, Magruder wrote to say that all the cotton at Laredo was needed to pay King, Kenedy, and Stillman, the company contracted to supply the Confederate Army in South Texas. The cotton assigned to Santos was to be turned over to the Cotton Bureau for sale.[85] A few days later, Magruder wrote again to say he was concerned about the growing depredations on the cotton road from San Antonio to Laredo, and he asked Santos to cooperate with Col. Charles Pyron in developing a plan to halt such robberies. The "marauders in the country must be swept away," the general told Santos.[86]

In late April, a little over a month after the Union attack on Laredo and just as Ford's Cavalry of the West was making its way across South Texas, Colonel Ford relayed the morale-boosting news that a large Union army had been turned back in Louisiana. "I suppose you have heard of our victory in Louisiana," Ford wrote from Rancho Los Angeles, not far from the Rio Grande. "It was great."[87] At the head of a large Confederate army, the very able general Richard Taylor had turned back the Federals at Mansfield in northwestern Louisana, south of Confederate headquarters at Shreveport. Although the rebels were bloodily blunted the following day at Pleasant Hill, the Federals had continued their retreat down the Red River. Ford was sure the news from Louisiana meant that East Texas, so valuable to the South because of its cotton and food production, was safe.[88] Ford even received a flag that had been made by women in Brownsville and carried by Gen. Hamilton P. Bee's Confederates at Mansfield and Pleasant Hill, and he asked his men to carry it to the Rio Grande with great pride. [89]

Taking a large part of Santos's command with him, including the Tejano companies of Capt. Refugio and Capt. Cristóbal Benavides, Ford proceeded east from Laredo back to Los Ojuelos. One day's march beyond the springs, where the road through the brush country turned abruptly to the southeast, he made camp near Rancho Las Ánimas, where he found abundant water. Continuing south, the column reached the Rio Grande a few miles above Roma.

About twenty-five miles above Rio Grande City, Lt. Eugenio Garza, part of Ford's vanguard, ran into a party of some thirty Mexican raiders who had left their horses on the south bank of the river and waded across. After a brief firefight, Garza reported killing the leader of the band while the remainder of the company fled back across the Rio Grande.[90] Advancing downriver, Garza and his advance party of Tejanos were able to pass themselves off as Federals, and they learned that a small Union scouting party was only a few miles away. Garza did not hesitate at Ringgold Barracks but continued downriver to within sight of the village of Las Cuevas. Upon hearing the sound of cannon upriver at Rio Grande City, Lieutenant Garza raced his men back to Ringgold Barracks only to learn that a noisy fiesta was under way across the river at Camargo.

Colonel Ford and the remainder of his command reached Ringgold

Barracks on May 4, and the next day he ordered all of Santos's men, except for one company, forward to join him. Here, he set up his headquarters and began to consolidate his Cavalry of the West for the final push against Brownsville. In preparation for the attack, Ford gave Capt. Refugio Benavides the unpopular task of impressing as many horses as possible from the area.[91] Units from his regiment were able to scout as far north as the Nueces and to within twenty miles of the coast, in many instances looking for cattle for Ford's hungry army.[92] Although greatly outnumbered, Ford was not deterred in his dogged determination to drive the Union Army out of the lower Rio Grande Valley. Once in the lower valley, Ford would be able to open negotiations with his old nemesis, Juan N. Cortina, who had taken power in Matamoros. "The present feeling in Tamaulipas is now more favorable to us than at any preceding period," Ford told General Slaughter,[93] and he was heartened to learn that Gen. Francis J. Herron had begun the process of transferring most of the Federals in the valley to Louisiana, leaving only a skeleton force to defend Fort Brown and Brownsville.[94]

In late June, Ford sent a reconnaissance in force to feel out the Federals and ascertain if they were indeed evacuating Brownsville. He first sent Lt. Col. Dan Showalter and Capt. Refugio Benavides to the Como Se Llama Ranch on the Arroyo Colorado north of Brownsville. With Colonel Giddings, Ford pushed along the river road to John and Salomé McAllen's San Tomás de la Blanca Ranch before turning north to Charles Stillman's Rancho Santa Rosa and then joining Showalter and Refugio Benavides at the Como Se Llama on June 23, 1864. The combined forces, about four hundred men in all, subsisting entirely on jerky, then moved toward the Rio Grande.

The soldiers reached the river at the Carricitos Ranch, just below the village of Las Rucias, little more than a stone's throw from where the Mexican War had begun in 1846. Learning that a sizeable Federal force was on picket at Las Rucias, Colonel Ford and 250 of his men used "an obscure trail through the chaparral" to advance on the Federals and were able to "get within a few hundred yards of the enemy without being discovered."[95] At eleven o'clock on the morning of June 25, the Confederates attacked.

Greatly outnumbered, the Union Texans hastily took up defensive positions in a large brick building and in several small jacales and mesquite fences.[96] The fighting opened with the charge of Capt. James Dunn, Capt. Cristóbal Benavides, and their men. Dunn, a Mexican War veteran, spurred his horse to a gallop and charged headlong into the Federal defenses, and he was killed instantly. Capt. Cristóbal Benavides had his horse shot from under him, and Sgt. Samuel Cockerel and Pvt. Eugenio Sanchez were killed.[97]

Outnumbered and outgunned, some of the Union soldiers fell back to the dense vegetation along a lagoon, whereas others fled into the tall cane and dense underbrush along the Rio Grande. Colonel Ford sent Capt. Refugio Benavides to a spot "behind a fence to the bank of the laguna [to] turn the right flank of the enemy and command the ground in [the] rear of the houses."[98] Captain Refugio Benavides evidently misunderstood the order, however, and moved to the extreme right and attempted to turn the enemy's left flank instead. With his men on horseback, the Laredo captain twice charged the Federals, but each time he was stopped by the sickle-shaped resaca. Refugio then ordered his men to dismount and join the remainder of Ford's command in a final assault on the Federals. Twelve of the Union Texans were able to escape by throwing their rifles into the river and swimming to the safety of the Mexican bank.

In thirty minutes of fighting, Ford estimated that twenty of the enemy were killed, ten or twelve wounded, and thirty-six taken prisoner.[99] Two wagons and teams, twenty-eight horses, and a number of saddles, as well as a considerable amount of commissary and quartermaster stores, fell into the hands of the Confederates.[100] Three Confederates were killed and four wounded at Las Rucias. Ford singled out Refugio and Cristóbal Benavides for their gallantry in the battle.[101]

From Las Rucias, the Confederates advanced downriver through a pouring rain. Ten miles from Brownsville, a small force of Union Texans fired on the Confederates, and the groups fought briefly before the Unionists fell back. Skirmishing as they slowly advanced, the Cavalry of the West was able to drive the Federal pickets back to the fortifications at Freeport.

The Federals, who were still evacuating the town, were in no position to engage the rebels in an open fight, and the Confederates were in no position to assault the Brownsville fortifications with Union artillery still in place. Ford thought of establishing a forward camp on the Arroyo Colorado but did not have the necessary supplies to sustain his men for any length of time. After five days, the Confederates broke camp and retreated back to their base at Ringgold Barracks.

At Rio Grande City, Ford continued to consolidate his forces and recruit additional men, while Union forces continued to depart the lower valley for New Orleans. On July 30, 1864, a Confederate reconnaissance approached Brownsville and found the outer defenses deserted. Somewhat surprised, the men cautiously rode into the town to discover the Federals gone. Two days earlier, the last of the Union forces had evacuated Fort Brown and departed for Brazos Island.

While the Federals were evacuating Fort Brown, Ford had written to Santos to order the men from Capt. Cristóbal Benavides's company who were not already with Ford to report to Ringgold Barracks, accompanied by an officer. Santos flatly refused Ford's request, saying the two lieutenants in the company at Laredo were "unfit for duty." Moreover, Santos complained, the recently recruited company of Capt. Julian García, which was at Laredo, was without arms.

While camped at San Ignacio in the third week of January, Santos had asked for fifty Enfield rifles from the ordnance depot in San Antonio. Many of his men, in addition to those in García's company, were without weapons. If the Enfield rifles were not available, he wanted the best weapons possible.[102] Santos did not think Ford was aware of the condition of his troops at Laredo, even though keeping the few soldiers he had was certainly in the "public interest."

Although General Magruder respected Santos and fully understood both the nature of his predicament at Laredo and his fierce independence, he did order the Laredo colonel not to interfere with any goods that were in transit, "except in extreme cases." Not only had Santos seized a wagon train of cotton, Lt. John Z. Leyendecker had seized a supply of leather.[103] Wagon masters with trains bound for Laredo heard that if they reached the river there, Santos would impress their cotton, and several began to cross at Rio Grande City or upriver at Eagle Pass instead.[104]

At Laredo on Christmas Day 1864, all the Masses at San Agustín Church were full, day and night, and a "great silence and respect reigned in the church." Santos was not there; he had departed to take command at Ringgold Barracks. In January 1865, a "great dying," most likely cholera, swept over the town, and fifteen children were dead within a week. The joy of Christmas gave way to mourning and pitiful processions to the Catholic cemetery. Then several adults became ill. In fact, Capt. Refugio Benavides was so sick he was bedridden for weeks, and his family thought he might die, too. The captain finally recovered but was unable to join Santos at Rio Grande City for several weeks. Uncle Basilio became seriously ill, as well, and few expected him to live; indeed, he would be dead within months. Amid the sickness and the sorrow persisted rumors that the "Yankies" were coming again.[105]

Within days of the Confederate reoccupation of Brownsville, sympathizers began crossing from Matamoros, and the lucrative arms and cotton trade resumed almost immediately. Just as Colonel Ford established his headquarters at Fort Brown, scouts brought word that the Federal rear guard was in camp eighteen miles east of the town on the road to Brazos Island. Although Ford had won a signal victory by reoccupying Brownsville, he was ill and unable to mount his horse, so he sent Lt. Col. Dan Showalter with several companies to attack the bluecoats. Spotting the Federals on the open prairie east of town, Showalter sent Capt. Refugio Benavides, who had recovered from his illness and who had reported for duty in the lower valley, out as part of a reconnaissance in force. Refugio charged into the Union lines, drove the bluecoats back, and captured several supply wagons. "We expected Colonel Showalter every moment," Refugio told Ford, but "at once we saw a heavy column of the enemy moving upon us. I then looked for Colonel Showalter, and saw his command going the other way, about a mile and a half off. The *carajos* came, and took all our wagons away from us."[106] When Showalter was "not under the influence of liquor," he was "as chivalrous a man as ever drew a sword," Ford later wrote.[107]

For the remainder of the war, soldiers skirmished along the river and on the windswept coastal plain between Brownsville and Brazos Santiago, where the Federals maintained a garrison and continued to construct fortifications. However, the area offered little more than "burning sands and unhealthy shrubs, broad prairies and uninteresting hills . . . sand crabs, fleas, flies and mosquitoes . . . for miles and miles in every direction," reported the *New York Herald*.[108] Because of the narrow and unpredictable waters of Boca Chica Pass and the large Federal guns on the island, Confederates were fearful of assaulting the entrenched Union forces.[109] Isolated and demoralized, the Union garrison of 1,590 men and officers chose not to attack Brownsville.

Following the Confederate reoccupation, Capt. Refugio Benavides was given the task of patrolling the area from Ringgold Barracks to Brownsville and, on occasion, scouting in the direction of Brazos Island. In August 1864, Refugio wrote Maj. Felix von Blücher, Colonel Ford's chief of staff and a third cousin of Field Marshal Gebhard Leberecht von Blücher of Battle of Waterloo fame, from his camp at Rancho de las Palmas, saying that any forward movement against the enemy would be impossible due to the incessant summer rains that had swept the lower valley. The entire countryside was one vast lake, especially the area near Boca Chica. "Nothing can be done," Refugio told Blücher. At the same time Refugio did not want anyone to interpret his report as a reluctance to fight the enemy. "In all of my battles I have never lost nor do I wish to now," he wrote.[110] Refugio went on to tell Blücher that he had scouted all the way to the coast and that any attempt to cross Boca Chica Pass against the Federals, who were well fortified on Brazos Island, would be suicidal since the Confederates would have to advance along a single road.

After receiving a letter from his wife back in Laredo, who had recently given birth, was seriously ill with a high fever, and was confined to her bed for days, Refugio asked for a leave of absence. The captain thought his wife's illness had something to do with the widely circulated rumor that he had been killed. He also reported that some of his men at Ringgold Barracks and Edinburg had been leaving because their wives had written to tell them that Colonel Santos Benavides had issued orders saying they were at liberty to return home. If something was not done, Refugio said, he would soon "not have a soldier left."[111]

The situation in the lower valley was becoming critical as supplies grew short, morale deteriorated, and the news from the East grew worse. In September 1864, Refugio sent a curt note to Lt. Col. George H. Giddings saying that he would not send a single man to the front until his company was properly supplied with ammunition.[112] He also heard that Giddings had made some disparaging remarks, perhaps racial, with respect to the Laredo captain and his younger brother's regiment. Hoping to calm the situation, Ford wrote to say that "full justice" would be done and if Refugio would come to his headquarters, Ford was sure he could explain everything to the captain's satisfaction.[113] He also asked Refugio to keep an eye on Cortina, in case he crossed the river with his army to join the Federals. "Appearances indicate that we shall again be confronted by our old enemy, the bandit Cortina," Ford told Refugio later in the war.[114]

Far to the west and north at Laredo, as Santos struggled to recruit his regiment and become a brigadier general, the rivalry between Santos and Ford grew into a full-fledged feud.[115] In early January 1864, Santos was told by General Magruder that Colonel Ford was to command all Confederate forces on the Rio Grande. Perhaps suspecting that Santos would be resentful, if not defiant, Magruder asked Santos to give Ford "his hearty assistance and cooperation." At the same time, Magruder continued to assure Santos that he would promote Santos to brigadier general and that he had "every confidence" in Santos's "ability and devotion."[116] General Bee had made arrangements for Santos to receive badly needed funds, but President Davis vetoed the appropriations. When Santos appealed for support, Magruder promised he would appropriate the funds through the Cotton Bureau.

In August 1864, Santos left Capt. Cristóbal Benavides in charge of his small army in Laredo and went to Houston to meet with General Magruder. Cristóbal was under orders not to move from the town until Santos returned. Not long after Santos left the border, however, Ford ordered his brother's company downriver. Cristóbal left Laredo, and Santos issued a severe reprimand. When Santos returned to Laredo and was ordered to send more men to the lower valley, he refused.

According to Colonel Ford, the troops at Laredo were performing little or no duty, were sleeping in their own houses, and were seldom attending roll call or dress parade. Santos had remained absent from his post for two months without orders, Ford asserted. In addition, Santos had seized cotton from the Cotton Bureau, crossed it to Nuevo Laredo in the night, and sold it. Money from the sale of the cotton had been used to pay officers in Laredo, whereas officers in the lower valley had not been paid in months.[117] To complete his regiment, Santos mustered into his cavalry men who were already in the infantry. Perhaps more seriously, Santos was guilty of disobeying orders and even "encouraging desertion." Besides his brothers and Basilio, Ford went on to say, witnesses to Santos's wrongdoings included F. W. Latham, collector of customs; Tomás Treviño; and other county officials.

On August 27, 1864, Colonel Ford wrote Santos demanding to know why the Laredo colonel was allowing men from his regiment to return to their homes "at their pleasure without the fear of being molested thereby causing trouble and exciting a spirit of insubordination."[118] As far as Ford was concerned, Santos had a disposition to ignore his authority. Ford, not Santos, was the ranking officer in command of the Rio Grande, and Santos was to order all soldiers to return to their units immediately. "You will be reported to Sub. Dist. Hd. Qrs. For disobedience of orders," Ford bluntly told Santos.[119] A few days later, Ford issued special orders prohibiting Capt. W. J. Weisenger, who was in DeWitt County at the time, from recruiting men for Santos's regiment. Ford issued a formal reprimand and threatened to court-martial Weisenger and Capt. A. C. Jones if they disobeyed orders in the future. He whipped off a terse note to Weisenger telling him that he was in violation of orders and that he was to report to Brownsville.[120]

Ford also had serious problems with Capt. Refugio Benavides. Irritated and fearful that Refugio would disobey orders, Ford demanded to know why the Laredo captain had not reported any news to headquarters at Fort Brown. "What is going on at the point you o[c]cupy? Rumors are thick."[121] Ford also wrote Cristóbal, who was in Laredo, warning that his leave of absence had expired and he was to rejoin his company at Brownsville immediately.[122]

In September 1864, Lt. W. L. Newsom, Ford's assistant inspector general, drew up a long litany of charges against Santos. Although Newsom failed to provide specifics, Santos had "endeavored to defeat the successful accomplishment of Col. Ford's Expedition." Moreover, Santos had, on more than one occasion, taken money by force from the customhouse officers. In fact, the colonel and his men were taking private property and using it without consent of the owners. When Colonel Ford learned that Santos was seizing Confederate cotton, he accused Santos of "doing things with a high hand." Ford was not alone, he said, in believing that "public property [was] not safe in the hands of Col. [Santos] Benavides." Ford asked General Magruder to have Santos arrested. The second week of October 1864, Ford heard that Santos was refusing to recognize any orders from him, and he pleaded again with headquarters in San Antonio to have Santos arrested.[123]

The confrontation between Ford and Santos peaked in September and October 1864 with Santos's continued attempts to recruit enough men to fill his regiment and obtain the appointment of brigadier general that was promised him. Santos did not respond to orders that newly formed companies in his regiment, who were then arriving at Ringgold Barracks, should report to Ford at Fort Brown, and he even allowed some of the men to visit their families in Laredo.[124] In early October Ford threatened to bring charges against Santos.[125] It was even rumored that Gen. E. Kirby Smith had decided to launch a court of inquiry into the problems between Ford and Santos. Albert Wood, a Texas refugee, perhaps not knowing that Santos and Leyendecker were related by marriage, wrote Leyendecker to say that Santos was fortunate Wood would not be able to testify at such an inquiry. "What a good thing for him that I cannot appear," he wrote.[126]

When he learned that Santos had authorized one of his officers to recruit men from Colonel Ford's command, men whose terms of enlistment were expiring, Ford was furious. The pressures of the war, evident in Ford's correspondence, may have added to the growing dispute between the two men. Ford feared the possibility of a sizeable Federal advance from Brazos Island with Cortina simultaneously crossing the river to join the Union force in an attack on Brownsville. Still, Ford was determined to hold the town "until the last brick [was] knocked from its place."[127] And Santos was ignoring "any authority or right" Ford may have had "to command."[128] According to Ford, Lt. Col. Matthew Nolan, who was acting as assistant inspector general for Santos, had come to the lower valley to recruit men from those whose terms of enlistment had expired. Ford called Nolan into his office at Fort Brown and ordered him not to recruit men who were likely to reenlist with Ford for "another tour of duty." The muster would "very materially diminish my command at a time when every man should be in front of the enemy who are reported to be reinforcing," Ford warned.[129]

Ford claimed that Santos would draw so many men away from his command that he might even be forced to evacuate the lower Rio Grande, should the Federals on Brazos Island move against Brownsville. The reoccupation of the Rio Grande Valley by the Federals "would be paying very dearly for the filling up of [Santos] Benavides' command." Ford rode with Nolan to Col. George Giddings's camp east of Brownsville, where Ford made an emotional speech imploring the men to reenlist with him and not with Santos, because he was fearful that his entire command in the lower valley would disintegrate. For the good of the Confederacy, the men should remain with him.[130] Ford claimed that after the speech not a single man was willing to muster into Santos's regiment. About a month later, on October 29, 1864, Ford gave Nolan explicit orders restricting his recruitment to the area west of the San Antonio River. A few weeks later, an entire company left for home, and Ford blamed recruiters and agents under the direction of Nolan.[131] Ford also demanded to know by what authority Santos, who was in Brownsville at the time, was signing himself as "Commander of the Line of the Rio Grande," although Ford in his correspondence had frequently referred to Santos as such.[132] By late November 1864, Ford was complaining that the growing demoralization within his command was due to the constant "disbanding, consolidating, re-organizing, and re-mustering" of companies.[133]

Hearing from Nolan what had happened in the lower valley, Santos hastened down the river from his headquarters to Ringgold Barracks to confront Ford personally. Ford admitted that the men whose terms of enlistment were expiring had the right to leave his command, but he insisted that Santos did not have the right to conscript them. If the men desired to reenlist, Ford argued, they would prefer him, not Santos. Santos suggested that his regiment was nearing completion. "Yes, you have them on paper," Ford claimed he told Santos, "but I dare you to show more than 500 men in actual service. If you have in your regiment so great a number of men why do you wish to take men I have raised and mustered."[134] "If a bee of the brigadier general species got in Benavides' hat and stung him, and caused insanity, he deserves our sympathy. He has not our condemnation or ill-will," Ford would sarcastically write years later.[135] But he later admitted that had Santos been allowed to recruit freely, the Laredo colonel could have mustered enough men to fill a brigade and would have fulfilled his desire of becoming a brigadier general.

In November 1864, Gen. James Slaughter arrived in the lower valley, and he set out to resolve the seemingly endless feuding and determine the organization of the Western Sub-District. Ford would be assigned to the Southern Division, while Santos would command the Western District from his headquarters at Ringgold Barracks. Col. Charles Pyron, a veteran of Sibley's New Mexico Campaign who commanded the Second Texas Cavalry, would have the Northern Division, and Col. Alexander C. Jones, a graduate of Virginia Military Institute who had served as chief of staff to General Magruder, would be in charge of the Eastern Division.[136] At the time, Santos had 323 officers and other men scattered along the river from Laredo to Eagle Pass. Pyron and Jones had similar numbers, but Ford had 1,838 men in the lower valley.[137]

After the war, Ford pushed his feud with Santos to the back of his mind, especially as he was crafting his lengthy memoirs. Much of what he wrote was a glowing tribute to the Tejano colonel and the Benavides family. "The services rendered by the family," Ford said, and the manner in which they "bore themselves on the battlefield" were unprecedented. "Santos Benavides could have transferred himself and his possessions across the river and lived a quiet and undisturbed life," but dedicated to the "American idea of personal freedom," he had remained a "patriot and true to his ideas of local self-government and state sovereignty, and he gave all he had, life, if necessary to the 'last cause.'"[138] Santos, however, never quite forgave Ford, whom he mistrusted and whom he blamed for his never becoming a general.

In early 1865, Santos reorganized his regiment and re-lettered the companies. The company of Capt. Joseph M. Peñaloza had previously been assigned to the Eighth Texas Infantry, was composed entirely of "Mexicans" from the San Antonio area, and had spent the early years of the war defending the Texas coast at places such as Saluria and Galveston. Although Peñaloza insisted that his men were "brave and reliable"—some of them had seized the enemy rifle pits at Saluria on the north end of Matagorda Island under fire—he had watched as his company melted away. More and more of his men had deserted, saying they had to return to their families in San Antonio, who were hungry and desperate.[139] By January of 1864, Peñaloza was down to seventeen men, and he asked that he and his men be allowed to join Santos's regiment, away from the Texas coast and the Eighth Infantry. If they could be stationed with Santos in the "West," in a part of Texas where they would feel more comfortable and be part of the cavalry instead of the infantry, Peñaloza was certain that many of his men would return. In early 1864, what was left of the company was sent to San Antonio. In San Antonio, the company failed to find any horses. Colonel Ford complained that soldiers were lacking in "discipline and good conduct," and he ordered them to join Santos at Laredo. Perhaps they would find horses on the road.[140]

With almost all of his regiment stationed in the lower valley, Santos made his headquarters at Ringgold Barracks.[141] Cristóbal remained in command of Company A, and Refugio commanded Company B. Both companies were composed of tough and dependable border Tejanos. Half of the regiment was commanded by men from San Antonio, such as Captain Peñaloza, who had been trusted with Ringgold Barracks for several months. Capt. George A. Gibson's Company D had been at Eagle Pass, but by September 1864 was at Fort Brown with Colonel Ford. At the age of twenty-eight, Gibson had first enlisted in San Antonio as a first sergeant in Capt. Pedro Cevallos's company of the Third Texas Infantry. At the same time that he was serving in Luckett's regiment, Gibson enlisted in Col. Samuel Gabriel Ragsdale's cavalry battalion. When the second enlistment was discovered, Gibson was hauled before a court-martial at Ringgold Barracks in October 1863, and when found guilty, he was reduced to private. Allowed to stay with Ragsdale's battalion, Gibson found himself helping to man the guns at Fort Manhassett, six miles west of Sabine Pass. At Laredo in April 1864, Santos wrote headquarters in Houston requesting that Gibson and his depleted company be transferred, and the request was granted.[142]

Capt. Sixto Eusebio Navarro came to command Company E. He had also been at Fort Brown with Colonel Ford. From Atascosa County, Navarro had enrolled early in the war in the Second Texas Mounted Rifles with Capt. Charles Pyron. At the same time, his older brother José Ángel had enlisted in Col. Hobby's Eighth Texas Infantry and after the retreat of the Texans from New Mexico Territory in the summer of 1862 was sent to occupy Fort Davis in far West Texas. While in camp at California Springs, the older Navarro wrote Gen. Hamilton P. Bee asking that his brother be able to join him. "I am very anxious to have my brother with me," Navarro told Bee, promising that his brother would bring fifteen to twenty "Mexicans" with him.[143]

Company F of the regiment was placed in the hands of a Tennessee-born San Antonio lawyer, N. A. Mitchel, who had enlisted early in the war at the age of thirty-two. Captain Mitchel was first stationed at Fort Duncan before being transferred to the lower valley. A wealthy Alabama-born planter from Matagorda named A. C. Jones came to command Company G. Jones had served in the Arizona Brigade of Col. Daniel Showalter's regiment in Colonel Ford's Cavalry of the West before he came over to Santos. Henry Clay Davis, a good friend and survivor of the Mier Expedition, was placed in command of Company H. Davis had married María Hilaria de la Garza, who came from a prominent landed family, and formed what came to be known as Davis Landing or Rancho Davis (modern Rio Grande City) during the war with Mexico in 1847. Rancho Davis became a prominent steamboat landing, and Davis prospered, especially after Ringgold Barracks was established adjacent to the town in 1848. An adventurous Kentuckian, Davis became a leading political force in Rio Grande City. He is listed as being sick at Rio Grande City for much of the war, but he was with Santos in Laredo for several months before he, too, was sent to the lower valley.[144]

Twenty-three-year-old captain Julian García, son of Bartolo García, a prominent Laredo stock raiser, was placed in command of Company I, while Capt. Pleasant B. Watson, a young Tennessee-born bookkeeper who had fought in Virginia early in the war, was in charge of Company K.[145] Three other companies were temporarily attached to Santos.

By April 1865, the Confederate Army on the Rio Grande was greatly reduced in numbers and was on the verge of breaking up. It was even rumored at Federal headquarters on Brazos Santiago that Santos had concluded the war was over and any further struggle against Union forces was senseless. Cortina's brother-in-law told Union officials that Santos was prepared to cross the Rio Grande with his small army to join Vidaurri, that he was likely to fight the Juaristas, or that he might even ally himself with Cortina.[146]

While in command of the "Line of the Rio Grande," Santos had been responsible for the entire Rio Grande frontier, which stretched from the occupied lower valley to the *despoblado* of Big Bend, upriver from Eagle Pass and west of Fort Clark. In the vast Trans-Pecos, the Confederates had been largely dependent on the eyes and ears of the notorious Henry Skillman. But on April 15, 1864, Union scouts out of Fort Bliss found and killed Skillman and several of his men at Spencer's Ranch at Presidio on the Rio Grande.[147] Two months earlier, Confederate scouts had been as far west as Fort Lancaster but had failed to find any Yankees.[148]

In late April 1865, the people of Brownsville learned that Gen. Robert E. Lee had surrendered his starving Army of Northern Virginia to General Ulysses S. Grant at Appomattox Court House, Virginia. "Everyone here is blue and despondent," Richard King wrote to a friend.[149] On May 1, 1865, a passenger on a steamer heading up the Rio Grande tossed a copy of the *New Orleans Times-Picayune* to Confederates camped at Palmito Ranch. The newspaper contained detailed accounts of Lee's surrender, Lincoln's assassination at Ford's Theatre, and Gen. Joseph E. Johnston's capitulation to Gen. William T. Sherman in a North Carolina farmhouse at Durham. Three days later, Gen. Richard Taylor surrendered what remained of the Confederate Army east of the Mississippi River. In Brownsville, a number of soldiers left for home or crossed the river to Matamoros.[150] Confederate officers hurried to cross as much cotton as possible into Mexico, and at Laredo, the Cotton Bureau agent absconded into Mexico with what funds were available.[151] Elsewhere in Texas, battle-hardened Confederate regiments degenerated into rowdy mobs that broke into stores and looted entire towns. Even the state treasury was rifled.[152]

Yet on the river, Ford and many of his men were determined to resist to the very end, although they would later claim they did not know the war was over. Gen. Edmund Kirby Smith, in command of the Confederate Trans-Mississippi Department, had yet to surrender, and Ford was not about to surrender to invading black troops. With a stubborn reluctance to admit defeat, Ford asserted that the "honor and manhood" of his men were at stake.[153] Of equal significance was the large quantity of King and Kenedy's cotton that remained to be sent across the river. If Ford did not resist, the cotton would be confiscated by the invading Yankees and thousands of dollars lost. As one northern newspaper put it, the Confederates "held out until the very last moment for the purpose of sending rebel cotton into Mexico."[154]

At 9:30 p.m. on May 11, 1865, Col. Theodore H. Barrett, commanding Union forces on Brazos Santiago, sent Lt. Col. David Branson with 250 men of the Sixty-second US Colored Infantry and fifty men of the dismounted Second Texas Cavalry across Boca Chica Pass on a "foraging expedition."[155] A stern disciplinarian, Branson respected his troops, and they respected him. After marching through the night, the Federals reached the Rio Grande at White's Ranch, where they bivouacked in the underbrush along the river. On arrival, however, they realized they had been spotted by civilians across the river in Mexico. Any hope of surprising the Confederate pickets on the river was lost, so Colonel Branson ordered his men upriver toward Palmito Ranch.

Stationed at Palmito Ranch were 190 men of Col. George H. Giddings's Texas Cavalry Battalion. After skirmishing, Federals overran the Confederate camp, captured three prisoners and some horses, and burned the abandoned rebel supplies. The Union reconnaissance then fell back to a small hill near the Rio Grande where they rested, cooked, and bivouacked for the evening. A few of the Federals who had been wounded and those "unable to make a heavy march," along with the captured cattle and horses, were sent back to Brazos Santiago.[156] Receiving orders from Colonel Ford to maintain contact with the Federals, Captain Robertson renewed the fighting before daylight on May 12.

After being pushed back to White's Ranch, Lieutenant Colonel Branson dispatched a courier to Brazos Island for reinforcements. Before daylight the next morning, May 13, 1865, Colonel Barrett had arrived with two hundred men of the Thirty-fourth Indiana Volunteer Infantry.[157] Taking command, Barrett cautiously sent the Sixty-second Infantry and the Second Texas Union Cavalry along the riverbank, while the Thirty-fourth Indiana advanced on the Union right. In continued skirmishing, the small Union army slowly pushed the outnumbered Confederates upriver to Palmito Ranch, where in the early morning a fierce skirmish erupted in a thicket along the river. Fearing he would be overrun, Robertson fell back across the open prairie in the direction of Brownsville. At the ranch, the black troopers shared their rations with the Indiana volunteers, and then both took time to destroy what rebel supplies had not been carried off or burned the previous day. They also torched several makeshift huts the Confederates had been using for barracks.[158]

After continuing their pursuit west along the river for several miles, the exhausted Federals fell back to a small sandy promontory about one mile west of Palmito Hill. From here, they sent a detachment to Brazos Island with their wounded and the prisoners taken in the skirmish, as well as those captured the previous day.

At three in the afternoon on May 13, Colonel Ford arrived from Fort Brown with three hundred cavalrymen, along with men from Col. Santos Benavides's regiment and additional men from Colonel Giddings's battalion. After pushing through the night, Capt. O. G. Jones's six-gun battery of field artillery also arrived on the scene. "This may be the last fight of the war," Ford later remembered thinking, "and from the number of Union men I see before me, I am going to be whipped." Dressed in civilian clothes and holding his spyglass, the fighting colonel made a short inspirational speech. He formed his men into a line for battle on the coastal plain. At four in the afternoon, three of Captain Jones's guns under Lt. William Gregory and Lt. Jesse Vineyard, assisted by volunteer French artillery, opened fire on the Federals from a mile away.

No sooner had the fighting commenced than a steamboat was spotted steadily moving upriver. Unable to see the "flag she bore" and fearful the boat might be from the Union Navy, one of the rebel cannons opened fire.[159] Two shots fell harmlessly in the muddy water before the Confederates realized the steamboat belonged to King and Kenedy. The artillerymen then turned their guns on the Federals. One rebel cannon, commanded by Lt. M. S. Smith, "threw several well-directed shells and round shot into the enemy's lines," Ford recalled, causing considerable confusion.[160] The Confederate barrage was followed by Captain Robertson and his men moving against the Union left near the river. At the same time, two companies of Giddings's battalion hit the Federal right, while the remainder of Ford's rebels charged the center. Ford was hoping the Confederate artillery could gain a position on the Federal flank and open an enfilading fire.[161]

The Confederates opened "a fire upon us with both artillery and small-arms," Colonel Barrett wrote.[162] "[With a] heavy body of cavalry and a section of a battery, under cover of the thick chaparral on our right," Barrett continued, "[the rebels] succeeded in flanking us with the evident intention of gaining our rear."[163] The situation for the Union forces was "extremely critical," he concluded.

Caught by surprise and in danger of being outflanked, the Federals had no alternative but to retreat. "Having no artillery to oppose the enemy's six twelve-pounder field pieces our position became untenable," Barrett continued. "We therefore fell back fighting."[164] In his memoirs, Ford remembered the Union forces having left the field in a "rather confused manner." Although Colonel Barrett had given the order to retreat "double quick," several times the men of the Sixty-second and a few men from the Second Texas were forced to halt to protect the skirmishers of the Thirty-fourth Indiana. The Hoosier riflemen, nevertheless, were surrounded by the pursuing Confederate cavalry and forced to surrender. Others in the Thirty-fourth Indiana panicked and fled the field. A few of the Thirty-fourth Indiana infantrymen who successfully crossed to the south bank of the Rio Grande later recrossed the river and returned safely to Brazos Santiago.

In command of the Sixty-second US Colored Infantry, Colonel Branson watched as the Hoosiers "broke ranks and forced their way through my regiment."[165] "For God's sake, men, don't break my ranks," Branson screamed out, hoping his men would not panic.[166] Before they reached Palmito Hill, some soldiers of the Second Texas Cavalry were sent out to skirmish, and these men, like the skirmishers of the Thirty-fourth Indiana, were overrun and captured. Only by deploying the more disciplined Sixty-second in a long skirmish line stretching for more than a mile from the river across the open prairie did the Federals avoid being completely overrun.

Totally exhausted, many of the stragglers in the Thirty-fourth Indiana fell out beside the road and were unable to continue on their blistered feet. For seven miles, to a point about halfway between White's Ranch and Boca Chica Pass, Ford continued to pursue them. So desperate and disorganized were the Indiana men that upon reaching Boca Chica Pass, they rushed into the water, desperate to seize any boat and cross the narrow pass to safety. Along the sandy road to Brazos Island, the footsore bluecoats had left "many stands of arms, threw others in the Rio Grande, and left clothing scattered on their whole line of retreat," Ford recalled.[167] Although the Sixty-second Infantry reached the safety of Brazos Island "with colors flying and music playing," the "34th Indiana crossed the same night in total confusion."[168] Capt. W. C. Durkee of the Sixty-second said that the Indiana regiment could not be restored to order and that the wounded could not be brought safely across the pass in the dark.[169] Their chaotic twelve-mile retreat lasted for four painfully long hours.

W. H. D. Carrington, who commanded the Confederate cavalry at Palmito Ranch, reported that the companies of Capt. Refugio Benavides and Capt. Sixto Navarro were "conspicuous in the charge in leading their men & in encouraging them."[170] In the fighting, Refugio had crossed a ravine that other Confederates thought impassible, and after dismounting his men, he was ready to charge. After other rebels had crossed the ravine, Refugio gave the signal to his bugler to sound "charge." As Refugio and Carrington charged into the chaparral at full speed, "Yankees & Mexicans were swept away like chaff before the wind." They pursued the Federals for almost a mile through the chaparral as shells rained down on them from the Union battery on the hill. Minié balls "seemed to come from every conceivable direction," one Confederate officer remembered.[171] As night fell, the Confederates halted and then fell back into the chaparral while Refugio and his men mounted their horses. They then rode to the edge of the prairie and fired a volley at the Federals before retreating to Martin's Ranch.

"Boys, we have done finely," Ford remembered saying as he sat on his horse within sight of Brazos Island. "We will let well enough alone and retire."[172] Late in the afternoon, General Slaughter arrived from Fort Brown and assumed command. The general had been delayed by his fear that Cortina, who had realigned himself with the Juaristas and who remained in close contact with the Federals, was preparing to attack Brownsville. Only after obtaining assurances from General Mejía that the Imperialists would cross the river to secure the city if Cortina did attack could Slaughter head east.[173]

Now in command, General Slaughter ordered the Confederates to continue their pursuit. But Ford, realizing the Federals were manning the large guns on Brazos Island and reinforcing its south end, only sent out skirmishers. After the Federals sent out their own skirmishers, the soldiers engaged in a brisk firefight in which John J. Williams, a private in Company B of the Thirty-fourth Indiana, was killed. Members of the regiment would later present his family with a medallion remembering the Indiana lad as the last soldier killed in the Civil War, and Colonel Barrett would claim that the "last volley of the war was fired by the 62nd U. S. Colored Infantry about sunset on the 13th of May 1865."[174] When the Confederates fell back, they were briefly shelled by a Union warship anchored off Brazos Santiago, and a seventeen-year-old Confederate blasted away in the direction of the exploding shell with his Enfield rifle, "using a very profane expletive for so small a boy, causing a hearty laugh from half a score of his comrades."[175] The last shot of the Civil War had indeed been fired.

Federal casualties from the fighting at Palmito Ranch and the retreat that followed included 111 men killed, captured, or wounded.[176] Ford reported that he had only five men wounded, although years later, Capt. W. H. D. Carrington, one of Ford's officers, recalled burying Confederate dead after the battle. On the march back to Fort Brown, a few of the Federal prisoners were able to escape. Captives from the Second Texas, several of them Unionists from central Texas, were afraid they would be declared traitors and executed. Prisoners from the Sixty-second US Colored Infantry were fearful they would be "either shot or returned to slavery."[177] But Capt. Harrison L. Dean, commander of Company E of the Thirty-fourth Indiana, who was on staff duty on Brazos Santiago at the time of the battle, was able to enter Brownsville under a flag of truce and obtain the release of the prisoners. All the captives, except two men General Slaughter ordered held because they were deserters from the Confederate Army, were set free. Although Slaughter admitted the war was over, several rebel officers said they intended to continue fighting and thought they could hold out in Texas for at least five years.[178]

Even General Slaughter remained defiant and combative. Hoping to cross as much cotton as possible and learning that General Brown was marching on Brownsville, he fired off a letter warning the Federals that any "forward or aggressive movement" was in violation of a previous agreement and that he would resist with force. Another battle like Palmito Ranch would "produce excitement throughout the State of Texas," Slaughter warned, and "prevent the speedy and peaceable settlement of difficulties." "Do not deceive yourself as to the strength of my command," he cautioned.[179] In response, Brown diplomatically but tersely told Slaughter that he was not aware of any prior agreement that prevented him from occupying Brownsville. The only way to end the war on the Rio Grande, Brown wrote, was for the "armed opponents of the government to yield to its demands and surrender.[180]

Angry soldiers who remained on the border—demoralized by the collapse of the Confederacy, hungry, and not having been paid in months—threatened to sack Brownsville or even Matamoros. Drunken mobs roamed everywhere. Officers quarreled among themselves and then turned on one another. As chaos and mayhem engulfed the once proud Confederate command, General Slaughter used the *Mexico*, a steamboat flying the Imperial flag, to rush cotton across the river. Simultaneously, he sent his artillery battery of six guns, along with considerable ammunition and military equipment, to Matamoros, where the weapons were sold to the Imperialists. Crowds cheered as the guns were dragged through the streets to the courtyard adjacent to the Imperial barracks.[181] In Brownsville, angry Confederates arrested General Slaughter, accusing him of embezzlement, and forced him to divide $20,000 with them.[182] A militia company composed of Tejanos, along with Mexican liberals who had taken refuge on the north bank, helped to restore order and patrol the streets.[183]

Weeks earlier, embittered Confederates on the south bank of the river were said to have publicly rejoiced upon hearing the details of Lincoln's assassination. Adjacent to the customhouse and not far from Imperial headquarters on Calle de Comercio, they dug a spurious grave for the martyred president and performed around it "buffooneries and gross indecencies" that would have "shamed an Apache or Comanche Indian," a Texas Unionist recalled.[184] A grave was also dug for Lincoln in the sand at Bagdad, where there was much celebration by drunken Confederates and soured Southern sympathizers.

Early on the morning of Saturday, May 21, 1865, three Union officers arrived in Brownsville under a flag of truce and were welcomed into the city "as guests of the Confederates." The Union officers were not only treated with eggnog at Colonel Ford's residence, but crossed on the ferry to Matamoros, where they were guests of General Mejía at a grand review of his Imperial Army.[185] However, General Slaughter, defiant to the end, was gone.

Nine days later, on May 30, the Union Army proudly marched into Brownsville at daylight, much as they had done in 1863. The army seized five hundred bales of cotton that the rebels had been unable to get across the river, along with several hundred cattle and a few horses and mules that had belonged to the vanquished Confederacy.[186] Within two weeks, 1,915 men, including soldiers from the Sixty-second US Colored Infantry and the Second Texas Union Cavalry, had made camp at Fort Brown.[187]

On June 2, 1865, fifty-four days after General Lee's surrender at Appomattox Court House, Gen. Edmund Kirby Smith strode aboard the USS *Fort Jackson* in Galveston harbor and formally, but reluctantly, surrendered the Confederate Trans-Mississippi Department. Among those representing the Union Army at the ceremony was Gen. Edmund J. Davis. Texas Civil War history had come full circle. But the surrender itself was a mere formality, since most of the hungry and battered soldiers in Smith's command had gone home weeks earlier. By this time, much of what remained of the once-proud Confederate Army on the Rio Grande had also melted away. As many of the men and boys in homespun and butternut struck north for home, some pillaging as they went, others crossed into Mexico and cast their lots with the French Imperialists or the Juaristas. Generals Smith and Magruder, along with Governor Pendleton Murrah, former governor Edward Clark, and two thousand other beleaguered Confederates, all fearing they would be prosecuted for treason or even hanged, also fled to Mexico.

Refusing to surrender, General Slaughter fled upriver to join Colonel Santos Benavides at Rio Grande City. Federal authorities had ordered his arrest, but with Santos's protection and assistance, he was able to confiscate 650 bales of cotton at Ringgold Barracks and send them across the river to Camargo, where they were promptly sold to Francisco Yturria.[188] Shortly thereafter, Slaughter, with the money from the sale of the cotton, rode south into permanent exile, leaving Santos as the last of the long-suffering Confederate soldiers on the Rio Grande.

From Ringgold Barracks, Santos wrote to his brother-in-law and quartermaster, Capt. John Z. Leyendecker: "Unfortunately our war is already terminated. I am doing all I can in order to protect the interests of the government and my soldiers. Have brother Refugio keep order and not allow the soldier to rob . . . I will do the same as the only commander of the line."[189] Within days, he had ridden home to Laredo, past Roma, where cotton was still being crossed into Mexico, and the village of Carrizo and Redmond's Ranch, where he had so decisively defeated Cortina at the beginning of the war. He probably did not realize it at the time, but Santos was one of the few rebel commanders who had never suffered a defeat during the entire war. Yet he was full of sadness, even despair.

In August 1865, Santos was on a scouting expedition with several of his men when a polite letter from Union officers in Brownsville arrived in Laredo, asking that he sign and forward his parole papers.[190] For Santos and his small band of Tejanos, the war was over. And with the end of the war came the challenge of peace. Although on paper its defeat was total, the Confederacy would live on as an exalted lost cause in the memories of those who would come to see the war as sublime and glorious. Reconstruction would come to Texas, the Rio Grande frontier, Santos Benavides, his brave brothers, and what had once been a singular corner of the defiant but now battered and vanquished Confederate States of America.

CHAPTER VI

PEACEMAKING ON THE BORDER

"In the race of life—in the great whirl for 'first place,' these old heroes of a lost cause, it is true—are forced to give way to the young and vigorous."

—Santos Benavides to Porfirio Díaz, July 4, 1886

As the Civil War in South Texas wound to a whimper after the Battle of Palmito Ranch, and the Confederate States of America ceased to exist, the fighting in Mexico raged on without end and, in fact, seemed only to intensify. "The chapparal [*sic*] on this side [of] the Rio Grande is literally filled with refugees from Mexico," Gardner W. Pierce wrote from Carrizo on May 4, 1865.[1] Many of the men who crossed the river into Texas were hoping to avoid conscription by the liberals, whereas others were simply fleeing the violence. Many brought their families. So many people from Guerrero sought safety in Texas that the alcalde of the town made a public announcement: unless the citizens of Mexico returned to Guerrero within two weeks, the government would confiscate their property.

The collapse of the Confederacy led to a great sense of fear and anarchy that threatened to engulf the towns all along the Rio Grande, including Laredo. The war had gone so badly in the end that the Confederate Army in the Trans-Mississippi had not really surrendered but had "disbanded themselves" and "no earthly power . . . could keep them together," Gen. Hamilton P. Bee wrote.[2] For many Texans, the loss of the war spawned a bitterness that would last for generations. Convinced that their antebellum way of life was lost and that they would be imprisoned or even hanged for treason, as many as eight to ten thousand former Confederates fled to Mexico. Some went all the way to Brazil. Prominent former rebels who crossed the Rio Grande included Gen. Edmund Kirby Smith, Gen. John B. Magruder, Gen. Joseph O. Shelby, former Texas governor Edward Clark, and Pendleton Murrah, the last rebel governor of the state, who died in Monterrey of tuberculosis, as well as former executives from Louisiana, Kentucky, and Missouri.[3]

General Shelby, after defiantly leading a large contingent of his Missouri brigade through Texas, paused at Eagle Pass to bury a Confederate battle flag in the murky waters of the Rio Grande.[4] In Mexico, Americans established colonies such as Carlota near Cordova in the state of Veracruz and small settlements near Tampico, Monterrey, and Cuernavaca, as well as in the state of Coahuila. Many rode with the armies of Maximilian. A few, such as Gen. Mosby Monroe Parsons, a veteran of Prairie Grove and the Red River Campaign, were less fortunate. After obtaining passports at Matamoros, Parsons, his staff, and their families, along with Aaron H. Conrow, a former Confederate congressman, headed south, only to be robbed and murdered by a band of Cortinistas near China in Nuevo León.[5] Their bodies were either buried in an unmarked grave or thrown into the San Juan River.

As Santos watched from Laredo, the Waterloo of the Mexican Imperial Army came on June 16, 1866, at Mesa de Santa Gertrudis near Camargo. In the sweltering heat of summer, the liberal forces of Gen. Mariano Escobedo decisively overwhelmed an army composed of Mexicans and Austrians and seized over two hundred wagons, two thousand mules, and more than $3 million in merchandise. The Battle of Santa Gertrudis was, the *Daily Ranchero* of Brownsville wrote, "a death blow to the reign of [the] Empire in Northern Mexico."[6] Fed by mounting support from the north, long a hotbed of liberalism in Mexico, Juaristas everywhere gathered strength. The war that had been seen as a dispute between two Mexican parties, conservatives and liberals, was evolving into a bloody struggle against a foreign invader.

After the disaster at Santa Gertrudis, Gen. Tomás Mejía, the Imperial

Army's commander in Matamoros, realized his situation was precarious. Facing a growing number of desertions and with his six-hundred-man garrison pressed on all sides, Mejía concluded he could no longer hold the city, and he reached an agreement with the newly proclaimed governor of Tamaulipas, José María de Jesús Carvajal.[7] Mejía would evacuate Matamoros within forty-eight hours, provided the Imperial Army be allowed to leave the city by land or by river without being molested.[8] In a meeting with Mejía, Gen. George Washington Getty, commanding the District of the Rio Grande at Fort Brown, agreed that Mejía and the Imperial Army could use American steamers to depart the city. With flags flying, drums beating, and plenty of pageantry, as if the soldiers had won the war on the river, the Imperial Army embarked from Matamoros with arms, ammunition, baggage, and two six-pounder artillery pieces on the *Colonel Holcomb*, *Eugenia*, and *Colonel Benedict*. No sooner were the men on board than church bells rang out and citizens rushed into the streets of Matamoros to celebrate.[9] No imperial armies remained on the Rio Grande.

In the spring of 1867, with Napoleon III ordering the French army out of Mexico, Emperor Maximilian and his Mexican conservatives were left to the mercy of Juárez and the liberals. On June 19, 1867, following the defeat of what remained of the Imperial Army at Querétaro, Emperor Maximilian, Gen. Tomás Mejía, and Miguel Miramón were executed on El Cerro de las Campanas outside the city. Three weeks after the death of the emperor and his generals, the once powerful and proud Santiago Vidaurri, who had become Maximilian's minister of finance, as well as Santos's friend and confidant, was found hiding in a house in Mexico City. After being dragged into the streets and beaten, he was executed by firing squad on a dung heap as several hundred citizens cheered and bands played.[10] News of Vidaurri's death, as well as the return of his remains to his beloved ranch on Mesa de Catujanes near Candela, was certain to have hit Santos hard. Santos and Vidaurri had formed a friendship that lasted for over a decade, and both had influenced the history of the middle border. The war had taken Comonfort and other friends, and now Vidaurri, too, was dead and disgraced. Moreover, the downfall of the empire would do little to end political intrigue and violence in Mexico.

Hoping to secure the Rio Grande frontier, Federal authorities planned to move troops upriver as far as Laredo and Eagle Pass, but they were unable to do so immediately for lack of adequate transportation.[11] Soldiers were eventually dispatched upriver by steamer to Ringgold Barracks and then by land to Fort McIntosh. On June 30, 1865, thirty-seven-year-old lieutenant Thomas A. James, a stock raiser in Caldwell County before the war, and forty men from Company A of the Second Texas Union Cavalry rode into Laredo from downriver. Thirty-year-old Kentucky-born major James Speed quietly followed a few days later with three hundred more cavalrymen from the same regiment.[12] Family legend holds that Santos and his brothers, fearing they would be arrested and severely prosecuted or even executed by the Federals, temporarily fled to Mexico, and that only John Z. Leyendecker was there to greet the Union troops. During some rather tense moments on the plaza—what amounted to a surrender of the town—Juliana Leyendecker, reflecting the fears of her brothers, worried that her husband would be seized and executed.

In the late summer of 1865, Santos did in fact go to Monterrey for a few weeks, until he was sure that Federal authorities in Texas were not mistreating former Confederate officers. Cristóbal traveled to New Orleans to report to Union authorities, one of his grandsons recalled years later, although he, too, feared he might be executed for sedition.[13] Weeks later, Cristóbal returned to Laredo and told family members he had never met anyone as friendly and respectful as the Union officers at army headquarters in the Crescent City. In the end, life in Laredo continued much as it had before the war.

Since so many of the buildings at Fort McIntosh had been sold early in the war and had been moved or torn down, Santos offered his new home on the plaza, said to be the most beautiful in Laredo, to the Federals for their headquarters. The officers politely refused, moving on to what remained of Fort McIntosh, west of town, but the post surgeon, Col. C. Allen, seized the home and turned it into an infirmary. Santos was forced to move his family to his ranch, fifteen miles upriver, where living conditions were far more primitive and the fear of Indian raids was constant.[14]

Most of the soldiers sent to the border at the conclusion of the war were black, seasoned veterans of the siege of Petersburg and the bloody battle of the Crater. They had also been the first to triumphantly enter Richmond in April 1865. "The line of the Rio Grande is growing dark with troops," one newspaper racially commented.[15] Within a year, the Fourth US Cavalry, along with the Thirty-eighth, 111th, and 114th US Colored Troops, plus one company of the First US Artillery, were stationed at Fort Brown. The Thirty-fourth Indiana, veterans of the debacle at Palmetto Ranch, occupied Ringgold Barracks in the early summer of 1865 but were replaced in July by 777 men of the Eighth and Twenty-ninth US Colored Troops under command of Gen. Richard Henry Jackson.[16] The black troopers were joined in August by two batteries of the First US Artillery.

In October, the 117th US Colored Troops arrived at Ringgold Barracks to replace the Eighth US Colored Troops, who were transferred to Fort Brown to be mustered out.[17] In the summer of 1866, Col. Thomas D. Sedgwick would arrive to patrol the border with 712 additional men of the 114th US Colored Troops. Besides garrisoning the more established military posts, Colonel Sedgwick stationed troops at Santa María, at Edinburg, and upriver at Redmond's Ranch near Carrizo.[18] During the summer of 1866, portly lieutenant colonel William R. Shafter arrived at Ringgold Barracks with four companies of the Forty-first US Infantry.

By late October 1865, besides the men of the Second Texas Union Cavalry, 365 men and officers of the Sixty-second US Colored Troops commanded by Capt. H. R. Parsons had arrived at Fort McIntosh.[19] As Santos watched two months later, Captain Parsons was relieved by Lt. Col. David Branson, who sent river patrols as far upriver as Eagle Pass. By early March 1866, one company of the Fourth Wisconsin Cavalry and one of the 117th US Colored Troops had also arrived in Laredo.[20]

In an election held four days before Christmas 1866, both Santos and

Edmund J. Davis and Santos Benavides were close political allies before and after the Civil War. During the war, Davis rose to the rank of brigadier general in the Union Army and tried unsuccessfully to lure Benavides into the Federal ranks. *Jerry Thompson Collection.*

Refugio were selected as notaries, much less exalted positions than those they held before the war, although their brother-in-law, John Z. Leyendecker, was selected as county treasurer.[21] But when Congress imposed Radical Reconstruction on the South in March 1867, Santos was prohibited from holding public office altogether. Yet several political officials in Laredo who had held office during the antebellum years continued to do so after the war. In Webb County, a number of the appointees of provisional governor Andrew J. Hamilton were friends or acquaintances of Edmund J. Davis, Santos's former ally, who was more than familiar with Laredo politics. The new government in Austin, however, was out of touch with Laredo, and named Basilio Benavides county judge, although he had been dead for two years. It was not until Basilio's son-in-law, José María Rodríguez, wrote Austin with news of his father-in-law's death that Benito García was named in his place.[22] So many individuals either did not qualify for office or declined to serve that county and city governments quietly ground to a halt.

In April 1869, after Santos and Agustina had returned to their home on the plaza, the military took control in Texas. Lt. Col. Nathaniel Prime of the Fourth US Cavalry, brevetted for his heroism at the battle of the Wilderness in 1864 and now in command of Fort McIntosh, issued orders requiring anyone carrying arms on the streets of Laredo, either openly or not, to turn the weapons over to the officer-of-the-day at the post or to the city marshal. Prime did not want to interfere with the traditional right of travelers in Texas to carry weapons, but he was determined to curtail the violence at the *bailes* and fandangos in Laredo.[23]

A few months later, the military at Fort McIntosh also became involved in an effort to improve sanitation conditions in Laredo. The community had no public privies or sinks, nor did many of the homes, and as a consequence, the air was "tainted with the noxious effects of human excrements and many of the streets [and] unoccupied lots" were "particularly offensive."[24] Garbage was frequently left in barrels near the plaza for weeks, and many feared an epidemic would again engulf the town. Despite the efforts to clean up the city, a smallpox epidemic swept over Laredo in December 1872, and every day several citizens died, largely as a result of the "sanitary condition of the city [that] invited and aggravated the disease."[25] Although officials renewed their efforts to cleanse the city, citizens continued to die at an alarming rate.

Samuel M. Jarvis, the radical Republican mayor of Laredo who had served as superintendent of the silver mines at Vallecitos, Nuevo León, took the situation seriously and issued rules for the proper disposal of all "human excrements." Offal, especially from slaughtered animals, was to be disposed of at least one mile from the town limits. Garbage was to be placed in barrels or boxes, and the city marshal was entrusted with seeing that it was properly disposed of.[26] Under Jarvis's guidance, the city council approved a new lease for Fort McIntosh, set out to curb the furious riding of horses through the streets, established a new cemetery, and gave one hundred lots in the eastern part of the town to the Rockport, Fulton, Laredo, and Mexican Pacific Railroad, which promised to build into the community within seven years.[27]

Perhaps Jarvis's most lasting legacy was his naming of the streets of Laredo. Drawing from his deep reverence for the history of both Mexico and the United States, Jarvis named many of the streets, in alternating fashion, for the military and political heroes of the two countries. He named other streets for early settlers of the town and two for his daughters.[28] In 1869, Jarvis also printed handbills promoting the celebration of George Washington's birthday and July 4 the following year. Born of wealthy New York parents, Jarvis was well educated and had served with the US Army during the war with Mexico, went with William Walker and the filibusters to Nicaragua, and was married to a Mexican woman. Appointed by the radicals and under the scrutiny of the military, Jarvis not only served as mayor but as collector of customs and county judge.[29] Although Reconstruction ended in Texas in 1873, the town and the Benavides brothers had not heard the last of Samuel M. Jarvis.

By 1872 Laredo had its first English-language newspaper: the weekly, four-page, Democratic *Two Eagles*. Anticipating the arrival of the railroad in Laredo, which was certain to make it the largest city in "Western Texas."

An 1873 view of Laredo from the Mexican bank of the Rio Grande, showing the Ursuline Convent on the far left and a yet-to-be-completed San Agustín Church on the far right. *Courtesy Ursuline Sisters.*

W. C. Carroll, a lawyer by profession and a Confederate veteran turned scalawag who had served as justice of the peace in Corpus Christi, was the owner and editor of the newspaper. Carroll was said to have failed at several endeavors, and with little advertising and a circulation of only 360 in a community that was predominantly Spanish speaking, his newspaper lasted for less than two years.[30]

Santos was one of the few who had gained materially from the war, and he had clearly become part of the landed and mercantile elite of Laredo. But the war had devastated others, particularly his close friend Hamilton P. Bee. From a distinguished South Carolina family—his grandfather had been a federal judge and his father secretary of state of the Republic of Texas—Bee, like so many other former Confederates, fled to Mexico after the war to avoid what was certain to be a "reign of terror." His distinguished brother, Barnard, had been killed at the first battle of Bull Run, and two of his sisters and all of their children except one had died of disease during the war. His brother-in-law Clem Stevens had been killed in the battle for Atlanta. Bee had lost everything he had in the war, and he and his wife, Mildred, and their six children traveled all over Mexico seeking economic security. Although he found Mexico "magnificent and delightful" and even went on to Cuba, he wanted to return to the United States.[31] Bee eventually settled at Saltillo but returned to Texas in 1876, living first in Laredo and then San

Antonio, where he practiced law and drank heavily. He never regained the wealth and influence he had possessed before the war.

Santos and his brothers watched during Reconstruction as banditry again became rampant in South Texas, especially the area south of the Nueces River, a no-man's-land where only Native Americans, outlaws, and the very daring ventured. To complicate matters, several of the counties in South Texas, such as Dimmit, Duval, McMullen, Encinal, and LaSalle, had no law enforcement officials to maintain order. Much of the violence in the area was traced to a gang of outlaws operating out of the village of Dog Town (modern day Tilden), located in a forest of mesquite at the mouth of Leoncita Creek along the Frio River. Camp Rio Frio, a Civil War home guard post, had been established here, where ragged soldiers huddled in picket houses with dirt floors and enjoyed a diet of prickly pear salad, turkey, quail, and deer. The village had been named for the dogs local cowboys used to help herd their cattle. Poker games abounded and liquor flowed freely at "Peg-Leg" Stewart's combination trading post and saloon, which seemed to be a magnet for men with bad reputations. The Dog Town outlaws bragged openly of murdering Mexicans, usually for their saddles or horses.[32] Leading the outlaws was thirty-five-year-old Thomas F. Green and brothers Richard and Malachi Gossett. All three had served in Capt. Lewis Maverick's Company E of Col. Peter C. Woods's Thirty-sixth Texas Cavalry, which had been recruited in DeWitt County during the Civil War. Unlike his companions, Richard Gossett had become a first lieutenant in Benavides's regiment and had actually commanded a company at one time. During the latter stages of the war, Santos had given him the job of gathering wild horses on the Nueces River, and the lieutenant had come to know the area well.[33]

To the residents of Dog Town, the three men were friendly, congenial, and sociable, but if they came across any Mexicans, "it was too bad for the Mexicans if they were riding a good horse or a good saddle that was worth the taking."[34] In the years following the war, the three men frequently took to the trails in the area between Dog Town and the Rio Grande, "becoming highwaymen in the old sense," and always, it was said, engaged in some "kind of devilment." They would do their "thievery or worse among the Mexicans and then take refuge among the Americans" in Dog Town.[35] The twenty-eight-year-old blonde-haired Malachi, the older of the two brothers, was the most vicious of the outlaws and was frequently seen at the gambling hall at old Fort Ewell on the south bank of the Nueces River. "Freckled blotches covered his pale sunburned face and seemed to shroud his pale blue eyes." Malachi sported a "flaming red handlebar mustache," and his red hair grew long over his ears and shoulders. The brothers were always seen together. Some found Dick Gossett, who first came to Dog Town after deserting from the army in 1864, to be charming and intelligent. Others remembered him being good with a six-gun and bragging that he had killed twenty-five men, mostly Mexicans and Indians.[36]

In December 1866, word reached Laredo that Juan Ortiz and three of his teamsters had been robbed and murdered while they camped on San Miguel Creek on the Laredo–San Antonio road in northeastern Frio County, about fifty miles southwest of San Antonio.[37] Their wagon train was looted of blankets, clothing, shoes, and a number of items Ortiz hoped to sell on the border. The assault was only the latest in a series of attacks on wagon trains in the preceding months. Maj. Andrew J. Hogan, commanding sixty-one men from the 114th US Colored Infantry at Fort McIntosh, reported that a group of bandits numbering between twelve and fifteen had been rampaging through the area, "murdering and robbing every one that they happened to meet with, having killed some seven or eight men within the last fifteen days."[38] Four of those killed were said to be citizens of Laredo.

Hearing of the death of their brother in December 1866, Plutarco and José Ortiz headed out from Laredo in the face of a bitterly cold norther. After pausing at A. J. Hall's La Mota Ranch, two miles downriver from old Fort Ewell, they were set upon by the Dog Town outlaws. Dick Gossett was wounded in a furious gun battle, and sometime during the melee, Plutarco Ortiz was sent back to Laredo to plea for assistance.

Major Hogan promised he would do everything possible to apprehend the outlaws, but very few of his sixty men at Fort McIntosh had horses. However, "Col. Santos Benavides came forward and offered his services with thirty Mexicans well mounted and armed," Hogan reported.[39] Santos assembled on the plaza a party of citizens who were "determined to apprehend and punish the murderers and robbers," the major went on to say. Hastily riding north with Santos were his two trusted brothers, Refugio and Cristóbal; his brother-in-law Francisco Farías; Dr. H. B. Butcher, the post surgeon; and several other friends and relatives. Santos and Major Hogan, one a Union veteran, the other a former Confederate, were in command, along with Capt. L. C. Drake.

Although suffering from hemorrhoids, the thirty-one-year-old Hogan was a tough army veteran of the Civil War who had led his black troopers from the time they enlisted in Kentucky through the bloodletting that was the siege of Petersburg and the surrender of the Army of Northern Virginia at Appomattox Court House.[40] Continuing through the night, the party reached La Mota Ranch early the next day. They found no bandits but heard rumors that the outlaws were intent on stealing a horse herd at El Sauz Ranch, several miles to the north. Continuing on, Santos and Hogan found the horses safely corralled and they posted pickets around the ranch. Clothing belonging to Tom Green, along with various items that were know to have been taken from the Ortiz wagon train, including pantaloons and Juan Ortiz's saddle, were found at the ranch.

The frigid night passed without incident, and early the next morning, the party was able to pick up the trail of the outlaws. Several more items stolen from the wagon train led them in the direction of Dog Town, forty miles to the northeast. Scouring the country for the desperadoes, Santos and Hogan rode to within fifteen miles of Dog Town, where they camped late at night. Hoping to catch the outlaws off guard, the party broke camp at three the next morning, and just as daylight settled over the brush country, less than a mile outside Dog Town, they met an unarmed "Mexican" who at first refused to talk but finally admitted that Tom Green, Malachi Gossett, and several others outlaws were in the village and were in possession of one of the Ortiz wagons they had stolen.[41] Santos and Hogan sent out flanking parties of six men each, as if in a Civil War skirmish, to make sure the outlaws did not escape. With Santos by his side, Hogan volunteered to lead the main party down the road to the village, and as soon as the outlaws were located, he would charge them. Santos later calculated that despite their caution, at least ten or twelve outlaws who were headquartered in the village escaped and raced off across the Rio Frio in the direction of Pleasanton.[42]

Finding the stolen wagon at the ranch house of Billy Franklin, Santos and Hogan quickly surrounded the premises, and Santos yelled out to the outlaws in Spanish to surrender, promising they would receive a fair trial back in Laredo. The three outlaws who were sleeping in the stolen wagon jumped out and raced for the safety of the ranch house, drawing their pistols as they ran. A volley of wild gunfire soon exploded from the doors and windows of the house, and one of Santos's men, Natividad Herrera, a trusted and courageous sergeant who had killed Octaviano Zapata in September 1863, was severely wounded.[43] Santos and his men dismounted and took cover behind several mesquite trees while they unleashed a blistering fusillade on the ranch house. "Soon the cries of women and children" could be heard, and a cease-fire was called. Major Hogan bravely rode up to within fifteen feet of the house and called on the women and children to come out. Several tearful women and frightened children soon emerged, as did Billy Franklin. Shortly thereafter, the outlaws could be seen peeking out the windows and doors, and the gun battle resumed. Dick Gossett soon lay dead, and Malachi was shot in the right arm. Determined to fight to the death, Malachi was said to have seized his pistol with his left hand, but Tom Green grabbed him and yelled out that the men were willing to surrender. Tom, his arms in the air, and Malachi, holding his shattered right arm to his side, emerged from the house.

Exactly what happened next is uncertain. One version of events holds that when a gun battle erupted in another part of the village, Tom and Malachi decided to make a run for it and were killed. Leaving the outlaws to be buried by their friends, Santos and his men placed the badly wounded Herrera in the stolen wagon and began the long ride back to Laredo. But other versions of what happened to Tom and Malachi have also come down through time. One version of the deadly Dog Town gun battle has the two men being captured and dragged to a small laguna near the village, beyond sight of the women and children, where Malachi was shot in the head and Tom was beaten to death with pistol butts. Another version agrees that the two men were executed about two miles outside Dog Town near a small creek, where their bullet-riddled bodies were later found and buried in unmarked graves in the village's Boot Hill Cemetery.[44]

In a brief report, Major Hogan said only that he and Santos found the outlaws, "made a charge upon them," and killed "three of the principal ones and captured twelve head of horses."[45] Santos later told the *San Antonio Herald* that the gun battle lasted for only a few minutes, at which time Tom and Malachi were captured and "both were punished," in "conformity with their crime." The citizens of Dog Town, he went on to say, "sanctioned and approved with pleasure the action."[46] In early February, when Major Hogan sent his report to headquarters, Gen. Charles Griffin recommended that Governor James W. Throckmorton write Santos a "complimentary letter" praising him for his "valuable assistance" in eliminating the "band of thieves" that had plagued the area.[47]

Despite the lawlessness in South Texas and the violence of Reconstruction, a correspondent for the *Austin Weekly State Gazette* reported in August 1869 that Laredo was one of the few places in the state where people slept "with their doors open and thefts from houses" were "almost unheard of." The "Mexicans of Webb County are brave, faithful, and reliable . . . and remarkable honest," the newspaper continued.[48]

In reality, the situation in South Texas in the summer of 1869 was desperate in a number of ways. Webb County was broke, and the tax assessor-collector reported he was unable to collect enough taxes to pay deputies to police Laredo, much less the entire county.[49] With mostly infantry at Fort McIntosh, as was the case before the war, the military was unable to curtail the Indian raids that consistently plagued the Laredo area. Not only were the Comanches and Lipan Apaches sweeping down on the Rio Grande, much as they had before the war, but outlaws were continuing to operate in Atascosa, Medina, and LaSalle Counties, killing cattle and skinning them for hides that were sold in Corpus Christi or San Antonio. Citizens of the county had a long history of conflict with Native Americans, and Santos, usually assisted by Refugio and Cristóbal, had fought the Indians successfully for more than two decades. For this reason and others, they were widely acknowledged by their community to be "gallant and true men."

After indigenous marauders killed seven citizens in the spring of 1869, the commanding officer at Fort McIntosh, New York-born colonel Nathaniel Prime, a grizzled veteran of the battle of the Wilderness and Spotsylvania, issued orders calling for four companies of civilians in Webb County, two companies in Duval County, and two in Encinal County to assist the military. Many of those who heeded the call to arms were former Confederate veterans such as Santos Benavides.[50] Prime reported to headquarters of the Fifth Military District, encompassing Texas and Louisiana, that a number of citizens were anxious to serve but had a "terrible fear of anything that resembled involuntary service," similar to Confederate conscription.[51] Although Prime explained that service would be voluntary, some men were still reluctant.

Companies were to be of "convenient size," and recruits were to be supplied with rations, although they were required to provide their "own horses and arms." Of the four companies authorized for Webb County, the first invitation to command went to Santos on May 23, 1869.[52] When Prime failed to hear from the former colonel, he drafted a second letter, again asking Santos to enroll "such men as [he] might be able to rely upon." Beyond fighting Indians, Santos's authority would be extended to the "arrest of all cattle thieves or persons engaged in illicit traf[f]ic in hides," and he would be able to inspect the papers of any "party in charge of a herd."[53] Finally, on July 17, Santos wrote to accept the position. He also included a list of the men he hoped to rely on, mostly Civil War veterans he had known and trusted.

Another company in Webb County was commanded by Bernardo Mendiola, who enrolled twenty-five men, all of whom were mounted and willing to "suppress any disorder." Mendiola said his men had agreed to serve at no cost to the government while "in pursuit of Indians."[54] Juan García Soto also accepted a commission and set out to raise a third company. At the same time, Santos's friend and Civil War subordinate, Charles Callaghan, confirmed he had twenty men who could "cheerfully aid him," and he accepted a commission to raise a militia company in Encinal County.[55] Later, the Texas Rangers would receive accolades for ending the banditry in the lawless Nueces Strip. In reality, it was the Tejanos on the middle border, often depicted in newspapers and dime novels as bandits and outlaws, who deserved most of the credit.

In August 1870, a party of forty-two Kickapoos crossed the Nueces River near old Fort Ewell and swept into Encinal County and down on Santos's Rancho Charco Largo, killing and stealing horses. Meanwhile, two individuals—a man and a woman—were killed at Gen. Julian Quiroga's Charco Largo de los Indios ranch, north of Laredo. Julian Quiroga Villarreal was a Santiago Vidaurri partisan who had risen to the rank of general in the army of the empire and later found refuge with Santos in Laredo. Four months later, raiders struck a wagon train on the Laredo–San Antonio road, killing Guadalupe Rosendo and carrying off Martina Díaz. The Indians proceeded south toward Laredo, where they killed a young herder named Aldama and another teenager, Pedro Cruz, before troops from Fort McIntosh chased them and rescued Díaz.[56]

In October 1871 yet another Indian raid out of Mexico swept across South Texas between Laredo and the Nueces River. A sheep herder was killed at a ranch above Laredo, and the raiders came close to killing General Quiroga after pursuing him for over a mile.[57] In March 1872 Santos was with Charles Callaghan on a survey party in the same area when they learned that a Kickapoo raiding party had crossed the river twenty-five miles above Laredo and attacked one of Cristóbal Benavides's sheep camps, killing several herders. Thirty miles north of Laredo, the Kickapoo killed Guadalupe

Elizario and Carlos Garza and the next morning struck the Callaghan Ranch, killing Felipe Gonzales. The raiders then turned south and rode down the Texas side of the Rio Grande before crossing back into Mexico.[58] In November of 1872 a party of ten Kickapoos struck across the river and killed two shepherds working for Callaghan, eighteen miles north of Laredo, before Santos and a party of citizens chased them away.[59]

Relations between the United States and Mexico were pushed to the breaking point several times, not only by the incessant cattle raids in the lower valley carried out by Juan Cortina and his followers, but also by Col. Ranald Slidell "Bad Hand" Mackenzie's dramatic raid into Mexico on May 18, 1873. Acting on unwritten orders and determined to stop the Indian raids emanating from south of the border, Mackenzie took 376 men of his Fourth US Cavalry across the Rio Grande in the night and on May 18, 1873, attacked three villages of Kickapoos and Lipan and Mescalero Apaches near Remolino, Coahuila, forty miles south of the border. Guided by twenty-four Seminole scouts, Mackenzie and his men burned 180 lodges, killed nineteen warriors, and took forty women and children as captives back to Fort Clark.

Although the Texas legislature extended its congratulations and Mackenzie's superiors applauded his daring, the government of Mexico was angry and embarrassed. South of the border, the Remolino Raid was seen as a clear and flagrant outrage against the national sovereignty of Mexico, a transgression that was not easily forgotten. In the end, the daring raid proved to be an impediment to peace and an open wound in the Mexican psyche. In June 1877 tensions along the border reached new heights when President Rutherford B. Hayes, under pressure from the Texas congressional delegation, authorized Gen. Edward O. C. Ord, commanding the army on the border, to cross into Mexico, if necessary.[60]

The military at Fort McIntosh tried gallantly to defend the outlying ranches as well as the small farmers along the river and above and below the town, but the infantry, in particular, was pitifully inadequate. Border raids continued for several years. Virtually unnoticed in the American press and in the halls of power in Washington, DC, however, was the fact that indigenous incursions into Mexico from Texas were far more numerous and deadly than Indian raids from Mexico into Texas. Such incursions had been addressed in the Treaty of Guadalupe Hidalgo in 1848 but had continued to agitate and alarm individuals on both sides of the border.[61]

So bad was the lawlessness in South Texas that Gov. Richard Coke commissioned Refugio Benavides, who was serving as mayor of Laredo at the time, as a lieutenant in the Texas Rangers with authority to raise twenty-five men and scout the area around the town.[62] In his oath, which he signed at Laredo on June 13, 1874, the words "and that I hold no other office under either the State or General Governments for which I receive pay" were carefully scratched out.[63] Refugio's appointment in the Texas Rangers preceded a deadly raid by outlaws and Indians who swept out of Mexico into Texas in November 1874.[64] It was one of the bloodiest raids in local memory. Twenty-five men, most of them herders, were killed in Webb and Duval Counties alone, while numerous others were seriously wounded. Hypolito Mendiola, a prominent citizen of Laredo, was among the dead, brutally killed at his ranch near the city.

Hearing of the attack, Lt. Refugio Benavides hastily gathered several men, most of them armed with Winchester or Sharps carbines and Colt or Smith & Wesson six-shooters, rode off in pursuit of the raiders, and caught up with them just as they were crossing back into Mexico. Although most of the raiders were able to escape, an old man who was wounded and left behind was captured and likely hanged.[65] Santos and Refugio Benavides had more than once "impressed on the invaders the lesson that the vicinity of Laredo was a bad region for the pursuit of their trade," a congressional report concluded.[66] But the raids continued unabated. As late as March 1879, a band of Kickapoos struck near Santos's ranch upriver from Laredo, killing two men, wounding a boy, and making off with several livestock. With ten days' rations, twenty men of the Eighth US Cavalry from Fort McIntosh went in pursuit, as did the Mexican military stationed in Nuevo Laredo, but the Kickapoos proved elusive.[67]

Refugio's appointment to the Texas Rangers attracted national at-

"Texas Rangers holding up Chaparral Bandits" by Frederick Remington. Although many Tejanos fell victim to the racism and violence of the Texas Rangers before and after the Civil War, the Benavides brothers were well respected by the Rangers as well as by the political leadership in Austin. In 1874, Refugio Benavides even became an officer in the Rangers. *Courtesy Library of Congress.*

tention when Governor Coke authorized him to cross the Rio Grande in pursuit of Native American raiders and cattle rustlers, if necessary. When the news came to the attention of Secretary of State Hamilton Fish, he promptly referred the matter to Attorney General George H. Williams, recommending that the federal government intervene. In response, Williams frankly told Governor Coke that if Refugio crossed the river, he would be in violation of federal law. Coke tried to explain, but few in Washington really understood the situation in South Texas.[68]

Upriver from Carrizo, citizens feared Indian marauders, but in the lower valley it was Cortina and his bands of cattle rustlers who drew all the attention. The Cortinistas unleashed a virtual reign of terror in South Texas in March 1875 when a large band rode across the uneven sands of the Wild Horse Desert with the intention of striking Corpus Christi. Robbing and murdering as they went, thirty of the raiders hit the small settlement of Nuecestown, thirteen miles northwest of Corpus Christi, instead. Here, 150 miles from the border, the raiders looted, humiliated, horsewhipped, and brutally killed several inhabitants. So terrorized were the inhabitants of Corpus Christi by the news from Nuecestown that hundreds of citizens rushed the town's municipal pier in hopes of boarding any boat they could find. Two posses were hastily organized at Corpus Christi and rode west to confront the raiders. After a fierce gun battle, one posse member was dead, and a Mexican raider who had been wounded was captured and taken to Corpus Christi, where he was lynched by a mob.[69]

In the wake of the Nuecestown raid, twenty-four Cortinistas crossed the Rio Grande at Paso Atrisco near Mier, rode upriver, and, on the morning of April 19, 1875, murdered a friend of Santos, the deputy collector of customs and postmaster at Carrizo, Dr. D. D. Lovell. He was "an old citizen of Texas and an estimable gentleman," Santos testified. Twelve of the raiders looted Lovell's store of $4,000 in goods. Later that month, Texas Rangers rode into the area and burned any ranches belonging to Tejanos. Fearing death by hanging, hundreds of rancheros crossed into Mexico or crowded into villages such as San Diego, north of the border, for protection.

During the height of the violence, Santos met with Gen. Nicanor Zapata, who had been sent to Nuevo Laredo by Gen. Mariano Escobedo. Santos had great faith that Escobedo, whom Santos knew, would do everything possible to restore order on the river and maintain peace between the two republics. For his part, Zapata promised to punish the Cortinistas operating in Texas.[70] Santos, who had been hailed as a "highly respected Mexican citizen of Texas" and a consistent "bulwark against disorder on the frontier," assured the public that Mexican authorities would punish those responsible for the crimes in Texas, and his statements were widely published.[71]

Citizens of South Texas had become accustomed to Cortinistas crossing into Texas and stealing horses and cattle, but the brutality and brazenness of the attack on Nuecestown coupled with the murder of Dr. Lovell at Carrizo sent shock waves across the area. What followed was an unsurpassed outbreak of hatred and violence in which Mexican Texans, the vast majority of whom had no association with Juan Cortina, were indiscriminately brutalized and killed. With a perverted sense of justice and retribution, "minute companies" of vigilantes roamed the countryside, committing untold acts of violence. In several counties such as Nueces and Duval, vigilantes drove Tejanos off their property, stole their livestock, and burned their homes to the ground. J. Frank Dobie, who knew as much about the South Texas brush country as anyone, estimated the number of Mexican Texans killed in the months following the raid on Nuecestown greatly exceeded the number of Mexicans who died at San Jacinto.[72] The San Antonio correspondent for the *New York Times* said that by October at least twelve to fifteen "Americans"—presumably meaning Texans of European descent—had been killed, and well over one hundred "Mexicans" hanged or shot. Much of the violence, the newspaper went on to report, had the purpose of "driving Mexican land owners out of the country" so that their lands could be bought "for a song."[73]

So widespread was the savagery that forty-eight Texas Rangers under Capt. Leander H. McNelly, a Civil War veteran who had served in the state police, had to be sent to the area to establish some semblance of law and order.[74] But the Rangers were themselves frequently responsible for numerous hangings and shootings of innocent Tejanos. Because Cortina's raiders were known to have taken twenty-five new saddles from the Thomas Noakes store at Nuecestown, any Mexican Texan with a new saddle was gunned down or hanged on the spot. In the weeks and months following the raid on Nuecestown, the decaying corpses of Tejanos hanging from mesquite trees became a common sight along the roads and trails of the region.

On the periphery of the brush country, Capt. Refugio Benavides and his men were also caught up in the violence. In August 1874 a man named Alanis, who was acting as a guide for a second company of Texas Rangers said to be cattle skinners, was apprehended by Refugio (also a Texas Ranger) and left hanging from a mesquite tree.[75] It was ironic that in a time when most Tejanos came to fear and hate the Texas Rangers, Refugio Benavides, with his brother by his side, proudly wore the five-pointed star of the Rangers.

Undeniably, the period from the early 1860s to the early 1870s was one of the most turbulent and significant in the history of the Rio Grande frontier. People on both banks of the lower Rio Grande had survived secession, political intrigue, civil war, revolution, and misguided foreign intervention, along with pestilence, guerrilla warfare, natural disasters, and seemingly unbounded and indiscriminate violence. On April 16, 1870, however, with the end of Reconstruction, civil government had at least been restored in Texas. Nine years after secession, the Lone Star State was back in the Union, and Brownsville and Laredo had begun to commemorate George Washington's birthday, as well as diez y seis de septiembre and the Fourth of July, with festive dinners, parades, and other lively festivities.[76]

The Benavides brothers continued to excel in politics, as they had before the Civil War, and it was here they came to have their greatest influence on Laredo and the middle border. With Reconstruction passing into memory and the Native Americans beaten back by genocidal warfare, former Confederates such as Santos once again rose to new political heights. But it was a difficult time for Tejanos. When Santos took the oath as state representative in 1879, he was the only Tejano in the state legislature. Ominous new challenges loomed on both the southern border and the northern horizon.

CHAPTER VII

BEYOND THE MEMORY OF LIVING MEN

"Santos Benavides, the Confederate robber, voted all his thieves and every other democratic thief, priest, and murderer."

—J. M. Flournoy to J. P. Newcomb, November 4, 1872

When Maj. William H. Emory of the US-Mexico boundary survey was on the bluff overlooking the Rio Grande at Roma in 1853, he was puzzled at how such "fine residences and warehouses, all recently built, could be sustained by trade." But when night crept over the river and Emory stepped outside to make an observation of latitude and longitude, he saw a long train of mules, heavily loaded with contraband goods, slowly winding their way across the river to Mexico.[1] When army inspector and colonel Joseph K. F. Mansfield came to Laredo to inspect Fort McIntosh in 1860, he also had strong suspicions of an extensive illegal trade. "It is difficult to say what sustains this town," he wrote.[2]

Since the Treaty of Guadalupe Hidalgo had established the boundary between the United States and Mexico at the Rio Grande in 1848, smuggling had become a way of life in border communities such as Laredo. Many individuals living on the river saw the international boundary as an artificial line imposed by governments from afar, and they saw nothing wrong with smuggling goods across the river.

Despite the untiring efforts of customs officials at Laredo to suppress the trade in contraband during Reconstruction, goods flowed across the river much as they had before the war. Smugglers took weapons and other

"Smuggling on the Rio Grande" by P. Frenzeny. Santos Benavides, like many citizens on the border at the time, actively indulged in smuggling. *Courtesy Library of Congress.*

goods into Mexico, usually at night, and moved other items into Texas. In many instances, corrupt customs officials in Mexico took bribes and helped falsify documents or simply turned their backs on the illicit trade. N. A. Jennings, who briefly served as town marshal of Laredo in 1876, asserted that in Laredo "seven-tenths of the people were smugglers, either chronic or occasional."[3] In fact, smuggling on the Rio Grande frontier became so rampant that in 1870 the Treasury Department sent a special agent to South Texas to investigate. In a matter of days the agent was able to conclude that there was "scarcely any limit" to the smuggling.[4] Another government official, echoing Jennings's claims, complained that as many as three-fourths of the people on the border were engaged in smuggling goods, mostly small items of an insignificant nature. On the Laredo bank of the river, as was the case in Roma in 1850, larger items were strapped to the backs of mules and the animals led across the river at night. In what proved to be an impossible task, one customs agent was assigned to watch the Rio Grande at Laredo, while two mounted guards were charged with policing a sixty-mile stretch of the river, above and below the town.

Since before the war, Santos and Cristóbal had been exporting a wide variety of foodstuffs, hardware, and dry goods to Mexico and importing rawhide and other items into the United States. The business became so successful the brothers opened a second retail and wholesale store in Nuevo Laredo.[5] Their exporting and importing business came to a screeching halt in February 1872, however, when Samuel M. Jarvis, collector of customs, mayor, and county judge at the time, accused the brothers of smuggling and bribing Nuevo Laredo customs officials.

The confrontation began when Jarvis issued orders prohibiting "Benavides and Brother" from importing seventy-six rawhides into the United States. The brothers, Jarvis argued, were acting under the authority of revolutionaries in Mexico who were attempting to overthrow the legitimate government of Benito Juárez.[6] At the same time, Santos's former friend Julian Quiroga, who owned a large ranch in Webb County and who commanded the Mexican army in Nuevo Laredo, issued orders denying Santos and Cristóbal the right to import goods into Mexico. The Benavides brothers were certainly not the only prominent Laredo businessmen who were involved in smuggling, but they found themselves at the center of a whirlwind of accusations and negative publicity.

Several prominent individuals on both sides of the Rio Grande thought politics was at the root of the Benavides-Jarvis feud. Jarvis was a dedicated and uncompromising radical Republican, while the Benavides brothers were loyal Democrats and former Confederates who resented the long arm of radical Republican rule. Although the strains of Reconstruction were real, the confrontation was undoubtedly fueled by the Benavides brothers' blatant smuggling and bribery. While calling for a thorough investigation, the *Corpus Christi Nueces Valley* also admitted that the case was one of "personal spite."[7] As tensions and hostilities grew, Santos and Cristóbal filed a complaint with the US commercial agent in Nuevo Laredo, Thomas Gilgan, arguing that customs officials there were bound by a treaty of commerce with the United States. The brothers maintained they had always paid the proper tariffs and had the right to conduct business across the border. There is little doubt they supported individuals in Mexico who controlled the Nuevo Laredo customhouse and who were hostile to the Juárez government.[8] When Gilgan refused to intervene, Santos promptly imported the rawhide and some other goods using a different customs broker.[9] Jarvis heard about it and was furious.

Tensions rose even more when several Mexican revolutionaries were arrested at Santos's Charco Largo Ranch for smuggling arms into Mexico. Santos was embarrassed by the resulting publicity, and he turned on Jarvis with a vengeance, commencing with a scurrilous attack in the *Matamoros El Fronterizo*.[10] Defending Jarvis, the pro-Republican *Nueces Valley* accused Santos of corruption, of using the cotton trade and his colonelcy to become rich during the war. The newspaper demanded a full investigation. There was little doubt Santos was deeply involved in the lucrative smuggling that was so rampant on the border, the *Nueces Valley* asserted. On the other hand, Jarvis was a dedicated public servant, "efficient, vigilant, and industrious."[11] In the "troubles at Laredo," as the newspaper called the confrontation, Cristóbal came to his brother's defense, arguing that the *Nueces Valley* was reckless and highly partisan. At the same time, the *Laredo Two Eagles* was publishing Santos's side of the dispute, although a few days later a spirited rebuttal by Jarvis was given equal coverage.[12] The feud finally subsided when Jarvis, sensing how much power the Republicans had lost in Texas, along with Washington's changing attitude toward Reconstruction, suddenly resigned as customs collector.

Despite the fact that Santos and Cristóbal were obviously guilty of smuggling goods, and even of gunrunning and bribing customs officers in Nuevo Laredo, their reputations remained untarnished. Smuggling continued to be seen by a large percentage of the population as acceptable, and in no way did it carry the social stigma it would in later decades. In fact, many in Laredo and Mexico admired the brothers for their tenacity and willingness to fight a system they viewed as heavy-handed and illegitimate. In time, the smuggling accusations against the Benavides brothers were largely forgotten.

Even before the Civil War had ended, Reconstruction laws allowed former Confederates to be pardoned, provided they took an oath of allegiance to the Union. However, high-ranking Confederate soldiers or government officials such as Santos, as well as plantation owners, were prohibited from holding government office. Although President Andrew Johnson pardoned hundreds of high-ranking former Confederates after 1865, Santos was not eligible through the general amnesty of May 1865. He simply returned home and continued much as he had before the war. It would be eight long years before he sought public office again.

Life in Laredo throughout the latter half of the nineteenth century was centered on the town's plazas, as it had been in the decades before the war. By 1873 a large and imposing church had been constructed on the east side of San Agustín Plaza, overlooking Santos's home and that of his brother-in-law, Leyendecker. The post office, courthouse, customhouse, and Santos's mercantile business on Flores Street, facing Market Plaza, were only blocks away. In 1881 Raymond Martin, who became the town's leading entrepreneur, constructed a large, modern two-story hotel at the intersection of Grant and Flores Streets, adjacent to San Agustín Plaza.[13] Martin, like Santos and other businessmen, was hoping to reap economic rewards from the arrival of the railroad. The twice-weekly mail service to San Antonio became daily, and communication with the Alamo City, which had taken a week before the war, now took only forty-eight hours. One of the principal activities of both the townspeople and the ever-present military was baseball. In October 1878, for example, thousands came on foot, on horseback, and by carriage, to watch the Laredo nine beat the bluecoats from Fort McIntosh, 26–16.[14]

In February 1869, Santos was able to purchase the remaining portion of porcion fourteen from Josefa Villarreal de Ugarte and Felipe Villarreal for $350.[15] A year later he purchased a small lot in Nuevo Laredo on the west side of the main plaza where he and Cristóbal could expand their mercantile

At the age of seventeen, Raymond Martin (1828–1900) followed two brothers to the United States, settling first at New Orleans and then Pensacola, Florida, before coming to the border in 1856, and marrying into the well-to-do García family. Martin opening a small mercantile business and within a decade become the wealthiest man in Webb County. A pioneer sheep raiser and wool producer, by 1882 he owned 130,000 acres of grazing land and 90,000 head of sheep. Serving in several offices, by the early 1880s he had become head of the Bota Democrats and the political rival of Santos Benavides and the Guaraches. *From* A Twentieth Century History of Southwest Texas, *published by the Lewis Publishing Company in 1907.*

business. At the same time, he bought and sold several pieces of property not far from San Agustín Plaza in Laredo.

In a meeting of the city council on February 7, 1872, it was decided the city should raise funds to construct a public school house. When Basilio was serving in the state legislature in 1860, the city had been authorized to dispose of six porciones the Visita General de la Villa de San Agustín de Laredo had given the village and Tómas Sanchez in 1767.[16] For three consecutive months, the land sale was advertised in the *San Antonio Herald, Austin Statesman*, and the *Brownsville Daily Ranchero and Republican*. At a highly anticipated auction in front of the mayor's office on June 1, 1874, Charles Callaghan outbid competitors for porciones one and two for $1,000 each, while Santos obtained Porcion three, sixteen miles above Laredo, for $500. A member of the city council, Peter Steffan, acquired Porcion four, also for $500.[17] A year later, Santos was able to purchase two sections of 640 acres each of railroad land on the headwaters of the Redamadero de los Tejones, thirty-two miles northwest of Laredo, for $300, or $4.26 per acre. In November 1869, he sold 160 acres in Encinal County, at what was called Charco de los Indios, ten miles southwest of old Fort Ewell, to Julian Quiroga for $100.[18] Several sections of land there had been granted to the Houston and Great Northern Railroad for building one mile of track in Houston County, north of Houston. Throughout the decade of the 1870s and into the 1880s, Santos also continued to buy and sell town lots. For example, four blocks on Flores Street was purchased from Lamar and Cristóbal Benavides while eight lots on Convent Street were sold to Daniel Milmo for 500 pesos. By 1880, Santos owned 16,796 acres, roughly 26 sections, of land in Webb County alone, and counting his town lots, he was in possession of sixty-five parcels of property. On the tax rolls, Santos listed 10,573 sheep, one hundred cattle worth $500, one thousand goats valued at $750, forty horses, and five hundred mules.[19]

In April 1879, a smallpox epidemic swept over Los Dos Laredos. The lethal disease was first contracted by soldiers at Fort McIntosh, who were promptly segregated according to medical protocol in a special ward at the post hospital. But in May a delirious soldier with a severe case of the disease managed to slip out of the hospital one night and wander aimlessly through the streets of the city until he was found near death early the next morning.[20] The smallpox rapidly spread to the poorer neighborhoods on the outskirts of the community, where many citizens lived in squalor and were particularly vulnerable. Death seemed to stalk the city, and quickly arranged funerals became routine. The dead were dressed in burial clothes and carried on biers to the new cemetery on the northeast side of the town, where gravediggers were hard at work in the sandy soil. Largely as a result of the smallpox, tensions between the towns and the fort grew a few weeks later when several soldiers were expelled from a "dance hall" near the post, and they began to riot. When the police arrived, a gun battle erupted.[21] Anxieties on both sides of the border were eased somewhat, however, when a friendly game of baseball was arranged between the Eighth US Cavalry, mostly men from California, and a team from Nuevo Laredo.[22]

But politics always seemed to dominate community life. After a four-day election in November 1872, Darío Gonzales, a former sergeant under Santos, was elected sheriff, while Cayetano de la Garza outpolled Jarvis for county surveyor, John Z. Leyendecker became county treasurer, and Santos's brother Eulalio was selected as inspector of hides and animals. In all, Democrats received more than double the votes of Samuel Jarvis's Republicans.[23] Several individuals, including Jarvis, Raymond Martin, and Hamilton Peterson, challenged the results of the election, asserting that Santos and his followers were guilty of numerous irregularities. "Santos Benavides, the Confederate robber, voted all his thieves and every other democratic thief, priest, and murderer," one angry nativist proclaimed.[24]

Besides complaining to state officials in Austin, the Republicans also challenged the results of the election in the local courts. Santos had brought as many as two hundred voters across the river from Nuevo Laredo, Jarvis and Martin alleged, to vote illegally in the election. Moreover, numerous voters were not listed in the registration books. Jarvis and Martin wanted Gov. Edmund J. Davis to declare the election null and void. But the highly eccentric Judge William H. Russell, who was known to be a partisan of Santos, ruled that aliens did not have to state their intentions of becoming US citizens when they voted, and he refused to invalidate the election.[25] Santos's resurgence in Laredo politics was well under way.

In 1873, despite the fact that in Webb County Governor Davis defeated the Democratic candidate, Richard Coke, by a vote of 512 to 91, his rout at the hands of the resurgent Democrats and "Southern Redeemers" statewide was decisive, and he lost by a vote of 85,549 to 42,663. As Santos watched from Laredo, the members of the state supreme court appointed by Davis declared the election unconstitutional, claiming that it had been held in one day instead of four, as specified by the constitution. But when President Ulysses S. Grant declined to intervene and an angry anti-Republican militia company took possession of the legislative chambers in the capital, Coke was triumphantly inaugurated as governor.[26] With no option other than armed resistance, Davis resigned four days later. Radical Republican rule in Texas was over. In Laredo, Samuel Jarvis was replaced as mayor and county judge. But the New Yorker had come to the border to stay, and he set out to build a competitive Republican Party in Webb, Encinal, and Zapata Counties.[27] Despite the bitterness of the election of 1873, as well as being on opposite sides during the war, Santos and Davis remained close friends, and the former governor continued to play an active role in the politics of the town.

By the time of the municipal election of December 8, 1873, Raymond Martin had given up on Jarvis and his Republicans and had formed a faction of the Democratic Party that challenged the Benavides Democrats for control of the town and county. The political atmosphere in Laredo became so charged that the city council discussed at length the "disturbances and affrays . . . owing to the feelings existing between the political parties of the city." As a result, Mayor Agustín Salinas was authorized to appoint "any number of extra police not to exceed fifty . . . to preserve the quiet and tranquility of the city."[28] In reality, the appointment of additional law enforcement officers was as much an attempt to trade employment for votes

Santos Benavides still had his chin whiskers when he sat for this pose in the late 1870s. *Jerry Thompson Collection.*

and intimidate opponents as it was a sincere effort to maintain law and order. On Election Day, with Refugio Benavides as candidate for mayor, the Benavides party swept to an easy victory by a vote of two to one.[29] In a hotly contested race for state representative, however, Santos was narrowly defeated by sixty-eight votes, despite the fact he was the clear favorite in Webb County.[30] He had been unable to campaign over a vast part of the district that encompassed twenty-two counties stretching all the way from El Paso in far West Texas to the Gulf of Mexico and north from the border to the Hill Country. His inability to communicate effectively in English did not help him either. Moreover, many Anglos, especially in counties north of Laredo, simply refused to vote for anyone named Benavides.

No sooner had Refugio taken office in January 1873 than Cristóbal was appointed city treasurer. A Benavides supporter became city marshal, while other supporters became clerks and policemen. In Laredo, the spoils system seemed to know no bounds. Furthermore, the new mayor was authorized to sue the previous mayor, Agustín Salinas, for two hundred dollars that Salinas "had paid out of the city funds for some purpose unknown to the present corporation."[31] Money was also missing from the office of the previous city treasurer.

As mayor, Refugio Benavides led the city council in passing ordinances to remove the sheep and goats that were known to roam freely in the town. Noisy and frequently violent fandangos, so common in South Texas and on the border, were first regulated and then prohibited outright. Other laws allowed for the arrest of vagrants and drunks. Anyone caught carrying a pistol or deadly weapon in the city limits would be fined from five to no more than ten dollars, and if unable to pay the fine, the miscreant was to be jailed with fifty cents' credit for each day of incarceration.[32] To the joy of many, Refugio built a new elementary school, Escuela Amarilla, in the northeast part of town. He also renewed efforts to complete the project Jarvis and military had begun of cleaning city lots and leveling streets. Perhaps more significant was a new city charter that redrew ward boundaries and established municipal elections in September rather than the traditional December.

With the approach of municipal elections in 1874, fifty policemen were hired to preserve the peace, and on Election Day, Refugio Benavides was easily reelected, as was the Benavides party's entire slate of candidates. In the general election in November, Eulalio was chosen as district clerk. Counting his antebellum service, Refugio was now serving his fourth term as mayor. The city council, "in consideration of his service as mayor," rewarded him with an entire block of city property on the eastern outskirts of the city, east of Zacate Creek, in what was being called the Heights.[33] The family was somewhat embarrassed, however, when the mayor's son, named Santos Benavides in honor of his well-known uncle, was arrested by US marshals and accused of buying stolen horses from Mexico.[34]

Opposition to the Benavides family and their political control of the city and county was again led by the indefatigable and avaricious Raymond Martin, who was gaining more and more political clout in Laredo. A peculiar-looking little man with a dark mustache, piercing brown eyes, and a receding hairline, Martin was a superb organizer, and he was able to attract a number of dedicated and determined men to his banner.[35] He had come to America with two older brothers, Paul and Joseph, living first in New Orleans, then moving on to Pensacola and San Antonio before finally settling on the border, where he established a mercantile business at Laredo in 1854. Sixteen years later, at the age of forty-two, he married seventeen-year-old Tirza García, daughter of the very prominent three-time mayor Bartolome García and his wife, Encarnación (Carmen) Benavides. Marrying into a well-to-do and extended family allowed him to make political alliances that were not possible when he was single, and within a decade of his arrival on the border, the French-born Martin had become the wealthiest man in Webb County, largely by turning consumer debts into land acquisitions. A pioneer sheep raiser and wool producer, he was also a leader in the South Texas livestock industry with 130,000 acres of grazing land in Webb and LaSalle Counties. At one time, Martin boasted of owning fifty thousand sheep and thousands of cattle. His political influence in Laredo grew steadily and was only rivaled by that of Santos Benavides.[36]

After consistently challenging the Benavides Democrats for control of the city and the county, Martin learned from his opponents, and he began providing plenty of alcohol to the hoards of ineligible voters he escorted to the polls.[37] In June 1870 he was arrested for selling liquor without a license, but the able José María Rodríguez obtained his release and had the charges dropped.[38] Drawing power and influence from his ranching and mercantile empire, Martin began to wage an all-out political war with Santos. By late 1875, Martin was able to field a full slate of candidates, including his father-in-law, Bartolo García, who ran against Refugio Benavides for mayor. In one of the closest elections in recent memory, Refugio was able to squeak out a narrow victory by a vote of 270 to 221. García challenged the results, alleging the Benavides brothers had escorted numerous illegal voters to the polls, but once again the district court was reluctant to act. Santos had an easier time in his race to become alderman from the Third Ward and received more than triple the votes of his opponent, Jesús Ramirez. Three of Martin's candidates were able to gain seats on the city council, however.[39]

The political tension between Santos Benavides and Raymond Martin was based, in part, on their no-holds-barred struggle for control of the lucrative ferry operating in the narrow waters between Laredo and Nuevo Laredo. Almost from the time Laredo was founded in 1755, a small ferry regularly had carried passengers and goods back and forth across the river. Pulled by several laborers, the ferry was little more than a flatboat attached to a cable that stretched across the river and was firmly anchored on both banks. Residents of Laredo and Nuevo Laredo had free passage, but strangers were charged a small sum, and revenues from the ferry were used to help build a church. After the Treaty of Guadalupe Hidalgo, the city council began to lease the ferry, usually on an annual basis, but sometimes for as long as five years, and whoever controlled the ferry franchise profited considerably. Paying $2,900 per annum, Cristóbal Benavides leased the ferry in 1874 and 1875, and the following year, Samuel M. Jarvis obtained the lease.[40] Problems developed when Martin and his business partners, Christopher

M. MacDonell and Edward F. Hall, two of the most powerful men on the middle border, began operating a ferry in competition with the city. Hall was the president of the company while Martin acted as secretary, although much of the brains and impetus behind the new enterprise came from MacDonell, the primary stockholder.

With an international bridge only a distant dream, the city of Laredo filed suit against Martin and the Laredo Ferry Company. Only the city, it was argued, had the authority to operate a ferry. In particular, the city wanted to revoke deeds on the north bank of the river along Water Street, from which Martin, MacDonell, and Hall operated the ferry. (Ironically, the ten lots had been inadvertently sold by Refugio Benavides when he was mayor.) Martin and his accomplices were also using several skiffs and smaller boats to rapidly transport passengers and merchandise across the river. Able to cut rates, since they paid none of their revenues to the city, the Laredo Ferry Company was slowly putting the city-operated ferry out of business. In fact, Agustín Salinas and Cayetano de la Garza, who leased the ferry in January 1877, asked the city council to nullify their contract.[41]

Santos was able to push a resolution through the city council that reaffirmed the city's ownership of the land on Water Street. In fact, all the land within two hundred yards of the river was considered city property. At the same meeting the city surveyor was directed to draft a map reflecting the council's new decree.[42] The city council also asked the district court to annul the deed signed by Refugio Benavides in 1875. Santos was authorized to inform Martin, Hall, and MacDonell that they were operating their ferry on city property and would have to cease operations. When Martin adamantly refused, Santos persuaded the council to retain the skillful Edmund J. Davis, a Benavides ally of long standing. Santos even agreed to spend thirty dollars of his own money to bring Davis down from the capital. Davis was given a lucrative retainer of five hundred dollars and one-third of the annual rent of the ferry for five years.[43] The former governor hurried south from Austin and promptly sued Martin and his partners.

In the case of *City of Laredo v. Raymond Martin et al.*, Santos was one of the first witnesses deposed by Davis. Fifty-four years old at the time, Santos recalled how he had ridden the ferry hundreds of times since he was a child. Relatives had told him that the ferry dated back to the time when Tomás Sánchez was alcalde. He was selected *procurador* (attorney) in 1843, when Mexico held the town, and one of his duties was to oversee the ferry's operations. Revenues were used to build a church, repair the streets, and pay policemen. By tradition, Santos said, the town had always been the exclusive owner of the ferry. Along with Michael Lidwell, he himself was given a two-year contract at five hundred dollars a year in 1859.[44] Partly because of the presence of soldiers at Fort McIntosh, the contract proved to be quite profitable. But when the fort was abandoned and the soldiers marched off to the western frontier, the economy of the town collapsed, and Santos and Lidwell began losing money. They had no alternative but to ask the city council to be relieved of the contract or have the amount of the lease reduced.[45]

Refugio testified to the same facts. The former mayor said he had "never knowingly or intentionally sold any land on the water's edge" and that under no circumstances would he sell land that "interfered with the ferry on the river." Refugio went on to say that he could not read or speak English, that when signing documents he always trusted his integrity to the city secretary. Under cross-examination, however, he admitted having sold the land along Water Street to MacDonell and Martin, just as he had signed deeds that granted both Santos and Cristóbal land along the waterfront.[46]

Cristóbal testified that he had obtained the ferry lease in 1874 for two years for $1,900 but that in 1876 Cayetano de la Garza and Agustín Salinas outbid him by $10. The year after Refugio had given the ferry company the land along the river, MacDonell presented a petition to the city council to confirm the deed. Although all four city councilmen were Martin partisans and voted to affirm the deed, Mayor Atanacio Vidaurri vetoed it. Edward Hall, the legal brains behind the new ferry company, had tried to intimidate the mayor during a verbal confrontation. "If you don't sign that document, I'll make you," Hall shouted.[47]

After five years of legal sparring, which included the district court ruling in favor of Martin and the Laredo Ferry Company, the case eventually reached the Supreme Court of Texas, which ruled in favor of the city. In February 1880 Martin and his partners were "perpetually enjoined from keeping and maintaining a ferry across the Rio Grande River [*sic*] opposite the city of Laredo."[48] The court had discovered that the original deed had been altered when someone inserted the figure "10" between the words "as" and "lots." The city of Laredo, the court went on to rule, had "maintained a ferry across the Rio Grande for a time beyond the memory of living men." Moreover, Refugio Benavides had had no authority to sell the land along the riverfront. Due to his "ignorance of the language," he had been overcome by those "more cunning and designing." Besides the fact that Refugio was not literate in English and did not know what he was signing, the $50 that was paid for the lots was "grossly inadequate" for land that was worth at least $50,000.[49] Santos and the city of Laredo had won a historic legal victory, but the lengthy and costly litigation only deepened the political wounds in the community and further polarized the competing parties.

In March 1875 Santos headed north to Austin by stage to testify before a joint committee of the Texas legislature on "frontier troubles." Also testifying was John S. Ford.[50] There is no evidence that the two men met or spoke. The *New York Times* reported that Santos, who testified with the help of an interpreter, was a "bulwark against disorder on the border." The *Galveston News* editorialized that he was a "highly respectable Mexican citizen of Texas." For his part, Santos said he thought a number of outlaws who lived on the south bank of the river could be extradited to Texas for punishment. A "crisis is close at hand," he warned. The 382-mile border from the mouth of the river to the canyonlands beyond Eagle Pass was virtually indefensible. Below Laredo, cattle rustlers and outlaws, primarily Cortinistas, crossed the border at will, and above Laredo, Lipan Apache and Kickapoo raids were deadly. The *New York Times*, echoing what was being said in Austin, claimed that stealing and raiding in Texas had "become a curse to the land."[51]

The sister cities of Laredo and Nuevo Laredo came to the attention of both nations in April 1876, when the revolution in Mexico spilled across the border. Needing money to feed and pay his troops, Col. Pablo Quintana, commander of the small federal army in Nuevo Laredo, decided to levy forced loans, *préstamos forzosos*, of $2,000 on ten of the largest merchants in Nuevo Laredo, five of them Americans. "Money is needed to support the military and if by 3 o'clock this afternoon you should fail to send to this office the sum of $2,000 . . . severe military measures will be taken, and double the amount will be taken by force," Colonel Quintana's subordinate, Capt. Anastacio Gonzales, brusquely told two of the defiant merchants.[52] When most of the entrepreneurs failed to respond, Quintana ordered them to give up the keys to their businesses, and when they again refused, he arrested and imprisoned several of the merchants.

James Haynes, US commercial agent in Nuevo Laredo and the son of John L. Haynes, not only wrote the State Department to complain of Quintana's forced loans but crossed the river to present the case of the perplexed merchants to Maj. Henry Merriam, who was in command of two companies of the Twenty-fourth US Infantry at Fort McIntosh.[53] Merriam crossed to Nuevo Laredo to confront Colonel Quintana. Allegedly, Quintana said he would not be responsible if several of the stores were broken into and robbed. "Some high words ensued," one correspondent reported, and Merriam bluntly told Quintana that it was his responsibility to protect American citizens at "all hazards." "You might do as you damned please," Quintana responded.[54]

As the crisis heightened, Merriam returned to Fort McIntosh, ordered his men to take up positions along the riverbank, and, in an obvious attempt to intimidate Quintana, trained two artillery pieces on Nuevo Laredo. Shortly thereafter, Mexican soldiers opened fire on men guarding the ferry, which was anchored on the north bank. As the guards fled to the safety of the town, Merriam had two shells lobbed into downtown Nuevo Laredo. "Great excitement prevails" in Laredo, a "curious city on American soil," a correspondent for the *New York Times* wrote.[55] In one version of the confrontation, the major met his Mexican counterpart on a rowboat in the middle of the Rio Grande, at which time Colonel Quintana demanded to know why Nuevo Laredo was being bombarded by the US Army. One of the reasons, Merriam asserted, was that bullets were flying across the river into Laredo. "If you must fight a battle over there," the major said, "you must contrive to do it as they fight on the stage—sideways. It won't do to shoot into the audience."[56]

Sensing that the federal defenders of Nuevo Laredo were preoccupied by the American troops on the north bank of the river, supporters of Gen. Porfirio Díaz, who had been lurking on the outskirts of the city for weeks, launched an all-out attack during the early morning hours of April 10, 1876. For two hours the defenders put up a ferocious fight, while most of the American businessmen fled across the river to the safety of Laredo. In Nuevo Laredo, the fighting raged from doorway to doorway and rooftop to rooftop. Hearing gunfire from across the river, Laredoans by the hundreds climbed to their rooftops to watch the battle for control of their sister city. Two soldiers could be seen dead in the streets, and several others who were seriously wounded were dragged off. But when bullets slammed into buildings in Laredo, the curious citizens ran for cover. Some thought the bullets had been fired deliberately into Laredo by the defenders of Nuevo Laredo out of "spite and vexation."[57]

With the defenders of Nuevo Laredo on the verge of defeat, soldiers fled across the river. One man drowned while attempting the swim. Fourteen of Colonel Quintana's men were disarmed by soldiers from Fort McIntosh. A newspaper correspondent found it ironic that the soldiers "gladly found refuge in the territory upon which they were lately firing."[58] Quintana and a handful of his men were seen in flight down the Mexican bank of the river.

Although Lerdo de Tejada's administration turned out to be one of the better ones in Mexican history, prominent politicians and even the press assailed him mercilessly. When he announced that he would seek reelection in 1876, José de la Cruz Porfirio Díaz Mori rose against him, calling for no reelection of the president and the governors, and saying Lerdo de Tejada had squandered public funds and violated the sovereignty of the states and municipalities. On the border, Santos joined with Mariano Escobedo, whom Santos had known and liked since before the Civil War, to obtain arms and raise a counterrevolutionary army in support of Lerdo de Tejada and against Díaz. Soldiers from a number of the states flocked to Díaz, and with Manuel González by his side, he and the insurgents defeated the Lerdistas at Tecoac in the state of Tlaxcala, and Lerdo fled into exile. On November 21, 1876, Díaz and his army occupied Mexico City, and for the next three decades, he directly or indirectly controlled the country. At the time, Santos was very much opposed to Díaz. Yet in time he came to admire Díaz and see him as a good friend.

On the Texas-Mexico border, Escobedo vowed to overthrow Porfirio Díaz. If the Mexican consul in San Antonio can be believed, in early 1876 Escobedo went to New York, where he received a considerable amount of cash and arranged through the export house of Frederick Probst and Company for a thousand rifles to be shipped to the Texas border. By April 1876, with Mexican agents closely following him, Escobedo arrived at New Orleans before going on to Galveston by steamer and finally to San Antonio. All the time, Escobedo was sending letters to individuals in Veracruz, Matamoros, and San Luis Potosí, attempting to foment revolution.

Escobedo planned to arm small bands of men who would cross the Rio Grande into Mexico and launch a guerrilla war against Díaz. Joined by other revolutionaries, Escobedo hoped to force the surrender of the federal garrison at Piedras Negras and then seize Nuevo Laredo.[59] When Escobedo arrived in Laredo, he met with Santos before setting up his headquarters at Rancho de Buenavista, on the river below the city. Shortly thereafter, the Mexican consul in San Antonio received a letter from a Díaz agent in

Born in Galeana, Nuevo León, Mariano Escobedo was promoted to colonel for his bravery at Puebla on Cinco de Mayo, 1862. Escobedo fought against the French invaders and was victorious at the Battle of Santa Gertrudis near Camargo in June 1866, when he overran Mexican and Austrian forces in what proved to be the Waterloo of the Imperialists in northern Mexico. He helped to capture Maximilian at Querétero in 1867, and under Benito Juárez commanded the Mexican army in northern Mexico and served as governor of several states. With the ascendancy of Gen. Porfirio Díaz, Escobedo was exiled to the United States, where Benavides helped him acquire arms and recruit men in an abortive uprising against Díaz. Escobedo was captured and then imprisoned in Mexico City. He died in the city in May 1902. *Courtesy Lawrence T. Jones III Collection, DeGolyer Library, SMU.*

Laredo saying everything was quiet and that spies were "keeping an eye" on Santos. "One can be pre-advised of any movement in the near future of the outside (Lerdist) party [simply by watching Santos]," the Díaz agents concluded.

In Laredo, Lázaro Garza Ayala, Santos's son-in-law, was to help amass weapons while Santos acted as a "revolutionary agent," using his business as a front to supply the rebels with arms. Aided by Cristóbal and Eulalio, Santos was "willing to advance money, arms, and horses to able-bodied men" who would "join the ranks of the Lerdaists." He was said to have been paid $5,000 by Escobedo. Forty men from Laredo, young and old, whom Mexican authorities in Nuevo Laredo claimed were "vagabonds of that neighborhood" and "criminals . . . unable to live in Mexico," were recruited and equipped by Santos. With his assistance, the rebels in Laredo were organizing in full view of the Americans accross the river. Authorities in Nuevo Laredo demanded the insurgents be arrested, pointing out that they were clearly in violation of American neutrality laws, but Webb County and federal officials turned their backs and in one instance flatly refused. On the day before the revolutionaries crossed the Rio Grande, "Don Santos," as Díaz's supporters called him, energetically addressed the men, saying they could keep the rifles they had been given, as well as any horses they could steal in Mexico. Moreover, once Nuevo Laredo had been taken, they would be allowed to plunder the city for two hours.[60] Ironically, Santos was plotting with Escobedo to overthrow General Díaz at the same time the general was in Brownsville meeting with Anglos to ask for their support in maintaining power and bringing peace to Mexico and the border.

Escobedo's men quietly crossed the river on the night of May 25 and posted themselves on the roads leading from Nuevo Laredo to Guerrero, Piedras Negras, and Monterrey. Travelers were robbed and kidnapped. Escobedo's revolutionaries even occupied a portion of Nuevo Laredo, but after twelve days of fighting they drew off, unable to take the town. In the end, Escobedo's revolution on the border collapsed, and many of the rebels were forced back across the river, where they again sought refuge with Santos and

An 1877 illustration in *Frank Leslie's Illustrated Newspaper* showing the fledgling town of Laredo on the north bank of the river and the ferry that connected Laredo and Nuevo Laredo. *Frank Leslie's Illustrated Newspaper*, May 12, 1877.

his brothers. Escobedo was apprehended in the desert at Cuatro Cienegas in Coahuila, and in September 1878 he was imprisoned at Santiago Tlatelolco in Mexico City.

Santos was a cousin of Manuel González, who was minister of war and of the navy under Díaz and who would be elected president of Mexico in 1880. During and after his presidency, González corresponded and exchanged gifts with Santos, and through González, Santos reached out to Díaz, after the US government had formally recognized the Díaz regime. In the years that followed, Santos's relationship with Díaz came to resemble what Santos had once had with Santiago Vidaurri, twenty years earlier.

As a guerrilla fighter against the French, Díaz had gained a reputation for personal integrity. During his first term, which lasted until 1880, he coaxed a degree of order out of the chaos that was Mexico by establishing the Rurales and waging a war on brigandage that Santos applauded. President Rutherford B. Hayes, convinced that the new president of Mexico meant to establish order and meet foreign obligations, extended diplomatic recognition to Díaz. To help promote diplomatic ties, Díaz opened Mexican consulates at Laredo, Rio Grande City, and Eagle Pass.[61]

In late November 1881, as Díaz stepped down, Santos made his way south to Mexico City, where he was able to meet with his cousin, the recently elected president, Manuel del Refugio González Flores. In Mexico City, Santos was also able to meet personally with General Díaz, the real power in Mexico. The *Two Republics* of Mexico City described Santos's visit to the capital by pointing out he was a "native of Texas" but of "Mexican origin." Moreover, he was one of the "most prominent men of this class of population in the state" and of "great wealth . . . great influence," a true "son of the South."[62] In late August 1882, Santos again returned to the Mexican capital for a six-week vacation and to visit old friends and prominent political figures there.[63]

If Díaz realized the extent of Santos's involvement in Escobedo's failed attempt to overthrow him, it is not evident in their correspondence or the historical record. How much Santos knew of Díaz's use of coercion, intimidation, repression, and even political assassination is equally unclear. In the end, the friendship proved mutually beneficial for both Santos and Díaz and served to greatly ease tensions along the border.

After his election in 1877, Díaz struggled to "fit the round peg of constitutional liberalism into the square hole of personalist traditions and practice."[64] As an authoritarian figure who presented a facade of liberal democracy, Díaz was famous for his suppression of civil society and public revolts, and Mexicans faced the choice during his reign between *pan o palo*, bread or a beating, benevolence or repression. And although the Porfiriato was marked by significant internal stability, the fight for profits kept the Mexican people in a constant state of uncertainty as thousands of the rural poor were dispossessed of their land in the midst of what seemed to be one of the golden ages of Mexican economics. The anger of the rural masses finally

Santos Benavides had a close and long-lasting friendship with Manuel González Flores, who was a Mexican general and liberal politician and the 36th president of Mexico from 1880–1884. González was also governor of Michoacán and Guanajuato and served as Secretary of War and Navy from 1878 to 1879. He fought with Gen. Porfirio Díaz at Puebla in 1862 and was wounded and taken prisoner by the French. Able to escape, he was taken prisoner a second time, but paroled. In continued fighting, he lost his right arm in an attack on Puebla. Born at El Moquete near Matamoros, he was the first president of Mexico from the state of Tamaulipas elected through popular vote. González died at the age of fifty-nine in 1893. *Courtesy Library of Congress.*

exploded in the Mexican Revolution of 1910, but by that time Santos had been dead for nineteen years.[65]

Santos and Díaz had much in common. Both were strong proponents of economic development and believed Mexico could only prosper with an infusion of foreign capital. Both agreed that international trade and cross-border business connections should be a priority. And both saw the coming of the railroads as a means of economic liberation that would not only transform Mexico and the American Southwest but unite the two republics.

Santos worked hard to promote friendly relations between the two countries. He frequently wrote brief and overblown biographical sketches of prominent Mexicans that were published in Texas newspapers such as the *Galveston News*. One sketch was of his cousin Manuel González shortly after he became president. Writing from Laredo on July 4, 1881, Santos wanted to help cement the "fraternal bonds which unite and should more closely bind" citizens of the United States to their "sister republic" with which they had and should have "much in common."[66] Santos assured anyone in Texas who was willing to listen that he knew, from personal and private correspondence plus personal interviews with González and members of his cabinet, as well as with several border governors and generals, of a "most happy disposition on the part of Mexico toward Texas and the United States." González, Santos argued, was a "progressive man" who had worked his way from poverty on the Rio Grande to become the "right man in the right place."[67]

During the time that González was president of Mexico and Santos was serving in the state legislature, the two frequently corresponded. In January 1881, for example, Santos wrote from Austin asking that twenty-five American railroad engineers and surveyors be granted permission to "explore the countryside from Laredo to Mexico City" to prepare for the linking of the railroad with the capital.[68] The party was willing to pay whatever was necessary to the officials at the border. Only days later, González telegraphed with permission for the men to enter Mexico. Santos responded with gratitude and told the president that he was working without "rest in favor of peace and exaltation of Mexico and the good relations between both republics." Only days earlier, Samuel Bell Maxey, who was a personal friend of Santos, had been selected as the US senator from Texas, and Santos assured González that the West Point graduate and former Confederate was also interested in building railroads that would connect the two republics, improve relations with Mexico, and help protect the settlers on the frontier.[69] After the legislature adjourned in early April, Santos was back on the border by April 12, and he promised to visit González in Mexico City as soon as he could take care of some personal business in Laredo.[70]

Santos assured the residents of Texas that under González, "peace reigned throughout Mexico."[71] As president, González undertook a program of economic reform and material progress. At the same time, he attempted to reform and modernize the armed forces and stimulate foreign investment, especially in the railroads and mining industry. Santos not only liked González personally, he identified with his government and his policies. Foreign capital investment was certain to be good for the border. Although considered a puppet of Díaz, González was able to make notable progress in the negotiation of treaties with the United States, and he tried earnestly to control the problems of smuggling, banditry, and border raids, all of which Santos thought would help stabilize the border and stimulate the frontier economy.[72]

Well into 1882, Santos continued his efforts to promote various Mexican political figures. In January he wrote a letter to the *Galveston News* praising the Mexican minister of war, Gen. Francisco Naranjo, and his friend Gen. Geronimo Treviño, who had been placed in command of the military in Tamaulipas, Nuevo León, Coahuila, and Chihuahua.[73] They had stood shoulder to shoulder in the struggle against the French, and they were strong supporters of President Díaz. Santos recalled how General Treviño had maintained his goodwill toward the United States, even when the two nations were on the verge of war due to the "invasion of Mexican soil in unwarrantable pursuit of Indians by military order." A "new era in the history of Mexico has begun," Santos assured Texans.[74]

Santos Benavides was a good friend of Gen. Geronimo Treviño, who served as governor of Nuevo León on three separate occasions. Born in Nuevo Laredo in 1836, Treviño fled across the border during the Mexican Revolution in 1913 and died in Laredo one year later. A town in Nuevo León honors his name today. *Courtesy Library of Congress.*

But it was always the politics of the border that dominated Santos's thoughts and actions and shaped his future. After losing the lengthy and costly contest to control the river ferry, Raymond Martin had become even more determined to gain control of the community and the county, and when Refugio Benavides chose not to seek reelection in 1876, the Martin Democrats swept into power. Some of the Benavides Democrats sensed a changing of the tide, and they joined Martin. The spoils system came full circle as Martin's men were appointed to key positions in the city government. In the county elections, Martin was also victorious, and a number of Benavides loyalists were forced out of office. In the systemic shift of power and influence, two of Martin's colleagues, Agustín Salinas and A. L. McLane, were elected to the House of Representatives from the newly created Seventy-Sixth District. So dominant was Martin that even José María

Rodríguez deserted the Benavides family and was rewarded by Martin with the office of county judge, a position he would hold for the next thirty-four years.[75] Many of Santos's closest friends, relatives, and long-time allies, some of them Civil War veterans, joined the Martin Democrats.

Yet Santos and his followers never gave up, and the community remained deeply divided between the Benavides Democrats and the Martin Democrats, each party refusing to have anything to do with the other. Samuel Jarvis and his small number of Republicans, many of them African American, remained on the political periphery.

If Santos was ever going to be elected state representative, it was obvious he would need support from outside Webb County. Santos first allowed himself to be nominated in the December 2, 1873, election.[76] At the time, the Thirtieth District stretched along the border all the way from the mouth of the Rio Grande to El Paso County in far west Texas, north to Nueces County, and east to Corpus Christi. In the six-man contest for three seats in the legislature, Santos did well, but not well enough, and he finished fourth. He ran poorly in El Paso, the lower valley, and Corpus Christi—the home turf of the other candidates—but, as expected, he did better in Webb County and rural Encinal County, although he was still outpolled in Laredo by Louis Cardis and Patrick Frances "Pat" Murphy, who had the support of the Martin Democrats.

But in defeat, Santos learned a number of useful lessons. Alliances with political bosses in other parts of South Texas were critical to any future political aspirations. This was particularly true of the young and energetic Brownsville attorney James Babbage Wells Jr. and his law partner, Stephen Powers. Powers had fought in Mexico with Gen. Zachary Taylor and had gone on to become collector of customs at Brazos Santiago, county judge of Cameron County, mayor of Brownsville, district judge during the Civil War, and, in 1872, state representative. Together, Wells and Powers created a coalition of influential ranchers, powerful businessmen, and hundreds of impoverished Tejano laborers to form the most powerful political machine in South Texas. Wells's skills as an accomplished linguist and his skill at unraveling difficult and often contentious land grant claims between the Rio Grande and the Nueces River only added to his clout in Cameron, Hidalgo, and Starr counties.[77] As an emerging political boss in Cameron County, especially after Powers's death in 1882, Wells quickly became a conservative spokesman for the Democratic Party in Texas.

Although Santos sought and ultimately gained the friendship of Powers and Wells and the blessings of their political machine, he remained obsessed with bringing down the Martin Democrats. In August of 1875 he allowed his name to be placed on the ballot as a delegate to a state constitutional convention. In the final tally, although Webb County had voted against even having a convention, Santos had received more votes in Laredo than both Cardis and Murphy, but finished behind the popular John S. Ford.[78] The well-liked Ford even outpolled Santos in Webb County, 169–162, and it was Santos's former commander who rode off to Austin.

First meeting in the capital on September 6, 1875, Ford and the other legislators adopted a new constitution that sought to reverse the perceived Republican excesses of Reconstruction. Restrictions were placed on salaries, expenditures, taxes, and the state debt. The new constitution also slashed the power of public officials and their terms of office. State banks were abolished, and the influence of railroads and other corporations was limited.[79] The constitution was submitted to voters the following year and was overwhelmingly approved, including in Webb County, where citizens approved of the new document by a vote of 611 to 12. In the decades that followed, the constitution was amended hundreds of times and is now considered one of the most disjointed and confusing of all such documents.[80]

When Agustín Salinas defeated José María Rodríguez in the race for state representative in 1876 and then promptly resigned, Santos contemplated competing in a special election that was scheduled for May. Realizing he faced an uphill battle, he declined at the last minute, and Albert L. McLane, a Martin Democrat, was selected instead. Yet Santos always kept out feelers, testing the political winds.[81] Because Laredo remained so deeply divided, he realized he would be unable to obtain a large enough majority in Webb County to overcome deficits elsewhere. Moreover, Martin continued to gain momentum until he even controlled a large chunk of the vote in Zapata County, especially in San Ignacio, which was controlled by Blas María Uribe.

In 1878 Noah Cox, a political boss from Starr County who was hoping to become district judge, rode upriver seeking votes. Cox badly wanted the support of the Martin Democrats, knowing that if he obtained Martin's endorsement, all his followers would fall in line. While in Laredo, Cox also sought Santos's endorsement. They had been friends since before the war and both realized the incumbent, Judge William H. Russell, had a serious problem with alcohol. But Russell was a friend, Santos said, who frequently visited him and stayed at his home in Laredo. If Russell decided not to run for reelection and Martin decided to support John S. Ford, Santos would most certainly throw his weight behind Cox.[82] Cox strategized that if Martin held back his endorsement, he would have no alternative but to "cling only to D[on] Santos." Cox had no doubt that Santos would work hard on his behalf, but he seemed reluctant to put himself in Santos's hands. Realizing the influence Governor Edmund J. Davis had with Santos, Cox asked the governor to persuade Santos to endorse Cox's candidacy.[83] Although reputed to be a drunkard, Judge Russell nevertheless was easily reelected. He went on such a prolonged binge in Rio Grande City the year after his reelection, however, that some talked of petitioning to have him removed. Stephen Powers, one of Russell's primary supporters, wrote Santos asking for his support in discouraging any such petition.[84]

In the same election in which Judge Russell was returned to office, Santos campaigned hard for the office of state representative in the new Seventy-Sixth District, from which two representatives were to be selected. The district no longer included the Trans-Pecos but Webb and Zapata Counties and the lower Rio Grande counties of Starr, Hidalgo, and Cameron, where Wells and Powers exerted considerable influence and where Santos felt at home. All were predominantly Spanish-speaking counties where he could easily campaign and renew old political ties from before the war. Although

Santos lost to Albert McLane and the Martin machine in Webb County by a vote of 807 to 478, he did well in Zapata County and in the lower valley, and he won a seat in the legislature.[85] His alliance with Powers and Wells and their machine was crucial to his political success. Santos would serve three consecutive terms in the legislature, an accomplishment unequaled by any other Tejano in the nineteenth century.

Santos took particular pride in being able to follow in the footsteps of Basilio Benavides. His uncle was one of only two Tejanos in the legislature before the war, and now Santos was the only Tejano in the Sixteenth Legislature.[86] During the cold January of 1879, Santos caught the stage north past Cotulla for San Antonio, then on to New Braunfels, San Marcos, and finally Austin, where he took his oath at the opening of the legislature on January 14. The long-bearded John Hughes Cochran, a former Texas Ranger and veteran of the Sixth Texas Cavalry and resident of Dallas, was selected as speaker. Santos was assigned to the Agriculture and Stock Raising Committee and the Public Health and Vital Statistics Committee, and History of Texas.[87]

Santos first caught the attention of the House of Representatives when he stood to request an official interpreter, much as Basilio had done twenty years earlier. H. B. Anderson was recommended for the position, but not before a contentious and long-winded debate ensued. Harriel G. "Hal" Geiger, a former slave from South Carolina and now a Republican turned Greenbacker from Robertson County, defiantly announced that he was "ashamed of such a resolution."[88] The debate became so personal and demeaning that the speaker demanded Geiger retract his disparaging statements. Several members of the House of Representatives complained of the cost, and the raucous debate, some of it racially rooted, continued. One member of the legislature mockingly requested for himself a translator with knowledge of Bohemian. When the motion failed by a vote of 33 to 57, a substitute motion was presented that would allow for an interpreter but no compensation. This motion also failed.

The *San Antonio Express* came to Santos's defense, arguing in an editorial that translators in the legislature had long been a tradition and a courtesy in a bilingual Texas, dating back to the days of the republic. The legislature's refusal to provide Santos with an interpreter would effectively disenfranchise twenty thousand citizens. Moreover, it would be an "exhibition of discourtesy to a very honorable gentleman who is thoroughly American in identity, who has long proved a power for good along the Rio Grande."[89] The newspaper pointed out that the vast majority of the population of South Texas was of Mexican descent and that Spanish was the universal language. To deny Santos an interpreter was to say to these citizens that their voices would not be heard. Finally, on January 20, 1879, a bill passed that allowed for a translator to be seated with Santos on the floor of the House of Representatives and paid $3.50 a day.

Santos was able to introduce and pass bills to adjust the boundaries of Webb, Dimmit, and Zavala Counties and to attach thinly populated Encinal County, established in 1856 but never organized, to Webb County for administrative purposes. Another of his acts called for issuing land patents to settlers south and west of the Nueces River.[90] Perhaps with the politics of Laredo and the border in mind, he also authored a bill that would "inquire what measures are necessary to prevent interference in elections in the counties bordering on the Rio Grande, on the part of persons residing in Mexico, and to prevent fraudulent voting in said counties by such persons."[91] The practice of bringing individuals from south of the border to vote in Texas had long been a tradition on the Rio Grande, especially in Laredo, and Santos was determined to stop it.[92] Mexicans voting illegally in Texas should be punished, he went on to say. But in Austin, few understood the problems of the border, and his bill gained little traction. Ironically, his political opponents back in Laredo had accused him on more than one occasion of the practice he now sought to prohibit.

Toward the end of the session, Santos also offered a bill designed to "prevent the importation of contagious diseases across the Rio Grande," though he did not specify how he hoped to enforce such a law. Santos was equally determined to somehow alleviate the wide-scale problem of cattle rustling and the practice of killing cattle and skinning the animals for their hides. With South Texas, as well as other areas, in mind, Santos passed a bill to "punish the unlawful taking, branding or killing of certain unbranded animals."[93] On March 14, it was announced, much to his displeasure, that the state treasury was dry and that his interpreter would no longer be paid. In response, George Preston Finlay, a former Confederate who had spent time on the Rio Grande frontier during the Mexican War and who was fluent in Spanish, agreed to interpret on his behalf.[94]

Although fiercely independent, Santos voted consistently with the Democrats, many of whom were former Confederates and who now dominated both branches of the legislature. In addition to the two committees he was initially appointed to, he was also placed on the Federal Relations Committee, the Committee on Indian Affairs, and a special committee on congressional districts. When José María Duran, Aniceto Gonzales, Bernardo Olguin, and Juan Severiano González, all leaders from Ysleta del Sur Pueblo near El Paso in far west Texas, visited the capital, Santos rose to ask that they be seated on the floor of the House. It was a way, Santos thought, of honoring the visitors and their unquestioned loyalty to Texas and their country. Ridiculing the motion, Joseph Chappell Hutcheson of Harris County, a former Confederate from Virginia who had ridden with Gen. Stonewall Jackson during the war, put forth an amendment recommending the visitors from Ysleta "as suitable parties for railroad commissioners." The amendment was quickly ruled out of order and the resolution passed.[95]

In March 1879, Santos was instrumental in pushing through a bill separating Zavala County from Maverick County.[96] Named after Lorenzo de Zavala, signer of the Texas Declaration of Independence and the first vice president of the Republic of Texas, Zavala County had been created before the Civil War, but like Encinal County it had never been formally organized. One day later, on March 13, Santos was excused because of illness; on April 1, still ill, he was granted an indefinite leave, and he returned to the border. In his absence, Otis Johnson of Leon County, acting on Santos's behalf, introduced a Senate bill that would set meeting times for the district courts in the Twenty-Fifth Judicial District. Several legislators objected, since Santos was not present, and the point of order was sustained.

The Sixteenth Legislature remained in session until April 24, when it adjourned *sine die*. By that time, Santos had been back in Laredo for three weeks. Six weeks later, in early June 1879, he hurried north by stage to Austin to attend a special session that convened on June 10, and he remained until the middle of July, when in the terrible heat of summer he returned to Laredo.[97]

In the November 1880 general election, the Martin Democrats threw their support behind Dr. Thomas W. Kennedy, a Pennsylvania-born physician from Rio Grande City. By campaigning hard and flooding the lower valley with circulars in Spanish, however, Santos was able to prevail, and he proudly returned to Austin in January 1881.[98] Again, Santos was beaten badly in Webb County by a vote of 925 to 508.[99] His rejection in his home county was embarrassing, and it only added to his disdain for the Martin political machine. By the time he took his oath in the Seventeenth Legislature, Santos had a much better understanding of Austin politics, and he played a more active role, even offering technical corrections to commerce and other important bills. It had taken time, but he had clearly mastered the legislative process.

Santos helped pass a bill to give veterans of the Texas Revolution 1,280 acres of state land, and in a night session, he introduced a bill that for unknown reasons exempted citizens of Cameron County from state taxes for 1881. In a funding bill for the Texas Rangers, he pushed through an amendment setting the appropriation at $75,000. His bill to fund the state "Lunatic Asylum" on north Guadalupe Street in Austin also passed. At the same time, Santos introduced an amendment reducing the school fund by one-fourth, but the amendment was promptly voted down.[100]

Perhaps the most dramatic vote in the Seventeenth Legislature followed the contentious debate over the prohibition of alcohol. Santos had always held strong opinions on the subject, and he took great pride in voting "nay"

This image of Benavides was taken by H. B. Hillyer at his gallery in Austin during the time Santos was serving in the Texas House of Representatives. *Jerry Thompson Collection.*

to any prohibition measure. He found himself in the minority, however, as the House voted 50–40 in favor of the bill, although the proposition lacked the two-thirds majority necessary for approval.[101] Contemplating the end of his political career in Austin, Santos rose on the afternoon of April 1, 1881, the sixty-seventh day of the legislature, for what amounted to an emotional good-bye. He made an "earnest expression of gratitude, respect and thanks" to his colleagues for their "uniform courtesy and consideration." "I bid you farewell, my fellow members, and as an old Texan who shall always be by your side until death do us part, in everything that relates to the interest of the state of my birth."[102] As it turned out, his speech would be premature.

For over a decade, much of Santos's attention had been devoted to the possibility of a railroad reaching Laredo from either San Antonio or Corpus Christi. While Samuel Jarvis was mayor in 1872, the Rockport, Fulton, Laredo, and Mexican Pacific Railroad had promised to build into the city within seven years and wanted land for a railyard. Jarvis and the city council, including the always astute José María Rodríguez, agreed to give the railroad as many as one hundred lots.[103]

Any railroad to the border required the assistance of US senator Richard Coke from Waco, whom Santos had come to know after Coke and the Democrats came to power in the contested election of 1873. As governor, Coke vetoed a subsidy to the International and Great Northern, which had planned to build to the border from San Antonio. As a US senator, Coke reversed course, however, and pushed hard for the building of a railroad to Laredo. Coke also lobbied for government assistance to the Galveston and Camargo Railroad, which hoped to build from Galveston and Houston along the coast to Rio Grande City. The construction of railroads to the border would greatly aid the US military on the Rio Grande, Coke argued. Commerce would flow and a lasting peace with Mexico would result.[104]

Exciting news finally came with the arrival of a survey crew of the Corpus Christi, San Diego, and Rio Grande Narrow Gauge Railroad Company, who were laying out a route from Corpus Christi to Laredo. After years of planning, the railroad had been chartered in March 1875, and work commenced west of Corpus Christi in the direction of Banquete. Caught up in the excitement of the time and hoping to reap the economic benefits, Santos invested heavily in the company and was listed as one of the original directors along with Richard King, Mifflin Kenedy, Uriah Lott, and even Samuel M. Jarvis.[105] He had little doubt that the arrival of the iron horse would rapidly transform Laredo and the economy of the border. "Warehouses [will] take the place of jacales," he and others thought.[106]

In fact, the arrival of what came to be known as the Texas Mexican Railway from Corpus Christi in 1881 did more to economically transform Laredo than any other event in the long history of the town. Large amounts of freight could now flow into Mexico at Laredo. As the construction crews reached Laredo from the east, Jay Gould's standard-gauge International-Great Northern Railroad was feverishly laying track south from Pearsall. Freight that was shipped to the end of the line and transferred to wagons was already beginning to arrive. By December 1, 1881, the I&GN was at Webb Station, only thirty miles from the border. On December 15, almost twelve months to the day since the railroad commenced construction south from San Antonio, the I&GN arrived at Laredo.[107] The railroad not only linked Laredo and the border to San Antonio, but the middle border to the rest of the United States.

Laredo and Nuevo Laredo celebrated the arrival of the railroads with a gigantic fiesta that lasted from Christmas Eve 1881 well into the New Year. Bullfights, cockfights, horse and mule races, concerts, and balls for the powerful and well-to-do were all part of the celebration. The liquor flowed freely.[108] It was one of the great moments in the long and tumultuous history of the city. Construction of a temporary low-water bridge commenced almost immediately, and on March 8, 1882, the first passenger train, carrying Civil War hero William Tecumseh Sherman, military officers from Fort McIntosh, and Laredo's leading businessmen and politicians, including Santos and other members of the state legislature, steamed across the river to be saluted by the Thirteenth Mexican Infantry. The famous railroad entrepreneur Jay Gould arrived on April 26 and was greeted by Santos and the city dignitaries.[109] The arrival of the train in Laredo had a profound and lasting influence on the town; the population of the community more than tripled in the decade that followed, from 3,521 in 1880 to 11,319 by 1890.[110] Laredo became a bustling city.

Santos was excited by the arrival of the railroad and the possibility that the Texas Mexican Railway Company would build an extension to the coal mines upriver from Laredo. "With a special appreciation of the advantages to be derived by the construction of the coal road," he agreed to give the Texas-Mexican a strip of land 100-feet wide across his properties upriver from Laredo.[111] The railroad company agreed to pay for any damages to houses, fences, fields, or other improvements, and to construct suitable cattle guards at all fence crossings. But funds were exhausted, and it was not until 1882 that the Rio Grande and Eagle Pass narrow gauge railroad was built to the mining camps of Dolores, Minera, Darwin, and Santo Tomás.

While the Texas-Mexican and the I&GN were building into Laredo from the east and north, respectively, the narrow-gauge Mexico Oriental Interoceanic & International, usually referred to as the Mexican National Railway, was rapidly building south into the Mexican interior with the help of American capital. Including the other construction crews laboring north of Mexico City, as many as sixteen thousand men were working on the railroad at one time. By November 1881 the Mexican National had reached Lampazos, and by the summer of 1882 it was nearing Monterrey. Finally, in late 1888, the link between Nuevo Laredo and the capital was complete.[112]

The development of coal mines twenty-seven miles upriver from Laredo also brought a frenzy of economic activity to the community. Coal was known to exist along the banks of the Rio Grande since the Spanish colonial era, but it was not until 1873 that Charles Callaghan and Refugio Benavides started a crude mining operation. The two aspiring entrepreneurs sent three large carts of coal to Corpus Christi for use on steamers running along the coast, with satisfactory results.[113] In 1881, at the same time as the arrival of the railroads, A. C. Hunt, former governor of Colorado, leased many of the coal deposits and began large-scale mining. By the following summer, the

Santo Tomás and Black Diamond Mines were producing as much as one hundred tons of coal daily. Mining camps such as Dolores, Minera, Santo Tomás, and Darwin sprang up overnight as hundreds of miners arrived from the towns and villages of northern Mexico.[114] By March 1882 one hundred men were laboring in twelve-hours shifts to build the narrow-gauge Rio Grande and Pecos to the coal mines. Three months later, Hunt arrived to drive a silver spike, commemorate the laying of the first rail, and brag of a day when the railroad would stretch along the banks of the Rio Grande all the way from Brownsville to El Paso. Within months, dirt was broken south of town on the Brownville line, but the railroad was never completed. Hunt had overextended his financial resources, and by 1885 he was broke.[115]

Even before he was elected to the House of Representatives in the late 1870s, when tensions between the United States and Mexico reached new heights, Santos had worked to repair his badly tarnished reputation in Nuevo Laredo. Within a decade, especially after he and Cristóbal opened a business in the sister city, his incursions into Mexico during the Civil War had largely been forgotten. In December 1882, following a hotly contested election in Nuevo Laredo, Santos arrived at the headquarters of Gen. Remal Cuellar leading a delegation of the "Texas-Mexican Club." Santos and his followers were met at the river by a company of Mexican troops and a brass band. One newspaper remarked on the novelty of seeing the "red, white, and blue and the green, white and red going up the street side by side." At General Cuellar's headquarters, Santos watched as the leaders of the two opposing parties embraced. Several Texas correspondents, including those from the Spanish-language newspapers *El Laredense* and *El Horizonte*, as well as the *Galveston Daily News* and *San Antonio Express*, watched a series of abrazos, speeches, and parties that lasted well into the night. Santos and his Laredoans, the *Galveston Daily News* curtly remarked, behaved themselves well.[116]

At three o'clock on the afternoon of September 29, 1883, Santos was at the head of a another delegation, this time welcoming the governor of Coahuila, Evaristo Madero, to a sumptuous banquet at Milmo Hall on Market Plaza in Laredo, that included eight meats and a wide variety of desserts. Prominent politicians from Nuevo Laredo, as well as officers from Fort McIntosh, joined a long list of local politicians and railroad executives in welcoming the governor. Musicians played "Yankee Doodle" and the Mexican national anthem, which were followed by endless toasts to the prosperity of the United States and Mexico. The highlight of the banquet was a stirring speech by Santos emphasizing the economic ties between Texas and Coahuila.[117] As was frequently his custom, Santos spoke in Spanish, and his son Juan translated his words into English. One reporter said the speech was offered in a "spirit of international fraternity." As everyone cheered loudly, "the old gentleman's benevolent face beamed with happiness."[118] Afterward, a long line of carriages followed Santos and Madero down Victoria Street and across the railroad tracks to Fort McIntosh, where the governor was greeted by a resounding seventeen-gun salute, a snappy dress parade, and a Gatling gun demonstration. The next day the large delegation boarded the Rio Grande and Eagle Pass narrow-gauge railroad for a tour of the coal-mining towns upriver from Laredo, where more than a thousand Mexican miners hacked away, many of them underground, at the rich coal seams along the river.

More than a decade earlier, Santos's and Agustina's daughter had wed Gen. Lázaro Garza Ayala in a gala ceremony at San Agustín Church on February 6, 1867. In the decade of the 1880s, Agustina Benavides Ayala and her husband, the former governor of Nuevo León, who was now serving as chief justice of the state supreme court, regularly came north for casual visits.[119] Likewise, Santos and his wife frequently traveled south to Monterrey, sometimes in a special car of the Mexican National Railway, to visit their daughter and her distinguished husband. Agustina and Santos were excited when their daughter gave birth to a son named Francisco. But the couple received a serious psychological blow in July 1882 when tragic news arrived from Matamoros that their beloved adopted daughter, Agustina, was dead of yellow fever at the age of thirty-four.[120] One year later, on June

27, 1883, Santos received equally bad news from Monterrey that Santos Eraclio Benavides y Villarreal, his faithful son who had gone to the city only a few months earlier for his health, was dead from the flu. Born out of wedlock in Guerrero in 1864, Eraclio was only eighteen years and seven months old at the time of his death. His coffin was carried from the family home at 26 Abasolo to the Basilica of Our Lady of Guadalupe for a funeral Mass and then to the Catholic cemetery, where he was laid to rest.[121] Eraclio's death was as much a blow to Agustina as it was to Santos. Agustina had nurtured the child since Santos brought him home from Guerrero, and she commissioned a tomb for young Eraclio, who in death had become "un hijo legítimo."[122] For years, Santos and Agustina would visit General Ayala in Monterrey and lay flowers at the grave of their adopted son.[123]

In September 1883, Santos and Agustina sold their home on San Agustín Plaza to Santos's younger brother Eulalio and moved to a larger,

A new Laredo City Hall and Market House was built in 1883–1884, just across the street from Benavides's second residence on Flores Street. *Courtesy Charles G. Downing Collection, Institute of Texas Cultures.*

more modern home three blocks north on Flores Street, opposite the new city hall on Market Plaza.[124]

In April 1881 Santos had gone north again to Austin, where the gray-bearded, South Carolina–born governor Oran Milo Roberts called the legislature back into session to deal with a large number of unsettled issues, including taxes and appropriations.[125] At the end of the session, Santos and his friend Edmund J. Davis caught the I&GN for the border, but the rails had yet to be laid all the way to Laredo, and twenty miles and north of the city the two old warriors turned politicians were forced to transfer to a stage. In Laredo, Davis was a guest in Santos's house, and the two celebrated July 4 together.

Despite his farewell address in the state legislature, Santos decided to seek reelection once again, and he was easily elected to a third term in November 1882. Santos appears to have agreed not to oppose any of Martin's candidates for local office in return for Martin's neutrality. Some had talked of Santos competing for a position in the more prestigious state senate, but he seemed content to stay in the House of Representatives because, as one observer remarked, "his constituency will always keep him there."[126]

In the newly formed Eighty-Third District, which excluded Cameron County but included Duval, Encinal, Hidalgo, Starr, Webb, and Zapata Counties, Santos was not as reliant as before on the Powers-Wells machine. He was pitted against Alejandro J. Leo Jr., a fellow Democrat from Hidalgo County, and Rafael Alderete, running as an independent Republican, in the three-man race for the two vacant seats. For a change, Santos carried Webb County, and he won Duval County decisively. As expected, Leo prevailed in Hidalgo County and nosed out Santos in Zapata and Starr Counties. When all the votes were counted, Leo had received 2,130 votes, Santos had 1,663, and Alderete finished a distant third with 692.[127]

In January 1883, Santos returned to Austin as one of 122 members of the House of Representatives of the Eighteenth Legislature. Once again, Santos was the only Tejano in either the Texas House or Senate. Surprisingly, he was one of only sixteen representatives born in Texas. The vast majority

Members of the House of Representatives of the Eighteenth Texas Legislature with Santos Benavides as the tenth member in the fourth row. He was the only Tejano in the legislature at the time and one of only five Tejanos to serve in the legislature in the nineteenth century. *Courtesy Texas State Library and Archives.*

of representatives at the time were either farmers or lawyers born in the Old South. He was one of only a handful of merchants and one of only seven stock raisers. At the age of fifty-nine, he was one of the older members of the House. With Reconstruction in the past, only two representatives were African American, and most of those elected, like Santos, were Democrats, except for a handful of Republicans and four fiery Greenbackers.[128]

No longer on the committees on stock raising and Indian affairs, Santos held positions on the Committee on Public Health, Vital Statistics, History of Texas, Insurance and Statistics, and the Military Affairs Committee, as well as the Federal Relations Committee.[129] Despite his growing seniority, his inability to communicate effectively in English kept him from chairing any of the committees. No sooner was the legislative session under way on January 9 than a resolution was introduced to honor George R. Reeves, who had served as speaker in the Seventeenth Legislature but who had died of hydrophobia after being bitten by a rabid dog. Speaking on Santos's behalf, John Hughes Cochran, the new speaker, said that Santos deeply regretted his "inability to speak the English language sufficiently plain." In carefully crafted remarks, Cochran quoted him as saying he would always remember Reeves as an "honorable man" whom he "loved dearly as a friend."[130] The legislature agreed to name Reeves County in far west Texas in his honor of the dead speaker.

One of the first motions Santos made in the new legislature was to have five hundred copies of Governor John Ireland's inaugural address printed in Spanish. In response, William John Caven from Marshall in Harrison County rose to offer an amendment that the copies be printed in Bohemian. The amendment was quickly defeated.[131]

On February 27, 1883, Santos was appointed as one of six senators and representatives to receive Gen. Porfirio Díaz, who would be visiting Austin while on a tour of the United States. Díaz also hoped to visit Galveston, and Santos drafted a letter to the citizens of the seaside city, asking that they give Díaz a warm welcome.[132] Díaz and his young bride, Carmen Ramos Rubio, had spent their honeymoon in the United States the previous year, attending balls and banquets in New York and Washington, DC. Certain to be elected president again, Díaz claimed his second visit to the United States was "recreational" and had no economic intent, but there was little doubt he was hoping to complete a commercial treaty with the United States.

From Veracruz, Díaz first traveled by steamer to New Orleans, where he was greeted by John W. Foster, the US Ambassador to Mexico. From the Crescent City, Díaz and his young wife traveled on to Washington, DC, in a special train offered by President Chester A. Arthur. Díaz spent three days at the White House, talking economics and loans and then touring the capital. Always the statesman, the former president went on to New York City, Niagara Falls, Boston, and Chicago, where he was greeted with a grand reception.[133] Díaz was well received everywhere he went because he was perceived to be pro-American. Arriving in St. Louis, he attended yet another elaborate reception and dinner before returning to Texas and the border. Late at night on March 6, Santos waited at the train station in Laredo to greet his friend and bid him good-bye as a special train of the Mexican National Railway waited to take him south to Monterrey and the capital. Santos's friend and former secretary of war, Gen. Geronimo Treviño, had come north from Monterrey to greet Díaz and escort him south.[134] Santos returned to Austin the next day.

Despite flashes of enlightened liberalism, Santos often backed legislation that was reactionary and repressive. In a kind of flashback to the antebellum period of slavery and peonage, he sponsored a socially regressive act designed to punish domestic servants who violated contracts. In a more progressive mode, however, he introduced an act to make vaccinations of schoolchildren compulsory.[135] The Eighteenth Legislature established a permanent university fund and a law mandating brand inspections for all cattle leaving the state. On February 6, 1884, the legislature adjourned *sine die*, and Santos left for the border. It was his last legislative session.

As the general election of 1884 approached, Santos openly campaigned for the reelection of Governor Ireland. Santos had known the governor since the Civil War, when Ireland was a lieutenant colonel stationed on the

This photograph of Santos Benavides appears to have been taken at the time he was serving in the Texas House of Representatives. *Jerry Thompson Collection.*

Texas coast and Santos was in command on the Rio Grande. The two were on opposite sides when Ireland opposed subsidies for the International-Great Northern Railroad and the governor earned the sobriquet "Ox Cart John." Santos had even supported Ireland's opponent, Gustav Schleicher, in the election for the US House of Representatives in 1878. But Santos campaigned for Ireland in 1882, asking his friends and all those who had fought with him "on Texas soil" to vote for Ireland.[136] "[Santos once] served Texas with his sword, so now he is devoting his influence to the same good cause," James Penn of the *Laredo Times* reported during the campaign.[137] Ox Cart John was easily reelected, and Santos was assured of having a friend in the governor's mansion.

With Santos's political influence growing, a number of prominent Texas Democrats sought his support, knowing that his endorsement could mean as many as eight hundred votes in Webb County. In October 1882, for example, George Preston Finlay, called the "Tall Sycamore" because he was six foot four, came to Laredo courting Santos's endorsement during his campaign to represent the Seventh Congressional District. On October 14, hundreds of citizens gathered at the Webb County Courthouse to hear Santos endorse Finlay, a Civil War veteran of Arkansas Post and Chickamauga. Finlay, who spoke no Spanish, was an able man, Santos said, who had devoted much of his life to improving the lives of the citizens of South Texas.[138] Although Finlay carried Webb County in November, Thomas P. Ochiltree was able to retain his seat in the House of Representatives.

Santos had decided not to seek office in the run-up to the general election of 1884, but several prominent politicians approached him to encourage him to run for the Senate as an independent Democrat against Edward F. Hall, the candidate of the Martin machine. Although the idea was tempting, Santos sensed the changing of the political winds; he declined the invitation and watched as Hall was reelected and E. A. Atlee, a Martin loyalist, took his old seat in the state legislature.[139]

Both during and after the time he was in the Texas legislature, Santos did much to improve relations with the government of Mexico. Porfirio Díaz, struggling to establish internal political stability after decades of domestic conflicts and international hostilities, made an inspection tour of the Rio Grande frontier in November 1878, and for the next decade Santos, as someone with political connections in both Texas and Mexico, acted as an intermediary on the border. In May 1884 he was rumored to be heading south to Monterrey on an "errand of peace" to help resolve a growing feud between Gen. Geronimo Treviño and President González, both of whom were good friends.[140] A few days later he handed the *Laredo Times* a letter he had received from Gen. Geronimo Treviño that was picked up by the *San Antonio Daily Express* and then by the *Galveston Daily News* and the *New York Times*. The letter denied rumors of a feud between Treviño on one side and President González and Porfirio Díaz on the other. The letter was also a strong rebuke of individuals who were circulating rumors that Mexico was on the eve of yet another revolution and that Treviño was the instigator. The general assured his "esteemed friend" Santos that he, the general, was the "last person to even entertain the idea of a revolutionary movement much less take part in it."[141]

Santos was honored in 1884 by being named a commissioner from Texas to the World's Industrial and Cotton Centennial Exposition in New Orleans. Santos and Agustina made their way to San Antonio on the I&GN and then east by rail through the night, arriving in the Crescent City on December 16, 1884, for the delayed opening of what amounted to be a spectacular world's fair. The exposition was designed to mark the one hundredth anniversary of the nation's cotton industry while highlighting the commercial revitalization of New Orleans as the world's largest cotton port. The entire exposition took up more than 245 acres in what is today Audubon Park, and its centerpiece was a thirty-three-acre Horticulture Hall, the largest greenhouse in the world. More than five thousand electric lights were used, a novelty at the time, and an electric elevator took Santos and Agustina to the top of an observation tower. President Porfirio Díaz and his young wife, Carmen Romero de Rubio, arrived and the two families toured the various exhibits. Santos and the president took particular pride in the Mexican exhibit, the largest and most elaborate of any Latin American country. Individual Mexican states showcased their wealth in natural resources with displays of iron, zinc, copper, and even stacks of gold and silver bars, as well as precious stones such as opals.[142]

With his extensive Mexican political connections, Santos's friendship was a prerequisite to gaining influence or business opportunities south of the border. When he served in the legislature, many saw him as little more than a token Mexican, while others, including many of the state's leading newspapers, took him far more seriously. Perhaps one of his most revealing and flattering interviews was conducted by the widely read *Galveston Weekly News* in 1882. Santos was five feet ten inches tall, the newspaper reported, although photographs of him seem to belie this measurement. He weighed 175 pounds and was one of the wealthiest men in South Texas. Santos and Agustina keep up the "old Castilian fashion of don and donna, occupying entirely separate apartments," the newspaper said. Their names were printed in large gilded letters over the doors of their rooms. The two enjoyed a lovely courtyard filled with fig trees, grapevines, banana trees, and orange trees.[143]

Santos was certainly the "most distinguished citizen" in Laredo, a gentleman of "high esteem" with "courtly and courteous manners" dating back to the Spanish era. Although he spoke English with "difficulty and hesitation," Santos understood the language well. As an independent Democrat, he had influence in Texas far beyond the Rio Grande. He "does not wear a brass collar of which somebody else carries the key," the newspaper continued. Santos knew everyone from Boca Chica to Eagle Pass and was "esteemed and respected by everyone." When asked how many sheep he owned, Santos replied, "Oh, I have not many now. I have sold a great many; I have now only fourteen to fifteen thousand head. Fifty thousand head is considered a very moderate flock in this country, you know."[144]

In his "declining years," Santos was praised by *Norton's Union Intelligencer* of Dallas for having "a reputation unspotted, unblemished" and "the unanimous verdict of his fellow man that he is beyond suspicion." Most importantly, Santos was a man "free from all demagoguery." When he was a soldier, Santos had gone "where duty called him, regardless of the danger." As a statesman he was always ready to "champion the cause of the people."[145]

CHAPTER VIII

BALLOTS AND BULLETS

"Last Wednesday night replete with joy and cheer.
Don Santos set up keg on keg of beer."

—*Laredo Daily Times*, October 18, 1884

During his many years in Texas politics, Santos Benavides befriended countless powerful and influential men in both the United States and Mexico. Certainly no one was more interesting than the German-born intellectual Gustav Schleicher. In 1848, during the Mexican-American War, Schleicher led a fraternity of highly educated German freethinkers to a site on the north bank of the Llano River so that they could establish a utopian socialist commune based on friendship, freedom, and equality. In time, however, the settlers at Bettina became disillusioned, and Schleicher moved to San Antonio, where he became a leading engineer, entrepreneur, and railroad promoter. A few years later in 1874, with Santos's support, he was elected to the US House of Representatives from the Sixth Congressional District, which included Webb County and a large part of the middle border. Santos and other Laredoans were beholden to Schleicher for bettering the mail service to San Antonio and for his attention to the problems on the border.[1] Throughout South Texas, Santos became known as a "Schleicher man" for his fervent support of the congressman. But on January 10, 1879, Schleicher died suddenly in Washington, DC.

At the Democratic congressional nominating convention in San Antonio two months later, there was considerable talk of nominating Santos.

He was a respected figure in "Western Texas," where relations with Mexico were of paramount importance, but once again he was hampered by his inability to communicate effectively in English.[2] And many of the delegates were not about to send someone who did not speak English to Washington. Moreover, the Cameron County delegates threw their support behind John S. Ford. Eventually, after hours of contentious debate and wrangling, it was the New York–born Christopher Columbus Upson, a former Confederate and a leading lawyer from San Antonio, who was nominated and who went on to replace the popular Schleicher in Washington, DC. Santos lost his opportunity to become the first Tejano elected to the US Congress.[3]

While serving in the state legislature, Santos remained determined to bring down Raymond Martin's political machine, which dominated Laredo and Webb County politics and was such an obstacle to his political aspirations. Energetically and unequivocally, Santos set out, with the assistance of James Saunders Penn and his English-language *Laredo Daily Times*, plus colleagues such as Darío Gonzales, to build a Reform Party that could put forth a slate of competent candidates for city and county elections in 1884.

James Penn arrived in Laredo from Austin with his printing press and other equipment in three prairie schooners in the early summer of 1881, and he and Santos became the best of friends. By 1883 his weekly edition of the *Times* had grown to twelve pages and had become the *Laredo Daily Times*.[4] From his office at the southeast corner of Flores and Farragut, Penn poured forth an endless stream of biting editorials, and in the process became a leading voice for municipal change and a strong supporter of Santos and the reformers.

In the campaign of 1884, the *Daily Times* compared Martin's corruption to that of Boss Tweed and Tammany Hall in New York City and chafed when Santos and the reformers were dismissed as pseudo-Republicans. Santos, Penn wrote, was a "life-long Democrat, a gallant soldier and wise legislator, and a man whose honor is as pure as the rays of the serenest gem." Besides "promoting" Colonel Benavides to general, the *Laredo Times* and other Texas newspapers pointed out that he was already well known on the border when his "loud-mouthed detractors were yet in their swaddling clothes." They proclaimed that Gen. Santos Benavides's name would shine with "luster when these supernumerary patriots shall have sunk into the oblivion of un-honored graves."[5]

One issue dividing Martin's Democrats and Santos's reformers was the construction of a streetcar line and international bridge. In September 1884, the Laredo Bridge and Street Railway Company, owned by Martin and several colleagues, was contracted by the city council to construct a streetcar line and bridge that would carry wagons and pedestrians. Santos's reformers presented to the city council a petition with the names of fifty-one citizens and asked that the projects be stopped. The construction was graft ridden, they contended, and little more than an opportunity for Martin and his business partners to ingratiate themselves financially and expand their already growing political influence. Martin's aldermen countered that the company was using "Laredo money" and that the projects were being built "by Laredo people for the benefit of the city of Laredo." To stop the construction would set the city back. When the pro-Martin mayor, Darío Sánchez, broke a tie within the council, the work continued. The county council also voted to construct a large enclosed market and an adjacent two-story city hall on Market Plaza. Within weeks the reformers were demanding an investigation into the quality of the construction, but once again they were rebuffed.

By late September 1884, small informal meetings at Santos's home on Flores Street, opposite the new city hall, had become large, formal assemblies in Milmo Hall at the Milmo National Bank, across the street, that were open to anyone wanting to help defeat the Martin Democrats at the upcoming election. Daniel Milmo and his brother Patricio, owners of the bank, had placed a large room at the disposal of the reformers, and with the November general election rapidly approaching, the new Reform Party began meeting every Saturday night. The reformers established an executive committee that included two sitting aldermen, a few prominent attorneys, Juan V. Benavides, and the aging warrior Refugio Benavides. Juan had returned to Laredo after completing his law degree at Washington and Lee

University and was admitted to the Texas bar in October 1877. Two years later he was selected as secretary of the Webb County Democratic Party.[6] With his political star rising, he was frequently by his father's side, always ready to offer an English translation if necessary.

With eloquence and energy, Santos struck hard at Martin and his machine. At Milmo Hall on October 18, 1884, Santos told an excited audience of several hundred citizens that all eligible Americans had a "duty of citizenship" that included voting. In "clear and forcible terms," voters must put a stop to the corruption that had engulfed the community. At every opportunity the crowd jumped to their feet and cheered the old warrior with "enthusiastic vivas." "General Benavides looms up as the colossus of the reform movement," Penn wrote in the *Laredo Daily Times*.[7]

In support of Santos and the Reform Party, Penn even tried his hand at poetry:

> Once more to the breach, dear friends, once more.
> Last Wednesday night replete with joy and cheer.
> When Don Santos set up keg on keg of beer.
> Come out to Milmo's hall again to-night,
> To pledge reform anew, justice home and right!
> Reform Club tonight!
> Milmo's—eight tonight!
> General Santos Benavides will be there to-night.
> I'll meet you at Milmo's Hall at 8 this evening . . .
> Mexican freemen, come out to-night and sign the roll of honor.
> We've got 'em on the run, and no mistake; press on the column and we'll sweep the field.[8]

But Penn was reaching only a small part of the Laredo electorate. A large number of the citizens were illiterate, and even those who could read did not subscribe to a newspaper or read English. Others received the more popular Spanish-language *La Voz del Pueblo*, which traditionally supported Martin.

Iturbide Street at the time of the Laredo Election Riot. The condition of the streets of Laredo well into the next century would be a source of criticism. As early as 1858, Santos Benavides complained to the city council of the stagnant water and rotten debris in the streets. *Courtesy Sam Johnson Collection, Webb County Heritage Foundation.*

For the reformers to be successful, they needed the support of several crucial coalitions. What the local Blaine and Logan Republican Club would do was largely settled when Santos lured J. J. Haynes, son of the staunchly Republican John L. Haynes of Civil War fame, to become the secretary of the Reform Club.[9] The reformer's success at the polls also depended on attracting the less fortunate, many of whom were economically dependent on city-, county-, or machine-owned businesses and ranches for their livelihoods. Many in the lower class belonged to the Club Azul Independiente Mejico-Tejano, which was headed by José María Vela, the city tax assessor-collector and a Martin loyalist. Another organization, the Sociedad Mutualista Union Mexicano, refused to make any promises.[10]

The Reform Party was hoping for support from Encinal County, the large, rural sheep- and cattle-ranching county east of Webb County. The sparsely populated county remained unorganized and had been attached to Webb County for administrative purposes, so party leaders were sent there promising to permanently separate the county from Webb. The reformers also hoped that several hundred Mexican miners at the small coal-mining towns upriver from Laredo—Santo Tomás, Dolores, Darwin, and Minera—would support them. Although the miners, all recent immigrants from Mexico, were subject to the whims and dictates of the mine owners, party leaders were dispatched to meet with the men.[11] A prominent citizen from La Jarita, Mexico, was rumored to have been hired by Santos to bring in large numbers of voters from Mexico.[12]

By early October the two parties had full slates of candidates and were preparing for battle. One of the races that attracted the most attention was that of county judge. The Martin Democrats ran the bright, articulate, and popular incumbent, José María Rodríguez, who had served as Basilio Benavides's interpreter in the legislature at the beginning of the Civil War. Rodríguez also doubled as chairman of the Webb County Democratic Party. Both positions gave him considerable political clout. To oppose Rodríguez, the reformers put up the equally bright and articulate Juan V. Benavides.[13]

As political tensions reached new heights, the Reform Club began meeting twice a week at the Milmo Bank, usually on Wednesdays and Saturdays. They also established a party headquarters at the corner of Flores Avenue and Matamoros Street, three blocks from Santos's house. Party leaders took turns denouncing the "ring" for every conceivable crime in the county. Part of their popularity stemmed from the fact that Santos always treated those assembled to beer at a local tavern after the political rallies. For example, on October 13 the reformers met at Milmo Hall to hear an "excellent brass band" from Nuevo Laredo, after which they patiently listened to Santos and others berate the Martin machine and then relocated to a saloon to "pledge success to the ticket in schooners of foaming beer."[14] Only three days later, "Don Santos treated the Reform crowd to 1,000 schooners of foaming beer." Politics "enjoys a monopoly in Laredo at the present," Penn wrote.[15]

By mid-October the campaign reached a fever pitch. On Saturday,

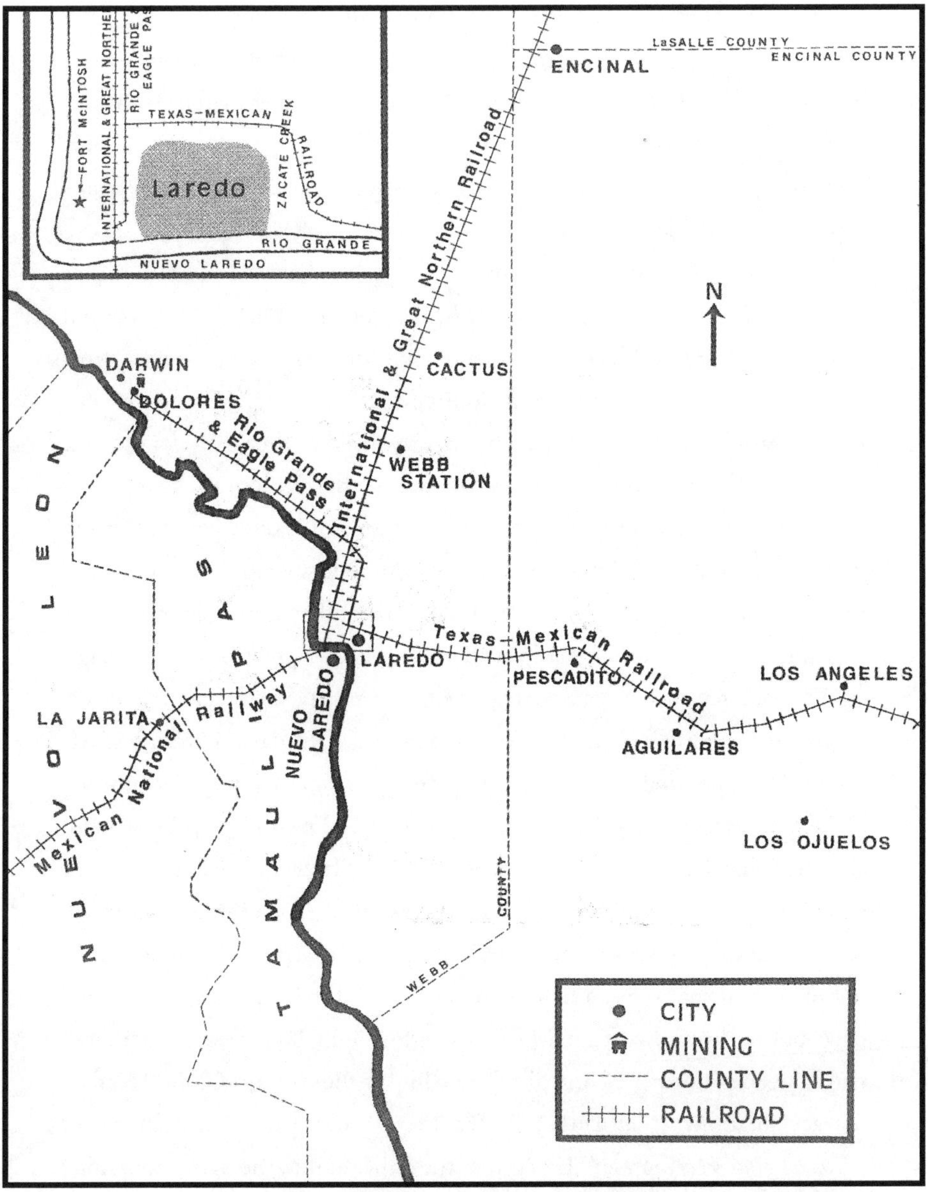

Map of the Laredo area at the time of the Laredo Election Riot, showing the recently completed railroads that connected the community to the outside world. *Warm Weather and Bad Whiskey.*

October 15, reformers gathered at Milmo Hall for a fiery meeting after which 350 partisans paraded through the streets for an hour before assembling again at Market Plaza, where they formed a large circle to hear a stirring appeal from Santos.[16] The crowd then retired for their usual beer. Someone less financially secure than Santos would surely have been bankrupted by the weekly bar bills.

Several violent confrontations between marchers from both camps helped to intensify the already emotional campaign. One fight broke out when a number of Martin Democrats stationed themselves on a street corner and commenced shouting "foul epithets" at the passing reformers. Leaders from both parties usually were at the head of the street demonstrations, a reflection of the oligarchical nature of the community. Santos was frequently seen on horseback at the head of the semi-weekly parades, sitting high in the saddle as if he was leading his Confederate regiment into war.[17] He was followed by large bandwagons with brightly painted signs and several hundred men on foot, many of them drunk, carrying banners and flags.

Despite recent heavy rains that turned the unpaved streets into a quagmire, the Reform Party met at Milmo Hall on Saturday, October 26. Although disappointed that a delegation from Encinal County had not arrived, the determined reformers listened to the Nuevo Laredo brass band and the usual speeches and consumed gallons of beer. The always eloquent Charles C. Pierce was the primary speaker for the evening and spoke in fluent Spanish. He strode forward with a guarache strapped to a pole, telling the crowd that the sandal was the symbol of the lower class, that it had been buried by the corrupt Martin ring for eight long years, but that it had now been unearthed and given new life by the Reform Club. "Deafening acclamations of applause" greeted Pierce's every word as a chorus of "*viva los guaraches*" echoed throughout the hall and into the dark and muddy streets. The Reform Party had unofficially and joyously become the Guarache Party. But Pierce was just beginning. He called forth two elderly men: a one-legged invalid in rags who hobbled forth on crutches and a second gray-haired man wretchedly bent over and obviously in the twilight of his life. As the two men stood silent, Pierce recalled how they had been abused and then dismissed by their employer, a prominent Martin Democrat, simply because they had stated their intentions to vote the reform ticket.[18]

With emotions boiling, 250 angry Guaraches filed out of Milmo Hall into the streets, marching through mud and water up to their ankles as they proudly carried their new banner aloft—"the ever glorious guarache." The men walked eleven blocks to the International-Great Northern depot, just east of Fort McIntosh, where they were treated to beer. The crowd then turned back to Milmo Hall. Several were too drunk to continue and fell out along the way. Juan Benavides, who was at the head of the crowd on horseback, tried to halt the parade, asking the men to retire for the evening, but a zealous Guarache seized the reins of his horse, and the march continued.[19]

The following week the Guaraches had just started their weekly parade in the central business district when a large group of Martin Democrats, who were now calling themselves Botas, gathered to taunt their rivals. They then began following the Guaraches, shouting curses at Santos, who was at the head of the procession. A number of Guaraches turned on the Botas and began to brawl. The Botas later argued that many of the Guaraches were drunk and that it had been the reformers who started the fracas.

Although the *bota* had long been the symbol of the ranch-owning elite of Texas and Mexico, just as the guarache symbolized the never-ending struggles of the poor and outcast laborers of the region, both parties counted among their supporters all classes of citizens. Neither were the parties drawn along ethnic lines, as both were made up primarily of Tejanos, as well as Mexicanos from across the river. In reality, the epic struggle that would turn bloody two years later was a contest for power and honor, a contest for the lucrative spoils of city and county government, and not a class struggle.[20]

With the election rapidly approaching, many in Laredo feared that the overly zealous partisans would arm themselves and fisticuffs would turn into gun battles. The Guaraches were rumored to be preparing to bring in several hundred men from Nuevo Laredo, and the Botas had plans to run a special train loaded with illegal voters all the way from Saltillo. On the Saturday before the Tuesday election, both parties were in the streets in large numbers, but there was no violence. The Guaraches, said to outnumber the Botas 680 to 440, were content to congregate in front of Santos's home on Flores Street and serenade the old soldier on his sixty-fourth birthday, while the Botas gathered in front of their headquarters on Iturbide Street.

As the campaign reached its climax, the *Laredo Times* became even bolder than before: "The old leprous conglomeration of mephitic garbage and reeking corruption which has for decades clung like eating cancer to the body politic of Laredo must be eradicated at all costs."[21] And Penn again tried to ridicule the Botas with poetry:

> Soon will be known the people's choice
> Against the Barnacles they shout;
> And all Laredo will rejoice
> To turn the mugwumps out.[22]

The biggest political demonstration was held on the night before the election. On horseback, Santos again led a large crowd of Guaraches through the streets. Just as the reformers were retiring to one of the saloons for their usual "eatables and drinkables," they received word that 250 miners had arrived by train to join them. Within minutes the Guaraches were in the streets again. Santos was in front, followed by a man carrying the Guarache flag and protected by three gunmen. Next came two large wagons drawn by several teams of horses. A number of clever signs adorned the wagons, one of which showed a Bota and a Guarache on a seesaw—the Bota high in the air and about to lose his balance. Behind the wagon came several hundred reformers carrying more signs. "Down with the Ring," read one sign, while another promised an international pedestrian bridge.[23] The shouts of the determined Botas could be heard blocks away.

At dawn on Election Day, November 4, 1884, Laredo was damp and overcast as a light mist clung to the city. As the polls opened, hacks, surreys, and wagons of all kinds sped through the dampened streets, carrying

Guarache and Bota voters to the polls. Men on horseback galloped with messages from party leaders to precinct chairmen and election officers. Within hours, it was evident the Martin Democrats were in complete control of the election process. Determined to win the election at any cost, Botas surrounded the polls with deputy sheriffs and special policemen brandishing guns. A few Guarache voters were even stoned as they approached the polls. A number of Botas also pelted the Guarache bandwagon.

During the day large numbers of men were arrested by deputy federal marshals for voting illegally. Most were from Nuevo Laredo and said they were poor and had been paid to vote by prominent citizens of Laredo. The *Laredo Times* blamed the illegal voting on the Botas and demanded that the individuals behind the scheme be arrested. The "poor devils" who voted illegally were not as guilty as the men who hired them, Penn proclaimed.[24] But it was the Bota zealots claiming to be deputy sheriffs and intimidating the voters who drew the most wrath. They stood with "murderous six-shooters . . . upon either side of the narrow entrance to the polls," the *Laredo Times* reported, "and each voter approached the ballot box . . . with fear and trembling."[25] Penn claimed that only one man at a time was allowed to approach the ballot box and that "in some instances ballots were snatched from the hands of voters, and their contents scanned."[26]

By late afternoon, as the skies cleared, the entire Guarache ticket had been crushed. Although the Bota election officials refused to release the voting totals, by sundown the results were well known on the streets. The Botas were already celebrating their victory with stewed chickens and kegs of beer. They even held a festive parade complete with a marching band. Someone brought forth a ragged guarache, the proud symbol of the fallen reformers, and buried it to the cheers of several hundred intoxicated partisans. Out of five county precincts, the Guaraches had managed to carry only one and even then by only a few votes. With almost everyone casting a straight party ticket, the totals for the various candidates rarely varied. Out of almost eighteen hundred voters, an all-time high for the county, the Botas had easily prevailed. Only in the business district had the Guaraches done well; they had even lost the small mining towns upriver from Laredo, as well as Encinal County.[27]

The election victory was a great personal triumph for Raymond Martin. For Santos, it was a dagger to the heart, a resounding defeat. Except for a single Guarache commissioner, the Botas now held all the county offices. In addition, New York–born Edward F. Hall, Martin's thirty-seven-year-old business associate and lawyer, was elected state senator, while thirty-six-year-old Tennessee-born E. A. Atlee, another lawyer and Bota colleague, took Santos's seat in the House of Representatives.[28]

Most political observers in Laredo and Webb County were certain the reform movement was dead. Santos had not given up, however; nor had many of his ardent supporters. "The Guarache is not dead," Penn proclaimed in the *Times*, "he only sleepeth; and it required neither the ken of a prophet, or the son of a prophet, to say that he will yet rise in the vehemence of his indestructible soul."[29] Although the election of 1884 had brought great drama and excitement to the thriving border city, it was only a dress rehearsal for the city election two years later, when the guarache would be hoisted aloft once more.

The Bota-Guarache confrontation and subsequent violence was part of a much bigger era of tension and violence on the border. A few days before Christmas, 1885, in the backyard of the Alice Morgan saloon, not far from San Agustín Plaza, Vicente Martinez shot and killed Fernando Lopez Montalbo, twenty-two-year-old editor of *El Horizonte*. The newspaper had been in publication for only a year and was one of several Spanish-language newspapers that was owned and edited by Mexican exiles who devoted considerable effort, much to Santos's disdain, vilifying Porfirio Díaz.[30] So charged were Laredo politics and tensions along the border that Fernando's brother, José, had been murdered in Nuevo Laredo six months earlier.

Another chapter in the tense relationship between the Botas and Guaraches opened in December 1885, when Hall, who succeeded Santos in the state legislature, was involved in a near-deadly altercation with Maj. O. M. Watkins, a Santos partisan. Hall and Watkins had exchanged angry words on more than one occasion, and Hall claimed he was peacefully walking by Watkins's office near San Agustín Plaza when Watkins fired three shots at him, one of which ripped through his coat and vest pocket and almost killed him. Watkins countered that Hall was the aggressor and that he was only defending himself. Watkins testified that he was peacefully sitting in his office when Hall entered angrily and struck him in the face with his fist while at the same time drawing his pistol and daring Watkins to resist. Watkins said he grabbed a pistol from his desk and as Hall stepped back onto the sidewalk, he fired three shots at him.[31]

As the April 1886 city elections approached, politics again came to dominate all public discourse. Once more, Santos was the driving force behind the Reform Party challenge to the entrenched Botas. He was toying with the idea of running as an independent Democrat for state representative or senator, but in the end, he agreed to support the party nominee and said he would concentrate on the city election instead.[32]

A number of Guaraches were preoccupied with removing the alcoholic Bota city attorney, J. P. C. Whitehead, from office. For six months, the Guaraches argued, Whitehead had been in a constant state of inebriation and "behaved in a highly boisterous and improper manner."[33] Whitehead was often so intoxicated he had to be carried out of council chambers feet first. In December 1884 he failed to appear at a meeting of the city council and was found "lying on the floor of his office" in a drunken stupor. Although Whitehead put up a fight and even hired Hall to represent him, the Botas finally gave up, and the city council agreed to dismiss him.[34]

Another issue was the conduct of city policeman. Many of the officers were observed to be drunk while on duty and were seen frequenting the city's saloons and houses of prostitution. After considerable debate, regulations were drafted requiring policemen to be of "good moral character." "No policeman, while on duty, shall be permitted to visit any saloon, gambling house or public resort, unless in the discharge of his official duty."[35] The reformist city marshal, Stephen Boyard, was able to remove several policemen, much to the displeasure of the Botas, charging them with drunkenness while on duty and conduct unbecoming an officer. At a stormy meeting of the city council on March 4, 1886, with Santos in attendance, the Botas retaliated by charging Boyard, who had previously been arrested for adultery, with "misconduct, corruption and malfeasance" for "knowingly permitting gaming against the laws of the city and state."[36] At a formal hearing one week later, Santos and so many angry Guaraches showed up that the council was forced to adjourn and seek a larger meeting room. Although the case dragged on for weeks, Boyard was eventually removed. Three days afterward, Santos led a large and angry crowd that denounced the Botas and drafted a protest petition. A few days later, Santos, with his son's legal assistance, was able to persuade Judge J. C. Russell, a personal friend, to issue an injunction prohibiting the Botas from removing Boyard, who returned to office.[37]

The fight between the Botas and Guaraches for control of the city in 1886 was similar to their conflict two years earlier. At the heart of Santos's passionate interest in this election, however, was his son Juan, who was hoping to become the new city attorney. The campaigning had opened in February with the usual speeches, torchlit parades, and excessive consumption of alcohol. With a much more bipartisan tone, Penn and the *Laredo Times* observed that "Laredo gets smashed on the Anheuser-Busch beers every election and the demand is as great as ever was." According to Penn, "Election bums are pouring in from the country, and stand in lively expectation in front of every bar in town."[38]

By 1886 party leaders and their supporters in the streets, both in defiance of city ordinances, were beginning to arm themselves. Both parties competed to see who could make the most noise with their weapons. The Botas seemed to take great pleasure in shooting their pistols at anvils. The Guaraches responded by acquiring an old cannon, dating back to before the Civil War, that had been given to the town for defense against Native Americans. When John Z. Leyendecker became postmaster after the war, he had placed the cannon in front of the post office with its barrel in the ground to make a convenient hitching post. The Guaraches cleaned

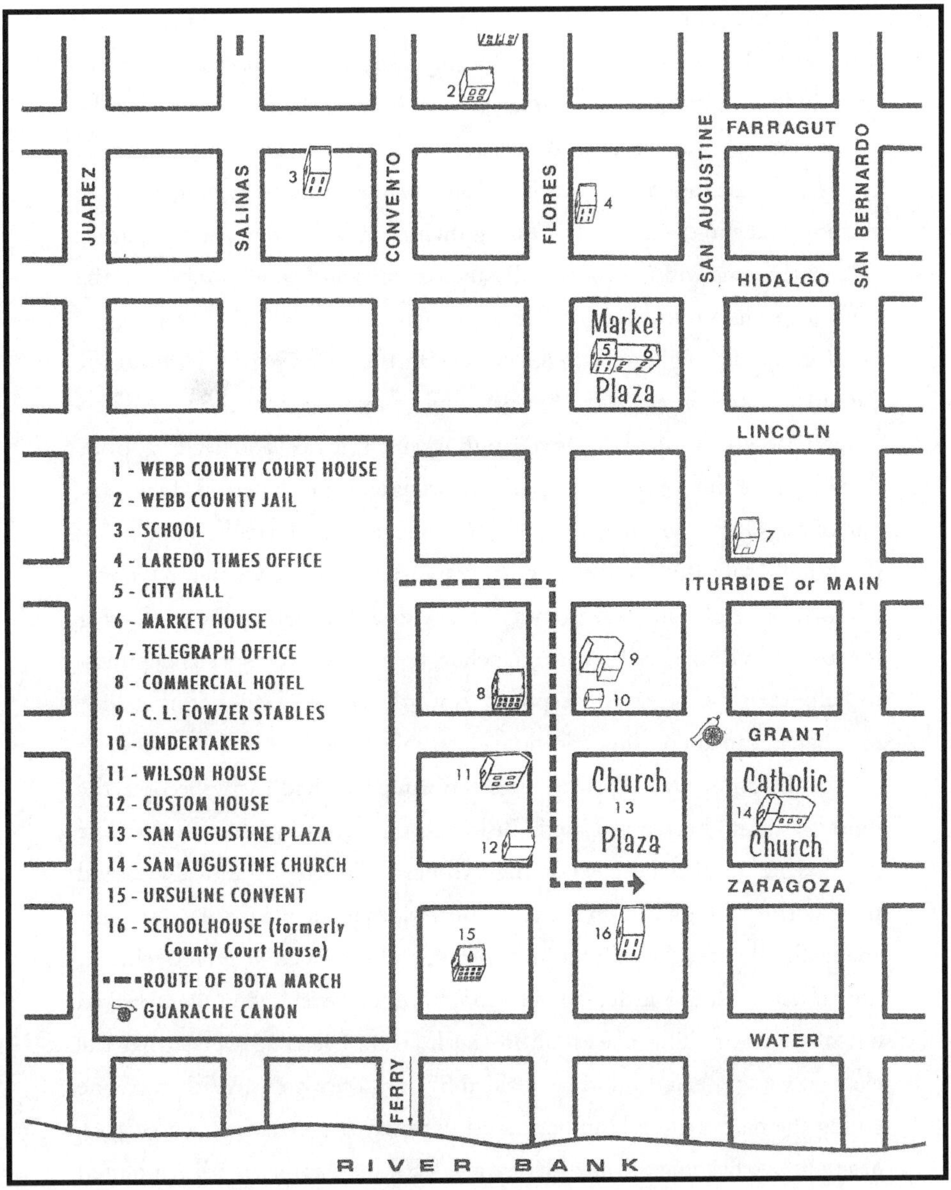

Map of downtown Laredo showing the route of the Bota victory parade on April 7, 1886. *Warm Weather and Bad Whiskey.*

and oiled the cannon, mounted it on a two-wheel carriage, and painted it a bright yellow to simulate brass. During their torchlit parades they frequently fired the cannon in an attempt to intimidate the Botas. A Guarache named Moran was designated the official cannoneer and was frequently seen astride the cannon in a bright red shirt as it was pulled by hand through the unpaved and dusty streets. During their nightly parades, the two parties frequently came within shouting distance of one another and exchanged the usual jeers and insults.[39]

On Sunday night, March 8, 1886, at Martin's Commercial Hotel at the corner of Grant Street and Flores Avenue, only blocks from Santos's new home, Alexander Meuly, a Swiss immigrant, rancher, and leading Bota, drew a pistol during a heated political argument and killed H. Douglass, one of the Guarache aldermen.[40] The Guaraches were furious and talked of lynching Meuly. But Meuly was quickly transferred to the Cameron County jail in Brownsville and was eventually sent to San Diego in Duval County for trial. The Bota sheriff, Darío Sánchez, appointed fifty "special deputies" to help keep the peace. In response, Boyard, who was still acting as city marshal, began appointing additional city policemen.[41]

By Election Day, April 6, 1886, the campaign had easily become the most bitter and heated in Laredo history, even surpassing that of 1884. The day dawned bright and clear as the two parties scurried frantically to and fro, escorting their voters to the polls. Both sides made the usual complaints about illegal voters, but few were arrested, and the election passed without the violence many had feared. Tensions rose, however, when word leaked out of several polling places, all in the homes of leading Botas, that the election was close and could be decided by only a few votes. With everyone voting the party ticket, Higinio García narrowly defeated Stephen Boyard, 629 to 618, to become the new city marshal. Santos was bitterly disappointed when Bota Charles A. McLane turned back Juan V. Benavides to become city attorney. Only two Guaraches, L. J. Christen and J. L. Bartlett, were elected to the council.[42] By 5:00 p.m., with the beer flowing freely, Bota party loyalists were celebrating in front of party headquarters and parading

Political parades in 1884 and 1886 would have been similar to this parade a decade later. *Courtesy collection of Federico E. Vidaurri. Digital restoration by Irene Vidaurri Zubeck.*

in the streets. Bands played throughout the night with only a brief respite now and then as men made their way to the nearest saloon. In the excitement, the Guaraches defiantly fired their cannon every five minutes, and many Laredoans spent a sleepless night.[43]

As the first rays of a new day shone into the streets, the yells of the "half drunken mob" could still be heard. Those who had been able to sleep awoke "ugly and pining for a scrap."[44] Children in the school on the south side of the plaza were so frightened by the noise that teachers dismissed classes. The Botas began to gather at party headquarters and agreed to hold another parade to celebrate their victory at the polls. As they had done two years earlier, some of the younger and more aggressive Botas decided to stage a mock funeral and bury a guarache. They all agreed that a good place to carry out the ritual would be in front of Darío Gonzales's house on San Agustín Plaza.[45] The Botas quickly drafted a funeral notice in Spanish, printed hundreds of copies, and distributed them on both sides of the river. Some of the "funeral invitations" were even posted on buildings around the plaza. The flyers bore a pathetic-looking weeping willow tree and in a sarcastic and mocking text announced the death of the Guarache Party. The "funeral cortege" would gather at the Bota Hall at 3:00 p.m. Invited to participate were "all Botas, all Bota sympathizers, all Botas indifferents, in fact every man that ever saw or heard of a boot."[46]

The invitations soon found their way into the hands of the Guaraches, and the hotheaded partisans, many of whom were still intoxicated, promised to retaliate. Gonzales told a group of party loyalists that he would not attempt to prevent the Botas from "celebrating or parading the streets," but he would never allow them "to bury the Guarache." "If you are on my side," Gonzales defiantly said, "I want you to help me protect my home." Some Guaraches were even more defiant: if the Botas tried to march, the Guaraches would spend the next few days "buying cemetery lots and improving them." "Someone else," besides the Guarache, was "going to be buried," Gonzales promised.[47] Other threats spewed forth when the Guaraches learned that the Bota band intended to insult several young women who had presented the Guaraches with a colorful banner only days before the election.

Other Guaraches, accompanied by cannoneer Moran in his red shirt, assembled on Iturbide Street and pointed their cannon directly at the Bota hall. One young Guarache defiantly waved their red and black banner, as if to challenge the Botas to mortal combat.[48] Many on both sides were armed with Colt revolvers and Winchester rifles. Promptly at 5:30 p.m., trumpets sounded, and the Bota band struck up a lively marching tune. A hundred jubilant voices could be heard, all speaking Spanish, as the Bota victory parade began. In front walked W. H. Adams carrying the party banner, followed by Sheriff Darío Sánchez and Judge José M. Rodríguez on horseback. Next came a procession of four men abreast followed by the Bota band. A line

AYER

a las seis de la tarde fallecieron

en está ciudad y en la FLOR de su edad,

El Club Gonzalez-Guarache

y sus organos La Voz del Pueblo y La Geringa.

[Q. E. P. D.]

Sus denodados partidarios, al participar al Gran Círculo Demócrata La Bota y la Sociedad "Union Mexicana," tan triste, prematuro y previsto acontecimiento, suplican a sus miembros y correligionarios, se dignen elevar al Sér Supremo las preces que su piedad les dicte, por el eterno descanso de los finados, y concurrir á los funerales y entierro que tendrán lugar hoy á las tres de la tarde.

El cortejo fúnebre se reunirá en el salon de Las Dos Republicas.

One of the events that precipitated the bloody 1886 Election Riot was the printing and distribution of a funeral notice by the Botas that celebrated the death of the Guarache Party.

YESTERDAY
At six in the evening died
In this city, and in the Flower of their age,
THE CLUB GONZALES-GUARACHE
May they Rest in Peace
Their devoted supporters, in announcing to the Grand Democratic Society, La Bota and the Society "Union Mexicano," such a sad premature and unforeseen occurrence beg their members and associates to have the goodness to raise to the Supreme Being the eternal rest of the deceased, and to attend the funeral services and burial which will take place at three in the afternoon. The funeral procession will assemble in the hall of Las Dos Republicas.
Laredo, Texas, April 7, 1886
Warm Weather and Bad Whiskey.

of men, two abreast and about sixty long, all armed with rifles and pistols, closely followed.[49] Thirty men on horseback, who were also armed, brought up the rear. The noisy procession made its way east on Iturbide Street and down Flores Avenue to the treeless San Agustín Plaza, as several of Martin's daughters showered the procession with flowers from the second story of the Commercial Hotel. Sheriff Darío Sánchez said that as he led the Bota procession down Flores Street, heading for the plaza, Santos emerged from Eulalio Benavides's house and stood defiantly on the street, "a belt of cartridges around his waist."[50]

A large, disorganized group of armed Guaraches, their band merrily playing "El Torito," followed the Botas.[51] One group broke off from the main body and rushed to San Agustín Avenue and Grant Street, where they planted their cannon in the middle of the intersection.

No one knows who fired the first shot. Darío Gonzales claimed that as the Botas were marching east along the south side of the plaza, a Guarache named Francisco García single-handedly rode forward and attempted to stop the procession. Sheriff Sánchez was heard to say, "Quico, go away, we don't want to fight, we are peacefully celebrating," but just as García turned to go, Plutarco Ortiz took aim and shot him off his horse.[52] Others claimed the gun battle erupted when Concepcion "Chono" Herrera, who was hurrying to join the Bota parade, fired two shots in the air, screaming that he was "going to kill [the] cabrón Guaraches."[53]

Regardless of who fired the first shot, rifle, pistol, and cannon fire began to echo across the plaza. The Guaraches, it was said, attacked the Botas from the front and rear, "breaking their ranks and scattering them in confusion."[54] The Botas had contemplated just such an attack, however, and had cleverly positioned snipers on the roofs of a number of homes and businesses in the vicinity of the plaza.

April 7, 1886, would long be remembered as the day the streets of Laredo ran red with blood. In less than five minutes, more than five thousand rounds of gunfire were exchanged in and around San Agustín Plaza in what is certain to have been one of the largest gun battles in the history of the

American West. As many as 250 men were involved in the fighting at one time or another. Bullets "whistled from all directions, from windows and from behind street corners."[55] Those who later walked through the scene of the fighting said the plaza and adjacent streets resembled a Civil War battlefield. Hundreds of shell casings littered the plaza, and the bodies of the dead and wounded lay scattered on the ground. After filling his cannon with nails, scrap iron, and rocks, Moran fired several salvos at the Botas on the south side of the plaza. Fortunately, his aim was inaccurate, and the cannon shots did little more than damage several buildings. During the heaviest of the fighting, a band of Botas attempted to capture the cannon, but one of the Guaraches rode forward on horseback and in a shower of gunfire, lassoed the cannon and pulled it to safety.[56]

Like the other merchants in the city, Cristóbal Benavides closed his store as soon as the Bota parade started. Natividad Herrera, a relative and Civil War comrade, was in the store at the time, however, and he rushed up the back stairs to get a better view of the fighting, just as a number of Botas fired at him. Recognizing one of the men, Herrera shouted, "José Mariano García! What are you shooting at me for, you idiot?" No sooner had Herrera finished than "a bullet ripped off his hat after which he raised his Winchester and emptied it into the crowd," Cristóbal recalled. At the same time, a number of Botas indiscriminately fired several shots into Cristóbal's residence a few blocks away, narrowly missing his wife, Lamar, and their children. Three days later, Cristóbal was still unable to control his anger. "We picked up a number of bullets in the house," he told a *San Antonio Express* reporter. "Here is one which struck within a few inches of [my wife's] head. I am keeping it and will remold it and return it, through my pistol, to the man who fired it at her."[57]

For two days following the bloodletting, the bells of San Agustín Church tolled as a number of funeral processions wound through the streets, carrying the victims of the violence to their final resting places. The day after the riot, the church held eight funeral Masses.[58] The names of sixteen of the victims are known, including a number of Santos's relatives and friends. Several of the victims were from Nuevo Laredo, men lured across the river by politics but buried in their native Mexico. Several of the dead were quietly buried without religious services.[59] Almost everyone in town admitted that the officially reported number of dead was perhaps only half of those actually killed. Bonnie Leyendecker, Santos's nephew and a leading Guarache who had witnessed much of the fighting, estimated the number of dead at sixty, with many more wounded.[60]

At Fort McIntosh a mile west of town, Bvt. Col. Ruben F. Bernard of the Eighth US Cavalry, a seasoned Civil War veteran of Cold Harbor and Appomattox Court House, had under his command eighty-four men of the Sixteenth US Infantry and fifty-three men of the Eighth Cavalry.[61] "Expecting . . . trouble for some time," Bernard had closely observed what he called "a horde of cutthroats and outlaws, both from Mexico and Laredo," who were awaiting any opportunity to "cross to the other side of the river to pillage either of the Laredos."[62] In the late afternoon, as the Botas began their victory parade, Bernard became particularly alarmed at the large number of Mexicans who were crossing the river.

When he heard the crack of gunfire and the booming of the Guarache cannon, Bernard knew the trouble had begun. He hurriedly dispatched a staff officer into the city, and the man came racing back with news that the violence was worse than anyone imagined. Twenty men were already dead. Leaving the cavalry under arms and on guard at the fort, Bernard took his two companies of infantry, formed them into columns of four, and double-timed them into the city. Heavily armed and carrying field-marching packs on their backs, the African American soldiers were not deterred. Several volleys of rifle fire passed close to them, but without looking right or left or breaking rank, they marched until they reached Market Hall. They quickly disarmed anyone carrying a gun and filled an army ambulance with an array of weapons, including shotguns, pistols, and rifles. Bernard declared martial law, and he ordered both the Guarache and Bota headquarters locked, the saloons closed, and the ferry to halt service. No one was permitted on the streets after dark unless they had a pass. Squads of soldiers patrolled the streets and riverbanks.[63]

As night settled in, Bernard sent squads of men to guard the post office, the customhouse, and Milmo National Bank. A number of city and county officials crowded the telegraph office near San Agustín Plaza to get their version of the battle out to the rest of the world. Governor John Ireland agreed to send the state militia at once. Senator Hall, while blaming the Guaraches for the violence, asked the governor to send an "unbiased force" to "aid the civil authorities." Still influential in state politics, Santos also wired the governor, asking him to immediately send troops.[64]

On the day after the riot, twenty-five men of the San Antonio Belknap Rifles received an urgent telegram from the governor: "Preserve and enforce the law. Use great precaution."[65] Later in the day, as more telegrams reached Austin, Ireland agreed to send twenty-five more men to the border city, this time from the San Antonio Rifles. The governor also diverted to Laredo a company of Rangers bound for North Texas to help quell the labor violence there. At 3:20 a.m. on April 9, a special train of the I&GN pulled out of San Antonio carrying militiamen, Rangers, and "war" correspondents, all bound for Laredo. Speeding across the South Texas countryside at twenty-seven miles an hour, the men reached Cotulla by sunup, and by 9:50 a.m., they were in Laredo.[66]

More than a thousand Laredo citizens watched and cheered as the militia assembled on San Agustín Plaza. Within two days, however, the militiamen were back on the train, returning to San Antonio, and the town was left in the hands of the Rangers. Ranger captain George H. Schmitt reported to Austin that although "considerable excitement" prevailed in Laredo, the "citizens was [*sic*] awful glad we came." Sleeping at the courthouse and taking their meals at the Commercial Hotel, the Rangers patrolled the town day and night. "Things is in a bad state of affairs here, but my presents assure order and everybody are so far well pleased with me. Things is worse here than published in the papers," Schmitt wrote Austin. "I am satisfied that a new fight would be most unavoidable if I would leave."[67] Fifty-nine citizens, almost all of them Guaraches and including Santos Benavides, Darío Gonzales, Daniel Milmo, James J. Haynes, L. J. Christen, Juan V. Benavides, and John Z. Leyendecker, petitioned to governor to leave the Rangers in Laredo indefinitely.[68] Three weeks after the election riot, the Rangers were still in Laredo, and Schmitt was not expecting to leave the border for six months. "Trouble are liable to be up any day," he wrote. "The feelings of the two parties are very bitter."[69]

The reaction to the Laredo Election Riot throughout Texas and the nation was one of shock and disbelief. That so much blood had been shed in the city he had fought more than once to defend was embarrassing for Santos. And as a leading reformer, he also helped instigate the violence. At the same time, he continued to see the cause of the Guarache Party as moral and righteous. In a letter to the *Galveston Daily News*, Santos referred to the riot as a "great disorder" while reminding readers that such violence was not a regular occurrence at Laredo. "The devil takes advantage of a weak spot," he continued.[70] Governor Ireland, too, found the riot disconcerting and vowed to prevent any repetition of the bloodshed. Any public official in Laredo who was guilty of any wrongdoing should be ousted from office, he argued.[71]

Several leading Texas newspapers, including the *Galveston Daily News* and the *San Antonio Express*, sent their best reporters to the border to cover the aftermath of the violence.[72] Laredo and Nuevo Laredo newspapers such as *El Horizonte, La Voz del Pueblo*, *El Laredense*, and the *Laredo Times* were certain to have done the same. Unfortunately, no copy of any Laredo or Nuevo Laredo newspaper survives for the entire month of April 1886.

The legal ramifications of the riot kept a host of leading Laredo and Texas attorneys busy for years afterward. As expected, Santos was in the middle of the litigation. The most widely publicized court battle began when Santos and the Guaraches attempted to remove Sheriff Darío Sánchez from office. Labeled *State of Texas, Ex. Rel. Daniel Milmo, Santos Benavides, et al. v. Darío Sánchez*, the struggle caught the imagination of the entire community, and sixteen leading Guaraches joined the case as plaintiffs.[73] The sheriff was accused of "incompetency and official misconduct" and with "prostituting his office." Prior to the election violence, Sánchez had appointed sixty-two deputies, forty-nine of whom were "ignorant of the English language."[74] On the day of the riot, moreover, Sánchez had led the deputies through the streets, knowing that his actions would lead to violence. The sheriff was also charged with directing the jailer not to receive any Botas who were arrested for voting illegally on the day of the election. The case opened in early June in the courtroom of the heavy-drinking judge John C. Russell, who was known to be a Guarache sympathizer, and Russell agreed to suspend Sánchez until the case could be decided. Bota attorneys tried unsuccessfully to persuade the state attorney general that the law Judge Russell used to suspend Sánchez was unconstitutional. They next asked Russell to dismiss the case, but he ruled the charges against the sheriff were "too grave for dismissal."[75]

Selecting an unbiased jury in politically charged Laredo was virtually impossible. After calling several hundred potential jurymen, nine Anglos and three African Americans were eventually chosen. Thirty-six witnesses were subpoenaed, including all the leading Botas. By mid-June the temperature in Laredo had soared well past 100 degrees, and witnesses were said to be sporting "palm fans" and "squirming under examination."[76] By late June, the case went to the jury, and hundreds gathered around the courthouse to await the verdict. Rumors on the street said that the jury stood eleven to one for acquittal and that the final verdict was expected momentarily. The next day, however, the jury reported they were hopelessly deadlocked, and Judge Russell declared a mistrial. At the time, the jury stood eight to four for acquittal.[77] Guarache attorneys asked that the case be transferred to Nueces County, but before Russell could act on the motion, the Bota county commissioners met and, in a bit of legal chicanery, declared the office of sheriff vacant, then, at the same meeting, reinstated Sánchez. After several more days of legal wrangling and maneuvering, Russell ruled their action legal, and Sánchez resumed his duties as sheriff.[78]

Throughout the summer, Judge Russell continued to hear cases resulting from the riot. A grand jury was impaneled, and the judge, in a "long and emphatic charge," asked that they give no quarter. Indictments were to be handed down against "all who took part in the late riot, all who supplied arms and all who encouraged the riot by word or gesture." Sometimes working into the night, the grand jury heard a seemingly endless line of witnesses—both Botas and Guaraches. Lists of individuals from both parties who were thought to be involved in the violence were checked and rechecked. The grand jury remained in session for five weeks and handed down over 350 indictments.[79] Although Marshall Stephen Boyard, County Judge José María Rodríguez, Mayor E. A. Atlee, and Sheriff Darío Sánchez were all indicted for malfeasance of office, their cases were eventually dismissed.[80] In the end, the court cases settled little between the two rival parties. Although the city council passed an ordinance prohibiting political processions, politics in Laredo remained confrontational and dangerous.[81]

Tempers were calmed somewhat when the political violence was followed by yet another smallpox scare. City officials hurried to quarantine parts of the city, and the lists of the dead, especially paupers, grew long. But it was the April riot that continued to haunt the city.

Well into the fall, the Democratic Party remained deeply divided, and Webb County sent two rival delegations to the state and congressional conventions. In June, José María Rodríguez, county judge and county chairman, had called the Democratic Party together to select delegates to the state convention. The meeting was scheduled for 5:00 p.m. at Market Hall, but while Judge Rodríguez was busy greeting and chatting with Bota partisans outside the meeting, the Guaraches gathered inside and hastily passed a motion to replace Chairman Rodríguez with Juan Benavides.[82] When Rodríguez finally entered the hall, those present were already in the process of selecting delegates. Following Rodríguez's lead, Botas flooded out of the hall in anger to stage a rump convention and select their own delegates.[83]

By early October numerous people, mostly from Laredo and Brownsville, had asked Santos to run as an independent Democrat against E. A.

Around 1900, men pose in front of the Western Union Telegraph and Cable Office on Iturbide Street, next to the jewelry store of Leon Daiches. Daiches later relocated to Flores Avenue. *Courtesy collection of Federico E. Vidaurri. Digital restoration by Irene Vidaurri Zubeck.*

Atlee for state senator. Atlee was a leading Laredo attorney and a Bota favorite who had been mayor of Laredo during the election riot and who was selected as senator following the death of E. F. Hall. The politically influential Guy B. Broadwater, a mounted customs inspector, was determined to persuade Santos once again to seek state office. Broadwater had toured Duval County, where it was said Santos would get a majority of at least 250 votes, including those of "all the best men of the county." In late September, Broadwater asked James B. Wells to visit both Hidalgo and Starr Counties and do everything he could for Santos. "You know as well as I do what old Santos is, but when dealing with the devil fight him with fire," Broadwater told Wells.[84] Although Santos's fighting spirit was still evident, he declined to seek office and pledged to support the regular Democrat nominee.[85]

In 1885, even before the election riot, Santos had been invited to visit Secretary of War Manuel González, a close friend, Tamaulipecan, and former president, but most important to Santos, a "blood relation." On November 17, 1885, with Agustina by his side, Santos headed downriver by stage to Matamoros, where he was greeted by Warren P. Sutton, US consul, and John W. Foster, the popular American minister to Mexico. Santos would later recall the "kindness and attention" Foster extended to him and Agustina.[86] Governor Servando Canales placed the gunboat *Libertad* at the travelers' disposal, and from Bagdad at the mouth of the river, the small boat sailed through the placid waters of the Gulf Coast, past Tampico and Tuxpan to historic Veracruz. Under a tropical sun, the party boarded the recently completed Ferrocarril Mexicano, which clattered west across the *tierra caliente*, past Córdoba and into the mountains at Orizaba, through tunnels and past streams and waterfalls, all the time climbing steadily upward. For Santos, son of the hot, dry, flat South Texas landscapes, it was a strange and magical land.

Leaving the verdant banana and coffee plantations for the more arid *tierra templada*, Santos looked to the north and saw the magnificent snow-clad volcanic cone of Pico de Orizaba, or Citlaltépetl, the third-highest mountain in North America. The train rattled on through the night past cornfields and small villages to Puebla, where Gen. Ignacio Zaragoza had stood against the French in 1862. Some 260 miles from the coast, the Ferrocarril Mexicano entered the great Valley of Mexico. Skirting the shallow, brackish waters of Lake Texcoco, the train rolled past ruined Aztec temples, past the hill where the Virgin Mary was said to have appeared before the young Indian Juan Diego, and finally into the bustling railroad station on Calle de las Estaciones in the heart of the capital. Here he was greeted by a delegation sent by President Díaz. "[Santos Benavides] naturally possesses a deep and sincere sympathy with our country and has ever been the friend of the Mexicans," wrote *El Partido Liberal*, one of Díaz's political organs.[87]

In Mexico City, Santos met on more than one occasion with Díaz, visited with Díaz's cabinet, and sat down with his old compatriot, Manuel González. In Santos's words, he also held "frequent conferences with many prominent senators." He had a friendly meeting with Gen. José Francisco Naranjo de la Garza, who had recently served as minister of war under González and who had only days earlier arrived in the capital from Monterrey. Santos was also able to observe the Mexican Congress in session, and he came away impressed. Everyone he met spoke of improving relations with their neighbor to the north. As a "native son" and someone markedly proud of his Mexican ancestry, Santos felt obligated to carry such feelings back to the United States.[88]

Back in Laredo, Santos wasted little time in writing Governor Oran Milo Roberts of his visit to Mexico and the friendly views of President Díaz and others toward Texas and the United States. In response, Roberts promised to do everything in his power to improve the relations between the two neighbors. Santos also took the time to write a lengthy, often rambling, letter to William M. Evarts, the former secretary of state and influential senator from New York. The letter was published in the *Galveston Daily News* under the headline "How the Mexicans Love Us." To improve relations with Mexico and the flow of commerce between the two countries, Santos was hoping the Harvard Law School–educated Evarts would do everything he could to push the pending US-Mexico reciprocity treaty through the Senate. Santos assured the former secretary that everyone in the Mexican capital, especially Porfirio Díaz, was anxious to "promote every measure calculated to more firmly establish and cement such international reciprocity as will tend to closer intimacy and happier relationships."[89]

Santos had no doubt that if the two republics would only cooperate, the "ripples of discord" that had characterized their relations for decades could be overcome, border raids stopped, "renegades and lawless" on the Rio Grande brought to justice, commerce promoted, and "general intercourse and business advanced."[90] Santos made it known that he was speaking from experience, having personally visited with President Díaz, former president González, several prominent Mexican senators, and border governors such as Servando Canales of Tamaulipas and Francisco Navarro of Nuevo León. All were interested in "promoting closer intimacy and [a] happier relationship" with the United States, he said.[91]

To impress Evarts, Santos pointed out that his great-great-grandfather had once been a captain in the service of the Spanish empire. He not only took great pride in his ancestry but pointed out that he had lived on the border for sixty-three years. The frontier "is as the land of the Pilgrims to me," he wrote. His ancestors had struggled to defend Laredo from the Native Americans and maintain a "foothold" until the "flag of the United States covered them as citizens and gave them protection." Playing somewhat loosely with the facts, Santos said that he and Servando Canales, who was born and reared in Camargo, had been "raised together." He had been friends with Gen. Francisco Naranjo since the two were children. Moreover, as he always emphasized, Manuel González was a "blood relation."[92]

At the same time that he worked to promote relations between the United States and Mexico, Santos worked to ease the leeriness in Mexico about railroad connections with the United States. Many in Mexico saw the north–south railroad lines as making the country more dependent on the United States and more susceptible to an invasion should the two countries ever come to war again.[93] In March 1887 Santos made yet another trip to Mexico City, this time traveling on the I&GN to San Antonio; then west on the Galveston, Harrisburg, and San Antonio, across the arid expanses and twisting canyons of the Trans-Pecos, to El Paso; then across the river to El Paso del Norte, or what would become Ciudad Juárez the following year, where he was able to obtain passage on the Mexican Central Railroad, the first such railroad to connect Mexico City to Texas. He rode south across the burning sands of the Chihuahuan Desert to Ciudad Chihuahua, Torreón, the old silver-mining city of Zacatecas, and Aguas Calientes, before turning southeast to the quaint old colonial city of Querétaro and, finally, the capital.[94] This time he would see more of Texas and Mexico than ever before.

Everywhere Santos went, he saw progress: railroads, "educational establishments, industrial enterprises," and other "material improvements of importance." For Santos, the Porforiato was a glorious epoch in Mexican history, and the "energetic hand" of Díaz was altogether evident. The Pax Porfiriana was supported by "safeguards and security," he said, intended to "attract foreign capitalists who with entire confidence" would be able "to assist and encourage the advancement of the country."[95] In reality, however, he was witnessing the growing might of American economic imperialism.

In the capital, Santos was greeted much as he had been before. Two military officers, both fluent in English, were assigned to see to his every need. "Born in Mexican territory, he naturally possesses a deep and sincere sympathy with our country and [he] has ever been the friend of the Mexicans," the pro-Díaz Mexico City press reported.[96] The *Two Republics* went as far as to say that Santos was "one of the most prominent men residing on the left bank of the Rio Grande." The Mexican press hoped that Santos would return to Texas with a "favorable impression of this country as will win . . . the respect and esteem of the people of that country." Back in Laredo, Santos wrote the *Galveston Daily News* with his impressions of Mexico, saying he was "full of pleasant impressions" of the progress of the country.[97] In many ways Santos had become the unofficial Mexican ambassador to the United States.

Well into the latter part of his life, Santos did much to promote the building and expansion of railroads in Texas and Mexico. He took a personal interest in the construction of the Mexican National Railway Company, headed by Gen. William Jackson Palmer, which was feverishly building a narrow-gauge track south from Nuevo Laredo to Lampazos, Monterrey, Saltillo, across the desert to San Luis Potosí, and then south through Morelia to Mexico City. He welcomed the general manager of the company, J. F. O'Brien, to his home and wrote him a letter of introduction to Porfirio Díaz. Santos considered O'Brien "an intimate friend" and told Díaz O'Brien was "a gentleman with good education and great capabilities" and "a friend of the Mexican people."[98]

Santos and Agustina even visited the American heartland. In June 1886, only weeks after the terrible election riot, the couple caught the I&GN

View looking north on Salinas Avenue. *Courtesy collection of Federico E. Vidaurri. Digital restoration by Irene Vidaurri Zubeck.*

to Burlington, Iowa, to see their old friend E. S. Edger, superintendent of the Burlington Northern Railroad. In Iowa the local press interviewed the "old Spanish nobleman of Old Mexico" and reported that Santos was a "fine looking old gentleman, full of the highbred courtesy of the traditional Spanish and [that he] enjoyed his visit thoroughly.[99] From Burlington, Santos and Agustina traveled by train to Washington, DC, for a tour of the nation's capital, where, Santos wrote President Díaz, he had "many friends."[100]

CHAPTER IX

INTERNATIONAL DIPLOMAT

"As the venerated old gentleman descended from the rostrum, cheer after cheer rent the air and the bands began to play."

—*San Antonio Daily Express*, April 8, 1889

In the twilight of his life, Santos continued to promote the causes of binational friendship and lasting peace with great vigor and determination. He worked hard on improving relations between Mexico and the United States ever since he was elected to the Texas House of Representatives and Porfirio Díaz had ascended to the presidency of Mexico. On January 2, 1886, Santos wrote a lengthy letter to the *Galveston Daily News* saying that because of his personal friendship with the people of Nuevo León, he could assure everyone north of the border that President Díaz had not intervened in the change of leadership in Nuevo León, as had been widely reported in the American press. Genaro Garza García had been removed by the National Congress in accordance with the Mexican Constitution, and Gen. Bernardo Reyes, a Díaz partisan, had been appointed as the provisional governor until elections could be held, Santos reported. He also claimed that the rumors of a rift between President Díaz and former president Manuel González were false. Santos even included two letters from González saying that he and Díaz continued to be good friends and that they were not in disagreement with one another. Despite considerable disorder in Monterrey, González assured Santos, the "public peace will not be disturbed."[1] Certainly Mexico was not in the midst of revolution, as had been reported in the United States.

In an exchange of letters with Díaz later in 1886, Santos pressed for the release of Mariano Arguindegui, a young Laredoan who enlisted in the Mexican army at the age of fourteen, only to desert. Captured by Mexican authorities, Arguindegui was promptly court-martialed, found guilty of desertion, and sentenced to three years in a military prison in Monterrey.[2] Santos learned from the young man's mother, who was a "very good and honorable woman," that Arguindegui was sick and near death, and Santos was hoping the president could make arrangements for Arguindegui to return to his "poor mother."[3] Assuming there were no extenuating circumstances and the case was simply one of desertion, Díaz saw no problem in granting a pardon, but he wanted Santos to petition the minister of war, Gen. Pedro Hinojosa, for Arguindegui's release.[4] Fortunately, Hinojosa, whom Santos knew personally for many years, was a Tamaulipecan by birth. On October 3, the president telegraphed Santos to say that a pardon had been granted. The case was difficult, the president said, but he was doing Santos a personal favor. "I give you the most gracious thanks for your kindness," Santos wrote Díaz, as he hurried south to escort Arguindegui to Laredo.[5]

In August 1886, Santos asked Díaz for a donation to help with the construction of a home for destitute Confederate veterans to be built on Sixth Street in Austin, which was being promoted by the John Bell Hood Camp of United Confederate Veterans and the Albert Sidney Johnston Chapter of the United Daughters of the Confederacy.[6] Will Lambert, a leading Texas journalist who had been on the staff of Gen. Edmund Kirby Smith during the war and whom Santos had known when Lambert was chief clerk and secretary to the Texas House of Representatives, asked Santos to contact Díaz. With Santos's blessing, Lambert wrote Díaz to ask for a contribution and reminded the president that the two men met when Díaz visited Austin. Impressed with Díaz's "democratic manners," Lambert described to the president the large number of wounded Confederate veterans who were "fast accumulating in . . . cities and towns." These "old heroes of a lost cause" were "indigent and disabled," Lambert went on to say; they were unable to

With his son-in-law Lázaro Garza Ayala by his side, Santos Benavides conspired with Mariano Escobedo in 1876 to smuggle arms into Mexico to support forces opposed to Porfirio Diáz. But as Diáz consolidated power in Mexico, Benavides befriended the Mexican strongman and the two became close. In the last decade of his life, Santos carried on a lively and warm correspondence with Diáz, frequently traveling by train to Mexico City for visits with the autocrat, even staying at the president's residence and exchanging gifts with him. Struggling to maintain law and order on the border and dispel racial stereotypes of Tejanos and Mexicans, Benavides aspired to become the American minister to Mexico but did not meet with success. Chased into exile in 1911, Diáz died in Paris four years later.
Courtesy Library of Congress.

care for themselves, had been caught in the "race of life," and were compelled to "give way to the young and vigorous."[7] Any people, Lambert said, who "forget their soldiers, whether in victory or defeat, are base ingrates." Lambert was hoping the president could somehow manage to make a contribution. With the endorsement of his son-in-law, Lázaro Garza Ayala, Santos also encouraged Díaz, with his "noble sentiments," to "contribute something."[8] There is no evidence that Díaz expressed any sympathy or responded to the plea for help from Texas: Mexico had bigger problems than decrepit Confederate veterans.

Throughout the decade of the 1880s, Santos acted as Díaz's emissary on the border, always keeping the Mexican dictator abreast of political events in Texas and the United States. Santos consistently sent Díaz newspapers from Texas, provided assessments of the latest news, and kept an eye on Mexican dissidents who had taken refuge in Texas and were agitating for the overthrow of the Díaz regime. In June 1886, Santos went as far as to warn the president that disgruntled Mexican revolutionaries on the Rio Grande were planning "some military preparations" against the president although he did not specify where. "Because of my affection for Mexico, for our friendship, and for the honor of the Mexican government," Santos promised he would do everything within his power to help curtail such "wrongs."[9] He had confidence US marshals would arrest anyone in Texas plotting against the president and in violation of the American neutrality laws.

In September 1886, there were some revolutionary Juaristas on the border, Santos said, but they were few in number and harmless and he would use his influence to see that they were investigated to determine if they were purchasing arms. In another instance, Santos assured the president he was "following the coyote closely" and would catch him.[10] Exactly who the coyote was Santos did not specify, although he may have been referring to Ruiz Sandoval, who owned a small store in Laredo and who in October 1886 was in the center of anti-Díaz agitation in Brownsville. Santos assured the president that the "good American citizens are all in favor of you" and there was nothing to worry about.[11] By 1887, opposition to the Díaz dictatorship emerged in Laredo with the publication of several Spanish-language newspapers. One such newspaper, *El Mutualista*, was owned and edited by Juan Zardeneta, who bluntly and consistently called for Díaz to be overthrown and referred to him as a tyrant.[12]

In early 1885, Santos was instrumental in arranging an invitation for Díaz to participate in the laying of the cornerstone for the new capitol in Austin that was to replace the old structure that burned in 1881. The president wrote Santos, however, that he was too busy with official business in Mexico City. Nevertheless, his letter "was replete with expressions of good wishes for the Lone Star State."[13]

There were endless advantages in having access to the president of Mexico. Once Santos devised a scheme to act as a middleman in an arms sale to the Díaz regime, telling the president he could provide weapons at the lowest price possible. There is no evidence such a deal was ever consummated, however. To cement his friendship with Díaz, Santos frequently sent the president gifts. Agustina even sent Díaz's second wife, Carmen Romero Rubio, a box of flower and garden seeds that she had promised during a visit to Mexico City.[14] Although she was thirty-four years younger than the president, Carmen Romero Rubio had married Díaz in November of 1881, and the two had traveled across the United States on their honeymoon, the young bride tutoring her husband in English as they went. Santos became so enthralled with Díaz he wrote the president asking for a photograph, and when the image arrived in Laredo several weeks later, Santos had it nicely framed and placed on the desk in his office.[15]

Santos and Agustina were able to visit Mexico City again in March 1886. After arriving in the capitol, they immediately took up residence in the president's mansion. Although the president was out of town, Santos wrote him with a copy of a letter he had written to the *Galveston Daily News*, promoting good relations between the United States and Mexico. Santos assured the autocrat that he had letters from both houses of the US Congress speaking highly of Díaz and his administration and wishing him well.[16] When Díaz ran for reelection two years later in 1888, Santos assured the president, "[All the] good and prominent men of the United States of America desire your reelection."[17] Several months later, Santos wrote the president again, this time to say that Governor Lawrence Sullivan "Sul" Ross of Texas, whom Santos called an "intimate friend," was hoping to visit Mexico City in the near future. Santos asked Díaz to receive Ross with great kindness and as a good friend of the Mexican Republic.[18]

Although growing old and frequently ill for weeks at a time, Santos dove headlong into the fight over prohibition in 1886 and 1887. The contentious issue had captured the nation's attention for decades, but it was not until the arrival of the Woman's Christian Temperance Union in 1883 that the movement came to the forefront of Texas politics. The constitution of 1876 allowed for local "wet-dry" elections, but the prohibitionists, who thought the consumption of alcohol was immoral and the root of much evil, wanted the manufacture and sale of all alcoholic beverages outlawed statewide. Both US senators, John H. Reagan and Samuel Bell Maxey, supported prohibition, but Santos's good friend Governor Ross was satisfied with local choice. So fervent were the prohibitionists that they formed a third party and nominated Ebenezer Lafayette Dohoney, a Kentucky-born lawyer, for governor. In November 1886, the popular Ross, whom Dohoney accused of being a "saloon stump speaker," received 78 percent of the vote, decisively defeating the Republican candidate, A. M. Cochran of Dallas, as well as Dohoney. In spite of their poor showing in the November election, the Prohibition party pushed for a constitutional amendment to prevent the production, sale, or exchange of alcoholic beverages. In the spring of 1887, the legislature decided to allow the "wets" and "drys" to settle their differences in a statewide referendum to be held on August 4, 1887.

On April 23, 1887, Santos called for a public meeting at Milmo Hall on Market Plaza. Hundreds flocked to the hall to hear him lash out at the prohibitionists in eloquent Spanish. Prohibition would have a negative influence on everyone, especially the poor, Santos said, since the rich "could easily find means to defeat the law."[19] Santos pledged to help defeat the proposed amendment, and he found a powerful ally in Raymond Martin, his old political adversary. At the conclusion of the meeting, as the applause subsided, Martin came forth to read a long letter asking the citizens in Webb and Encinal Counties to vote against the proposed amendment. In Webb County, where few fundamentalist Protestants lived, the proposed amendment was decisively defeated 194 to 56. To the east in sparsely settled Encinal County, all twelve voters cast their ballots for the "wets."[20] Statewide, the election drew more voters than the contest for governor the previous year. With minorities voting heavily against the amendment, the "wets" won easily: 220,627 to 129,270.[21]

A few days before Christmas 1887, Santos received a letter from Lewis E. Daniell saying he would be featured, along with Sam Houston, Richard Coke, and John H. Reagan, in an illustrated book entitled *Types of Successful Men of Texas*. Although Daniell wanted as much biographical information as possible, as well as a photograph, Santos did not provide either.[22] The book was not published for another three years, and even then Santos was only one of 172 Texans to be featured.[23]

In 1890, Santos received a letter from his old Civil War commander and nemesis, John S. "Rip" Ford. Ford was certainly one of the most important individuals on the nineteenth-century Texas frontier, and in the nostalgic years of his later life, he began to prepare his memoirs for publication. Ford drew from his personal archive, which he collected over the decades, but he could not find a copy of Santos's account of his gallant defense of Laredo in March 1864, nor did Ford have any information on Santos's application to become a brigadier general. In the months that followed, Ford repeatedly asked Santos for his assistance, but Santos, still bitter about never being promoted to brigadier general, did not bother to reply. Frustrated, Ford bluntly warned Santos that if he wanted to be in the book, he must furnish the information requested. If Santos refused, his "reputation as an officer" could be negatively affected.[24] Because of ill health or possibly out of spite, Santos again failed to respond. Although Ford was still peeved at Santos for refusing to answer his repeated requests for information, Ford remained amazingly objective, eventually writing that Santos was "one of the best known, most trusted, influential citizens of Southwest Texas" and giving him full credit for the exceptional role he had played on the border during the Civil War. Ford even included a copy of Santos's official report of his defense of Laredo, which Ford had managed to find somewhere.[25]

For years, starting in October 1884, the *Laredo Times* and other Texas newspapers, along with a handful of Texas politicians, had been suggesting that Santos head a "mission to Mexico" meant to improve relations between the two republics. Although such a position would be "a just tribute of an old veteran who has rendered in the past invaluable service to Texas," Santos said he had no interest in "that direction, preferring to remain among the people he [had] known and loved so long."[26] However, even rumors of such an appointment were a "tribute to an old warrior," the *Laredo Times* proclaimed.[27]

In 1887, Roger Quarles Mills, Texas congressman and chairman of the powerful House Ways and Means Committee, began promoting Santos to President Grover Cleveland as minister to Mexico. Mills told the president that he and Santos had been friends since they were in their youth and that no citizen of Texas was more honorable than Santos. Cleveland bluntly responded that he had no intention of appointing a Texan. Instead, he named a North Carolina jurist and party hack, Thomas Courtland Manning, who had little knowledge of Mexico and who spoke no Spanish.[28]

In May 1888, Santos traveled north to Austin for the last time. General Garza Ayala had received an invitation to attend the dedication of the spectacular new capitol building but unable to attend, he asked his father-in-law to represent him instead. Carrying a congratulatory letter from Garza Ayala to Governor Ross, Santos arrived in the capital only hours before crowds began lining Congress Avenue and filling the capitol grounds for the dedication, a grand parade, and festive ceremonies.[29] As an honored guest representing the state of Nuevo León, Santos was treated with great respect and shown every "possible courtesy and attention by Governor Ross."

The Goddess of Liberty was already placed on the dome as Temple Houston, son of Sam Houston, accepted the 310-foot-high, 392-room red

The much decorated Lázaro Garza Ayala, three time governor of Nuevo León, married Santos Benavides's adopted daughter, Agustina, at San Agustín Church in February 1867. Agustina died of yellow fever at the age of thirty-four in the summer of 1882. Garza Ayala fought with Santiago Vidaurri in the War of the Reform and with Benito Juárez and the Liberals against the Imperialists. Garza Ayala outlived his wife by thirty-one years, dying in May 1913. *Courtesy Library of Congress.*

granite building, which was larger than the Capitol Building in Washington, DC, on behalf of the state of Texas. "This building fires the heart and excites reflections in the minds of all," Houston was quoted as saying.[30] Santos took particular pride in the state legislature, in session in the new capitol for the first time, passing a resolution honoring him for his service as state representative.[31] Special streetcar lines had been built to encampment grounds one mile from the city, where Santos watched drill teams compete, bands play a variety of lively and patriotic tunes, and fireworks lit the Austin sky. Thrilled but exhausted, Santos returned to Laredo with several souvenir albums containing photographs of the capitol and leading state officials. The "grandeur of the mammoth capital building, the vast amphitheater," along with the pomp and pageantry, were overwhelming," Santos said, but his description of the Austin festivities showed that he had "highly enjoyed" his trip to Austin.[32]

Back in Laredo, serious problems were again erupting on the border. At Rio Grande City in September 1888, the Starr County sheriff W. W. Shelby, notorious for being involved in the lynching of several alleged Mexican bandits, arrested Abraham Reséndez for robbery. Shortly thereafter, Reséndez was shot and killed by the US inspector of customs, Victor Sebree, while supposedly trying to escape. The incident sparked a violent public outrage. Two activists, Agustín and Silverio de la Peña, charged the sheriff with racism, and they vowed to defeat him at the next election. They were helped by Catarino Erasmo Garza, a bright and articulate Mexican journalist who was active in the Corpus Christi area, agitating against Porfirio Díaz. Garza arrived in Rio Grande City for the September elections and during a confrontation with Sebree at a barbershop was shot and wounded by the customs inspector. Inflamed by the shooting as well as the cronyism and racism endemic in Starr County, Garza's sympathizers, said to number as many as two hundred, threatened to lynch Sebree and even pursued him to Ringgold Barracks, where he found refuge with the military.[33]

Exaggerated reports of anarchy in the streets of Rio Grande City quickly spread across Texas. To the Texas press, it was the 1886 Laredo Election

Riot all over again. The US Army rushed reinforcements to the border, and Governor Ross instructed the sheriffs of Bexar, Cameron, Hidalgo, and Zapata Counties to proceed with their deputies to Rio Grande City.[34] In all, as many as 250 heavily armed lawmen headed for Starr County. Meantime the governor ordered three companies of state militia—the San Antonio Rifles, Belknap Rifles, and Houston Light Guards—to be ready to march for the border at a moment's notice. Because Rio Grande City was little more than an armed camp, the threat of violence quickly dissipated, although Garza would later launch a revolution against Díaz in the area. From Laredo, Santos whipped out a letter to Governor Ross, complimenting the governor for preventing bloodshed at Rio Grande City.[35]

In November 1888, Santos received an urgent telegram from the Mexican consul in San Antonio saying that Gen. Enrique Guillermo Antonio Mexía—a Texan by birth whose father had been executed by Santa Anna, a veteran of the war against the French imperialists, and a friend of Santos for many years—was very sick and on the train headed for the border. The consul asked Santos to meet Mexía at the train station and escort him across the river. Not only did Santos meet the old general, he accompanied Mexía to Monterrey, after which Mexía continued on by train to Mexico City, where he lived for another eight years.[36]

Santos was honored once more on April 6, 1890, at the opening of the magnificent foot and wagon bridge across the Rio Grande. Five sturdy steel trusses, each 150 feet long, supported the new bridge, which stretched 18 feet wide and rose 30 feet above the waters of the Rio Grande. Promptly at 10:00 a.m. a procession of several thousand citizens and dignitaries left Market Plaza. At the same time, an equally large delegation departed Plaza Principal in Nuevo Laredo. The Americans were led by the Sixteenth US Infantry band, which came south by train from San Antonio along with the Laredo Amateur Brass Band, while the citizens of Nuevo Laredo followed a military band that had arrived from Lampazos. Within minutes of one another, the two delegations met at the center of the bridge, where a speakers' stand was erected. The entire bridge was decorated with colorful bunting

After the Civil War, a new Fort McIntosh was constructed that included four barracks buildings, three of which are shown in this image. The brick was procured locally, but the timbers were brought overland in wagons from Corpus Christi. Only one of the barracks buildings stands today as Arechiga Hall at Laredo Community College. Benavides initially set up his headquarters at the fort early in the Civil War. *Courtesy National Archives.*

and hundreds of small Mexican and American flags, and a huge streamer completely covering the Mexican end of the bridge bore the imperial cross of Saint George. Cannon from Fort McIntosh placed along the riverbank boomed out a twenty-one-gun salute that echoed up and down the Rio Grande. After the Mexican band had played the "Himno Nacional Mexicano," "Hail, Columbia" was ably performed by the Sixteenth US Infantry Band. Citizens from both sides of the river were seen to wipe tears from their eyes. Pedro Arguëlles, representing Mexico, gave a stirring speech in Spanish, after which Capt. Thomas Dodd, a prominent Laredo attorney, delivered an equally patriotic speech in English.

Although quite ill, Santos had been named the international orator by a committee made up of citizens from both sides of the river. As four thousand people listened quietly, he read a carefully prepared speech, not in Spanish, as was his custom, but in English. The dedication of the bridge, Santos said, was a "celebration of great significance" to both Mexicans and Americans. But the bridge across the Rio Grande represented much more:

"It represents the band of union that binds more firmly the friendly relations of two people" destined to "live in peace and fraternity." "As the venerated old gentleman descended from the rostrum, cheer after cheer rent the air and the bands began to play," the *San Antonio Daily Express* reported. After the music had finally quieted, letters were read from President Díaz, Governor Ross, the commander of the Department of Texas, and the governor of Tamaulipas. Following the ceremony, the people of the two nations respectfully exchanged places. Laredoans marched into Nuevo Laredo, and Mexicans crossed into Laredo. After decades of war, hostility, and mistrust, the two republics were joined anew.[37]

As twilight crept over the Rio Grande, the bridge was illuminated with hundreds of electric lights and Chinese lanterns from one end to the other. People lined the riverbanks, and fireworks lit the night sky. Bands played as two thousand couples danced until midnight, and "champagne, wine and beer flowed freely." It was the "grandest ball ever witnessed in the state of Texas," one newspaper reported.[38] Santos was so proud and excited he clipped from the *San Antonio Daily Express* a lengthy account of the event that included his short speech and rushed it off to President Díaz.[39]

As Santos's health began to decline, he closed his mercantile store on Flores Avenue and sold most of his sheep and cattle. He remained, nevertheless, one of the wealthiest men in the county.[40] In November 1890 his health took a turn for the worse. "His legion of friends in Laredo hope for his speedy recovery," the *Laredo Times* reported.[41] But Santos did not recover. Bedridden and ill for almost a year, he slowly slipped into unconsciousness and finally died early on the morning of Sunday, November 9, 1891, eight days after his sixty-eighth birthday.[42]

The news of Santos's death spread quickly over the city. At nine the next morning a large, somber crowd gathered on Market Plaza in front of his residence to escort his remains to San Agustín Church, where a lengthy high Mass was conducted before a large congregation, rich and poor, who filled the cathedral to capacity and spilled over into the plaza. During the service, Juan, who was exhausted from having sat with his father for several nights, fainted and was carried unconscious from the church. At the conclusion of the Mass, a long line of carriages carrying relatives and the elites of the city, along with hundreds of mourners on foot, including men who had ridden and fought with Santos in the Civil War, followed a black-draped hearse holding Santos's body to the Catholic cemetery.[43]

Newspapers all over the state carried his obituary. The *Fort Worth Gazette* said he was one of the great pioneers of the Rio Grande: "He leaves many friends and relatives in this state and also in Mexico."[44] Under the heading "A Pioneer of the Rio Grande Answers the Bugle Call," the newspaper wrote simply that Santos had been "identified with Laredo from his birth until death." "[He commanded] the Confederate forces in this section of the state during the rebellion, and after the cause was lost, settled down under the stars and stripes and was a law-abiding citizen."[45] His life was an incredible march through the stormy history of the Texas-Mexico border. Through all the sound and fury that characterized the nineteenth century in the two republics, this astonishing man carved out a life for himself and made his mark on history.

In his *Types of Successful Men of Texas*, published the year before Santos's death, Lewis E. Daniell captured the life of the old soldier. Santos had "lived free from blame and reciprocity." "When that last summer comes, he can calmly and undismayed 'wrap the drapery of his couch about him and lie down to pleasant slumber.'"[46] A century later in his *Farías Chronicles: A History and Genealogy of a Portuguese/Spanish Family*, George Farías seemed to grasp what made Santos Benavides so special. Santos was "kindhearted and considerate of the rights and feelings of others. He acceded the end of the Civil War gracefully, and cooperated during Reconstruction. He was known for his direct and sound logic. He was cool and deliberate in expressing his opinions, but was always well-mannered and a polished gentleman."[47]

EPILOGUE

Not long after Santos's death in 1891, the local camp of Confederate veterans was named in his honor. Decades later, in 1937, a street at Fort McIntosh was also named for him. Over time, however, his legacy was largely forgotten, like those of so many other nineteenth-century borderlanders, until a state historical marker was dedicated in San Agustín Plaza honoring Santos and his remarkable brothers as part of the American bicentennial in 1976. Twenty years later, Federico Peña—a descendant, former mayor of Denver, Colorado, and the secretary of energy—came to Laredo to dedicate an elementary school in Santos's honor.[1] A few years later, a historical marker was erected by the Webb County Historical Commission at his gravesite in the Catholic cemetery, and a small plaza was dedicated at the entrance to Laredo's busy Juárez-Lincoln International Bridge.

In January 1871, Santos and Agustina made out a will giving their property upon their deaths to Agustina Benavides Ayala, Juan V. Benavides, Santos Eraclio, and Santos Jr., whom they acknowledged as their legally adopted children. With the help of Ángel Navarro in May 1876, Santos revoked the previous will and drafted a second document giving all his property to his wife. In yet another legal document created in July 1881, while Santos was in the legislature, he and Agustina, with Edmund J. Davis, Eulalio Benavides, and Sixto E. Navarro as witnesses, cancelled all their previous wills and "revoked, cancelled, and declared void" the adoptions of Agustina, Juan, and Eraclio. Each bequeathed the other their real and personal property, valued at $40,000.[2] Yet in another will written in July 1887, Santos and Agustina gave their property to their son Juan and to Francisco Gar-

This photograph labeled "Santos Benavides, adopted son of Santos Benavides," has caused considerable confusion. One scholar even misidentified the individual as the colonel himself. Santos Benavides did have two nephews, sons of brothers Refugio and Cristóbal, both of whom were named in his honor, but neither was ever a sergeant in the regular US Army as was the unknown individual in this photograph. *Courtesy Laredo Public Library.*

za Ayala Benavides, son of their adopted daughter, Agustina, but the will was never probated and years of litigation followed.[3] After Santos's death, Agustina was finally named the executor, but largely through the legal chicanery so common in South Texas at the time, she lost virtually all the family property.[4] Twenty-five years after Santos's death, in a heart-rending reversal of fortunes, his heirs filed a bill with Congress asking for financial relief.[5]

Although older, José del Refugio outlived his brother by eight years, dying of chronic diarrhea at the age of seventy-eight on June 29, 1899. At the time of his death, he was remembered as "a member of one of the old-

Unlike his older brothers, Cristóbal Benavides (1839–1904) never sought political office. After the war, he helped to run the mercantile business of "S. Benavides and Brother." He became sole proprietor of the firm at 815 Grant Street in 1875. Cristóbal and his wife, Lamar Bee, the daughter of Gen. Hamilton P. Bee, raised six daughters and four sons. The 1995 Texas state historical marker at Santos's gravesite can be seen on the right in the background. *Author photo.*

est, largest and most respected families" in South Texas.[6] Santos's younger half-brother, Cristóbal, died on the night of September 2, 1904, at the age of sixty-five years, four months, and twenty-seven days.[7] Cristóbal was said to have been one of the "solid men of Laredo," and his death caused considerable "sorrow and regret" among his family, relatives, and friends. He was a "gallant Confederate," who, along with his two brothers, was among the last of the rebels to lay down their arms in the summer of 1865.[8]

Agustina Villarreal de Benavides, the loyal wife who endured both infidelity and war, outlived her famous husband by seventeen years, dying at the family home on Flores Street at the age of eighty-six on the morning of February 2, 1908. Juan, who was county attorney at the time, was by her side, as was her grandson, Francisco G. Benavides, who hurried north by train with his father, Lázaro Garza Ayala.[9] Three years later, when revolution engulfed Mexico, Santos's friend Porfirio Díaz, who had ruled Mexico with an iron fist for thirty-five years, fled into exile.[10]

Santos's faithful brother-in-law, John Z. Leyendecker, died on August 29, 1902. After Bishop Peter Verdaguer celebrated Mass the following morning before a congregation that filled San Agustín Church, Leyendecker was buried in the family burial grounds in the old Catholic cemetery.[11] Santos's sister and Leyendecker's second wife, Juliana, perhaps the most remarkable of all the Benavides children, had cared lovingly for her sister's five children and gave birth to ten children of her own. She outlasted her soldier-merchant-postmaster husband by twenty-four years, dying in June of 1926.[12]

Santos's beloved son Juan moved into the family home on Flores Street after the death of his father and was elected county attorney several times. Married to Canadian-born Laura Allen, the well-educated Juan died of pneumonia at the family home on the morning of May 20, 1920. Known affectionately throughout Laredo as "Chaclas" for the slippers he wore in public while on official business, he was buried in the city cemetery next to his wife. In honor of his passing, flags at city hall and the county courthouse were lowered to half-staff. Juan, it was said, never turned his back on anyone who was poor and in need.[13] After the death of his father, Santos M. Bena-

Santos Benavides's half-sister, Juliana Benavides Leyendecker, born on June 19, 1837, was the second wife of John Z. Leyendecker. This image was taken in 1924 on her eighty-seventh birthday. Shown are her sons Boni J., Peter Paul, Joseph Patrick, Miguel Mauricio, Thomas de Aquino, and daughters Pauline Agnes Mullally and Petronila Maria Magdalena Leyendecker. *Courtesy of the Leyendecker Family.*

vides Jr. managed the family ranches near Webb Station and Encinal and served as city treasurer and district attorney and in a clerical position with the Texas Railroad Commission.[14]

Following the election riot of 1886, the Botas continued to control Laredo and Webb County politics until Danish-born Andrew Hans Thaison, an independent Republican and Guarache, headed the reform ticket and was elected mayor in 1895. When the Botas mounted a comeback in 1896, the two parties were able to settle their differences and create the Independent Club, or what came to be known as the Partido Viejo. With Laredo's ranching, banking, and mercantile elite at the heart and helm of the party, the Independent Club survived numerous corruption charges. Entrenched

Santos Benavides's remains, along with those of Agustina and his brothers and relatives, were removed from the old city cemetery on Moctezuma Street in the late 1930s and reinterred in the new Calvary Catholic Cemetery in east central Laredo. *Author photo.*

and resilient, the club dominated Laredo and Webb County politics for the next eighty-two years.[15]

With the passage of time, Santos has come to be seen as acting, in many ways, on the wrong side of history. Although he considered himself a reformer, many of his political views were those of an entrenched oligarch. In the twenty-first century, not only his views on slavery, secession, and the Civil War, but also his never-ending wars with Native Americans are seen as wrong. Perhaps his true importance stems from his efforts to create a lasting peace on the Texas-Mexico border. With an identity drawn from both sides of the border, he possessed a binational view of history that made him uniquely qualified to be an ambassador of goodwill in Austin, Mexico City, the halls of Congress, and beyond. While remaining proud of his Mexican ancestry, he was American by destiny, and he lived and died in a place and time that set him apart from many of his contemporaries.

Over six decades, Santos watched as the small and impoverished village he had come to love and so gallantly defend survived disease, disaster, war, and politics. Thirty-eight years after his death, Santos's remains were moved, along with those of Agustina, his brothers, and hundreds of friends and relatives, to a new Catholic cemetery on Meadow Street in the northeastern outskirts of Laredo. Santos rests there today in the sunbaked red soil of South Texas, beneath a historical marker that proclaims him to be the honorable public servant and indefatigable warrior he was.[16]

NOTES

Acknowledgments

1. Broadside, November 26, 1859, Letters Received, Adjutant General's Office, Record Group 94, National Archives, Washington, DC.

2. Few if any Tejanos served in public office in Brownsville or Cameron County in the period from 1848 until 1861. In Laredo, unlike the lower valley, most of the Tejanos never lost control of their land and their political influence. The Benavides family, Santos and his uncle Basilio in particular, mastered the American political system and by 1861, were in political control of both Laredo and Webb County.

Introduction

1. José Felipe de la Peña, ed., *Los Benavides de Nuevo León, Tamaulipas, y Texas, 1619–1010* (Ventura, Cal., n.p., 1995), 1–10; and José de la Peña, ed., *Los Benavides de Revilla, 1754–1876* (Ventura, Cal., n.p., 1995), 1–6.

Chapter I

1. Certificate of Baptism, José de los Santos Benavides, July 28, 1986. This particular document by Rev. Thomas A. Davis mistakenly lists his birth as October 31, 1823. Teodocio was later killed by Comanches.

2. Graves of early Laredo citizens are still interred near San Agustín Cathedral, beneath concrete and asphalt parking lots, sidewalks and streets. Archeologists and historians believe the founder of the village, Tomás Sanchez, is interred near the foundation altar of the old church, just northwest of the larger, present day cathedral.

3. Margarita Ramón, Probated Will by José de Jesús Benavides, May 5, 1835, document F 114, Laredo Archives, St. Mary's University, San Antonio, Texas. For the English translation, see Robert D. Wood, trans., Death and Taxes (San Antonio: St. Mary's University Duplication Services, 2001), pp. 47–48.

4. José de Jesús Benavides Last Will and Testament, September 28, 1844. Courtesy of George Farías; José Cristóbal Benavides, Certificate of Baptism, Fr. Thomas A. Davis, July 23, 1986, Author's files. Cristóbal was born on April 2, 1839 and baptized at San Agustín eight days later.

5. José de Jesús Benavides Last Will and Testament, September 28, 1844, Laredo Archives.

6. Ford, "The Benavides Family," n. d., John S. Ford Papers, Haley Memorial Library and History Center, Midland Texas.

7. Declaration of Independence, September 18, 1821, Laredo Archives, St. Mary's University, San Antonio, Texas. Robert D. Wood, comp., *Indexes to the Laredo Archives* (San Antonio: St. Mary's University Duplication Services, 1993), 17.

8. Gregg Cantrell, *Stephen F. Austin: Empresario of Texas* (New Haven: Yale University Press, 1999), 111.

9. Stephen F. Austin to J. E. B. Austin, March 23, 1822, quoted in Gregg Cantrell, *Stephen F. Austin: Empresario of Texas* (New Haven: Yale University Press, 2001) , 112.

10. Robert D. Wood, ed., *Documentos Para La Genealogia* (San Antonio: St. Mary's University, 2010), 69.

11. Alwyn Barr, *Texans in Revolt: The Battle for San Antonio, 1835* (Austin: University of Texas Press, 1990), 57.

12. Basilio Benavides and María Encarnación García, Marriage Record, February 22, 1822, San Agustín Parish Archives, Laredo, Texas. Also, Odie Arambula, "The image problems of Don Basilio Benavides," and "Benavides was border achiever," both at http://madmax.lmtonline.com/textarchives/032308/13.htm and http://madmax.lmtonline.comtextarchives/090405/11.htm. Arambula has Basilio's birth as five years earlier in 1795. José Antonio Garcia was captain of the militia in Laredo in 1809.

13. In 1937, State Representative B. J. Leyendecker passed a resolution in the House of Representatives placing a portrait of Basilio in the State Hall of Fame. Basilio had four sisters and three brothers and was one of only five Tejanos to serve in the Texas legislature in the nineteenth century.

14. Jerry Thompson, *Warm Weather and Bad Whiskey: The 1886 Laredo Election Riot* (El Paso: Texas Western Press, 1991), 9–12.

15. J. Garza and J. Flores to Comandancia de Tamaulipas, February 1836, Laredo Archives, (F 121, D 1–6); translated in Robert D. Wood, *Archivos de Laredo: Documentos Referentes a Los Indios,* (San Antonio: St. Mary's University, 1998), 48.

16. B[acilio] B[enavides], April 11, 1836, Laredo Archives (F 121, D1–21); Wood, *Documentos Referentes a Los Indios*, 49

17. Ford, *Rip Ford's Texas*, 134.

18. Ibid.

19. *El Mercurio del Pueblo de Matamoros*, April 22, 1836, quoted in Wilcox, "Laredo during the Texas Revolution,"; and Wilkinson, *Laredo and the Rio Grande Frontier*, 145–46; and in Wilcox, *Papers on Laredo History*, 44–45. Shortly after the decisive Battle of San Jacinto, on July 4, 1836, Basilio's fourteen-year-old daughter María del Refugio, was married to José Ángel Benavides. José Ángel Benavides and María del Refugio Benavides, Marriage Record, July 4, 1836, San Agustín Parish Archives, Laredo, Texas. For Matamoros during the Texas Revolution, see: Craig H. Roell, *Matamoros and the Texas Revolution* (Denton: Texas State Historical Association, 2013).

20. John Milton Nance, *After San Jacinto*: *The Texas-Mexico Frontier, 1836–1837* (Austin: University of Texas Press, 1963), 34. In many ways, Nance's lengthy book remains the definitive study of this crucial period of border history.

21. D. W. Smith to John Forsyth, December 10, 1838, Matamoros Consular Dispatches, Records of the Department of State RG 59, NA.

22. Deposition, Santos Venibedas [sic], n.d. by Mirabeau Buonaparte Lamar, *Papers of Mirabeau Buonaparte Lamar*. Ed. Charles Adams Gulick, Jr., and Winnie Allen (Austin: Pemberton Press, 1968), 6: 128–29.

23. Ibid., 129.

24. Nance, *After San Jacinto*, 175–76.

25. Ibid.

26. His complete name was Pedro Nolasco Martín de la Candelaria Francisco Javier Ampudia y Grimarest.

27. Nance, *After San Jacinto*, 175–76,

28. Ibid.

29. Ibid., 410.

30. John C. Hays to B. T. Archer, April 14, 1841, in *Telegraph and Texas Register*, April 28, 1841; Nance, *After San Jacinto*, 312–14. John S. Ford wrote years later that nine Mexicans died in the battle. Ford, *Rip Ford's Texas*, 61. The San Agustín Archives contain the names of the three men who were known to have died in the fighting: Juan Hinojosa, forty-eight, who is listed as part of the Compañia de Lampazos; Antonio Zuniga, thirty-five; and Magdaleno Gutierrez, thirty-four. Also, James Kimmins Greer, *Colonel Jack Hays: Texas Frontier Leader and California Builder* (College Station: Texas A&M University Press, 1987), 37–38.

31. Paul N. Spellman, *Forgotten Texas Leader: Hugh McLeon and the Texan Santa Fe Expedition* (College Station: Texas A&M University Press, 1999), 72–129.

32. Frank de la Teja, ed.

33. Joseph Milton Nance, *Attack and Counter-Attack: The Texas-Mexican Frontier, 1842* (Austin: University of Texas Press, 1964), 384–85.

34. Jerry Thompson, *Sabers on the Rio Grande* (Austin: Presidial Press, 1974), 117.

35. Baptismal Record, April 29, 1842. San Agustín Parish Archives. Courtesy of Olee Rodriguez.

36. Matrimonios, Libro I, 1790–1858, San Agustín Parish Archives.

37. Lewis E. Daniell, *Types of Successful Men of Texas* (Austin: E. Von Boeckmann, 1890), 327–28.

38. Robert D. Wood, ed., *Documentos Para La Genealogia* (San Antonio: St. Mary's University, 2010), 163.

39. Nance, *Attack and Counter-Attack, 444–96;* Sam W. Haynes, *Soldiers of Misfortune: The Somervell and Mier Expeditions* (Austin: University of Texas Press, 1990), 24–65; and J. M. Nance, *Dare-Devils All: Texas Mier Expedition*, (Austin: Eakin Press, 1998) ed. Archie P. McDonald, 17–29.

40. John Henry Brown, *History of Texas, from 1685 to 1892* (St. Louis: L. E. Daniell, 1892, 2: 484.

41. www.lrl.state.tx.us/scanned/CongressJournals/House7Con.cfm (accessed December 26, 2015). The orders can also be found in Stanley Brown Hendricks, "The Somervell Expedition to the Rio Grande," *Southwestern Historical Quarterly* 23 (October 1919), 112–13.

42. Nance, *Attack and Counter-Attack*, 511.

43. Ibid.

44. Hayes, *Soldiers of Misfortune*, 53.

45. Thompson, *Sabers on the Rio Grande*, 124.

46. Harvey Alexander Adams, "Expedition Against the Southwest in 1842 and 1843," December 8, 1842, ms., CAH. Adams is quoted extensively in Nance, *Attack and Counter-Attack.*

47. List of items plundered from citizens of Laredo, Laredo Archives, n. d., Roll no. 15.

48. Ibid.

49. Ibid.

50. Hayes, *Solders of Misfortune*, 54; and Thomas J. Green, *Journal of the Texian Expedition Against Mier* (Austin; W. Thomas Taylor, 1993), 21–22.

51. William Preston Stapp, *Prisoners of Perote: Containing a Journal Kept by the Author Who Was Captured by the Mexicans, at Mier, December 25, 1842, and Released from Perote, May 16, 1844* (Philadelphia: G. B. Zeiber, and Company, 1845), 25. Also, quoted in Nance, *Attack and Counter-Attack*, 525. Albert G. Brackett to Brother [Charles Brackett], June 8, 1857, Library of the Daughters of the Republic of Texas at the Alamo, San Antonio, Texas.

52. A. Somervell to Alcalde of Laredo, December 9, 1842, quoted in Nance, *Attack and Counter-Attack*, 526.

53. Joseph D. McCutchan, *Mier Expedition Diary: The Texan Prisoner's Account* (Austin: University of Texas Press, 1978), 25–26.

54. Thomas J. Green, *Journal of the Texian Expedition Against Mier* (Austin: W. Thomas Taylor, 1993), 22.

55. Sam Houston, "Speech on Thomas Jefferson Green," August 1, 1854, *Writings of Sam Houston* (Austin: Jenkins Publishing Company), ed. Amelia Williams and Eugene C. Barker, 6: 77–78.

56. For comprehensive and scholarly studies of the Mier Expedition, see: Haynes, *Soldiers of Misfortune*, and Nance, *Dare Devils All.*

57. Thompson, *Sabers on the Rio Grande*, 139.

Chapter II

1. Thompson, *Warm Weather and Bad Whiskey*, 1–2.

2. R. A. Gillespie to John C. Hays, March 23, 1846, Letters Received (LR), Adjutant General's Office (AGO), Record Group (RG) 94, National Archives, Washington DC (NA). This letter can be viewed at http://www.fold3.com/image/248/292592066/.

3. Ibid.

4. Bryan P. Tilden Jr., *Notes on the Upper Rio Grande*, 36. Also, B. P. Tilden Jr. to Geo. A. McCall, October 28, 1846; McCall to Tilden, November 7, 1846; and McCall to Lamar, November 7, 1846; all in LR, Army of Occupation, AGO, RG 94, NA. The arrival of the *Major Brown* is discussed in Hinojosa, *A Borderlands Town in Transition*, 55–58; and Thompson, *Sabers on the Rio Grande*, 146–50.

5. [Lamar] to Zachary Taylor, December 24, 1846, Gulick, *Papers of Mirabeau Buonaparte Lamar*, vol. 4, pt. 1, 69–70 (hereafter *Lamar Papers*, 4:1:69–70).

6. [Lamar] to Taylor, December 24, 1846, *Lamar Papers*, 4:1:69–70.

7. W. W. S. Bliss to M. B. Lamar, October 15, 1846, *Lamar Papers*, 4:1:143.

8. Order for an Election Held at Laredo, Texas, July 13, 1847, *Lamar Papers*, 4:1:173–74.

9. Returns of an Election Held at Laredo, Texas, July 13, 1847, *Lamar Papers*, 4:1:173.

10. Florencio Villarreal to Z. Taylor, March 13, 1847, LR, AGO, RG 94, NA.

11. Santos Venibedas [*sic*], Recollections, n.d., *Lamar Papers*, 6:128–29.

12. Basilio Benavides Statement, n.d., *Lamar Papers*, 6:90.

13. Sam'l F. Boyd, et al., to Lamar, [March 15, 1847?], *Lamar Papers*, 4:1:164.

14. Lamar to Bliss, May 21, 1847, LR, AGO, RG 94, NA.

15. José Ma. Ramón, Bracillio [*sic*] Benavides and José Ma. Gonzales, April 8, 1848, *Lamar Papers*, 4:1:196.

16. Ibid.

17. Lamar to Ramón, Benavides, and Gonzales, April 11, 1848, *Lamar Papers*, 4:1:197.

18. Ibid.

19. Ibid.

20. *General Laws of the Second Legislature of the State of Texas (1847–1854)*, 3:28.

21. The town on the north bank was approximately twice the size of what became Nuevo Laredo on the south. Lamar's 1847 census counted a population of 1,891 on both sides of the river, while the seventh US census for 1850 found 1,173 citizens living on the north bank. Even after the small exodus of families to the south bank following the Treaty of Guadalupe Hidalgo, little more than seven hundred citizens comprised Nuevo Laredo. Laredo Census, *Lamar Papers*, 6:44–65; 7th Census (1850), Webb County, Texas, NA. See also, Hinojosa, *Borderlands Town in Transition*, 55–58; and Thompson, *Warm Weather and Bad Whiskey*, 152–53.

22. Hamilton P. Bee to J. P. Garesche, August 2, 1848, LR, AGO, RG 94, NA. Lewis, a survivor of the 1842 Black Bean Incident, went to great lengths to deny his involvement in the plunder of Sabinas. He later died from the gunshot blast of a jealous husband. *Corpus Christi Star*, December 23, 1848; and see Cox, *Texas Ranger Tales*, 19–20.

23. *Brownsville American Flag*, June 2, 1847.

24. Armando C. Alonzo, "Mexican-American Land Grant Adjudication," accessed April 15, 2016, http://www.thshaonline.org/handbook/online/articles/pqmck. Also, Galen D. Greaser and Jesus de la Teja, "Quieting Title to Spanish and Mexican Land Grants in the Trans-Nueces: The Bourland and Miller Commission, 1850–1852, *Southwestern Historical Quarterly* 61 (April, 1992), 455–56.

25. Ibid. Many of the land titles from the lower valley were lost when the *Anson Jones*, bound from Port Isabel to Galveston, went down in heavy seas fifteen miles from Matagorda. Greaser and Teja, "Quieting Title to Spanish and Mexican Land Grants," 455–56.

26. Ibid.

27. Post Returns, Fort McIntosh, Texas, 1848–1861, AGO, RG 94, NA.

28. *New York Times*, April 14, 1876.

29. Ibid.

30. John H. King to George Deas, April 10, 1850, LR, Western Department, Letters of the Adjutant General's Office (LAGO), RG 393, NA; see also, Secrest, *The Man from the Rio Grande*, 68–69.

31. Post Returns, April 1850, Fort McIntosh, Texas, AGO, RG 94, NA.

32. Thompson, *Sabers on the Rio Grande*, 168; Heitman, *Historical Register and Dictionary of the United States Army*, 1:551; and Smith, *The U.S. Army and the Texas Frontier Economy*, dedication page.

33. Ford, *Rip Ford's Texas*, 173–79; and McCaslin, *Fighting Stock*, 41–42. In the months preceding their arrival in Laredo, Ford and his men were stationed near Corpus Christi; then at San Antonio Viejo, forty-five miles north of Rio Grande City; and then at Los Ojuelos, thirty-three miles east of Laredo.

34. Ford, *Rip Ford's Texas*, 142.

35. Ibid., 222.

36. A. Soto, et al., to P. H. Bell, [August 1852], Peter H. Bell Papers, Texas State Library and Archives.

37. H. P. Bee to P. H. Bell, August 26, 1852, Bell Papers, TSA.

38. Owen Shaw to Bell, August 27, 1852, Bell Papers, TSA.

39. Bell to Henry Redmond, December 13, 1852, Bell Papers, TSA. At the time, Carrizo was frequently referred to as "Bellville" in honor of Governor Bell.

40. Smith, *U.S. Army and the Texas Frontier Economy*, 86; and Thompson, *Sabers on the Rio Grande*, 177.

41. Post Returns, Fort McIntosh, Texas, 1850–1861, AGO, RG 94, NA.

42. Ibid.; see also, Thompson, *Sabers on the Rio Grande*, 176; and Thompson, *Warm Weather and Bad Whiskey*, 6.

43. Resolution, June 24, 1854, Laredo Archives, microfilm roll no. 15; see also, Hinojosa, *A Borderlands Town in Transition*, 70.

44. James E. Slaughter to Robert Jones, August 8, 1855, Albert G. Brackett Papers, Library of the Daughters of the Republic of Texas, San Antonio, Texas.

45. *New York Daily Times*, July 11, 1854. It was generally thought that the August 14, 1885, hanging of Celedonio Chivarria, who was convicted of murdering Guadalupe Treviño and a second individual named Crisento Aldava, was the first such hanging in Webb County. *State of Texas v. Celedonio Chivarria*, Webb County Criminal Court Case No. 535, Special Collections, Killam Library, Texas A&M International University.

46. *New York Daily Times*, July 25, 1854, quoting *New Orleans Bulletin*, July 17, 1854, which in turn obtained the information from the *Brownsville Flag*, July 8, 1854.

47. *New York Daily Times*, July 20, 1854.

48. Lydia Spencer Lane, *I Married a Soldier*, 42.

49. Randolph B. Marcy to Nellie Marcy, July 14, 1856, George B. McClellan Papers, Library of Congress, Washington DC.

50. Albert G. Brackett to Brother [Charles Brackett], June 8, 1857, Daughters of the Republic of Texas Library at the Alamo, San Antonio, Texas.

51. H. P. Bee to E. M. Pease, March 13, 1856, Elisha M. Pease Papers, TSA (hereafter Pease Papers).

52. Benavides to Santiago Vidaurri, March 9, 1856, enclosing statement of Victor Botello, n.d. [February 25, 1856], Correspondencia de Santiago Vidaurri, Archivo General del Estado de Nuevo León, Monterrey, Nuevo León, Mexico (hereafter referred to as Correspondencia de Vidaurri, AGNL).

53. Benavides to Santiago Vidaurri, March 9, 1856, Correspondencia de Vidaurri, AGNL.

54. Ibid.

55. Proceedings of a Public Meeting of the Citizens of Webb County, March 11, 1856, Pease Papers, TSA.

56. Ibid.

57. Ibid.

58. Albert G. Brackett to Brother [Charles Brackett], June 8, 1857, Library of the Daughters of the Republic of Texas at the Alamo, San Antonio, Texas.

59. Ibid.

60. E. M. Pease to Edmund J. Davis, March 24, 1856; Pease to Jefferson Davis, March 24, 1856; both letters in Pease Papers, TSA.

61. Benavides to Vidaurri, n.d., Correspondencia de Vidaurri, AGNL. Although undated, this particular document is filed between letters dated July 14, 1855, and March 1, 1856.

62. Lewis E. Daniell, *Types of Successful Men of Texas*, 325.

63. Benavides to Santiago Vidaurri, February 20, 1859, Correspondencia de Vidaurri, AGNL.

64. Benavides to Vidaurri, February 27, 1859, Correspondencia de Vidaurri, AGNL.

65. *San Antonio Herald*, September 22, 1859.

66. *San Antonio Herald*, September 17, 1859; Bartolo García Deposition, Testimony before the Thomas P. Robb Commission (1873), vol. 10, Records of Boundary and Claims Commissions and Arbitration, RG 76, NA.

67. Vidaurri to John R. Baylor, June 29, 1861, in *New York Times*, October 31, 1861.

68. "An Act for the Incorporation of the City of Laredo," *Laws of Texas*, 3:176.

69. 7th Census (1850), Webb County, Texas, NA.

70. James A. Wilkinson to W. D. Miller, January 20, 1849, Election Returns, Webb County, Secretary of State Records, RG 307, TSA.

71. *Report of Mail Contracts*, Vol. 580, 31st Cong., 1st Sess., House Ex. Doc. 88, 345, 351, 353. Under the directions of Col. Juan N. Seguín in 1836, it was Cazneau who had gathered the remains of the Alamo defenders and saw to their burial. Along with his wife Jane, Cazneau had also helped to establish Eagle Pass.

72. *Abstract of Bids Under Advertisement of January 15, 1851*, Vol. 643, 32nd Cong., 1st Sess., House Ex. Doc. 56, 390.

73. *Report of Mail Contracts*, Vol. 789, 33rd Cong., 2nd Sess., House Ex. Doc. 86, 518.

74. Ibid., 522–23, 528; *Mail Contracts*, Vol. 860, 34th Cong., 2nd Sess., House Ex. Doc. 122, 447; and 7th Census (1850), Rio Grande Valley, NA.

75. Laredo Election Return (fragment), June 28, 1850, Laredo Archives, microfilm roll no. 15. Refugio was reelected alderman in 1852. Election Returns, 1852, Laredo Archives, microfilm roll no. 15; *Corpus Christi Weekly Caller*, July 7, 1899; *Laredo Daily Times*, June 30, July 1, 1899; newspaper obituary, n.d., courtesy of Genoveva B. Vela and María B. Saenz; Jerry Thompson, "José del Refugio Benavides," application for a historical marker, Texas State Historical Commission, 1989, author's files. Only four months after taking office, Refugio surprisingly resigned.

76. Minutebook 1, January 12, April 2, 1852, Special Collections, Laredo Public Library, Laredo, Texas.

77. Ordinances Approved by the City Council of Laredo, January 15, 1856, Ordinance no. 1, Laredo Archives, microfilm roll no. 15.

78. Ordinances Approved by the City Council of Laredo, January 18, 1856, Ordinance no. 2, Laredo Archives, microfilm roll no. 15.

79. Ordinances Approved by the City Council of Laredo, January 20, 1856, Ordinance no. 3, Laredo Archives, microfilm roll no. 15.

80. Ordinances Approved by the City Council of Laredo, June 9, 1857, Ordinance no. 3, Laredo Archives, microfilm roll no. 15.

81. Santos Benavides, John Z. Leyendecker, et al. to the Honorable Mayor and the Board of Aldermen, February 10, 1858, Laredo Archives.

82. Ibid.

83. Minutebook No. 1, April 1, 1856 to April 1, 1857, Special Collections, City Library, Laredo, Texas; and Election Returns, 1856 and 1857, Laredo Archives, microfilm roll no. 15.

84. Santos Benavides to the Mayor and Council of the Corporation of Laredo, October 14, 1859, Laredo Archives, microfilm roll no. 15.

85. D. E. Twiggs to L. Thomas, January 11, 1859, and General Order no. 4, February 5, 1859, "Difficulties on Southwestern Frontier," 36th Cong., 1st sess., no. 1050, 8. As soon as the Bluecoats were gone, townsmen descended on Fort McIntosh, ripping out windows, tearing down doors, and even taking off roofs and hauling away some of the walls. Thompson, *Texas and New Mexico on the Eve of the Civil War*, 144.

86. Santos Benavides to the Mayor and Council of the Corporation of Laredo, October 14, 1859, Laredo Archives, microfilm roll no. 15.

87. Basilio Benavides to Santiago Vidaurri, n.d., Correspondencia de Vidaurri, AGNL.

88. Luis García, "Santiago Vidaurri and Santos Benavides," 2.

89. Basilio Benavides to Santiago Vidaurri, December 30, 1859, Correspondencia de Vidaurri, AGNL.

90. Basilio Benavides to Vidaurri, May 16, 1860, Correspondencia de Vidaurri, AGNL.

91. *Laredo Daily Times*, September 3, 4, 1904; and *A Twentieth Century History of Southwest Texas*, 2:77.

92. "Sketch of the Life of J. M. Rodríguez," San Agustín Parish Archives, Laredo, Texas; and [Rodríguez], *Rodríguez Reports of Early Texas*, 43–51.

93. DeRyee and Moore, *Texas Album of the Eighth Legislature*, 34. Rodríguez died in Laredo on February 22, 1913. *Laredo Weekly Times*, March 2, 1913.

94. *Contracts for Carrying the Mail*, Vol. 1013, 35th Cong., 2nd Sess., House Ex. Doc. 109, 292–93.

95. *Fines and Deductions*, Vol. 1097, 36th Cong., 2nd Sess., House Ex. Doc. 27, 11.

96. *Contracts for Carrying the Mail*, Vol. 1013, 35th Cong., 2nd Sess., House Ex. Doc. 109, 284.

97. García, *The Children of John Z. Leyendecker*, 9–11, 20–24; and Sepulveda Brown and Villa Cadena, *San Agustín Parish of Laredo*, 238. Leyendecker was born on September 10, 1827, at Kadenback Sayner Holz Walderodt in the Duchy of Nassau and was baptized in the parish church of Mendt.

98. Maria Isabela was born on July 2, 1858, Maria Juana on October 23, 1859, and Lucia Pragedis on July 21, 1861. On November 2, 1862, while Leyendecker and María Andrea were in Fredericksburg during the early days of the Civil War, she bore a son, John, but the child was "sickly," died five days later, and was buried in the Catholic cemetery. 8th Census (1860), Gillespie County, Texas, NA. Leyendecker lists no real estate on the census but a personal estate valued at $2,500, probably the inventory from his small store. The building for the store was owned by his father, a farmer also named John, who was serving as justice of the peace in Fredericksburg at the time. From Fredericksburg in September 1851, the father petitioned Governor Peter H. Bell on behalf of some fifty individuals living in the community who had been on the frontier for five years and, having declared their intent to become citizens two years

earlier, asked the governor to expedite their citizenship. John Leyendecker to P. H. Bell, September 2, 1851, Bell Papers, TSA.

99. Moseley, "The Public Career of Santiago Vidaurri," 222–27.

100. Ibid., 233–34.

101. Benavides to Vidaurri, July 14, 1855, Correspondencia de Vidaurri, AGNL.

102. Benavides to Vidaurri, September 23, 1856, Correspondencia de Vidaurri, AGNL.

103. Benavides to Vidaurri, February 27, 1859, Correspondencia de Vidaurri, AGNL.

104. Benavides to Vidaurri, January 12, 1857; Vidaurri to Benavides, July 31, 1858; both in Correspondencia de Vidaurri, AGNL.

105. Benavides to Vidaurri, March 1, 1856, Correspondencia de Vidaurri, AGNL.

106. Benavides to Vidaurri, July 18, 1856, Correspondencia de Vidaurri, AGNL.

107. Benavides to Vidaurri, August 17, 1856, Correspondencia de Vidaurri, AGNL.

108. Benavides to Vidaurri, September 23, 1856, Correspondencia de Vidaurri, AGNL.

109. 1851 Webb County Tax Roll, courtesy of Olivia "Olee" Rodriguez. The term *sitio* was commonly used in Spanish Texas to designate parcels of land. At the same time, Santos was paying taxes on the property he owned in Encinal and La Salle counties. For example, in 1871, he paid $2.56 for the 160 acres he owned at Charco Largo. La Salle Assessment Roll of Lands, 1871, Courtesy of Olee Rodriguez.

110. Deed Book No. 8, 549–50, Webb County Clerk's Office, Laredo, Texas. The property had originally been granted to Henry Bayes by the General Land Office of the Republic of Texas for his services during the Texas Revolution.

111. Deed Book No. 5, 369, Webb County Clerk's Office.

112. Deed Book No. 4, 384, 399–400, Webb County Clerk's Office. The acquisition in Porción fifteen was 100 varas frontage on the Rio Grande and extending back into the interior some 30,000 varas while the property in Porción was 125 varas wide and the same distance away from the river. During the Civil War, Santos had purchased 320 acres on the Nueces River but later sold the land to Charles Callaghan.

113. Benavides to Vidaurri, July 3, 1859, Correspondencia de Vidaurri, AGNL. For Agustina and the children spending the summer in San Antonio, see Benavides to Vidaurri, April 28, 1854, Correspondencia de Vidaurri, AGNL.

114. Benavides to Vidaurri, July 3, 1859, Correspondencia de Vidaurri, AGNL. For the sale of animals, see Benavides to Vidaurri, May 15, 1859; Benavides to Vidaurri, January 21, 1860; and John Fonda to Benavides, January 10, 1860, all in Correspondencia de Vidaurri, AGNL.

115. See, for example, Augustine Gaudet to John Mary Odin, December 19, 1861, Odin Papers, University of Notre Dame Archives, http://archives.nd.edu/calendar/cal1861l.htm, accessed April 15, 2015; and Foley, *Missionary Bishop*, 43–154.

116. Benavides to Vidaurri, March 3, 1859; and Vidaurri to Dear Friend, March 26, 1859, both in Correspondencia de Vidaurri, AGNL.

117. Benavides to Vidaurri, April 28, 1859, Correspondencia de Vidaurri, AGNL.

118. Benavides to Vidaurri, April 28, 1854, Correspondencia de Vidaurri, AGNL.

119. Davis and Grobe, *New Encyclopedia of Texas*; Daniell, *Successful Men of Texas*, 327.

120. 7th Census (1850), Webb County, Texas, NA. Surprisingly, Santos's two neighbors—Santiago Treviño, a farmer, and José María Ramirez, a shoemaker—listed far more wealth.

121. 8th Census (1860), Webb County, Texas, NA.

122. 9th Census (1870), Webb County, Texas, NA.

123. Ibid.

124. Benavides to Vidaurri, September 4, 1860, Correspondencia de Vidaurri, AGNL.

125. Benavides to Vidaurri, August 11, 1860, Correspondencia de Vidaurri, AGNL.

126. *San Antonio Daily Ledger and Texan*, October 10, 1860.

127. Maria Tomása Cameros to John Z. Leyendecker, October 21, 1860, Leyendecker Papers, Center for American History, University of Texas at Austin (CAH). In her letters, Cameros address her son-in-law as "Dearest unforgettable son."

128. Cameros to Leyendecker, November 18, 1860, Leyendecker Papers, CAH.

129. *San Antonio Herald*, January 7, February 6, May 19, 1858.

130. De León, *They Called Them Greasers*, 49–50; see also Nichols, "The Line of Liberty," 413–33.

131. *Corpus Christi Ranchero*, March 17, 1860; 8th Census (1860), Nueces County, Texas, NA.

132. Ford, *Rip Ford's Texas*, 196.

133. Deposition of David M. Level, Testimony before the Thomas P. Robb Commission (1873), vol. 10, Records of Boundary and Claims Commissions and Arbitrations, RG 76, NA. The three murderers, according to Level, were Zenabio Vaca, José María Salinas, and José Galindo.

134. *Corpus Christi Ranchero*, November 17, 1860. Typescript of article courtesy of Ron Tyler. For a history of the *Ranchero*, see Norman C. Delaney, *The Maltby Brothers' Civil War* (College Station: Texas A&M University Press, 2013), 45–112, 126–170.

135. *Corpus Christi Ranchero*, November 17, 1860.

136. Ibid.

137. Benavides to Vidaurri, January 25, 1861; and Benavides to Vidaurri, February 1, 1863, both in Correspondencia de Vidaurri, AGNL.

138. *State Gazette Appendix*, 11, 15.

139. *House Journal, 8th Legislature, Regular Session*, 65. Considering the influence Basilio had with Governor Vidaurri, Rodríguez wrote the governor in November 1860 seeking to obtain a position for his sister in one of the convent schools in Monterrey. The sister was fluent in Spanish, English, and French and could also teach geography and arithmetic, besides embroidery and sewing. Should his sister find employment in Monterrey, Rodríguez thought of finding a job there also. J. M. Rodríguez to Vidaurri, November 15, 1860, Correspondencia de Vidaurri, AGNL.

140. Benavides to Vidaurri, January 25, 1861, Correspondencia de Vidaurri, AGNL.

141. Basilio Benavides to Vidaurri, November 25, 1860, Correspondencia de Vidaurri, AGNL.

142. *Galveston Civilian and Gazette*, April 2, 1861; and *Hancock Jeffersonian* [Findlay, Ohio], April 12, 1861. Where the latter newspaper obtained the information "From Texas" is uncertain.

143. Cristóbal Benavides to Leyendecker, March 26, 1861, Leyendecker Papers, CAH.

144. *Galveston Civilian and Gazette*, April 2, 1861.

Chapter III

1. Basilio Benavides to Santiago Vidaurri, November 25, 1860, Correspondencia de Vidaurri, AGNL.

2. *Corpus Christi Ranchero*, January 12, 1861.

3. Ford, "The Benavides Family," n.d., Ford Papers, Nita Stewart Haley Library and J. Evetts Haley History Center, Midland, Texas; Ford, *Rip Ford's Texas*, 323.

4. Ibid.

5. "Influence of the Benavides Family," n.d., Ford Papers, Haley Library.

6. Benavides to Vidaurri, January 23, 1861, Correspondencia de Vidaurri, AGNL.

7. Maverick County voted 80–3 against secession, but the returns from Eagle Pass arrived in Austin too late to be tabulated. Glen Sample Ely, *Where the West Begins* (Lubbock: Texas Tech University Press, 2011), 28, 139; and Jesse Sumter, *Paso del Aguila: A Chronicle of Frontier Days on the Texas Border*, ed. Ben E. Pingenot (Austin, TX: Encino Press, 1969), 83. In the Trans-Pecos, where a large percentage of the population was dependent on federal protection and federal expenditures, Presidio County voted 364–0 against secession. To the west in El Paso County, where fraud and intimidation were rampant, the vote was 871–2 in favor of secession, however. Glen Sample Ely, *The Texas Frontier and the Butterfield Overland Mail, 1858–1861* (Norman: University of Oklahoma Press, 2016), 342–43.

8. Quoted in Ralph A. Wooster, *Texas and Texans in the Civil War* (Austin, TX: Eakin Press, 1995), 17–18. Also, Russell Brown, "An Old Woman with a Broomstick: General David E. Twiggs and the Surrender in Texas, 1861," *Military Affairs* 48 (April 1984): 57–61.

9. *Dallas Herald*, May 30, 1861; Francis Richard Lubbock, *Six Decades in Texas: Memoirs of Francis Richard Lubbock* (Austin, TX: Ben C. Jones, 1900), 232 (quote).

10. C. C. Sibley to W. A. Nichols, March 11, 1861, *War of the Rebellion: A Compilation of the Official Records of the Union and Confederate Armies* (Washington, DC: Government Printing Office, 1889), ser. I, 1:534–45 (hereafter referred to as *OR*, by series, volume, and part); also, Sibley to A. G., April 25, 1861, *OR*, I, 1:561–62; Sibley to Authorities of the Confederate States of America, April 25, 1861, *OR*, I, 1:562–63; and Sibley to L. Thomas, June 3, 1861, *OR*, I, 1:563–64.

11. G. W. Pierce to John Z. Leyendecker, March 25, 1861, Leyendecker Papers, CAH.

12. Cristóbal Benavides to Leyendecker, April 7, 1861, Leyendecker Papers, CAH.

13. Ford to Benavides, April 17, 1861, Ford Papers, Haley Library.

14. Jerry Thompson, *Juan Cortina and the Texas-Mexico Frontier, 1859–1877* (El Paso: Texas Western Press, 1994), 11–12.

15. Jerry Thompson, ed., *Fifty Miles and a Fight: Major Samuel Peter Heintzelman's Journal of Texas and the Cortina War* (Austin: Texas State Historical Association, 1998), 155–56.

16. *New York Times*, May 27, 1861, quoting the *Fort Brown Flag* (Brownsville), May 9, 1861. Cortina's movements were reported by H. Clay Davis from Rio Grande City, who sent an express to Brownsville.

17. Virgil N. Lott and Mercurio Martinez, *The Kingdom of Zapata* (Austin, TX: Eakin Press, 1983), 42–43.

18. Gardner W. Pierce to [Leyendecker], June 1, 1861, Leyendecker Papers, CAH; also, Baum, *The Shattering of Texas Unionism*, 75–76.

19. *Corpus Christi Ranchero*, April 20, 1861.

20. Pierce to [Leyendecker], June 1, 1861, Leyendecker Papers, CAH.

21. *Corpus Christi Ranchero*, April 20, 1861.

22. Henry Redmond to John S. Ford, April 12, 1861, Edward Clark Papers, Texas State Archives, Austin, Texas. Also, John D. Mussett to Captain Brown, October 18, 1861, LR, Confederate District of Texas, New Mexico, and Arizona, RG 109, NA.

23. Ford to Redmond, April 15, 1861, Ford Papers, Haley Library.

24. Eighth Census (1860), Zapata County, Texas, NA.

25. *Corpus Christi Ranchero*, April 27, 1861. As a result of his service during the Mexican War, Nolan was known in South Texas as the "Boy Bugler of the Battle of Cerro Gordo." In the years after the Mexican-Amercan War, Nolan had served with Ford's company of rangers in the Nueces Strip as a bugler. Later he was elected sheriff of Nueces County. Nolan was murdered in Corpus Christi on December 22, 1864. Bill Walraven, *Corpus Christi: The History of a Texas Seaport* (Woodland Hills, CA: Windsor, 1982), 53.

26. Gardner Pierce to [Leyendecker], June 1, 1861, Leyendecker Papers, CAH.

27. *Corpus Christi Ranchero*, April 27, 1861. Santiago Vela, fifty-seven, a victim of "una armada de aquel estado," was buried in Guerrero at 10:00 a.m. on the same day, April 15, 1861. Registro Civil de Guerrero, *Libro de Defunciones, 1860–1861*, 26–27, Guerrero Archives, Nuevo Guerrero, Tamaulipas. Copy courtesy of Stanley Green.

28. *Reports of the Committee of Investigation Sent in 1873 by the Mexican Government to the Frontier of Texas* (New York: Baker and Godwin, 1875), 66. For a more detailed study of the turmoil in Zapata County, see Jerry Thompson, *Vaqueros in Blue and Gray* (Austin, TX: State House Press, 2000), 15–23; and Jerry Thompson, *Mexican Texans in the Union Army* (El Paso: Texas Western Press, 1986), 1–7.

29. Ford to Benavides, April 19, 1861, Ford Papers, Haley Library.

30. Henry Redmond to John S. Ford, May 14, 1861, Ford Papers, Haley Library. Besides the originals of the Ford Papers at the Haley Library, copies are available at the Texas State Archives in Austin.

31. *Austin Weekly State Gazette*, June 8, 1861, TSA.

32. Ysidro Vela to Ford, May 14, 1861, Ford Papers, Haley Library.

33. [Juan G. Garza] to Gefe Politico del Distrito del Norte, May 19, 1861, Correspondencia del Alcalde de Guerrero, Guerrero Archives, Nuevo Guerrero, Tamaulipas.

34. [Juan G. Garza] to Santos Benavides, May 18, 1861, Correspondencia del Alcalde de Guerrero.

35. Pierce to [Leyendecker], June 1, 1861, Leyendecker Papers, CAH.

36. Redmond to Ford, May 23, 1861, Broadside File, TSA.

37. *Galveston Weekly News*, June 18, 1861.

38. Benavides to Ford, May 14, 1861, Ford Papers, Haley Library; *Corpus Christi Ranchero,* June 1, 8, 1861. "I have no prisoners," Santos said in his official report. Santos told José María Hinojosa that ten of Cortina's "men were left dead on the field

and that the others were dispersed in all directions." [Juan G. Garza] to Gefe Politico del Distrito del Norte, May 22, 1861, Correspondencia del Alcalde de Guerrero. Yet in a letter to his friend Vidaurri, Santos said seven Cortinistas were killed. Benavides to Vidaurri, June 10, 1861, Correspondencia de Vidaurri, AGNL. Also, *Galveston Weekly News*, June 15, 18, 1861.

39. Benavides to Ford, May 14, 1861, Ford Papers, Haley Library.

40. Daniell, *Successful Men of Texas*, 327.

41. Ibid.

42. Francis Richard Lubbock, *Six Decades in Texas or the Memoirs of Francis Richard Lubbock*, ed. C. W. Raines (Austin, TX: Pemberton Press, 1968), 380.

43. "Rout of Cortina," May 29, 1861, contained with Benavides to Ford, May 23, 1861, Ford Papers, Haley Library.

44. Ford, Orders No. 21, May 27, 1861, Ford Papers, Haley Library.

45. L. E. Daniell, *Types of Successful Men of Texas* (Austin, TX: 1890), 327.

46. Ibid. Wallace E. Oakes, a friend of the governor, gave the pistol to Benavides personally in November 1861. Wallace E. Oakes to Clark, August 27, 1861; and Benavides to Clark, October 24, 1861, Clark Papers, TSA.

47. Vidaurri to Benavides, June 22, 1864, Correspondencia de Vidaurri, AGNL.

48. Laredo City Council Resolution, November 25, 1862, in Fort McIntosh Consolidated File, Quartermaster General's Office, Record Group 92, NA.

49. "Sale of houses in camp to the persons noted down," December 11, 1862; and C. Callaghan to Capt. Parsons, November 19, 1865; both in ibid.

50. *Houston Tri-Weekly Telegraph*, July 30, 1862, quoting *San Antonio Herald*, July 26, 1862. Leaving Austin, Hamilton and his party traveled only at night and resting during the day before reaching the Rio Grande. Hamilton was commissioned a brigadier general and named military governor of Texas. John L. Waller, *Colossal Hamilton of Texas* (El Paso: Texas Western Press, 1968). Tennessee-born James R. Hord, a stockman by trade, enlisted in the First Texas Cavalry (Union) before deserting at Monganza, Louisiana, on July 18, 1864. Hord CMSR, RG 109, NA. Also, Benavides to Vidaurri, February 1, 1862, Correspondencia de Vidaurri, AGNL.

51. Benavides to Vidaurri, February 1, 1862, Correspondencia de Vidaurri, AGNL.

52. Ford to Benavides, July 19, 1861, Ford Papers.

53. Benavides to Earl Van Dorn, September 5, 1861, Benavides CMSR, RG 109, CAGO, NA.

54. Charles Løvenskiold to Clark, October 10, 1861, Clark Papers, TSA.

55. Benavides to Clark, October 24, 1861, Clark Papers, TSA.

56. Løvenskiold to Francis Lubbock, November 6, 1861, Lubbock Papers, TSA.

57. Løvenskiold to Lubbock, November 6, 1861, Lubbock Papers, TSA.

58. Callahan to Løvenskiold, November 6, 1861, Lubbock Papers, TSA.

59. *New York Times*, October 18, 1861.

60. Løvenskiold to Lubbock, December 5, 1861, Lubbock Papers, TSA.

61. Ibid. The Laredo deserters were Francisco Flores, Nicolás Flores, Manuel Pruneda, and Nestor Filan.

62. Løvenskiold to Lubbock, January 19, 1862, Lubbock Papers, TSA.

63. G. W. Pierce to John Z. Leyendecker, March 25, 1861, Leyendecker Papers, CAH.

64. Løvenskiold to Lubbock, January 19, 1862, Lubbock Papers, TSA.

65. Lubbock to Hébert, December 10, 1861, LR, Dist. of Texas, NM, and Ariz., RG 109, NA.

66. Benavides to Lubbock, December 28, 1861, Lubbock Papers, TSA.

67. Testimony of Carlos Salinas before the Robb Commission, Records of Boundary and Claims Commissions and Arbitrations, RG 76, NA.

68. Testimony of José María Rodríguez before the Robb Commission, Records of Boundary and Claims Commissions and Arbitrations, RG 76, NA. Joseph A. Durand testified that the Kickapoos also struck into Atascosa County in 1862, killing and carrying off captives. Joseph A. Durand, Testimony before the Robb Commission, Records of Boundary Commissions and Arbitrations, RG 76, NA.

69. Løvenskiold to Benavides, January 25, 1862, Ford Papers, Haley Library.

70. Daniell, *Types of Successful Men of Texas*, 325.

71. Muster Roll of Refugio Benavides's Company, CAH.

72. S. W. Pease, *They Came to San Antonio, 1794–1865* (n.p., n.d.), 153–56; Eighth Census (1860), Nueces County, Texas, NA.

73. Thompson, *Vaqueros in Blue and Gray*, 23.

74. [Juan G. Garza] to Santos Benavides and Cristóbal Benavides, May 31, 1861, Correspondencia del Alcalde de Guerrero, Nuevo Guerrero Archives.

75. Ford to Clark, July 14, 1861, Clark Papers, Texas State Archives.

76. M. Capistran to [John S. Ford?], October 19, 1861, LR, Dist. of Texas, N. M., and Arizona, RG 109, NA.

77. Benavides to Vidaurri, June 10, 1861, Correspondencia de Vidaurri, AGNL. Santos was writing in response to a letter from Vidaurri inquiring if Santos could find buyers for part of his horse herd, which was reproducing faster than he could sell the animals. Few could offer "well bred mares at favorable prices" like his, the governor wrote. Vidaurri to Benavides, May 30, 1861, Correspondencia de Vidaurri, AGNL.

78. Vidaurri to Benavides, June 22, 1861, Vidaurri Papers, AGNL.

79. Ford to Benavides, May 29, 1861, Ford Papers, Haley Library.

80. G. García to Benavides, May 29, 1861, Correspondencia de Vidaurri, AGNL.

81. Ford to Benavides, May 29, 1861 (first letter), Ford Papers, Haley Library.

82. Ford to Benavides, May 29, 1861 (second letter), Ford Papers, Haley Library. Also, Ford to Benavides, June 2, 1861, Ford Papers; McCaslin, *Fighting Stock*, 119; Ford, *Rip Ford's Texas*, 325; Hughes, *Rebellious Ranger*, 199; and Thompson, *Cortina*, 101.

83. Benavides to Vidaurri, July 11, 1861, Correspondencia de Vidaurri, AGNL. Also, Andrea Leyendecker to John Z. Leyendecker, July 6, 1861, Leyendecker Papers, CAH.

84. Ford to Clark, July 14, 1861, Clark Papers, TSA. Also, McCaslin, *Fighting Stock*, 127; Thompson and Jones, *Civil War and Revolution*, 45–56; and Tyler, *Santiago Vidaurri and the Southern Confederacy*, 50–52, 59.

85. Rosaura Hernández Rodríguez, "Comonfort y la intervención francesca," *Historia Mexicana* 13 (July–September 1963): 60.

86. After becoming a general in the liberal army, Comonfort was killed by guerrillas on the road from Querétaro to San Luis Potosí, near San Juan de la Vega, on

November 13, 1862. He was only fifty-one. President Juárez had his remains taken to Mexico City, where he was interred in the Panteón de San Fernando, where Juárez himself would be buried ten years later.

87. Ignacio Comonfort to Vidaurri, July 21, 1861, Correspondencia de Vidaurri, AGNL.

88. Tyler, *Santiago Vidaurri and the Southern Confederacy*, 59.

89. Andrea Leyendecker to John Z. Leyendecker, August 5, 1861, Leyendecker Papers, CAH.

90. Benavides to Earl Van Dorn, September 5, 1861, in Benavides, CMSR, RG 109, NA.

91. Vidaurri to Benavides, February 4, 1862, Correspondencia de Vidaurri, AGNL.

92. Vidaurri to Ángel Navarro, April 6, 1862, Correspondencia de Vidaurri, AGNL.

93. Benavides to Vidaurri, February 7, 1862, Correspondencia de Vidaurri, AGNL.

94. Benavides to Vidaurri, February 6, 1862, Correspondencia de Vidaurri, AGNL.

95. José M. J. Carvajal to Ford, March 15, 1862, Ford Papers, Haley Library; Vidaurri to Lubbock, April 6, 1862, Lubbock Papers, TSA. Also, Joseph E. Chance, *José María Jesús Carvajal: The Life and Times of a Mexican* Revolutionary (San Antonio, TX: Trinity University Press, 2006), 174–75; Tyler, *Santiago Vidaurri and the Southern* Confederacy, 50–53; Thompson, *Cortina*, 162–64; and McCaslin, *Fighting Stock*, 129.

96. Chance, *José María de Jesús Carvajal*, 174–75; and McCaslin, *Fighting Stock*, 128–29.

97. Vidaurri to Benavides, February 4, 1862, Correspondencia de Vidaurri, AGNL.

98. Benavides to Vidaurri, February 7, 1862, Correspondencia de Vidaurri, AGNL.

99. Vidaurri to Benavides, February 16, 1862, Correspondencia de Vidaurri, AGNL.

100. Ford, *Rip Ford's Texas*, 331–32.

101. For Santos Benavides's invoices, see January 16, May 25, June 23, August 1 and 29, September 22, October 31, and December 16, 1862. For those of Eulalio, see January 21, June 1, and December 31, 1862. For invoices of Cristóbal, see August 25, September 15, and December 31, 1862. For those of Basilio, see May 9, 1862. The invoice signed by Teresa Benavides is dated April 30, 1863. All are in Confederate Citizens File, RG 109, War Department Collection of Confederate Records, NA.

102. Benavides to Vidaurri, March 28, 1862, Correspondencia de Vidaurri, AGNL.

103. Vidaurri to Benavides, April 7, 1862, Correspondencia de Vidaurri, AGNL.

104. List of forces in the Sub-Military District of the Rio Grande, November 1, 1862, *OR*, I, 15: 851.

105. Benavides to Vidaurri, July 12, 1862, Correspondencia de Vidaurri, AGNL. Also, McCaslin, *Fighting Stock*, 130; and Chance, *José María de Jesús Carvajal*, 174–75.

106. Vidaurri to Benavides, July 29, 1862, Correspondencia de Vidaurri, AGNL.

107. Vidaurri to Benavides, May 14, 1862, Correspondencia de Vidaurri, AGNL.

108. Benavides to Vidaurri, July 3, 1862, Correspondencia de Vidaurri, AGNL.

109. Benavides to Vidaurri, October 30, 1862, Correspondencia de Vidaurri, AGNL.

110. Benavides to Vidaurri, October 14, 1862, Correspondencia de Vidaurri, AGNL.

111. Benavides to Vidaurri, October 24, 1862, Correspondencia de Vidaurri, AGNL.

112. Benavides to Vidaurri, December 15, 1862, Correspondencia de Vidaurri, AGNL.

113. Benavides to Vidaurri, February 1, 7, 20, 26, 1863, Correspondencia de Vidaurri, AGNL.

114. Benavides to Vidaurri, March 10, 1863, Correspondencia de Vidaurri, AGNL.

115. Llano to Señor Lienciado, n.d. [March, 1863], Correspondencia de Vidaurri, AGNL.

116. Benavides to Vidaurri, March 10, 1863, Correspondencia de Vidaurri, AGNL.

117. Vidaurri to Benavides, February 7, 1863, Correspondencia de Vidaurri, AGNL.

118. Benavides to Vidaurri, August 15, 1863, Correspondencia de Vidaurri, AGNL.

119. Benavides to Vidaurri, February 1, 1863, Correspondencia de Vidaurri, AGNL.

120. Bee to López, February 25, 1863, *OR*, I, 15: 99.

121. Thompson, *Mexican Texans in the Union Army*, 13.

122. Pierce to Seward, March 21, 1862, Matamoros Consular Dispatches, RG 59, NA.

123. Pierce to Seward, August 26, 1862, Matamoros Consular Dispatches, RG 59, NA.

124. *Dallas Herald* quoted in James Marten, "True to the Union: Texans in the U.S. Army," *North and South: The Magazine of the Civil War Conflict* 3 (November 1999): 83.

125. William Huster to E. J. Davis, December 12, 1863, William Huster CMSR, US Department of War, RG 94, NA. For the Nueces Massacre, see Rodman L. Underwood, *Death on the Nueces: German Texans, Treue der Union* (Austin, TX: Eakin Press, 2000); Robert W. Shook, "The Battle of the Nueces, August 10, 1862," *Southwestern Historical Quarterly* 66 (July 1962): 31–42; John W. Sansom, "The Desperate Battle of the Nueces River, August 10, 186[2]," *Hunter's Magazine* 1 (September 1911): 22–24; see also Pierce to Seward, September 22, 1862, Matamoros Consular Dispatches, RG 59, NA. For the flight of Texas Unionists to Mexico, see Pierce to Seward, March 1, 21, 24, April 8, 21, 22, 30, May 5, August 26, and September 21, 22, 1862, Monterrey Consular Dispatches, RG 59, NA. For accounts of Texas refugees arriving in Monterrey, see Caleb B. H. Blood to Seward, May 23, 1862; M. M. Kimmey to Seward, October 29, November 21, 1862, April 7, 17, June 4, September 21, 28, 1863, and May 21, 1864, Monterrey Consular Dispatches, RG 59, NA.

126. Thompson, *Mexican Texans in the Civil War*, 13.

127. E. Dorsey Etchinson to W. A. Pile, December 7, 1864, Matamoros Consular Dispatches, RG 59, NA.

128. Juan Leyendecker to Dear Family, n.d., Leyendecker Papers, CAH. This letters appears to be an addendum to Andrea's letter of September 27, 1862.

129. Andrea Leyendecker to John Z. Leyendecker, July 6, 1861, Leyendecker Papers, CAH.

130. Juan Leyendecker to Dear Family, n.d., Leyendecker Papers, CAH.

131. Jacob Leyendecker, CMSR, CAGO, RG 109, NA; Martin Hardwick Hall, *Confederate Army of New Mexico* (Austin, TX: Presidial Press, 1978), 171.

132. Benavides to Vidaurri, August 23, 1863, Correspondencia de Vidaurri, AGNL.

133. Benavides to Vidaurri, October 30, 1863, Correspondencia de Vidaurri, AGNL.

134. Ibid.

135. Benavides to Vidaurri, April 15, 1862, Correspondencia de Vidaurri, AGNL.

136. Gilberto Miguel Hinojosa, *A Borderlands Town in Transition: Laredo, 1755–1870* (College Station: Texas A&M University Press, 1983), 83.

137. *Bandera Americana* (Brownsville), February 2, 1863, quoted in the *Boletín Oficial* (Monterrey), n.d., copy in Pickett Papers, LC.

138. Journal of James Hampton Kuykendall, December 27, 28, 1863, CAH.

139. *Fort Brown Flag* (Brownsville), February 2, 1863, quoted in the *Corpus Christi Ranchero,* January 22, 1863; *Bandera Americana* (Brownsville), February 2, 1863, quoted in the *Boletin Oficial* (Monterrey), n.d., copy in Pickett Papers, LC.

140. Bee to Albino López, February 3, 1863, *OR*, I, 15, 966–67.

141. López to Bee, March 20, 1863, Cotton Bureau Records, Treasury Department, RG 365, NA. There is no evidence the two men were ever captured, and both became officers in the Union Army.

142. Vidaurri to Benavides, August 30, 1863, Correspondencia de Vidaurri, AGNL.

143. *Reports of the Committee of Investigation Sent in 1873*, 69; Bee to López, April 22, 1863, *OR*, I, 15, 1,051–53.

144. *Corpus Christi Ranchero,* January 15, 23; February 5, 1863; *Houston Tri-Weekly Telegraph*, February 2, 1863; *Confederate Veteran* (1922): 473. Ford also recalls the fight in his "Influence of the Benavides Family," n.d., Ford Papers, Haley Library.

145. Ford, "Influence of the Benavides Family," n.d., Ford Papers, Haley Library.

146. Benavides to P. N. Luckett, February 15, 1863, in Benavides, CMSR, RG 109, CAGO, NA.

147. Miguel Gonzales, quoted in Carroll, "Texas Collection," 455.

148. Bee to López, March 19, 1863; López to [Bee], March 20, 1863, *OR*, I, 15, Pt. 1,133; Octaviano Zapata to Antonio Pérez, July 24, 1863, Correspondencia de Santiago Vidaurri, Archivo General del Estado de Nuevo León. At this time, Leonard Pierce Jr., the American consul in Matamoros, reported he had three hundred muskets in his possession. It is probable these arms were intended for Zapata's guerrillas. Pierce to Seward, April 10, 1863, Matamoros Consular Dispatches, RG 59, NA.

149. Bee to Manuel Ruiz, September 7, 1863, Bee Letterbook, Library, United States Military Academy, West Point, New York.

150. Vidaurri to Benavides, August 15, 1863, Correspondencia de Vidaurri, AGNL.

151. Benavides to E. J. Gray, March 13, 1863, Cotton Bureau Records, Confederate Department of the Treasury, RG 395, NA.

152. Benavides Statement, [March 12, 1863], in Encarnación García, CMSR, RG 109, NA.

153. López to Bee, March 15, 1863, *OR*, I, 15: 1,128–29,

154. Benavides to Gray, March 13, 1863, Cotton Bureau Records, RG 393, NA.

155. Ibid.

156. Ibid.

157. Ibid.

158. López to Bee, March 15, 1863, *OR*, I, 15: 1,129 (first quote); López to Bee, March 17, 1863, *OR*, I, 15: 1,131 (second quote).

159. Bee to López, March 22, 1863, *OR*, I, 4, 1,135.

160. Juan Cortina to Miguel Negrete, May 15, 1864; Alberto María Carreño, ed.,

Archivo del General Porfirio Díaz: Memorias y Documentos (Mexico City: Editorial "Elede," 1949), 3:302.

161. G. W. Hagler, "Charges and Specifications preferred against Private Benjamin Thompson," Benjamin Thompson CMSR, RG 109, CAGO, NA.

162. Lt. Martin Gonzales lived to the end of the war and beyond. Moreover, there is no record of a sergeant named Zertuche having enlisted with Santos or having served in the Confederate Army. Martin Gonzales, CMSR, RG 109, CAGO, NA.

163. The Thompson legend is repeated in W. M. Walton, *Life and Adventures of Ben Thompson* (Austin, TX: Steck, 1956), 37–45; J. B. Wilkinson, *Laredo and the Rio Grande Frontier* (Austin, TX: Jenkins, 1975), 285; Thompson, *Vaqueros in Blue and Gray*, 52–53; and Miscellaneous Notes, Seb Wilcox Papers, St. Mary's University Library, San Antonio, Texas. There is no definitive biography of the notorious gunman, and Tom Bicknell and Anne Beck fail to mention any such incident in their entry in the *Handbook of Texas History*, http://www.tshaonline.org/handbook/online/articles/fth16, accessed May 22, 2015.

164. Benavides to Gray, April 13, 1863, *OR*, I, 15: 1,040–41.

165. Ibid.

166. López to Bee, April 17, 1863, *OR*, I, 15: 1,044–45.

167. Bee to López, April 22, 2863, *OR*, I, 15: 1052.

168. James Duff to J. H. Earle, July 1, 1864, in Santos Benavides, CMSR, RG 109, CAGO, NA.

169. Benavides to William O. Yager, September 3, 1863, *OR*, I, 14, 285. Also, *Reports of the Committee of Investigation Sent in 1873*, 200–203; *Corpus Christi Ranchero*, September 17, 1863. Although there is no record of Zapata as officially part of the First or Second Texas (Union) Cavalry, there is little doubt that he saw himself as part of the Union Army.

170. Bee to Edmund P. Turner, September 11, 1863, OR, I, 26, 2: 284. This same letter is in the Bee Letterbook, Library, USMA.

171. [Octaviano Zapata] to Antonio Perez, n.d., 1863, Correspondencia de Vidaurri, AGNL.

172. [Zapata] to Antonio Perez, July 24, 1863, Correspondencia de Vidaurri, AGNL.

173. Benavides to Vidaurri, October 30, 1863, Correspondencia de Vidaurri, AGNL.

174. Bee to Turner, September 11, 1863, *OR*, I, 14, 284.

175. Joint resolution of thanks to Major-General Magruder, C. S. Army, and others," *Official Records of the Union and Confederate Navies in the War of the Rebellion*, I, 19:468, http://texashistory.unt.edu/ark:/67531/metapth192854/m1/493/?=santos benavides, accessed November 11, 2015; also, Joint Resolution of the Texas Legislature, quoted in General Order No. 56, March 30, 1863, *OR*, I, 15: 221; and *Texas Almanac for 1864*, 19, http://texashistory.unt.edu/ark21/?q=s67531/meta/m1/21/?q=santos7531/meta/m1/21/?q=santos, accessed November 21, 2015.

176. Stephen D. Yancey, endorsement on GO 56, March 30, 1863, *OR*, I, 15, 221.

177. Ibid.

Chapter IV

1. W. M. Perkins to W. J. Hutchins, June 3, 1864, LR, Records of the Trans-Mississippi Cotton Bureau, Confederate Treasury Dept., RG 365, NA.

2. The best study of Confederate diplomacy remains Frank Lawrence Owsley, *King Cotton Diplomacy: Foreign Relations of the Confederate States of America* (Chicago: University of Chicago Press, 1959); also see J. M. Callahan, *Diplomatic History of the Southern Confederacy* (Baltimore, MD: Johns Hopkins Press, 1901).

3. *New York Times*, February 8, 1863.

4. Eliza Ripley, *From Flag to Flag: A Woman's Adventures and Experiences in the South during the War, in Mexico and in Cuba* (New York: D. Appleton, 1889), 95–96.

5. John Warren Hunter, "The Fall of Brownsville on the Rio Grande, November 1863," typescript, CAH, 4–5; see also John Warren Hunter, *Heel-Fly Time in Texas* (Bandera, TX: Frontier Times, 1931), 11–12; and Ronnie C. Tyler, "Cotton on the Border, 1861–1865," *Southwestern Historical Quarterly* 73 (April 1970): 456.

6. Hunter, "The Fall of Brownsville," 4–5; and Tyler, "Cotton on the Border," 456.

7. Hunter, "The Fall of Brownsville," 4–5. Some of the larger firms operating on the Rio Grande were those of Droege, Oetling and Company; King, Kenedy, and Stillman; Brown, Fleming and Company; Harding, Pullin and Company of London; Lloyd's of London; Treviño Brothers; Oliver Brothers of Monterrey; Attrill and Lacosta; and Marks and Company. See Daddysman, *Matamoros Trade*, 31. For an excellent account of Matamoros during the war, see Robert W. Delaney, "Matamoros: Port for Texas during the Civil War," *Southwestern Historical Quarterly* 58 (April 1955): 473–87.

8. Pierce to Seward, March 1, 1862, *OR*, I, 9, 674.

9. Ed. J. Allen to John Price, January 12, 1866, LR, AGO, RG 94, NA.

10. Daddysman, *Matamoros Trade*, 33.

11. James Arthur Lyon Fremantle, *Fremantle Diary: Being the Journal of Lieutenant Colonel James Arthur Lyon Fremantle, Coldstream Guards, on His Three Months in the Southern States*, ed. Walter Lord (London: Andre Deutsch, 1956), 6.

12. Theodorus Bailey to Gideon Welles, eds., *Official Records of the Union and Confederate Navies in the War of the Rebellion*, 30 vols. (Washington, DC: Government Printing Office, 1894–1927), I, 17, 403. Hereafter referred to as *ORN*, by series and volume. Also, *Daily Ranchero* (Brownsville), December 16, 1866.

13. *New York Herald*, July 29, 1865.

14. *Daily Ranchero* (Matamoros), January 18, 1866 (first quote); and *New York Herald*, July 2, 1865 (second quote).

15. *New York Herald*, July 2, 1865.

16. William Watson, *Adventures of a Blockade Runner; or, Trade in Time of War* (London: Unwin, 1892), 26.

17. The voluminous José San Román Papers at the CAH have yet to be thoroughly studied by scholars.

18. Wooster, *Texas and Texans in the Civil War*, 119–20; Daddysman, *Matamoros Trade*, 35; and J. Fred Rippy, *United States and Mexico* (New York: Alfred A. Knopf, 1926), 238.

19. Jesse Gillam to W. A. Broadwell, July 28, 1864, Trans-Mississippi Cotton Bureau, Confederate Treasury Dept., RG 365, NA.

20. Tyler, *Santiago Vidaurri and the Southern Confederacy*, 34.

21. Ibid.

22. For an excellent overview of the cotton trade on the Rio Grande, see: S. L. James to C. M. Fontleroy, October 18, 1863, LR, Houston Bureau, Trans-Mississippi Cotton Bureau, Confederate Treasury Dept., RG 365, NA.

23. S. Hart to Lieutenant Phillips, May 29, 1863, LR, Dist. of Texas, N. M., and Arizona, RG 109, NA.

24. F. E. Mitchell to Leyendecker, September 9, 1864, Leyendecker Papers, CAH.

25. GO No. 142, July 23, 1864; and GO No. 51, July 11, 1864; both in Trans-Mississippi Cotton Bureau, Confederate Treasury Dept., RG 365, NA.

26. *Houston Tri-Weekly Telegraph*, December 30, 1863.

27. Bee to A. M. Hobby, March 29, 1863; Hobby to James A. Ware, April 11, 1863; both in LR, Dist. of Texas, N. M., and Arizona, RG 109, NA.

28. Magruder endorsement, n.d., Index to LR, Trans-Mississippi Cotton Bureau, Confederate Treasury Dept., RG 365, NA.

29. Benavides to Vidaurri, December 29, 1863, Correspondencia de Vidaurri, AGNL.

30. S. Hart to J. E. Slaughter, March 7, 1864, LR, Dist. of Texas, N. M., and Arizona, RG 109, NA. Also, J. M. Peñaloza, SO No. 4, November 3, 1864, General Correspondence, Shreveport Office of the Trans-Mississippi Cotton Bureau, Confederate Treasury Dept., RG 365, NA.

31. LR, Santos Benavides, January 9, 1864, Records of the Cotton Bureau of the Trans Mississippi, Confederate Treasury Dept., RG 365, NA.

32. Clayton L. Jewett, *Texas in the Confederacy: An Experiment in Nation Building* (Columbia: University of Missouri Press, 2002), 193–94.

33. Benavides to Vidaurri, February 1, 1862, Correspondencia de Vidaurri, AGNL.

34. Vidaurri to Benavides, February 4, 1862, Correspondencia de Vidaurri, AGNL.

35. Thompson, *Mexican Texans in the Union Army*, 10–15.

36. A. Lincoln to Edwin M. Stanton, August 4, 1862, *The Collected Works of Abraham Lincoln* (New Brunswick, NJ: Rutgers University Press, 1953), 5:357.

37. *Harper's Weekly*, November 28, 1863. The storm forced some of the men to throw their mules overboard, as well as wagons and forage for the animals.

38. Banks to Lincoln, November 3, 1863, *OR*, I, 26, Pt. 1, 396. Also, Banks to Halleck, November 4, 1863, *OR*, I, 25, Pt. 1, 397–98; Banks to Halleck, November 6, 1863, *OR*, I, 26, Pt. 1, 399–400.

39. Ibid.

40. Ford to Turner, January 24, 1864, *OR*, I, 26, Pt. I: 955.

41. Davis to [Banks], n.d., John L. Haynes CMSR, RG 94, NA.

42. Haynes to Banks, August 26, 1863, John L. Haynes, CSR, RG 94, NA.

43. Haynes to Cortina, September 12, 1863. Letter in private collection. Also, Thompson, *Mexican Texans in the Union Army*, 10–15; and Thompson, *Cortina*, 110–11.

44. Edmund P. Turner to Bee, June 5, 1863, *OR*, I, 26, Pt. 2, 37.

45. Bee to Turner, April 27, 1863, LR, Dist. of Texas, N. M., and Arizona, RG 109, NA.

46. Bee to Turner, August 15, 1863, Bee Letterbook, Library, USMA.

47. Bee to Turner, August 24, 1863, Bee Letterbook, Library, USMA.

48. Henry T. Davis to George W. Caldwell, November 11, 1863, *OR*, I, 26, Pt. 1,

444–45. The bluecoats had come to the Rio Grande frontier "to enlist the Mexicans and arm the negroes as they march[ed] through Texas." Bee to Turner, November 15, 1863, *OR*, I, 26, Pt. 2, 414.

49. Bee to Turner, November 5, 1863, *OR,* I, 26, Pt. 1, 433.

50. *Houston Tri-Weekly Telegraph*, November 12, 1863, quoting the *Fort Brown Flag* (Brownsville), October 30, 1863.

51. Several of Vidal's men were later arrested for murders committed in Mexico and were executed by firing squad in Matamoros in January 1867. *Brownsville Daily Ranchero*, January 18, 1867.

52. Jerry Thompson, "Mutiny and Desertion on the Rio Grande: The Strange Case of Captain Adrian J. Vidal," *Military History of Texas and the Southwest* 11 (1975), 160–69; Jerry Thompson, "Adrian J. Vidal: Soldier of Three Republics," *Hispanic Genealogical Journal*, 14 (1996), 74–84; *Houston Tri-Weekly Telegraph*, June 16, 1865; and Jane Clements Monday and Frances Brannen Vick, *Petra's Legacy: The South Texas Ranching Empire of Petra Vela and Mifflin Kenedy* (College Station: Texas A&M University Press, 2007), 104–106.

53. Bee to Turner, November 8, 1863, *OR,* I, 26, Pt. 1, 434.

54. Ibid.

55. Ibid., 435.

56. Bee to Benavides, November 3, 1863, *OR*, I, 26, 2: 399.

57. Special Orders No. 108, November 26, 1863, Ford Papers Haley Library. Copies of Ford's letters can be found at the Harold B. Simpson Research Center, Hill College, Hillsboro, Texas, and at the Texas State Archives.

58. Charles Russell to Turner, November 18, 1863, LR, Dist. of N.M., Ariz., and Texas, RG 109, NA.

59. Magruder to Cortina, May 22, 1864, *OR*, I, 34, Pt. 3, 835; and P. Murrah, June 23, 1864, endorsement on same, *OR*, I, 34, Pt. 3, 836.

60. M. M. Kimmey to Seward, May 21, 1864, *OR*, I, 34, Pt. 4, 467.

61. Bee and Slaughter to Turner, September 14, 1863, Bee Letterbook, Library, USMA.

62. Bee and Slaughter to Turner, September 14, 1863, Bee Letterbook, Library, USMA; Ford, "Influence of the Benavides Family," n.d., Ford Papers, Haley Library.

63. W. R. Boggs to Benavides, November 3, 1865, Ford Papers, Haley Library.

64. Benavides to Bee, November 11, 1863, *OR*, I, 26, Pt. 2: 405–6.

65. Ibid. For Bee's promises to Santos, see also Bee to Turner, November 15, 1863, *OR*, 1, 26: 2, 414–15

66. Turner to Bee, December 5, 1863, *OR*, I, 26, 2: 483.

67. Antonio Abad Dias to Pedro Gonzalez Uriegas, January 7, 1864, Ford Papers, Haley Library.

68. Magruder to Boggs, January 6, 1864, *OR*, 1, 34, Pt. 2, 834.

69. Ibid.

70. Turner to Bee, December 5, 1863, *OR*, 1, 26, 2: 483.

71. Slaughter to Benavides, March 24, 1864, LS, Dist. of Tex., NM, and Ariz., RG 109, NA.

72. Magruder to Boggs, January 6, 1864, *OR*, I, 34, Pt. 2, 834.

73. Magruder to Boggs, December 5, 1863, *OR*, I, 26, 2: 404.

74. Charles Russell to B. Bloomfield, November 28, 1863, *OR*, I, 53: 917.

75. Thompson, *Mexican Texans in the Civil War*, 15.

76. N. J. T. Dana to Pierce December 1, 1863, *OR*, I, 26, Pt. 1: 830.

77. Ford, "Influence of the Benavides Family," n.d., Ford Papers, Haley Library.

78. Vicki Betts, "'Private and Amateur Hangings': The Lynching of W. W. Montgomery, March 15, 1863," *Southwestern Historical Quarterly* 88 (October 1984), 147.

79. Houston *Tri-Weekly Telegraph*, January 20, February 1, 1864; Tom Lea, *The King Ranch* (Boston: Little, Brown and Co., 1957), I, 215–18; James Speed CMSR, RG 94, NA.

80. Ford, *Rip Ford's Texas*, 638–39; John S. Ford "Memoirs," CAH, 1,058.

81. Ford, *Rip Ford's Texas*, 355.

82. In 2001, Homero Vera, editor of *Los Mesteños* for a number of years and a resident of Premont at the time, after much effort, located what is thought to be the site of Los Patricios twelve miles northwest of Premont.

83. Nolan to Ford, March 15, 1864, *OR*, I, 34, Pt. I, 642–43; *Corpus Christi Caller*, November 22, December 6, 1976.

84. *Houston Tri-Weekly Telegraph*, December 18, 1863, quoting *Austin State Gazette*, n.d.

85. Ibid.; also, John Adams, *Conflict and Commerce on the Rio Grande: Laredo, 1755–1955* (College Station: Texas A&M University Press, 2008), 90.

86. Benavides to Vidaurri, December 2, 1863, Correspondencia de Vidaurri, AGNL.

87. Benavides to Vidaurri, December 25, 1863, Correspondencia de Vidaurri, AGNL. The scheme to save his property is also mentioned in Nicolas Sanchez to [Vidaurri], January 1, 1864, Correspondencia de Vidaurri, AGNL.

Chapter V

1. Ford, *Rip Ford's Texas*, 344.

2. Edmund P. Turner to Ford, December 22, 1863, *OR*, I, 26, Pt. 2, 525–26.

3. Ford to Benavides, December 28, 1863, Ford Papers.

4. Ford to Comdg. Officer of the Post at Eagle Pass, February 18, 1864; Ford to Theodore Herman, February 21, 1864; both in Ford Letterbook I (February 18, 1864–April 25, 1864), Ford Papers, Haley Library.

5. N. P. Banks to F. J. Herron, December 25, 1863, *OR*, I, 26, Pt. 1: 880.

6. Dana to Charles P. Stone, December 24, 1863, *OR*, I, 26, Pt. 1: 877.

7. T. P. Macmanus to N. J. T. Dana, February 13, 1864, *OR*, I, 34, 2: 316–20. Also, Jerry Thompson and Lawrence T. Jones III, *Civil War and Revolution on the Rio Grande Frontier: A Narrative and Photographic History* (Austin: Texas State Historical Association, 2004), 70; Stephen A. Townsend, *The Yankee Invasion of Texas* (College Station: Texas A&M University Press, 2006), 143–44; and Jerry Thompson, ed., *New Mexico Territory during the Civil War: Wallen and Evans Inspection Reports, 1862–1863* (Albuquerque: University of New Mexico Press, 2008), 12–13.

8. N. P. Banks to Carleton, November 5, 1863; and R. W. Creel to J. R. West, December 7, 1863, both in Letters Received, Department of New Mexico, RG 393, AGO, NA.

9. H. W. Halleck to Carleton, April 11, 1864, *OR*, I, 34: 135–36; Thompson, *New Mexico Territory during the Civil War*, 13.

10. Ford reported on March 9, 1864, that Skillman had "gone above for Eagle Pass."

Ford to E. P. Turner, March 9, 1864, Ford Letterbook I, Ford Papers. For Skillman, see Glen Sample Ely, "Skullduggery at Spencer's Ranch: Civil War Intrigue in West Texas," *Journal of Big Bend Studies* 21 (2009): 9–29; and Jerry Thompson, "Drama in the Desert: The Hunt of Henry Skillman in the Trans-Pecos, 1862–1864," *Password* 37 (Fall 1992): 107–26. For a thorough discussion of Carleton's plans for defending New Mexico Territory, see Jerry Thompson, *A Civil War History of the New Mexico Volunteers and Militia* (Albuquerque: University of New Mexico Press, 2016), 229–53.

11. José Quintero to Judah Benjamin, December 23, 1863; and Quintero to Simeon Hart, December 23, 1863, Pickett Papers; Clarence C. Thayer to E. Kirby Smith, December 20, 1863; and Patricio Milmo to Thayer, December 17, 1863, *OR*, I, 53, 931–33. One of the more scholarly accounts of the "Milmo difficulty" can be found in Tyler, *Santiago Vidaurri and the Southern Confederacy*, 123–27.

12. Vidaurri to Benavides, October 29, 1864, Correspondencia de Vidaurri, AGNL. At the same time, Vidaurri sent one of his servants who was ill, Sebastian Samaniego, to Laredo in a cart, hoping that he could receive better treatment in Texas.

13. Special Orders No. 12, January 24, 1864, Ford Papers.

14. Quintero to Benjamin, January 25, February 1, 1864, Pickett Papers; Tyler, *Santiago Vidaurri and the Southern Confederacy*, 124–25; Joseph Howard Parks, *General Edmund Kirby Smith, C. S. A.* (Baton Rouge: Louisiana State University Press, 1954), 302–5, 352–53.

15. Slaughter to Benavides, March 2, 1864, LS, Dist. of Tex., NM, and Ariz., RG 109, NA.

16. Benavides to Magruder, April 4, 1864, RG 365, Treasury Department Collection of Confederate Records, NA. Also, James Arthur Irby, "Line of the Rio Grande: War and Trade on the Confederate Frontier" (Ph.D. diss., University of Georgia, 1969), 131–32; Thompson, *Vaqueros in Blue and Gray*, 100–101.

17. Special Orders No. 12, June 25, 1864, Ford Papers, Haley Library.

18. Ford to Comdg. Officer of the Post at Eagle Pass, Letterbook I, Ford Papers, Haley Library.

19. Ángel Navarro to Vidaurri, December 1, 1863, Correspondencia de Vidaurri, AGNL. Early in the war, Navarro was instrumental in recruiting a company in San Antonio that became Co. H of Col. Alfred Marmaduke Hobby's Eighth Texas Infantry. Also, David McDonald, *José Antonio Navarro: In Search of the American Dream in Nineteenth Century Texas* (Denton: Texas State Historical Association, 2010), 255.

20. Vidaurri to Ángel Navarro, December 5, 1863, Correspondencia de Vidaurri, AGNL. The elder Navarro had also written to say he was willing to assist Vidaurri but that he was too old and he had become an American. José Antonio Navarro to Vidaurri, May 24, 1860, Correspondencia de Vidaurri, AGNL.

21. McDonald, *José Antonio Navarro*, 256.

22. Ángel Navarro to Vidaurri, May 13, 1860, Correspondencia de Vidaurri, AGNL.

23. *Galveston Tri-Weekly News*, January 24, 1864, quoting *San Antonio Herald*, January 15, 1864.

24. Quoted in Ford, *Rip Ford's Texas*, 347–48. For the drought, see National Oceanic and Atmospheric Administration, United States Department of Commerce, "Reconstruction of Past Drought across the Coterminous United States from a Network of Climatically Sensitive Tree-Ring Data," www.ngdc.noaa.gov/paleo@

pdsiyear.html, accessed December 24, 2005. With the exception of 1861, when the rainfall was normal in South Texas, every year from 1859 to 1864 had rainfall from two to three inches below normal. Not until 1865 was the drought in the region broken by adequate precipitation.

25. Benavides to Ford, January 27, 1864, Ford Papers, Haley Library.

26. Benavides to Ford, January 29, 1864, Ford Papers, Haley Library.

27. Magruder to Benavides, February 3, 1864, LR, Dist. of Tex., NM, and Ariz., RG 109, NA.

28. George Pfeiffer to Benavides, February 20, 1864, Ford Papers, Haley Library.

29. Ford to Nolan, March 5, 1864, Ford Letterbook I, Ford Papers, Haley Library.

30. Ford to Benavides, March 5, 1864, Ford Letterbook I, Ford Papers, Haley Library. Presumably "the mountains" refers to the Texas Hill Country.

31. Benavides to Ford, January 27, 1864, Ford Papers, Haley Library.

32. Benavides to Ford, February 15, 1864, Ford Papers, Haley Library.

33. R. Benavides to Santos Benavides, February 22, 1864, Ford Papers, Haley Library; R. Benavides to Ford, February 22, 1864, Ford Papers, Haley Library.

34. Benavides to Slaughter, March 14, 1864, *OR*, I, 34, 2: 1042–43.

35. Thomas A. Dwyer to Ford, March 21, 1861, Ford Papers, Haley Library.

36. Election Returns, November 24, 1862, Webb County, Tex., TSA.

37. Ford, *Rip Ford's Texas*, 357. Santos's defiant order would be recalled in a speech by Attorney General Robert Lee Babbitt when he was dedicating a historical marker in San Agustín Plaza for the Texas centennial on October 16, 1936. *Laredo Times*, October 18, 1936.

38. Benavides to Ford, March 21, 1864, *OR*, I, 34, 1, 648; Thomas A. Dwyer to John S. Ford, March 21, 1864, Ford Papers, Haley Library; Jerry Thompson, "A Stand Along the Border: Santos Benavides and the Battle for Laredo," *Civil War Times Illustrated* 26 (August 1980): 26–33; Thompson, *Vaqueros in Blue and Gray*, 107–10. The Union version of the battle, if it exists, has been lost or has yet to be found.

39. Thomas A. Dwyer to Ford, March 21, 1863, Ford Papers, Haley Library.

40. Santos Benavides to John S. Ford, March 21, 1864, *OR*, 1, 34, Pt. 1, 648.

41. Dwyer to Ford, March 21, 1864, Ford Papers, Haley Library.

42. Benavides to Ford, March 19, 1864, I, 34, 1: 647–48.

43. Thompson, *Mexican Texans in the Civil War*, 24.

44. Ford to Showalter, March 22, 1864, Ford Letterbook I, Ford Papers, Haley Library.

45. Ford to John Littleton, March 22, 1864, Ford Letterbook I, Ford Papers, Haley Library.

46. Ford to Turner, March 24, 1864, Ford Letterbook I, Ford Papers, Haley Library.

47. Ford to Benavides, March 31, 1864, Ford Letterbook I, Ford Papers, Haley Library.

48. Ford to Turner, March 31, 1864, Ford Letterbook I, Ford Papers, Haley Library.

49. Ibid.

50. W. W. Camp to Ford, March 20, 1864, Ford Papers, Haley Library.

51. Ibid.

52. Ford to Benavides, April 7, 1864; and Ford to Benavides, April 8, 1864 (quote); both in Ford Letterbook I, Ford Papers, Haley Library.

53. Benavides to Ford, February 25, 1864, Ford Papers, Haley Library.

54. F. J. Herron to Charles P. Stone, January 15, 1864, *OR*, I, 34, 2, 84–87.

55. T. P. McManus to N. J. T. Dana, February 13, 1864, *OR*, I, 34, 2, 316–20.

56. H. P. Bee to A. G. Dickinson, November 13, 1863, *OR*, I, 26, 2, 413.

57. F. J. Herron to William Dwight, July 2, 1864, *OR*, I, 34, 1, 1,054.

58. J. B. Weyman to E. P. Turner, April 5, 1864, *OR*, I, 34, 3, 736.

59. James A. Ware to Bart J. DeWitt, June 20, 1864, *OR*, I, 34, 1, 1,034.

60. Ford to Benavides, February 4, 1864; Ford to Theodore Herman, February 21, 1864, Ford Letterbook I; both in Ford Papers, Haley Library.

61. Ford to Benavides, January 22, 1864, Ford Papers, Haley Library.

62. Ford to Benavides, December 28, 1863, Ford Papers, Haley Library.

63. Ford to Benavides, January 23, 1864, Ford Papers, Haley Library.

64. Ford to Nolan February 28, 1864, Ford Letterbook I, Ford Papers, Haley Library.

65. Ford to Benavides, Ware, and Giddings, February 4, 1864, LR, Dist. of Texas, N. M., and Arizona, RG 109, NA.

66. Ford, *Rip Ford's Texas*, 350.

67. Ford to Nolan, March 5, 1864, LR, Dist. of Texas, N. M., and Arizona, RG 109, NA. Also, Ford to Benavides, March 5, 1864; Ford to Giddings, March 5, 1864; Ford to Turner, March 6, 1864; all in Ford Papers, Haley Library. Nolan was later murdered in Corpus Christi on December 19, 1864. *Houston Tri-Weekly Telegraph*, January 6, 1865.

68. John S. Ford to E. P. Turner, April 9, 1964, *OR*, I, 34, Pt. 3, 754.

69. Ford to Turner, April 17, 1864, Ford Letterbook I, Ford Papers, Haley Library.

70. Benavides to James E. Slaughter, April 10, 1863, *OR*, I, 53: 980–91; also see M. Kimmey to Seward, March 29, 1863, Monterrey Consular Dispatches, RG 59, State Department Records, NA; and Tyler, *Santiago Vidaurri and the Southern Confederacy*, 141–42.

71. Charles Allen Smart, *Viva Juárez: A Biography* (New York: J. B. Lippincott, 1964), 277; Ralph Roeder, *Juárez and His Mexico* (New York: Viking Press, 1947), 512–13.

72. J. A. Quintero to J. P. Benjamin, January 25, 1864, Pickett Papers, LC; Tyler, *Santiago Vidaurri and the Southern Confederacy*, 137.

73. Smart, *Viva Juárez*, 303; Tyler, *Santiago Vidaurri and the Southern Confederacy*, 139.

74. Slaughter to [Benavides], March 24, 1864, Confidential Letters and Telegrams and Special Orders Issued, Dept. of Tex., NM, and Ariz., RG 109, NA.

75. Benavides to Slaughter, April 10, 1864, *OR* I, 53: 980–81, Haley Library.

76. Benavides to Slaughter, April 10, 1863, *OR*, I, 53: 981.

77. Tyler, *Santiago Vidaurri and the Southern Confederacy*, 139.

78. Ibid.

79. Ford to Turner, April 17, 1864, Ford Letterbook I, Ford Papers, Haley Library

80. Ford to Turner, April 17, 1864, *OR*, I, 53, 980–81. This letter is in Ford's Letterbook I and is quoted in Ford, *Rip Ford's Texas*, 359.

81. Ford to Turner, April 17, 1864, *OR*, I, 53, 980–01; also, McCaslin, *Fighting Stock*, 159.

82. Ford, *Rip Ford's Texas*, 359.

83. Ibid., 360.

84. Ford to C. H. Merritt, April 23, 1864, Ford Letterbook I, Ford Papers, Haley Library.

85. Aldrich to Benavides, May 3, 1864, LS, Dist. of Tex., NM, and Ariz., RG 109, NA.

86. Aldrich to Benavides, May 8, 1864, LS, Dist. of Tex., NM, and Ariz., RG 109, NA.

87. Ford to Benavides, April 24, 1864, Ford Letterbook I, Ford Papers, Haley Library.

88. Ford to Benavides, April 24, 1864, Ford Letterbook I, April 24, 1864, Ford Papers, Haley Library.

89. Ford to H. P. Bee, September 21, 1864, Ford Letterbook II, Ford Papers, Haley Library.

90. Ford to Turner, May 5, 1864, *OR*, I, 34, Pt. 3, 807; and Thompson, *Vaqueros in Blue and Gray*, 112.

91. Thompson, *Vaqueros in Blue and Gray*, 112.

92. Ford, Special Orders No. 69, May 17, 1864, Ford Papers, Haley Library.

93. John S. Ford to J. E. Slaughter, June 20, 1864, *OR*, I, 34, Pt. 4, 684–85.

94. Thompson, *Vaqueros in Blue and Gray*, 362.

95. Ford to J. E. Slaughter, July 2, 1864, *OR*, I, 34, Pt. 1, 1,055.

96. Thompson, *Mexican Texans in the Union Army*, 30.

97. Killed and Wounded at Las Rucias, [Texas,] June 25, 1864, Confederate Army Casualties and Narrative Reports, RG 109, NA; see also Frank Wilson Kiel, ed., "'Wir waren unser 20 Mann gegen 150' ('We were 20 men against 150'): The Battle of Las Rucias; A Civil War Letter from a German-Texan Soldier in the 1864 Union Invasion of the Lower Rio Grande Valley," *Southwestern Historical Quarterly* 105 (January 2002): 465–78.

98. Ford to Slaughter, July 2, 1864, OR, I, 34, Pt. 1, 1,055.

99. General Herron reported the Union losses at "15 to 20 killed and wounded." Francis J. Herron to William Dwight, June 26, 1864, *OR*, I, 34, Pt. 1, 1,055–56.

100. Ford to Slaughter, July 2, 1864, *OR*, I, 34, Pt. 1, 1,056.

101. Ibid., 1055. The fight at Las Rucias is also covered in McCaslin, *Fighting Stock*, 165–66.

102. Benavides to A. G. Dickinson, January 18, 1864, Ford Papers, Haley Library.

103. Aldrich to Benavides, June 28, 1864, LR, Dist. of Tex., NM, and Ariz., RG 109, NA.

104. Statement of G. J. Brown, n. d., Ford Papers, Haley Library.

105. A. M. Sanchez to Dear Friend [John Z. Leyendecker], January 26, 1865, Leyendecker Papers (translation from French courtesy of Elisabeth Butzer). Reports that Basilio Benavides had died in 1863 were premature.

106. Ford, *Rip Ford's Texas*, 365–66.

107. Ibid.

108. *New York Herald*, July 2, 1865.

109. As of May 1864, the weapons overlooking Boca Chica and on the south end of Brazos Santiago consisted of both light and heavy artillery, including two 20-pounder Parrots, two 30-pounders, one 24-pounder brass howitzer, one 24-pound-

er smoothbore, one 18-pounder smoothbore, and three 12-pounders. Post Returns, Brazos Santiago, August 1864, RG 393, AGO, NA.

110. Refugio Benavides to Felix Blücher, August 19, 1864, Ford Papers, Haley Library.

111. Ibid.

112. A. L. Cashell to [George H.] Giddings, September 15, 1864, Ford Papers, Haley Library.

113. Ford to R. Benavides and Other Officers of Benavides's Batt., September 22, 1864, Ford Letterbook III (September 22, 1864 to November 29, 1864), Ford Papers, Haley Library.

114. Ford to Refugio Benavides, April 6, 1865, Ford Papers.

115. Magruder to W. R. Boggs, January 6, 1864, *OR*, I, 34, 2: 835.

116. L. G. Aldrick to Benavides, January 21, 1864, Letters Sent, District of Tex., NM, and Ariz., RG 109 NA.

117. W. L. Newsom to W. Kearney, September 4, 1864, Ford Papers, Haley Library.

118. James H. Fry to Benavides, August 27, 1864, Ford Letterbook II, August 24, 1864–December 30, 1864, Ford Papers, Haley Library.

119. James H. Fry to Benavides, September 2, 1864, Ford Letterbook II, Ford Papers, Haley Library.

120. Ford to A. C. Jones, September 2, 1864; and Ford to W. J. Weisinger, September 2, 1864.Ford Letterbook II, Ford Papers, Haley Library.

121. Fry to R. Benavides, September 1, 1864, Ford Letterbook II, Ford Papers, Haley Library.

122. Fry to Cristóbal Benavides, August 27, 1864, Ford Letterbook II, Ford Papers, Haley Library.

123. Ford to J. E. Dwyer, October 11, 1864, Ford Letterbook II, Ford Papers, Haley Library.

124. Ford to Benavides, September 2, 1864, Ford Letterbook II, Ford Papers, Haley Library.

125. Ford to Wm. M. Perkins, October 6, 1864, Ford Letterbook II, Ford Papers, Haley Library.

126. Albert Wood to Friend Leyendecker, January 22, 1864, Leyendecker Papers, CAH.

127. Ford to Rose, September 9, 1864, Ford Letterbook II, Ford Papers, Haley Library.

128. Ford to Unknown (incomplete letter), Ford Letterbook II, Ford Papers, Haley Library.

129. Ford, *Rip Ford's Texas*, 383–84. These remarks are largely taken from Ford to Nolan, October 30, 1864, Ford Letterbook III, Ford Papers, Haley Library.

130. Ibid.

131. Ford to Nolan, October 29, 1864; and Ford to Nolan, October 30, 1864; Ford Letterbook III, Ford Papers, Haley Library.

132. Ford to Benavides, October 31, 1864, Ford Letterbook III, Ford Papers, Haley Library.

133. Ford to L. G. Aldrich, November 29, 1864, Ford Letterbook III, Ford Papers.

134. Ford, *Rip Ford's Texas*, 385.

135. Ibid., 385–86. Ford was also upset that Capt. Cristóbal Benavides had gone home to Laredo on a leave of absence and had not rejoined his command. In late August 1864, Ford ordered him back. Ford to Christobal [*sic*] Benavides, August 27, 1864, Ford Letterbook II, Ford Papers, Haley Library.

136. McCaslin, *Fighting Stock*, 187.

137. "Abstract from return of the Eastern Sub-District of Texas," November 1864, *OR*, I, 41, Pt. 4: 1,085.

138. Davis, Ellis A., and Edwin H. Grobe, *New Encyclopedia of Texas* (Dallas, Texas Development Bureau, 1926), 2: 963.

139. J. M. Peñaloza to General, December 19, 1863; Peñaloza to E. P. Turner, January 24, 1864; and Peñaloza to Theodore Lohmann, January 27, 1864; all in J. M. Peñaloza, CMSR, RG 109, CAGO.

140. Ford to Turner, March 11, 1864, Ford Letterbook I, Ford Papers, Haley Library.

141. J. E. Slaughter, Special Orders No. 22, February 7, 1865, Ford Papers, Haley Library.

142. George A. Gibson, CMSR, RG 109, CAGO, NA. In particular, see "Charges and Specifications preferred against Private G. A. Gibson of Co. 'E,' 3rd Regt., Tex. Vol. Inf., CSA" and Benavides to Edmund P. Turner, April 2, 1864, in ibid.

143. Sexton [Sixto] E. Navarro, CMSR, RG 109, CAGO, NA; Ángel Navarro, CMSR, RG 109, CAGO, NA; and 8th Census (1860), Atascosa County, Tex., NA.

144. H. C. Davis, CMSR, RG 109, CAGO, NA; and Garna L. Christian, "Rio Grande City," at https://www.tshaonline.org/handbook/online/articles/hfr05.

145. Julian Garica, CMSR, RG 109, CAGO, NA; P. B. Watson, CMSR, RG 109, CAGO, NA; and 8th Census (1860), Webb County, Tex., NA.

146. M. Dolan to S. A. Hurlbut, April 3, 1865, *OR*, I, 48, Pt. 2: 17–18.

147. Glen Sample Ely, "Skullduggery at Spencer's Ranch: Civil War Intrigue in West Texas," *Journal of Big Bend Studies* 21 (2009) 9–29; Ely, "What to Do about Texas? Texas and the Department of New Mexico in the Civil War." *New Mexico Historical Review* 85 (Fall 2010), 375–408; Ely, *The Frontier and the Butterfield Overland Mail, 1858–1861* (Norman: University of Oklahoma Press, 2016), 389; and Jerry Thompson, "Drama in the Desert: The Hunt for Henry Skillman in the Trans-Pecos, 1862–1864," *Password* 37 (Fall 1992), 107–62.

148. Ford to Benavides, February 26, 1864, Ford Papers, Haley Library.

149. Richard King to Green Hall, April 26, 1865, King Ranch Archives, Kingsville, Texas.

150. L. G. Aldrich to George Patrick, May 20, 1865, in *New York Tribune*, July 2, 1865.

151. *New York Tribune*, July 2, 1865.

152. William L. Richter, *The Army in Texas during Reconstruction, 1865–1870* (College Station: Texas A&M University Press, 1987), 13.

153. Ford, *Rip Ford's Texas*, 396.

154. *New York Herald*, July 2, 1865.

155. Testimony of Col. Theodore H. Barrett, Court Martial Records in the Case of Robert G. Morrison, July 21–August 29, 1865, JAGO, RG 153, NA.

156. Ibid.

157. Eight companies of the Thirty-fourth Indiana Infantry had arrived on Brazos Santiago three days before Christmas 1864, replacing the Ninety-first Illinois Infantry, which embarked for New Orleans on the *Clinton*. Post Returns, Brazos Santiago, December 1864, RG 393, AGO, NA.

158. Theodore H. Barrett to L. Thomas, August 10, 1865, *OR*, I, 48, Pt. 1, 266.

159. Ford, *Rip Ford's Texas*, 390.

160. Ibid., 391.

161. Ibid.

162. Theodore H. Barrett to L. Thomas, August 10, 1865, *OR*, I, 48, Pt. 1, 266.

163. Ibid.

164. Ibid.

165. David Branson Testimony, Morrison Court-Martial, JAGO, RG 153, NA.

166. Charles A. Jones Testimony, Morrison Court-Martial, JAGO, RG 153, NA.

167. Ford, *Rip Ford's Texas*, 390.

168. Barrett Testimony, Morrison Court-Martial, JAGO, RG, 153, NA.

169. Testimony of Capt. W. C. Dukee, Morrison Court-Martial, JAGO, RG, 153, NA.

170. W. H. Carrington to G. H. Giddings, n. d., Ford Papers, Haley Library.

171. Ibid.

172. Ford, *Rip Ford's Texas*, 391.

173. L. G. Aldrich to John S. Ford, October 21, 1890, in Ford, *Rip Ford's Texas*, 394–95.

174. Theodore Barrett to L. Thomas, August 10, 1865, *OR*, I, 48, 1, 267.

175. Noah Andre Trudeau, "The Last Gun Had Been Fired," *Civil War Times Illustrated* 29 (July–August 1990), 63.

176. Theodore Barrett to L. Thomas, August 10, 1865, *OR*, I, 48, Pt. 1, 267; also Noah Andre Trudeau, *Out of the Storm: The End of the Civil War, April–June 1865* (Baton Rouge: Louisiana State University Press, 1994), 309–10. For a detailed discussion of the confusion over the casualties at Palmito Ranch, see Phillip Thomas Tucker, *The Final Fury: Palmito Ranch, The Last Battle of the Civil War* (Mechanicsburg, PA: Stackpole Books, 2001), 156–63. For an excellent and comprehensive study of the battle, see Jeffrey Wm Hunt, *The Last Battle of the Civil War: Palmetto Ranch* (Austin: University of Texas Press, 2002).

177. Ford, *Rip Ford's Texas*, 393.

178. Hunt, *Last Battle of the Civil War*, 132

179. J. E. Slaughter to Commanding Officer, US Forces on the March, May 29, 1865, LR, AGO, RG 94, NA.

180. E. B. Brown to Slaughter, May 30, 1865, LR, AGO, RG 94, NA.

181. D. Finley to John Price, January 13, 1866; William Griffin to Price, January 13, 1866; Ed. J. Allen to Price, January 12, 1866; all in LR, AGO, RG 94, NA.

182. Brown to J. Schuyler Crosby, May 28, June 2, 1865, LR, AGO, RG 94, NA.

183. *Matamoros Daily Ranchero*, May 31, 1865.

184. Ed. J. Allen to John Price, January 12, 1866, LR. AGO, RG 94, NA.

185. Thompson and Jones, *Civil War and Revolution*, 94–95.

186. Brown to Crosby, May 30, 1865, LR, AGO, RG 94, NA.

187. F. Steele to P. H. Sheridan, June 10, 1866, LR, AGO, RG 94, NA.

188. W. G. Wiley to Headquarters, Military District of the Gulf, June 13, 1865, LR, AGO, RG 94, NA.

189. Benavides to Leyendecker, May 16, 1865, Leyendecker Papers, CAH.

190. Santos Benavides Parole, August 11, 1865, Benavides CMSR, CAGO, RG 109, NA.

Chapter VI

1. Gardner W. Pierce to Friend Leyendecker, May 4, 1865, Leyendecker Papers, CAH.

2. H. P. Bee to Jonah Randall, December 22, 1863, Bee Pardon File, Case files of applications from former Confederates for Presidential Pardons, RG 94, NA.

3. Ben Z. Grant, "A Texas Governor Buried in Mexico," *Marshall News Messenger*, January 3, 1999; Ben Z. Grant, "Finding Governor Murrah," *Marshall News Messenger*, March 14, 1999.

4. Edwin Adams Davis, *Fallen Guidon: The Saga of Confederate General Jo Shelby's March to Mexico* (College Station: Texas A&M University Press, 1995), 71.

5. Thompson, *Cortina*, 151. In 1868 Parsons's son and sister, along with the family of Aaron Conrow, sued the Mexican government via the General Claims Commission (United States and Mexico) and in 1875 received a judgment amounting to $50,000 in gold.

6. *Daily Ranchero* (Brownsville), September 26, 1866; also, *San Antonio Daily Herald*, July 6, 1866.

7. *Daily Ranchero* (Brownsville), September 26, 1866. "Sporting a huge moustache and huger whiskers," Carvajal had just arrived on the border from New York.

8. Tomás Mejía, José María J. Carvajal, et al., Agreement for the surrender of Matamoros, agreed to on June 22 and signed on June 23, *Conditions of Affairs in Mexico*, 233.

9. *Galveston Tri-Weekly Telegraph*, July 28, 1866; *San Antonio Daily Herald*, July 6, 1866.

10. For details of the execution, see *Daily Ranchero* (Brownsville), September 27, 1867; also, H. Montgomery Hyde, *Mexican Empire: The History of Maximilian and Carlota of Mexico* (London: Macmillan, 1946), 311; J. J. Gallegos, "Santiago Vidaurri: Regional Power, Trade and Capital Formation in Northern Mexico" (PhD diss., University of Houston, 2003), copy courtesy of the author.

11. Richter, *Army in Texas during Reconstruction*, 17.

12. C. Callaghan to Capt. Parsons, November 17, 1865, in Fort McIntosh Consolidated File, QGO, RG 92, NA; *Galveston Daily News*, July 21, 1865, quoting *San Antonio News*, July 5, 1865; and Thomas A. James and James Speed, CMSRs, RG 109, AGO, NA. Speed had been dismissed from the army at Brazos Santiago in June 1864 but had been reinstated in February 1865.

13. Cristóbal Benavides, interview by author, February 10, 1969.

14. Daniell, *Types of Successful Men of Texas*, 329–30. Presumably, Daniell obtained the information from Santos.

15. *New York Tribune*, September 1, 1865.

16. PR, Fort Ringgold, July, 1865, AGO, RG 393, NA. The Irish-born Jackson was a dedicated officer and combat veteran who rose from private to brigadier general during the Civil War.

17. PR, Fort Ringgold, October, 1865, AGO, RG 393, NA.

18. PR, Fort Ringgold, August, 1866, AGO, RG 393, NA.

19. PR, Fort McIntosh, October 1865, AGO, RG 393, NA.

20. PR, Fort McIntosh, March 1866, AGO, RG 393, NA. For a history of the 4th Wisconsin, see Michael J. Martin *A History of the 4th Wisconsin Infantry and Cavalry in the American Civil War* (New York: Savan Beatie, 2006).

21. Election Returns, December 21, 1866, Webb County, RG 307, TSA.

22. J. M. Rodríguez to A. J. Hamilton, February 7, 1866, Webb County Election Returns, RG 307, TSA.

23. A. F. Bayard, Special Order, n.d., March 29, 1869, Fort McIntosh, LS, RG 393, AGO, NA.

24. T. M. Anderson to Samuel M. Jarvis, September 26, 1869, Fort McIntosh, LS, RG 393, AGO, NA.

25 . *Nueces Valley* (Corpus Christi), December 14, 1872.

26. Tom Green, "Daughters Recall Early Laredo Days," *Laredo Times*, January 11, 1948.

27. Minutebook A, July 24, 1872, Special Collections, City Library, Laredo, Texas.

28. Green, "Daughters Recall Early Laredo Days," *Laredo Times*, January 11, 1948; also, Thompson, *Warm Weather and Bad Whiskey*, 34. Santa Clotilde was named for Clotilde Jarvis Withoff, Santa Maria for Maria Jarvis Diáz, and Sarita for another daughter. Sarita was later changed to Main Street, however.

29. Thompson, *Warm Weather and Bad Whiskey*, 33.

30. *Nueces Valley* (Corpus Christi), October 26, 1872; also, *Dallas Herald*, February 7, 1872, March 9, 1872, September 7, 1872, October 5, 1872, and April 27, 1873; and *Weekly Democratic Statesman* (Austin), July 3, 1873. Carroll appears to have been assisted by James Tucker, who at the age of seventeen was working for William Maltby on the *Corpus Christi Ranchero*. No copies of the *Two Eagles* are known to exist. 9th Census (1870), Nueces County, Texas, NA. For a list of newspapers quoting the *Two Eagles*, see William F. Walsh II, *The Sharpshooter, El Tirador de Primera: The Untold Story of Hamilton Cobb Peterson, U.S. Commissioner for the Justice Department, Laredo, Texas* (N.p., 2012).

31. Bee to Randall, December 22, 1865, Bee Pardon file, Case files of applications from former Confederates, RG 94, NA.

32. Henry Martin, comp., "Boothill Stories Taken from Dogtown: Stories of a Frontier Village with a Past," (n.p., n.d.), 78, courtesy of Martin Callahan.

33. Richard Gossett, Malachi Gossett, and Thomas F. Green, CMR, RG 109, CAGO, NA. Historians are often confused by the fact the Thirty-sixth Texas Cavalry was frequently referred to at the time as the Thirty-second Texas Cavalry.

34. Millard F. Martin Sr., *Zachariah Martin II, 1790–1873, Louisiana and Texas Pioneer: His Parents and His Descendants*. (n.p., 1976), 78.

35. Duaine, *Dead Men Wore Boots*, 100–101. The name of the community was changed to Tilden following the election of 1876 in honor of the defeated Samuel J. Tilden, who won the popular vote but lost the electoral vote and who many Democrats thought had been cheated out of the presidency. A street in Laredo was also named in Tilden's honor.

36. Martin, "Boothill Stories," 78.

37. Carl L. Duaine, *The Dead Men Wore Boots: An Account of the 32nd Texas Volun-*

teer Cavalry, C.S.A (Austin, TX: San Felipe Press, 1966), 100–101. Although created by the legislature in 1858, Frio County was not formally organized until 1871.

38. A. J. Hogan to Burton Drew, January 12, 1867, James Throckmorton Papers, TSA.

39. Cristóbal Benavides, Santos Benavides, et al., Affidavit, December 24, 1872, Throckmorton Papers, TSA.

40. PR, Fort McIntosh, December 1866, March 1867, AGO, RG 393, NA.

41. Charles Griffin to J. W. Throckmorton, February 2, 1867, Throckmorton Papers, TSA.

42. Ibid.

43. Ibid.

44. Duaine, *Dead Men Wore Boots*, 100–101.

45. Hogan to Drew, January 12, 1867, Throckmorton Papers, TSA.

46. *San Antonio Herald*, January 17, 1867.

47. Griffin to Throckmorton, February 2, 1867, Throckmorton Papers, TSA. If Governor Throckmorton did indeed write such a letter, it has long since disappeared from the historical record.

48. *Weekly State Gazette* (Austin), August 21, 1869.

49. C. E. Morse, letter, July 30, 1869, Register of LR, Fort McIntosh, AGO, RG 393, NA.

50. Nathaniel Prime, Order No. 3, May 23, 1869, LR, Dept. of Texas, AGO, RG 393, NA.

51. N. Prime to C. E. Morse, July 28, 1869, LS, Fort McIntosh, AGO, RG 393, NA.

52. General Orders No. 75, May 23, 1869, PR, Fort McIntosh, AGO, RG 393, NA.

53. Prime to Benavides, July 8, 1869, LS, Fort McIntosh, AGO, RG 393, NA.

54. Bernardo Mendiola to [Prime], July 17, 1869, Register of LR, Fort McIntosh, AGO, RG 393, NA.

55. Charles Callaghan to [Prime], July 19, 1869, Register of LR, Fort McIntosh, RG 393, AGO, NA.

56. James O. Luby, deposition, n.d., Records of Boundary and Claims Commissions and Arbitrations, Records of the Dept. of State, RG 76, NA. Julian Quiroga Villarreal was the former governor of Nuevo León.

57. *Nueces Valley* (Corpus Christi), October 14, 1871.

58. *Two Eagles* (Laredo), n.d., quoted in the *Dallas Daily Herald*, April 27, 1872.

59. David M. Level deposition, March 27, 1873, Records of Boundary and Claims Commissions and Arbitrations, Dept. of State, RG 76, NA.

60. *San Antonio Express*, October 22, 29, 1878.

61. *San Antonio Express*, October 31, 1878.

62. Refugio Benavides Oath, June 13, 1874, AGO, TSA. Santos's loyal sergeant from the Civil War, Darío Gonzales, was commissioned a second lieutenant. Gonzales Appointment Certification, AGO, TSA.

63. Refugio Benavides Oath, June 13, 1874, AGO, TSA.

64. *Report of the Special Committee on Texas Frontier Trouble*, House of Representatives, Report No. 343, 44th Cong., 1st Sess., 162.

65. Ibid., 51.

66. Ibid., x.

67. *San Antonio Express*, March 8, 1879.

68. Richard Coke to George H. Williams, August 6, 1874, *Texas Frontier Troubles*, 164–66.

69. Thompson, *Cortina*, 224.

70. *New York Times*, April 23, 1875. Also, McCaslin, *Fighting Stock*, 225.

71. *New Orleans Bulletin*, April 23, 1875; *New Orleans Republican*, April 23, 1875; and *Memphis Daily Appeal*, April 23, 1875.

72. J. Frank Dobie, *Vaquero of the Brush Country* (Austin: University of Texas Press, 1998), 62.

73. *New York Times*, October 22, 1875.

74. Chuck Parsons, and Marianne E. Hall Little, *Captain L. H. McNelly, Texas Ranger: The Life and Times of a Fighting Man* (Austin, TX: State House Press, 2001), 192; George Durham, *Taming the Nueces Strip: The Story of McNelly's Rangers* (Austin: University of Texas Press, 1962), 54; and Robert M. Utley, *Lone Star Justice: The First Century of the Texas Rangers* (New York: Oxford University Press, 2002), 162.

75. William H. Hager, "The Nuecestown Raid of 1875: A Border Incident," *Arizona and the West* 1 (autumn 1959): 267–78,

76. *Daily Ranchero* (Brownsville), February 17, 19, 1869; and Jerry Thompson, *Laredo, A Pictorial History* (Norfolk, VA: Donning, 1986), 195.

Chapter VII

1. William H. Emory, *Report on the United States and Mexican Boundary Survey Made under the Direction of the Secretary of the Interior* (Austin: Texas State Historical Association, 1987) 1:63–64.

2. Thompson, *Texas and New Mexico on the Eve of the Civil War*, 144.

3. N. A. Jennings, *A Texas Ranger* (New York: Charles Scribner's Sons, 1899), 40–41.

4. *Nueces Valley* (Corpus Christi), January 7, 1871.

5. *Memorial and Genealogical Record of Southwest Texas* (Chicago: Goodspeed Brothers, 1894), 477–79.

6. Thomas Gilgan to William Hunter, February 26, 1872, Consular Dispatches, Nuevo Laredo, RG 59, NA. For a thorough treatment of the incident and feud between Santos and Jarvis, see George T. Díaz, *Border Contraband: A History of Smuggling across the Rio Grande* (Austin: University of Texas Press, 2015), 33–34.

7. *Nueces Valley* (Corpus Christi), February 24, 1872; March 9, 1872 (quote); and May 18, 1872.

8. Santos and Cristóbal Benavides to US Consul, Monterrey, Mexico, February 21, 1872, Despatcher from US Consuls in Nuevo Laredo, RG 59, NA.

9. Santos and Cristóbal Benavides to Gilgan, February 21, 1872; and Gilgan to Julian Cerda, February 21, 1872; both in Consular Dispatches, Nuevo Laredo, RG 59, NA.

10. *Nueces Valley* (Corpus Christi), April 27, 1873.

11. *Nueces Valley* (Corpus Christi), January 7, 1871.

12. *Nueces Valley* (Corpus Christi), May 18, 1872, quoting *Two Eagles* (Laredo), n.d.

13. Thompson, *Pictorial History*, 16–47. For a description of the town at the time, see *San Antonio Express*, March 9, 1879.

14. *San Antonio Express*, October 24, 1878; and February 20, 1879.

15. Deed Book No. 4, 92–94; and Deed Book No. 5, 369, Webb County Clerk's Office.

16. Galen D. Greaser, comp., *New Guide to Spanish and Mexican Land Grants in South Texas* (Austin: Texas General Land Office, 2009), 259–60.

17. Deed Book No. 10 388, Webb County Clerk's Office. Each porción was 1,000 varas wide at the river and stretched into the interior some 30,000 varas. A Mexican or Spanish vara, also used by the early Anglo settlers in Texas, was equivalent to 33⅓ inches.

18. Deed Book No. 6, 2–3, Webb County Clerk's Office. Records indicate the property had two water holes.

19. 1880 Webb County Assessment Roll of Property, courtesy of Olee Rodriguez. Also, Warranty Deed, City of Laredo to Santos Benavides, July 19, 1875, Webb County Clerk's Office, Laredo, Texas.

20. *San Antonio Express*, May 9, 1879.

21. *San Antonio Express*, May 27, 1879.

22. *San Antonio Express*, June, 7, 1879.

23. Election Returns, Webb County, December 2, 1872, County Clerk's Office, Laredo, Texas.

24. J. M. Flournoy to J. P. Newcomb, November 4, 1872, in Election Returns, Webb County, RG 307, TSA.

25. Ibid.

26. Carl H. Moneyhon, *Texas after the Civil War: The Struggle for Reconstruction* (College Station: Texas A&M University Press, 2004), 197–98; Moneyhon, *Edmund J. Davis of Texas*, 265; Ford, *Rip Ford's Texas*, 417–20; and *Frank Leslie's Illustrated Weekly*, February 21, 1874.

27. *Nueces Valley* (Corpus Christi), July 20, 1872. For Jarvis's efforts to build a Republican Party in South Texas, see *Nueces Valley* (Corpus Christi), July 8, 1871; September 7, 1872; and August 29, 1874.

28. Minutebook A, November 27, 1873, Special Collections, City Library, Laredo, Texas.

29. Minutebook A, December 8, 1873, Special Collections, City Library, Laredo, Texas. Also, Thompson, *Warm Weather and Bad Whiskey*, 38.

30. *Nueces Valley* (Corpus Christi), January 3, 1874.

31. Minutebook A, January 5, 1873, Special Collections, City Library, Laredo, Texas.

32. Ibid.

33. Minutebook A, May 28, 1875, Special Collections, City Library, Laredo, Texas.

34. *San Antonio Light*, April 12, 1884.

35. Thompson, *Warm Weather and Bad Whiskey*, 40.

36. Carmina Danini, "The Immigrants Who Built Laredo," *Saludos* 3 (July 1976): 4. Martin died on March 2, 1900, and Tirza García on December 10, 1910. For Martin's obituary, see *Laredo Daily Times*, March 3, 1900. Ten children, five boys and five girls, were born into the Martin family. For Martin's economic influence on Laredo and South Texas, see Calderon, "Mexican Politics in the American Era," 618–19.

37. At the time of his death on March 2, 1900, Martin had amassed a fortune: personal property and real estate valued at $101,246. Besides 67,366 acres or approximately seventy-six sections of land, as well as 10,056 sheep, 3,591 goats, 159 horses,

and 2,365 cattle. "Inventory, Appraisement and List of Claims," June 18, 1900, Probate Record No. 341, County Clerk's Office, Webb County, Texas.

38. *State of Texas v. R. Martin*, June 6, 1870, 12th District Court Docket Book, District Clerk's Records, Special Collections, TAMIU, Laredo, Texas.

39. Minutebook A, December 13, 1875, Special Collections, City Library, Laredo, Texas.

40. Jose Moreno, "Laredo's First International Bridge," 8.

41. Minutebook A, January 8, 1877, Laredo Public Library; Moreno, "Laredo's First International Bridge," 11; and John A. Adams, *Conflict and Commerce on the Rio Grande, Laredo, 1755–1955* (College Station: Texas A&M University Press, 2008), 126–28.

42. Moreno, "Laredo's First International Bridge," 10.

43. Minutebook A, January 4, 1876, Laredo Public Library; Thompson, *Warm Weather and Bad Whiskey*, 42–43.

44. Ibid., 514

45. WPA Historical Records Survey, Webb County, Box 4H120; *Texas Reports* (Texas Supreme Court), 52: 511, 548.

46. *City of Laredo v. Macdonnel* in "Cases argued and declared in the Supreme Court of the State of Texas, during the Tyler term, 1879, and part of the Galveston term, 1880, vol. 52, 513 (first quote), 525 (second quote), 526, at http://texasjostpru/imt/edi/arl:/67531/metapth28522/m/521/?q=santos benavides, accessed December 24, 2013.

47. Ibid., 414.

48. *City of Laredo v. Raymond Martin and Laredo Ferry Company*, Texas Supreme Court Records, TSA; *City of Laredo v. Raymond Martin, et al.*; and *City of Laredo v. C. M. MacDonnell, et al.*, District Court Records, Special Collections, Texas A&M International University, Laredo, Texas; and *City of Laredo v. C. M. MacDonnell and the Ferry Company* in *Cases Argued and Decided in the Supreme Court of Texas* (San Louis: Gilbert Book, 1880), 52:511–12, 514, 520.

49. *City of Laredo v. Macdonnell*, 521 (first quote), 523 (second quote), District Court Records, Special Collections, TAMIU.

50. McCaslin, *Fighting Stock*, 225.

51. *New York Times*, February 2, 1876.

52. *New York Times*, May 10, 1876. Among the largest merchants were Daniel Milmo, L. G. Levy, Diamond and Hirsch, and Alderete and Son.

53. *New York Times*, April 20, 1876: Post Returns, Fort McIntosh, Tex., May 1876, AGO, RG 393, NA.

54. *New York Times*, April 12, 1876.

55. *New York Times*, May 10, 1876, quoting a letter from Laredo dated April 19, 1876.

56. Jennings, *Texas Ranger*, 66.

57. *New York Times*, April 11, 12; and May 10 with unsigned letter dated April 19, 1876

58. *New York Times*, April 12, 1876.

59. M. de Zamacona to W. M. Evarts, July 31, 1878, LR, AGO, RG 94, NA.

60. Ibid.

61. Michael C. Meyer, William L. Sherman, and Susan M. Deds, *Course of Mexican History* (New York: Oxford University Press, 1999), 421.

62. *Galveston Daily News*, December 7, 1881 quoting the *Two Republics* (Mexico City), n.d.

63. *Galveston Weekly News*, August 24, 1882.

64. Paul Garner, *Porfirio Díaz: Profiles in Power* (White Plains, NY: Longman, 2001), 93.

65. Impressive scholarship on the Porforiato includes Paul Vanderwood, "Genesis of the Rurales: Mexico's Early Struggle for Public Security," *American Historical Review* 50 (1970): 323–44; Enrique Krauze, *Porfirio Díaz: Mistico de la Autoridad* (Mexico City: Fondo de Cultura Económica, 1987); John Mason Hart's very readable *Revolutionary Mexico: The Coming and Process of the Mexican Revolution* (Berkeley: University of California Press, 1989); Laurens Ballard Perry, *Juárez and Díaz: Machine Politics in Mexico* (DeKalb: Northern Illinois University Press, 1978); Daniel Cosio Villegas, *The United States versus Porfirio Díaz* (Lincoln: University of Nebraska Press, 1963); and Paul Garner's more recent *Porfirio Díaz: Profile in Power* (New York: Routledge, 2001).

66. *Galveston Weekly News*, July 10, 1881.

67. Ibid.

68. Benavides to Manuel González, January 18, 1881 (telegram), Manuel González Papers, Universidad Iberoamerica, Mexico City, DF.

69. Benavides to González, January 26, 1881 (telegram), González Papers.

70. Benavides to González, April 12, 1881, González Papers.

71. *Galveston Weekly News*, April 18, 1881.

72. Garner, *Porfirio Díaz*, 91. The best biography of González remains Dan Coerver, *The Porfirian Interregnum: The Presidency of Manuel González of Mexico, 1880–1884* (Fort Worth: TCU Press, 1979).

73. *Galveston Weekly News*, January 24, 1882.

74. *Galveston Weekly News*, February 2, 1882.

75. *Laredo Weekly Times*, March 2, 1913. For Martin's rise to power, see Noah Cox to S. Powers July 22, 1878, James B. Wells Papers, Center for American History, University of Texas, Austin; also, Thompson, *Warm Weather and Bad Whiskey*, 44–45.

76. *Galveston Daily News*, October 22, 1873.

77. Roberto Ramón Calderón, "Mexican Politics in the American Era, 1846–1900: Laredo, Texas" (PhD diss., University of California, Los Angeles, 1993), 697.

78. Election Returns, Webb County, August 2, 1875, County Clerk's Office, Laredo, Texas. The county, by a vote of 611 to 12, did approve the new constitution in February 1876.

79. Alwyn Barr, *Reconstruction to Reform: Texas Politics, 1876–1906* (Austin: University of Texas Press, 1971).

80. See https://www.tsl.texas.gov/treasures/constitution/index.html; and Joe Ericson and Ernest Wallace, "Constitution of 1876," *Handbook of Texas Online*, https://tshaonline.org/handbook/online/articles/mhc07, accessed July 28, 2015.

81. F. W. Latham to Stephen Powers, September 28, 1875, Stephen B. Powers Papers, CAH.

82. Noah Cox to S. Powers, July 22, 1878, James B. Wells Papers, CAH.

83. Cox to Powers, May 28, 1878, Wells Papers, CAH.

84. Wells to Powers, April 1, 1879, Wells Papers, CAH.

85. Amusingly, the cunning McLane and Santos shared the same birthday.

86. Election Returns, Webb County, November 1878, November 1880, November 1882, Webb County Clerk's Office, Laredo, Texas.

87. *Journal of the House of Representatives of the State of Texas, Being the First Session of the Sixteenth Legislature Begun and Held at the City of Austin, January 14, 1879* (Galveston, TX: A. H. Belo, 1879). Also, "Santos Benavides," *Legislative Reference Library of Texas*, http://www.lrl.state.tx.us/legal.eaders/members/membersdisplay.dfm?memberId=4058, accessed July 5, 2015; also see http://www.lrl.state.tx.us/legeLeaders/members/chargesDisplay.cfm?cmteID=5560, accessed July 4, 2015.

88. *Journal of the House of Representatives . . . Sixteenth Legislature*, 16.

89. *San Antonio Express*, January 21, March 12, 1879.

90. *Journal of the House of Representatives . . . Sixteenth Legislature*, 100, 183, 301, 216–17.

91. Ibid., 362.

92. *San Antonio Express*, February 14, 15, 1879

93. *San Antonio Express*, February 27, 1879.

94. *Journal of the House of Representatives of the Sixteenth Legislature of the State of Texas, Convened in Austin, June 10, 1879* (Extra Session) (Galveston, TX: News Book and Job Establishment, 1879), 383, 498, 674.

95. Ibid., 78.

96. *Journal of the House of Representatives of the Sixteenth Legislature of the State of Texas, Convened in Austin, June 10, 1879* (Extra Session) (Galveston, TX: News Book and Job Establishment, 1879), 201.

97. *San Antonio Express*, June 8, 1879. On the 1880 Webb County census Santos and Agustina are enumerated along with eight servants. Sons Juan and Santos Jr. were listed as working as clerks in the family mercantile business. 10th Census (1880), Webb County, Texas, NA. Sometime in the late 1870s or early 1880s, Santos and Cristóbal had decided to separate their mercantile business.

98. A. J. Leo to James Wells, October 1880, James B. Wells Papers, CAH.

99. Webb County Election Returns, November 1880, Webb County Clerk's Office, Laredo, Texas.

100. *Galveston Weekly News,* March 17, 14, 31, 1881; and *Journal of the House of Representatives . . . Seventeenth Legislature*, 131, 150.

101. *Galveston Weekly News*, March 31, 1881.

102. *Journal of the House of Representatives Being the First Session of the Seventeenth Legislature of the State of Texas Begun and Held at the City of Austin, January 11, 1881* (Galveston, TX: A. H. Belo, 1881), 378.

103. Minutebook A, May 1872, City Secretary's Office.

104. *San Antonio Express*, January 1, 4, February 12, April 11, 1879.

105. *Nueces Valley* (Corpus Christi), April 25, 1874. Articles on the origins of the railroad can be found in the *Nueces Valley*, January 20, 1871, and February 24, 1872.

106. John F. Jenne to William Hunter, December 20, 1880, Consular Dispatches, Nuevo Laredo, RG 59, NA.

107. *Galveston Daily News*, February 16, 18, March 8, April 1, 18, 21, 1882; and *San Antonio Express*, September 28, 1882.

108. Wilkinson, *Laredo and the Rio Grande Frontier*, 367; and Thompson, *Warm Weather and Bad Whiskey*, 46.

109. *Galveston Daily News*, February 16, 18, and March 9, 1882.

110. Seb S. Wilcox, "Laredo through 182 Years of Growth," author's files.

111. Deed Book No. 8, 284–85, Webb County Clerks' Office.

112. *Laredo Times,* August 24, 1881; May 23, 25, 1882; and *Galveston Daily News*, May 25, June 11, 1882; Wilkinson, *Laredo and the Rio Grande Frontier*, 362–67; and Edwin A. Atlee, *Description of Laredo, Texas, the Acknowledged International Gate Way between the Two Republics, Early History, Manufactories, Progress, Wealth, Population, Climate and Prospects* (Laredo: Gate City Printing House, 1888), 6.

113. Miscellaneous newspaper clipping, *Laredo Times*, n.d., "Santo Tomás Coal Mine," Author's files.

114. Jerry Thompson and A. Joachim McGraw, *Campfires and Coal Dust on the Rio Grande* (Austin: Texas Department of Transportation, 1997), 29–42.

115. Thompson, *Warm Weather and Bad Whiskey*, 48.

116. *Galveston Daily News*, October 2, 1884.

117. *Laredo Daily Times*, June 14, 1883.

118. *San Marcos Free Press*, May 31, 1883.

119. *McKinney Gazette*, December 19, 1885.

120. *Galveston Daily News*, August 1, 4, 1882.

121. Esquela, Santos Eraclio Benavides y Villarreal, copy courtesy of George Farías.

122. Santos Benavides, Affidavit, July 10, 1883, copy courtesy of Hector Farías; also, folio 87, Rollo 691 (quote), copy courtesy of George Farías. Eracilio died at 3:00 a.m. on June 27.

123. *Laredo Daily Times*, August 22, 1888.

124. Casa Vidaurri Historical Marker Application, http://texashistory.unt.edu/ark:/67531/metapth435170/m1/70, accessed June 26, 2015. When Eulalio died in 1907, the property passed to his four daughters.

125. *Journal of the House of Representatives of the State of Texas Being a Called Session of the Seventeenth Legislature Begun and Held at the City of Austin, April 6, 1882* (Galveston, TX: A. H. Belo, 1882).

125. William Headen to M. Kenedy, March 23, 1882, James B. Wells Papers, CAH.

127. Election Returns, 83rd District, TSA. In Encinal County, Santos received ninety-three votes, Leo ninety-one, and Alderete only one. At the municipal elections on December 11, 1883, Santos not only served as presiding judge for Ward No. 4, but gave up his house for polling. Minutebook No. 2, December 18, 1883, City Secretary's Office.

128. *Pocket Directory of the Eighteenth Legislature of Texas, with Names and Address of Members, Their Nativity, Age, Occupation and Politics* (Austin, TX: Deffenbaugh, 1883), 2–9. The data also reflects that of the Seventeenth Legislature. See *Pocket Directory of the Seventeenth Legislature with Names and Address of Members, Their Nativity, Age, Occupation and Politics* (Austin, TX: E. W. Swindells' Book and Job Office, 1881), 3–7.

129. See http://www.lrl.state.tx.us/legeLeaders/members/chargesDisplay.efm?cmtelId=4852, accessed July 4, 2015.

130. *Journal of the House of Representatives of the State of Texas Being the Regular Session of the Eighteenth Legislature Begun and Held at the City of Austin, January 9, 1883* (Austin, TX: E. W. Swindells, 1883), 97.

131. Ibid., 52.

132. *Galveston Daily News*, February 24, 1883.

133. *Fort Worth Daily Gazette*, March 22, 14, 1883; and *Dallas Daily Herald*, March 17, May 5, 1883.

134. *San Antonio Daily Express*, March 6. 15, 1883.

135. Ibid., 37, 59,

136. *Galveston Daily News*, October 2, 1884, quoting *Laredo Times*, n.d.

137. *Laredo Times*, September 26, 1884.

138. *Galveston Weekly News*, October 19, 1882.

139. *Galveston Daily News*, September 20, 1884.

140. *Dunkirk Evening Observer*, May 6, 1884.

141. *New York Times*, May 25, 1884, quoting the *Galveston Daily News*, which obtained a copy of the letter from the *Laredo Times*. Also, *San Antonio Daily Express*, May 10, 1884.

142. *Times-Picayune* (New Orleans), September 18, 2011; Garner, *Porfirio Díaz,* 143,–44; Herbert S. Fairall, *The World's Industrial and Cotton Centennial Exposition,* í, *1884–85* (Iowa City, IA: Republican, 1998); and http://www.neworleanspubliclibrary.org/~nopl/exhibits/gateway/1884.htm.

143. *Galveston Weekly News*, June 8, 1882.

144. Ibid.

145. *Norton's Union Intelligencer* (Dallas), April 5, 1884.

Chapter VIII

1. *San Antonio Express*, July 6, 7, 1878. The community was named after Bettina Brentono von Arnin, a liberal German writer. Elen E. Lich, "Bettina, TX." *Handbook of Texas Online,* http://www.tshaonline.org/handbook/online/articles/hub55, accessed April 30, 2016.

2. *Galveston Daily News*, March 21, 1879.

3. In 1961 Henry B. Gonzáles became the first Tejano elected to the US Congress.

4. Violet Cearley, "Laredo Times," *Handbook of Texas Online*, http://www.tshaonline.org/handbook/online/articles/ee104, accessed September 3, 2015.

5. *Laredo Daily Times*, October 20, 1884.

6. *San Antonio Express*, March 18, 1879.

7. *Laredo Daily Times*, October 16, 1884.

8. *Laredo Daily Times*, October 18, 1884.

9. *Laredo Daily Times*, October 9, 1884.

10. Thompson, *Pictorial History*, 180; and Thompson, *Warm Weather and Bad Whiskey*, 62–63.

11. *Laredo Daily Times*, November 4, 1884.

12. *Laredo Daily Times*, October 28, 1884.

13. *Laredo Daily Times*, November 3, 1884.

14. *Laredo Daily Times*, October 18, 1884.

15. *Laredo Daily Times*, October 16, 1884.

16. Ibid.

17. *Laredo Daily Times*, October 27, 1884.

18. Ibid.

19. Ibid.

20. In his dissertation, Roberto Calderon erroneously views the political struggle

in Laredo as largely ethnic. In reality, the conflict was not Anglos versus Tejanos, but an oligarchical contest for power, influence, and wealth. Undoubtedly, the number of Anglos and European immigrants competing for political influence had greatly increased after the arrival of the railroads in 1881, but they were divided among the two competing parties. Calderon, "Mexican Politics in the American Era, 1846–1900, Laredo, Texas," 683, 709–35.

21. *Laredo Daily Times,* October 3, 1884.

22. Ibid.

23. *Laredo Daily Times*, November 4, 1884.

24. Ibid.

25. *Laredo Daily Times* November 5, 1884.

26. *Laredo Daily Times*, November 4, 1884.

27. Ibid.

28. Webb County Election Returns, November 4, 1884, County Clerk's Office. At one time, Hall and Martin had been on opposite sides of the political struggle in Laredo. See *San Antonio Express*, March 28, 1879; also, 10th Census (1880), Webb County, Texas, NA.

29. *Laredo Daily Times*, November 5, 1884.

30. Calderon, "Mexican Politics in the American Era," 718. Martinez fled but was apprehended, and with the crime only hours old, Judge Russell recalled a grand jury that promptly indicted him for murder.

31. *Galveston Daily News*, December 21, 1885; and Calderon, "Mexican Politics in the American Era," 716–17.

32. *Laredo Daily Times*, September 12, 1886.

33. Minutebook no. 2, December 5, 1884, Laredo Public Library.

34. Minutebook no. 2, December 13, 1884, Laredo Public Library.

35. Minutebook no. 2, September 5, 1884, Laredo Public Library.

36. Minutebook no. 2, March 4, 1886, Laredo Public Library.

37. *Galveston Daily News*, April 2, 1886; and *San Antonio Express*, April 15, 1886.

38. *Laredo Daily Times*, March 7, 1886.

39. *San Antonio Express*, April 10, 1886.

40. *State of Texas v. Alexander Meuly*, Case no. 693, District Court, Criminal Cases, Special Collections, TAMIU; and *Alexander Meuly v. State of Texas*, vol. 26., Texas Court of Appeals, 274–308. After a change of venue to Duval County, Meuly was convicted of second-degree murder and given ten years in the state prison. In October 1888 the Texas Court of Appeals reversed and remanded the case, and Meuly eventually went free.

41. *State of Texas v. Stephen Boyard*, Case no. 807, District Court, Civil Cases, Special Collections, TAMIU.

42. Minutebook no. 2, April 7, 1886, Laredo Public Library.

43. *San Antonio Express*, April 15, 1886.

44. *San Antonio Express,* April 8, 1886.

45. María Gonzales Dovalina, "Reminiscences of Laredo through the Years," (1965), 3–4. Author's files.

46. *San Antonio Express*, April 8, 1886.

47. Dovalina, "Reminiscences of Laredo through the Years," 5.

48. *San Antonio Express*, April 15, 1886.

49. *San Antonio Express*, April 9, 1886.

50. *Laredo Times*, April 12, 1886. Typescript in Sebron Wilcox Papers, Special Collections, University of Texas at San Antonio. Copy courtesy of Olivia "Olee" Rodriguez. Although Wilcox compiled a transcript of much of the evidence in *State of Texas vs. Darío Sánchez*, the original documents in the case have unfortunately been lost.

51. Seb S. Wilcox, "Laredo City Election and Riot of 1886," *Southwestern Historical Quarterly* 45 (July 1941): 13.

52. Dovalina, "Reminiscences of Laredo through the Years," 5.

53. Grand Jury Testimony, Laredo Election Riot, County Clerk's Office.

54. *San Antonio Express*, April 15, 1886.

55. *Austin Daily Statesman*, April 9, 1886. For a complete account of the Laredo Election Riot, see Thompson, *Warm Weather and Bad Whiskey*, 71–195. Roberto Ramón Calderón also devotes considerable space to the election riot in his dissertation, "Mexican Politics in the American Era: 1845–1900: Laredo, Texas," 710–42. Seb Wilcox's 1942 article, "Laredo City Election and Riot of 1886," was the first scholarly study of the subject.

56. *Galveston Daily News*, April 9, 188.

57. *San Antonio Express*, April 11, 1886.

58. Funeral Book, 1886, San Agustín Parish Archives, Laredo; also, *New York Times*, April 10, 1865.

59. *San Antonio Express*, April 10, 1886.

60. Wilcox, "Laredo City Election and Riot of 1886," 15.

61. Fort McIntosh Post Returns, April, 1886, AGO, RG 393, NA.

62. *San Antonio Express*, April 11, 1886.

63. Don Russell, *One Hundred and Three Fights and Scrimmages: The Story of General Reuben F. Bernard* (Washington, DC: United States Cavalry Association, 1936), 167–68.

64. *Galveston Daily News*, April 8, 9, 1886.

65. Ibid.

66. *San Antonio Express*, April 10, 1886.

67. Geo. H. Schmitt to L. P. Sieker, April 9, 1886, Adjutant General's Records, TSA.

68. Citizens of Laredo to John Ireland, April 15, 1886, AGR, TSA.

69. Schmitt to Sieker, April 30, 1886, AGR, TSA.

70. *Galveston Daily News*, April 20, 1886.

71. *Corpus Christi Caller*, April 25, 1886.

72. The *Galveston Daily News* headlined the riot for several days with articles such as, "Battle on the Border," "Bloody Border Battle," and "The Great Laredo Riot." The *San Antonio Express* rushed "war correspondents" to the "front" to write of "Blood Lust," "The Woeful War on the Rolling Rio Bravo," "The Charge of the Light Brigade," and "Bloody Streets." Sensational headlines in other newspapers were also common.

73. *State of Texas, Ex. Rel. Daniel Milmo, Santos Benavides, et al. v. Darío Sánchez*, Case No. 566, District Court Civil Cases, Special Collections, TAMIU. Also, *Laredo Daily Times*, June 13, 1886.

74. *State of Texas, Ex. Rel. Daniel Milmo, Santos Benavides, et al. v. Dario Sanchez*, TAMIU.

75. Minutes of District Court, Book no. 2, June 11, 12, 1886, County Clerk's Office.

76. *San Antonio Express*, June 11, 1886.

77. *Laredo Daily Times*, June 13, 1886.

78. County Court Minutes, Book no. 2, June 24, 1886, TAMIU; also, *Laredo Weekly Times*, June 4, 1886.

79. *Laredo Weekly Times*, April 13, 1928. This article was written to commemorate the forty-second anniversary of the election riot.

80. Case nos. 708–49, 754–58, 760–825, District Court, Civil Cases, TAMIU; also, Thompson, *Warm Weather and Bad Whiskey*, 103–5.

81. Minutebook No. 2, July 13, September 16, 1886, Special Collections, City Library, Laredo, Texas.

82. J. S. Penn to J. B. Wells, July 7, 1886, James B. Wells Papers, CAH.

83. *Galveston Daily News*, June 22, 1886.

84. G. B. Broadwater to James B. Wells, September 20, 1886, James B. Wells Papers, CAH.

85. *Laredo Daily Times*, October 17, 1886.

86. *Galveston Daily News*, April 20, 1886.

87. Ibid.

88. Ibid.

89. Ibid.

90. Ibid. Benavides's letter to Evarts is dated February 25, 1886.

91. Ibid.

92. Ibid.

93. For Mexico's concerns about railroad connections with the US, see: *San Antonio Express*, March 29, 1879.

94. *Galveston Daily News*, March 23, 1887.

95. Ibid.

96. *El Partido Liberal*, n.d., quoted in *Galveston Daily News*, March 23, 1887.

97. *Galveston Daily News*, March 11, 1887, quoting Mexico City *Two Eagles*, n.d.

98. Benavides to Díaz, December 2, 1888, Díaz Papers, Universidad Iberoamerica.

99. *Laredo Daily Times*, June 27, 1886, quoting the *Burlington Hawk Eye*, n.d.

100. Benavides to Díaz, June 11, 1886, Díaz Papers, Universidad Iberoamericana. Away from the border, most Americans instinctively thought all Mexicans were from "Old Mexico."

Chapter IX

1. *Galveston Daily News*, January 3, 1886.

2. Benavides to Díaz, June 11, 1886, Díaz Papers, Universidad Iberoamericana.

3. Benavides to Díaz, June 11, 1886 (first quote), and August 20 (second quote), 29, 1886, Díaz Papers, Universidad Iberoamericana.

4. Díaz to Benavides, June 19, 1886, Díaz Papers, Universidad Iberoamericana.

5. Benavides to Díaz, October 4, 1886, Díaz Papers, Universidad Iberoamericana. A brother of the young deserter, Manuel Arguindegui, had previously been involved in a fracas with the proprietor of a Nuevo Laredo newspaper in Monterrey on July 30, 1882. Alcohol and jealousy involving a young woman led to Arguindegui pulling a

pistol and killing Procopio Cardenas. *La Patria* (Mexico City), August 30, 1882; and *La Voz de Mexico* (Mexico City), August 24, 25, 1882.

6. Benavides to Díaz, August 9, 1886, Díaz Papers, Universidad Iberoamericana.

7. Will Lambert to Díaz, July 4, 1886, Díaz Papers, Universidad Iberoamericna. For Lambert, see Thomas W. Cutrer, "Will Lambert," *Handbook of Texas Online*, http:www.tshaonline.org/handbook/online/articles/fla28, accessed October 12, 2015. For the Confederate Home, see Cynthia J. Beeman, "Texas Confederate Home," *Handbook of Texas Online*, http://www.tshaonline.org/handook/online/articles/ynt05, accessed October 12, 2015. During its first two years of operation, the home had 113 veterans. From 1887 to 1953, more than two thousand former Confederates were housed at the facility. By 1943, however, only six Confederates were still in residence. Thomas Riddle, the last veteran at the home, died in 1954 at the age of 108.

8. Benavides to Díaz, September 21, 1886, Díaz Papers, Universidad Iberoamericana.

9. Benavides to Díaz, June 10, 1886, Díaz Papers, Universidad Iberoamericana. At the bottom of the letter, in the hand of an aide was written:, "He will continue being vigilant of the advances of certain gullible people."

10. Benavides to Díaz, September 10, 1886, Díaz Papers, Universidad Iberoamericana.

11. Benavides to Díaz, October 4, 1886, Díaz Papers, Universidad Iberoamericana.

12. For anti-Díaz agitation in Laredo after 1890, see: Carlos Cuellar and Stan Green, *Mexican Revolutionaries in Laredo, 1890–1891* (Laredo, TX: Border Studies, 1991).

13. *Galveston Daily News*, February 18, 1885.

14. Benavides to Díaz, May 5, 1887, Díaz to Benavides, May 17, 1887; both in Díaz Papers, Universidad Iberoamericana.

15. Benavides to Díaz, February 10, 1889, Díaz Papers, Universidad Iberoamericana.

16. Benavides to Díaz, March 26, 1886, Díaz Papers, Universidad Iberoamericana.

17. Benavides to Díaz, February 25, 1888, Díaz Papers, Universidad Iberoamericana.

18. Benavides to Díaz, November 22, 1888; Díaz to Benavides, November 27, 1888; both in Díaz Papers, Universidad Iberoamericana.

19. *Laredo Times*, April 25, 1887.

20. *Texas Almanac and State Industrial Guide for 1912* (Dallas, TX: Galveston-Dallas News, 1912), 45.

21. Randolph B. Campbell, *Gone to Texas* (New York: Oxford University Press, 2012), 319; also, Jared Paul Sutton, "Ethnic Minorities and Prohibition in Texas, 1887–1919" (MA thesis, University of North Texas, 2006); and the Legislative Reference Library of Texas, http://www.lrl.state.tx.us/legis/ConstAmends/electiondates.dfm, accessed September 16, 2015. The cause of prohibition would reemerge during the Progressive Era and would be first approved in Texas in 1908 and then defeated three years later, before the 18th Amendment to the US Constitution was approved in 1919.

22. *Austin Statesman*, December 26, 1887.

23. Daniell, *Successful Men of Texas*, 322–28.

24. Ford to Benavides, December 25, 1890, Ford Papers, Haley Museum and Library; also, McCaslin, *Fighting Stock*, 258. Ford outlived Santos by six years, dying

in San Antonio at the age of eighty-two on November 3, 1897. He was buried in the Confederate Cemetery.

25. Ford, "Benavides Family," Ford Papers, Haley Museum and Library.

26. *Laredo Daily Times*, October 1, 1884.

27. *Laredo Times*, October 1, 1884.

28. *Galveston Daily News*, March 18, 1893, quoting *Laredo Times*, n.d. This same article also appeared in the *Brownsville Daily Herald*, March 18, 1893.

29. *Austin Weekly Statesman*, May 10, 1888.

30. See http://www.tspb.state.tx.us/SPH/capitol/history/history.htm, accessed June 15, 2015.

31. *Laredo Times*, May 18, 1888.

32. *Galveston Daily News*, May 23, 1888, quoting the *Laredo Times*, n.d.

33. Elliott Young, *Catarino Garza's Revolution on the Texas-Mexico Border* (Durham, NC: Duke University Press, 2004), 65–78

34. Arnoldo De Leon, *They Called Them Greasers: Anglo Attitudes toward Mexicans in Texas, 1821–1900* (Austin: University of Texas Press, 1983), 93–94; and Alicia A. Garza, "Rio Grande City Riot of 1888," *Handbook of Texas Online*, http://wwwtshaonline.org/handbook/online/articles/jcr03, accessed June 20, 2015.

35. *Austin Weekly Statesman*, October 4, 1888.

36. *Laredo Daily Times*, November 20, 1888; also, C. Alan Hutchinson, "General Guillermo Antonio Mexía and his Texas Interests," *Southwestern Historical Quarterly* 82 (October 1978): 117–42,

37. *San Antonio Daily Express*, April 8, 1889.

38. *Galveston Daily News*, April 7, 1889.

39. Benavides to Díaz, April 9, 1889, Díaz Papers, Universidad Iberoamericana.

40. *Laredo Daily Times*, September 12, 1886.

41. *Laredo Times*, November 12, 1890.

42. *Laredo Times*, November 10, 1891.

43. *Laredo Times*, November 11, 1891. During the Great Depression his remains were removed to the new Catholic Cemetery, just behind the more impressive tombs of Cristóbal and Lamar Benavides.

44. *Fort Worth Gazette*, November 10, 1891.

45. Ibid. Benavides's death was also reported in the *Laredo Times*, November 1, 2, 1891; and Dallas *Southern Mercury*, November 19, 1891.

46. Daniell, *Successful Men of Texas*, 330.

47. Farías, *Farías Chronicles*, 148.

Epilogue

1. The school was later converted and a new school in the Winfield subdivision several blocks to the north was named in his honor.

2. Santos Benavides & Wife to the Public, July 18, 1881, Deed Records, Vol. 12, 301–3, Webb County, Texas.

3. *Rosetti v. Benavides*, Case no. 5844, Court of Civil Appeals, *Southwestern Reporter* (St. Paul, MN: West, 1917), 208–11. Francisco would go on to become a prominent physician and marry Cristóbal's daughter, Aurelia "Lila" Benavides, in San Agustín Church on February 6, 1895, with Bishop Peter Verdaguer y Prat presiding. Olee

Rodriguez to author, May 25, 2016. Email in author's files.

4. Entry No. 214, "In the matter of the Estate of Santos Benavides, deceased," December 7, 1891, County Clerk's Office, Laredo, Texas.

5. Heirs of Santos Benavides, 64th Congress, 1st Session, House of Representatives, No. 231, (February 21, 1916), 1; and Heirs of Santos Benavides, 64th Congress, 1st Session, Senate, No. 271 (March 18, 1916), 1.

6. Deathly ill, Refugio was taken to the home of his son, Miguel, in the fashionable "heights" of the city, just east of Zacate Creek, where he managed to make out a last will and testament dividing his land and property between his second wife, Anastacia García, and his son by his second marriage, Miguel G. Benavides, who was police chief at the time. After a late afternoon funeral Mass at San Agustín Church, a long line of buggies and people on horseback followed the hearse carrying his remains to the Catholic cemetery. Of the five children from his first marriage to Teresa Pizaña, only three children were still living. The old Civil War warrior and former Texas Ranger had managed to hold on to over $100,000 in property, including 4,251 acres of valuable land that included the valuable and rapidly developing coal deposits at the village of Santo Tomás, upriver from Laredo. In addition, Refugio owned twenty-three lots in the city. *Weekly Caller* (Corpus Christi), July 7, 1899; Death Notice, Health Department Records, City of Laredo, June 28, 1899; Esquela (death notice), Sr. Don Refugio Benavides, June 30, 1899, courtesy of Genoveva Vela; and "Statement of Inventory and Appraisement of Property," October 28, 1899, Probate Records, Webb County, Texas. Because of the large number of Anglo property owners in the heights, Roberto Calderon refers to this section of the city as the "American quarter." Calderon, "Mexican Politics in the American Era," 579.

7. After Cristóbal and Santos divided their mercantile business of S. Benavides and Brother in 1875, Cristóbal went on to become one of the leading merchants as simply "C. Benavides." Besides his large wholesale and retail business on Matamoros Street, he became director of the Milmo Bank, as well as a leading stock raiser, managing forty-five thousand acres, several hundred Durham cattle, and twenty thousand sheep. Although considered as a "man of the highest honor," he consistently refused to seek or hold public office, unlike Santos and Refugio. After his death, his remains were taken the next day from the mortuary on Grant Street to San Agustín Church. At the church, his casket was almost hidden by the numerous floral arrangements. After three priests performed a high Mass, a long funeral procession of friends and relatives in buggies and on foot, led by his grieving wife, Lamar Bee de Benavides, their ten children, and their families, followed his remains to the Catholic cemetery. It was said to have been the largest such gathering of mourners in Laredo history. Esquela, Cristóbal Benavides, September 3, 1904, courtesy of Stanley Green.

8. *Laredo Daily Times*, September 3, 4, 1904. Younger brother Eulalio died in 1907.

9. Ibid. Webb County Probate Minutes, vol. 3, 188–94; Agustina Villarreal de Benavides, Last Will and Testament, July 18, 1881 and January 1887, Volume 12, 301–3. For Gen. Garza Ayala's death, see *Laredo Weekly Times,* February 11, 1913.

10. *Laredo Weekly Times*, February 2, 1908.

11. *Laredo Daily Times*, August 20, 1902.

12. Baptismal Records, San Agustín Parish Archives, Laredo, Texas; also, García, *Descendants of John Z. Leyendecker*, 20–33. After the Civil War, he established a

mercantile store in Laredo and served as postmaster and city secretary for six years.

13. *Laredo Daily Times*, May 23, 1920; and List of Diseased, May 20, 1920, Health Department Records, City of Laredo.

14. *Laredo Daily Times*, October 10, 1888; and *Laredo Times*, February 21, 1936. At the same time, he became one of the city's leading baseball players, journeying to cities such as Corpus Christi and San Antonio to compete.

15. *Laredo Weekly Times*, April 13, 1928; and Thompson, *Warm Weather and Bad Whiskey*, 129–33.

16. Santos would even make it onto the cover of a 1979 Southwestern Bell telephone directory. Farías, *Farías Chronicles*, 148.

BIBLIOGRAPHY

Manuscripts and Archival Collections

Adams, Harvey Alexander. Manuscript copy. Center for the Study of American History, University of Texas at Austin.

"Amnesty Papers." Applications from Former Confederates for Presidential Pardons, Record Group 94. National Archives, Washington, DC.

Bee, Hamilton P. Letterbook. Special Collections, Library, United States Military Academy, West Point, New York.

Bee, Hamilton P. Papers. Center for the Study of American History, University of Texas at Austin.

Broadside File. Texas State Archives, Austin, Texas.

Clark, Edward. Papers. Texas State Archives, Austin, Texas.

Comonfort, Igancio. Papers. Benson Latin American Collection, University of Texas at Austin.

Confidential Letters and Telegrams Sent and Special Orders Issued, March 1864 to May 1865, Record Group 109, National Archives, Washington, DC.

Consular Dispatches, Monterrey, Mexico. Records of the United States Department of State. Record Group 59. National Archives, Washington, DC.

Consular Dispatches, Nuevo Laredo, Mexico. Records of the United States Department of State. Record Group 59. National Archives, Washington, DC.

Cotton Bureau Records. Confederate Department of the Treasury. Record Group 395. National Archives, Washington, DC.

Correspondencia del Alcalde de Guerrero. Nuevo Guerrero Archives, Nuevo Guerrero, Tamaulipas.

Correspondencia de Santiago Vidaurri. Archivo General del Estado de Nuevo León, Monterrey, Nuevo León.

Davis, Edmund J. Papers. Texas State Archives, Austin, Texas.

Death Records. Health Department, City of Laredo, Laredo, Texas.

Díaz, Porfirio. Papers. Universidad Iberoamericana, Mexico, D. F.

Eighth Census (1860), Zapata County, Texas. National Archives, Washington, DC.

Eighth Census (1860), Cameron County, Texas. National Archives, Washington, DC.

Eighth Census (1860), Webb County, Texas. National Archives, Washington, DC.

Election Returns. Laredo Archives. St. Mary's University Library, San Antonio, Texas.

Ford, John S. Papers. Texas State Archives, Austin, Texas.

Ford, John Salmon. "Memoirs of John Salmon Ford." Seven volumes. Center for American History, University of Texas at Austin.

Election Returns. Webb County, 1851–1856. Records of the Secretary of State, Record Group 307. Texas State Archives, Austin, Texas.
Ford, John S. Memoirs. Center for American History, University of Texas at Austin.
González, Manuel. Papers. Universidad Iberoamericana, Mexico, D. F.
Hamilton, Andrew J. Papers. Texas State Archives, Austin, Texas.
Heintzelman, Samuel Peter. Papers. Library of Congress, Washington, DC.
Haynes, John L. Compiled Service Record. United States Department of War. Record Group 94. National Archives, Washington, DC.
Haynes, John L. Papers. Center for American History, University of Texas at Austin.
Herron, Francis J. Papers. New York Historical Society, New York, New York.
Kenedy, Mifflin. Letterbook. King Ranch Archives, Kingsville, Texas.
Killed and Wounded at Las Rucias. Confederate Army Casualties and Narrative Reports. Record Group 109. National Archives, Washington, DC.
King, Richard. Letters. King Ranch Archives, Kingsville, Texas.
Kingsbury, Gilbert D. Papers. Center for American History, University of Texas at Austin.
Kuykendall, James Hampton. Journal. Center for American History, University of Texas at Austin.
Letters Received. Confederate Adjutant General's Office. Records of the Confederate War Department. Record Group 109. National Archives, Washington, DC.
Letters Received. Confederate Trans-Mississippi Department. Records of the Confederate War Department. Record Group 109. National Archives, Washington, DC.
Letters Received. Confederate District of Texas, New Mexico, and Arizona. Records of the Confederate War Department. Record Group 109. National Archives, Washington, DC.
Letters Received. Department of Texas. Record Group 393. National Archives, Washington, DC.
Letters Received. Western Department. Record Group 393, National Archives, Washington, DC.
Leyendecker, John Z. Papers. Center for American History, University of Texas at Austin.
Lubbock, Francis R. Papers. Texas State Archives, Austin, Texas.
Military Commission Appointed to Investigate and Report Upon the Facts Relative to the Capture of the Town of Bagdad on the Mexican Side of the Rio Grande on January 5, 1866. Records of the Adjutant General's Office. Record Group 393. National Archives, Washington, DC.
Pickett, John T. Papers. Domestic Correspondence of the Confederacy. Office of the Secretary of State. Manuscript Division, Library of Congress, Washington, DC.
Post Returns. Fort McIntosh. Records of the Adjutant General's Office. Record Group 393. National Archives, Washington, DC.
Post Returns. Ringgold Barracks. Records of the Adjutant General's Office. Record Group 393. National Archives, Washington, DC.
Record Book of the Second Texas Cavalry, 1863–1864. Adjutant General's Office, Texas State Archives, Austin, Texas.

Registro Civil de Guerrero, Nuevo Guerrero Archives, Nuevo Guerrero, Tamaulipas.
Robertson, George Lee. Papers. Center for American History, University of Texas at Austin.
San Román, José. Papers. Center for American History, University of Texas at Austin.
Tenth Census (1880), Webb County, Texas, National Archives, Washington, DC.
Webb County:
County Court Minutes, 1884–1887.
District Court Minutes, 1851–1911.
District Clerk, Criminal Court Case Papers, 1853–1920.
Deed Records, 1848–1887.
Filing Book, Civil Docket, Fol. 1, District Court, 1870–1891.
Marriage Records, 1852–1909.
Probate Minutes, 1851–1911.
Tax Rolls, 1851–1910.
Wilcox, Seb. Papers. San Mary's University Library, San Antonio, Texas.

Newspapers

Austin Southern Intelligencer
Austin Weekly State Gazette
Brownsville Daily Ranchero
Brownsville Daily Ranchero and Republican
Brownsville Rio Grande Sentinel
Brownsville Union Journal
Corpus Christi Advertiser
Corpus Christi Caller
Corpus Christi Ranchero
Dallas Daily Herald
El Correo de Laredo
Flake's Daily Galveston Bulletin
Galveston News
Galveston Tri-Weekly News
Galveston Daily News
Galveston Weekly News
Harpers Weekly
Houston Tri-Weekly Telegraph
Laredo Times
Laredo Weekly Times
Laredo El Diputado
Laredo El Figaro
Laredo El Horizonte
Laredo El Mutualista
Laredo El Progreso
Laredo La Colonia Mexicana
Loyal National Union Journal
Matamoros Daily Morning Caller
Matamoros Daily Ranchero
Matamoros El Orden
Matamoros Monitor
Matamoros Ranchero
Matamoros El Ranchero Diario
Mexico City El Siglo
Mexico City La Patria
Mexico City La Voz de Mexico
Mexico City Two Republics
Monterrey Boletin Oficial
New Orleans Daily Crescent
New Orleans Daily True Delta
New Orleans Daily Picayune
New Orleans Times
New York Herald
New York Tribune
New York World
San Antonio Herald
San Antonio Daily Ledger and Texan
San Antonio El Regidor
San Antonio Weekly Herald

Books

A Compendium of the War of the Rebellion, Compiled and Arranged From Official Records of the Federal and Confederate Armies Reports of the Adjutant Generals of the Several States, The Army Registers and Other Reliable Documents and Sources. Dayton: Morningside Bookshop, 1978.

Adams, John A. *Conflict and Commerce on the Rio Grande: Laredo, 1755–1955.* College Station: Texas A&M University Press, 2008.

Adjutant General's Report, 1873. Austin, 1875.

Atlee, Edwin A. *Description of Laredo, Texas, the Acknowledged International Gate Way between the Two Republics, Early History, Manufactories, Progress, Wealth, Population, Climate and Prospects.* Laredo: Gate City Printing House, 1888.

Ávila, Jesús, Leticia Martinez, and César Morado, *Santiago Vidaurri: La formación de un liderazgo regional desde Monterrey (1809–1867).* Monterrey, Nuevo León: Universidad Autönoma de Nuevo Leön, 2012.

Bailey, Theodorus, and Welles, eds. *Official Records of the Union and Confederate Navies in the War of the Rebellion.* 30 Volumes. Washington, DC: Government Printing Office, 1894–1927.

Barr, Alwyn. *Texans in Revolt: The Battle for San Antonio, 1835.* Austin: University of Texas Press, 1990.

Baum, Dale. *The Shattering of Texas Unionism: Politics in the Lone Star State during the Civil War Era.* Baton Rouge: Louisiana State University Press, 1998.

Bender, Steven W. *Greasers and Gringos: Latinos, Law, and the American Imagination.* New York: New York University Press, 2003.

Benito Juárez: Documentos, Discursos y Correspondencia. Mexico City: Secretaria del Patrimonio Nacional, 1964–69.

Bowden, J. J. *The Exodus of Federal Forces from Texas, 1861.* Austin: Eakin Press, 1986.

Brown, John Henry. *History of Texas, 1685–1892.* St. Louis: L. E. Danielle, 1892.

Buenger, Walter L. *Secession and the Union in Texas.* Austin: University of Texas Press, 1984.

Callahan, James M. *The Diplomatic History of the Southern Confederacy.* Baltimore: Johns Hopkins Press, 1901.

Campbell, John R., comp., *Ramón Family of Laredo, Texas.* Laredo, n.p., 2001.

Cantrell, Gregg. *Stephen F. Austin: Empresario of Texas.* New Haven: Yale University Press, 1999.

Carreño, Alberto María, ed. *Archivo del General Porfirio Díaz: Memorias y Documentos.* Mexico City: Editorial "Elede," 1949.

Chance, Joseph E. *José María de Jesús Carvajal: The Life and Times of a Mexican Revolutionary.* San Antonio: Trinity University Press, 2006.

Daddysman, James W. *The Matamoros Trade: Confederate Commerce, Diplomacy and Intrigue.* Newark: University of Delaware Press, 1984.

Daniell, L. E. *Types of Successful Men of Texas.* Austin: E. Von Boeckmann, 1890.

Davis, Edwin Adams. *Fallen Guidon: The Story of Confederate General Jo Shelby's March to Mexico.* College Station: Texas A&M University Press, 1995.

Davis, William C., ed. *The South Besieged, The Image of War, 1861–1865.* Garden City: Doubleday and Company, 1983.

Delaney, Norman C. *The Maltby Brothers' Civil War.* College Station: Texas A&M University Press, 2013.

De la Peña, José, ed., *Los Benavides de Nuevo León, Tamaulipas y Texas, 1619–1910.* Ventura, California, 1995.

De Leon, Arnoldo, ed., *Apuntes Tejanos.* Vol. 1. Austin: Texas State Historical Association, 1978.

———, ed., *Apuntes Tejanos.* Vol. 2. Austin: Texas State Historical Association, 1978.

———. *They Called them Greasers: Anglo Attitudes Towards Mexicans in Texas, 1821–1900.* Albuquerque: University of New Mexico Press, 1981.

———. *The Tejano Community, 1836–1900.* Albuquerque: University of New Mexico Press, 1989.

Depredations on the Frontiers of Texas. 42nd Cong., 3rd sess., no. 39.

Díaz, George T. *Border Contraband: A History of Smuggling across the Rio Grande.* Austin: University of Texas Press, 2015.

Duaine, Carl L. *The Dead Men Wore Boots: An Account of the 32nd Texas Volunteer Cavalry, C.S.A.* Austin: San Felipe Press, 1966.

Ely, Glen Sample. *Where the West Begins.* Lubbock: Texas Tech University Press, 2011.

———. *The Texas Frontier and the Butterfield Overland Mail, 1858–1861* (Norman: University of Oklahoma Press, 2016).

Farías, George. *The Farías Chronicles, A History and Genealogy of a Portuguese-Spanish Family*

Foley, Patrick. *Missionary Bishop: Jean-Marie Odin in Galveston and New Orleans.* College Station: Texas A&M University Press, 1913.

Ford, John S. *Rip Ford's Texas.* Edited by Stephen B. Oates. Austin: University of Texas Press, 1963.

Fremantle, James Arthur Lyon. *The Fremantle Diary: Being the Journal of Lieutenant Colonel James Arthur Lyon Fremantle, Coldstream Guards, on his Three Months in the Southern States.* Edited by Walter Lord. London: Andre Deutsch, 1956.

Gallaway, B. P., ed. *Dark Corner of the Confederacy.* Dubuque, Iowa: Kendall-Hunt Publishing, 1972.

García, Felix. *The Children of John Z. Leyendecker.* Laredo, n. p., 1984.

García, Genaro, ed. *Documentos inéditos o muy raros para la historia de México.* Mexico City, 1910.

García, Luis Alberto. *Guerra y Frontera: El Ejercito del Norte Entre 1855–1858.* Monterrey. Archivo General del Estado de Nuevo León, 2006,

Garner, Paul. *Porfirio Diáz: Profiles in Power.* White Plains, NY: Longman Publishing, 2001.

Giese, William Royston. *The Confederate Military Forces in the Trans-Mississippi West, 1861–1865: A Study in Command.* Austin: University of Texas Press, 1974.

Green, Stan, ed. *Border Biographies.* Laredo: Border Studies, 1991.

Green, Thomas J. *Journal of the Texian Expedition Against Mier.* Austin: W. Thomas Taylor, 1993.

Greer, James Kimmins. *Colonel Jack Hays: Texas Frontier Leader and California Builder.* College Station: Texas A&M University Press, 1987.

Haley, James L. *Sam Houston.* Norman: University of Oklahoma Press, 2002.

Hayes, Sam W. *Soldiers of Misfortune: The Somervell and Mier Expeditions.* Austin: University of Texas Press, 1990.

Hébert, Rachel Bluntzer. *The Forgotten Colony: San Patricio de Hibernia: The History, the People and the Legends of the Irish Colony of McMullen-McGloin*. Austin: Eakin Press, 1981.

Hernández Rodríguez, Rosaura. *Ignacio Comonfort: Trayectoria Politica. Documentos.* Mexico City: Universidad Nacional Autónoma de Mexico, Instituto de Investigaciones Históricas, 1967.

Hinojosa, Artemio Benavides. *Santiago Vidaurri: Caudillo del noreste mexicano (1855–1864)*. Mexico City: Tusquets Editores Mexico, 2012.

Hinojosa, Gilberto Miguel. *A Borderlands Town in Transition: Laredo, 1755–1870*. College Station: Texas A&M University Press, 1983.

Historia del Noreste Mexicano: Correspondencia Benito Juárez—Santiago Vidaurri, 1855–1864. Monterrey: Anuario del Archivo General del Estado de Nuevo León, 2005.

Houston, Sam. *Writings of Sam Houston*. Ed. by Amelia Williams and Eugene C. Barker. 8 vols. Austin: Jenkins Publishing Company, 1970.

Hughes, W. J. *Rebellious Ranger: Rip Ford and the Old Southwest* Norman: University of Oklahoma Press, 1964.

Hunt, Jeffrey Wm, *The Last Battle of the Civil War: Palmetto Ranch*. Austin: University of Texas Press, 2002.

Hunter, John Warren. *Heel-Fly Time in Texas*. Bandera: Frontier Times, 1931.

Irby, James. *Backdoor to Bagdad.* El Paso: Texas Western Press, 1977.

Journal of the House of Representatives of the State of Texas Being the First Session of the Sixteenth Legislature Begun and Held at the City of Austin, January 14, 1879. Galveston: A. H. Belo & Co., 1879.

Journal of the House of Representatives of the Sixteenth Legislature of the State of Texas (Extra Session) Convened in Austin, June 10, 1879. Galveston: Galveston News Book and Job Establishment, 1879.

Journal of the House of Representatives Being the First Session of the Seventeenth Legislature of the State of Texas Begun and Held at the City of Austin, January 11, 1881. Galveston: A. H. Belo & Co., 1881.

Journal of the House of Representatives of the State of Texas Being a Called Session of the Seventeenth Legislature Begun and Held at the City of Austin, April 6, 1882. Galveston: A. H. Belo & Co., 1882.

Kelly, Pat. *River of Lost Dreams: Navigation on the Rio Grande*. Lincoln: University of Nebraska Press, 1986.

Kennedy, Roger B. *Cotton and Conquest: How the Plantation System Acquired Texas.* Norman: University of Oklahoma Press, 2013.

Kerby, Robert L. *Kirby Smith's Confederacy: The Trans-Mississippi South, 1863–1865.* New York: Columbia University Press, 1972.

Knapp, Frank A. Jr., *Sebastian Lerdo de Tejada*. Xalapa: Universidad Veracruzana, 1962.

Lambert, Will, comp., *Pocket Directory of the Seventeenth Legislature of Texas*. Austin: Swindells' Book and Job Office, 1881.

Lambert, Will, comp., *Pocket Directory of the Eighteenth Legislature of Texas*. Austin: Deffenbaugh & Co. 1883.

Lea, Tom. *The King Ranch*. 2 Volumes. Boston: Little, Brown and Co., 1957.

Leiker, James N. *Racial Borders: Black Soldiers Along the Rio Grande*. College Station: Texas A&M University Press, 2002.

Lonn, Ella. *Foreigners in the Confederacy*. Gloucester, Mass., 1965.

———. *Foreigners in the Union Army and Navy*. Baton Rouge: Louisiana State University Press, 1952.

Lott, Virgil N., and Mercurio Martinez. *The Kingdom of Zapata*. Austin: Eakin Press, 1983.

Lubbock, Francis R. *Six Decades in Texas: The Memoirs of Francis R. Lubbock, Confederate Governor of Texas*. Edited by C. W. Raines. Austin: Ben C. Jones and Co., 1900.

McCaslin, Richard B. *Fighting Stock: John S. "Rip" Ford of Texas*; Fort Worth: TCU Press, 2011.

McCutchan, Joseph D. *Mier Expedition Diary: A Texan Prisoner's Account*. Austin: University of Texas Press, 1978, ed. Joseph Milton Nance.

Mahoney, Harry Thayer and Marjorie Locke. *Mexico and the Confederacy, 1860–1867*. San Francisco: Austin and Winfield, 1998.

Malsch, Brownson. *Indianola, The Mother of Western Texas*. Austin: State House Press, 1988.

Marbán, Jorge A. *Confederate Patriot, Journalist, and Poet: The Multifaceted Life of José Agustín Quintero*. Victoria, BC: Friesen Press, 2014.

Marten, James. *Texas Divided: Loyalty and Dissent in the Lone Star State, 1856–1874*. Lexington: University of Kentucky Press, 1990.

Martin, Millard F. Sr., *Zachariah Martin II, 1790–1873: Louisiana and Texas Pioneer, His Parents and His Descendants*. N. p., 1976.

May, Robert E. *Manifest Destiny's Underworld: Filibustering in Antebellum America*. Chapel Hill: University of North Carolina Press, 2002.

Medrano, Arturo Gálvez. *Regionalismo y Gobierno General: El Caso de Nuevo León y Coahuila, 1855–1864*. Monterrey: Gobierno del Estado de Nuevo León, 1993.

Memorial and Genealogical Record of Southwest Texas. Chicago: Goodspeed Brothers, 1894.

Moneyhon, Carl and Bobby Roberts. *Portraits of Conflict: A Photographic History of Texas in the Civil War*. Fayetteville: University of Arkansas Press, 1998.

Mora-Torres, Juan. *The Making of the Mexican Border: The State, Capitalism, and Society in Nuevo León, 1848–1910*. Austin: University of Texas Press, 2001.

Murphy, Douglas A. *Two Armies on the Rio Grande: The First Campaign of the US-Mexican War*. College Station: Texas A&M University Press, 2014.

Nance, Joseph Milton. *After San Jacinto: The Texas-Mexico Frontier, 1836–1841*. Austin: University of Texas Press, 1963.

———. *Attack and Counter-Attack: The Texas-Mexican Frontier, 1841*. Austin: University of Texas Press, 1964.

———. *Dare-Devils All: Texas Mier Expedition, 1842–1844*. Ed. Archie P. McDonald. Austin: Eakin Press, 1998.

Newton, Alexander H. *Out of the Briars*. Ayer Publishers, 1910.

Oates, Stephen B. *Confederate Cavalry West of the River*. Austin: University of Texas Press, 1961.

Owsley, Frank Lawrence. *King Cotton Diplomacy: Foreign Relations of the Confederate States of America*. Chicago: University of Chicago Press, 1959.

Palmquist, Peter E., and Thomas R. Kailbourn. *Pioneer Photographers of the Far West*,

A Biographical Dictionary, 1840–1865. Palo Alto: Stanford University Press, 2000.
———. *Pioneer Photographers from the Mississippi to the Continental Divide.* Stanford: Stanford University Press, 2005.
Pierce, Frank F. *A Brief History of the Lower Rio Grande Valley.* Menasha, Wisconsin, 1917.
Rayburn, John C., and Virginia Kemp Rayburn. *Century of Conflict, 1821–1913: Incidents in the Lives of William Neale and William A. Neale, Early Settlers in South Texas.* Waco: Texian Press, 1966.
Reports of the Committee of Investigation Sent in 1873 by the Mexican Government to the Frontier of Texas. New York: Baker and Godwin Publishers, 1875.
Report of the Investigative Commission of the Northern Frontier: La informe de la comisión pesquisidora. Introduction by Timothy Bowman. Dallas: William P. Clements Center for Southwest Studies, Southern Methodist University, 2015.
Reséndez, Andrés. *Changing National Identities at the Frontier: Texas and New Mexico, 1800–1850.* Cambridge: Cambridge University Press, 2005.
Richardson, Chad. *Batos, Bolillos, Pochos, and Pelados: Class and Culture on the South Texas Border.* Austin: University of Texas Press, 1999.
Richardson, James D., ed. *A Compilation of the Messages and Papers of the Confederacy.* Nashville: United States Publishing Company, 1906.
Richter, William L. *The Army in Texas During Reconstruction, 1865–1870.* College Station: Texas A&M University Press, 1987.
Ripley, Eliza More McHatton, *From Flag to Flag: A Woman's Adventures and Experiences in the South During the War, in Mexico, and in Cuba.* New York: D. Appleton, 1889.
Rippy, Fred J. *The United States and Mexico.* New York: Alfred A. Knopf, 1926.
Roel, Santiago. *Correspondencia Particular de D. Santiago Vidaurri, Gobernador de Nuevo León, (1855–1864), Tomo primero, Juárez-Vidaurri.* Monterrey: Impresora Monterrey, 1946.
Roell, Craig H. *Matamoros and the Texas Revolution.* Denton: Texas State Historical Association, 2013.
Schoonover, Thomas, ed., *A Mexican View of American in the 1860s: A Foreign Diplomat Describes the Civil War and Reconstruction.* Rutherford: Fairleigh Dickinson University Press, 1991.
———, ed., *Mexican Lobby: Matías Romero in Washington, 1861–1867.* Lexington: University of Kentucky Press, 1986.
Schuler, Louis J. *The Last Battle in the War Between the States, May 13, 1865.* Brownsville: Springman-King, 1960.
Secrest, William B. *The Man from the Rio Grande: A Biography of Harry Love, Leader of the California Rangers who tracked down Joaquin Murietta.* Spokane: Arthur H. Clark, 2005.
Smith, Thomas T. *The U. S. Army & the Texas Frontier Economy, 1845–1900.* College Station: Texas A&M University Press, 1999.
———. *The Old Army in Texas: A Research Guide to the U. S. Army in Nineteenth-Century Texas.* Austin: Texas State Historical Association, 2000.
Spellman, Paul. *Forgotten Texas Leader: Hugh McLeod and the Texan Santa Fe Expedition.* College Station: Texas A&M University Press, 1999.

Stabb, William Preston. *The Prisoners of Perote: Containing a Journal Kept by the Author Who Was Captured by the Mexicans at Mier, December 25, 1842, and Released from Perote, May 16, 1844.* Philadelphia: G. B. Zieber and Company, 1845.

Stevens, Thomas N. *Dear Carrie.* Mount Pleasant, Michigan: Central Michigan University, 1984.

Stout, Joseph A. Jr., *Schemers & Dreamers: Filibustering in Mexico, 1848–1921.* Fort Worth: TCU Press, 2002.

Sumter, Jesse. *Paso del Aguila: A Chronicle of Frontier Days on the Texas Border.* Ed. Ben E. Pingenot. Austin: Encino Press, 1969.

Texas Almanac and State Industrial Guide for 1912. Dallas: Galveston-Dallas News, 1912.

Texas Frontier Troubles. 44th Cong., 1st sess., no. 343.

Thompson, Jerry. *Juan Cortina and the Texas-Mexico Frontier, 1859–1877.* El Paso: Texas Western Press, 1994.

———. *Vaqueros in Blue and Gray.* Austin: State House Press, 2000.

———. *Mexican Texans in the Union Army.* El Paso: Texas Western Press, 1986.

———, ed. *Fifty Miles and a Fight: Major Samuel Peter Heintzelman's Journal of Texas and the Cortina War.* Austin: Texas State Historical Association, 1998.

———. *Warm Weather and Bad Whiskey.* El Paso: Texas Western Press, 1991.

———. *A Wild and Vivid Land: An Illustrated History of the South Texas Border.* Austin: Texas State Historical Association, 1997.

———, ed. *Texas & New Mexico on the Eve of the Civil War: The Mansfield & Johnston Inspections, 1859–1861.* Albuquerque: University of New Mexico Press, 2001.

——— and Lawrence Jones III. *Civil War and Revolution on the Texas-Mexico Border, A Narrative and Photographic History.* Austin: Texas State Historical Association, 2004.

———. *Cortina: Defending the Mexican Name in Texas.* College Station: Texas A&M University Press, 2007.

Tilley, Nannie M., ed. *Federals on the Frontier: The Diary of Benjamin F. McIntyre, 1862–1864.* Austin: University of Texas Press, 1963.

Toral, Jesus de León, ed. *Historia Documental Militar de la Intervencion Francesa en Mexico & El Denominado Segundo Imperio.* Mexico City: Secretaria de la Defensa Nacional, 1967.

Torget, Andrew J. *Seeds of Empire: Cotton, Slavery and the Transformation of the Texas Borderlands, 1800–1850.* Chapel Hill: University of North Carolina Press, 2015. Truett, Samuel. *Fugitive Landscapes: The Forgotten History of the U.S.-Mexico Borderlands.* New Haven: Yale University Press, 2006.

Townsend, Stephen A. *Yankee Invasion of Texas.* College Station: Texas A&M University Press, 2006.

Tucker, Phillip Thomas. *The Final Fury: Palmito Ranch, The Last Battle of the Civil War.* Mechanicsburg, Pa.: Stackpole Books, 2001.

Trudeau, Noah Andre. *Out of the Storm: The End of the Civil War, April–June 1865.* Baton Rouge: Louisiana State University Press, 1994.

Truett, Samuel. *Fugitive Landscapes: The Forgotten History of the U.S.-Mexico Borderlands.* New Haven: Yale University Press, 2006.

Tyler, Ronnie C. *Santiago Vidaurri and the Southern Confederacy.* Austin: Texas State Historical Association, 1973.

Undersood, Rodman L. *Death on the Nueces: German Texans, Treue der Union.* Austin: Eakin Press, 2000.

US War Department. *The War of the Rebellion: A Compilation of the Official Records of the Union and Confederate Armies.* 128 Volumes. Washington: US Government Printing Office, 1880–1901.

Waller, John L. *Colossal Hamilton of Texas: A Biography of Andrew Jackson Hamilton, Militant Unionist and Reconstruction Governor.* El Paso: Texas Western Press, 1968.

Walsh, William F. II. *The Sharpshooter: El Tirador de Primera. The Untold Story of Hamilton Cobb Peterson, US Commissioner for the Justice Department, Laredo, Texas.* N.p., 2012.

Weber, David J. *The Spanish Frontier in North America.* New Haven: Yale University Press, 1994,

Wilcox, Sebron Sneed. *Papers on Laredo History.* Edited by Robert D. Wood. San Antonio: St. Mary's University Duplicating Service, 2005.

Williams, R. H. *With the Border Ruffians, Memories of the Far West, 1852–1868.* Edited by E. W. Williams. Lincoln: University of Texas Press, 1982.

Winsor, Bill. *Texas in the Confederacy: Military Installations, Economy, and People.* Hillsboro: Hill College Press, 1978.

Wood, Robert D., ed. *Archivos de Laredo: Documentos Referentes a Los Indios.* San Antonio: St. Mary's University, 1998.

———. *Archivos de Laredo: Index to the Municipal Correspondence, 1825–1845, and Verbal Arbitrations and Decisions, 1832–1842.* San Antonio: St. Mary's University, 2000.

———. *Archivos de Laredo: The History of Mexico, 1809–1845, In the Laredo Archives.* San Antonio: St. Mary's University, 2000.

———. *Archivos de Laredo: Death and Taxes.* San Antonio: St. Mary's University, 2001.

———, comp. *Index to the Laredo Archives.* San Antonio: St. Mary's University, n.d.

Woodman, Lyman L. *Cortina, Rogue of the Rio Grande.* San Antonio: Naylor, 1950.

Wooster, Ralph A. *Texas and Texans in the Civil War.* Austin: Eakin Press, 1995.

———. *Lone Star Generals in Gray.* Austin: Eakin Press, 2000.

Wright, Marcus J., comp. *Texas in the War, 1861–1865.* Edited by Harold B. Simpson. Hillsboro: Hill College Press, 1965.

Yeary, Mamie. *Reminiscences of the Boys in Gray, 1861–1865.* Dayton, Ohio: Morningside, 1986.

Young, Elliott. *Catarino Garza's Revolution on the Texas-Mexico Border.* Durham: Duke University Press, 2004.

Zorrilla, Juan Fidel. *Governadores, Obispos y Rectores.* Ciudad Victoria: Universidad Autónoma de Tamaulipas, 1979.

Articles and Other Published Materials

Ashcraft, Allan C. "The Union Occupation of the Lower Rio Grande Valley in the Civil War." *Texas Military History* 8 (1970).

Barr, Alwyn. "Texas Coastal Defense, 1861–1875." *Southwestern Historical Quarterly* 65 (July, 1961).

Betts, Vicki. "'Private and Amateur Hangings': The Lynching of W. W. Montgomery, March 15, 1863." *Southwestern Historical Quarterly* 88 (October, 1984).

Broussard, Ray F. "Vidaurri, Juárez, Comonfort's Return from Exile." *Hispanic American Historical Review* 69 (May, 1969).

Brown, Russell. "An Old Woman with a Broomstick: General David E. Twiggs and the Surrender in Texas, 1861." *Military Affairs* 48 (April, 1984).

Cantrell, Gregg. "'Our Very Pronounced Theory of Equal Rights to All': Race, Citizenship, and Populism I the South Texas Borderlands." *Journal of American History* 100 (December, 2013).

Champion, A. A. "The Miller Hotel in the Antebellum Period." *More Studies in Brownsville History*. Edited by Milo Kearny. Brownsville: Pan American University at Brownsville, 1989.

Cheeseman, Bruce S. "Let us have 500 good determined Texans": Richard King's Account of the Union Invasion of South Texas, November 12, 1863, to January 20, 1864." *Southwestern Historical Quarterly* 101 (July, 1997).

Clendenen, Clarence C. "Mexican Unionists: A Forgotten Incident of the War Between the States." *New Mexico Historical Review* 39 (1964).

Cohen, Barry M. "The Texas-Mexico Border, 1858–1867." *Texana* 6 (Summer, 1968).

Danini, Carmina. "The Immigrants who Built Laredo." *Saludos* 3 (July 1, 1976).

Davenport, Herbert. "General José María Jesús Carvajal." *Southwestern Historical Quarterly* 55 (April, 1952).

Delaney, Robert W. "Matamoros: Port for Texas during the Civil War." *Southwestern Historical Quarterly* 58 (April, 1955).

Delaney, Robert W. "Corpus Christi–The Vicksburg of Texas." *Civil War Times Illustrated* 16 (July, 1977).

Elliott, Claude. "Union Sentiment in Texas, 1861–1865." *Southwestern Historical Quarterly* 50 (April, 1947).

Ewing, Floyd F. Jr. "Origins of Unionist Sentiment on the West Texas Frontier." *West Texas Historical Association Year Book* 32 (October, 1957).

Farías, Hector Jr. "Col. Santos Benavides: The Emergence of a Dynamic Military and Political Leader." *LareDos* 15 (October, 2010).

Fitzhugh, Lester N. "Saluria, Fort Esperanza, and Military Operations on the Texas Coast, 1861–1864." *Southwestern Historical Quarterly* 61 (July, 1957).

Heidler, Jeanne T. "'Embarrassing Situation': David E. Twiggs and the Surrender of United States Forces in Texas, 1861." *Military History of the Southwest* 21 (Fall, 1991).

Hendricks, Stanley Brown. "The Somervell Expedition to the Rio Grande." *Southwestern Historical Quarterly* 2 (October, 1919).

Kelly, Patrick J. "Is he a Mexican or a Texan," Paper delivered at the Texas State Historical Association Conference (2000).

Kiel, Frank Wilson, ed., "'Wir Waren unser 20 Mann gegen 150' ('We were 20 men against 150') The Battle of Las Rucias: A Civil War Letter from a German-Texan Soldier in the 1864 Union Invasion of the Lower Rio Grande Valley." *Southwestern Historical Quarterly* 105 (January, 2002).

Marshall, Bruce. "Santos Benavides: 'The Confederacy on the Rio Grande.'" Magazine of the *Civil War Society* 8 (May–June, 1990).

Marten, James. "True to the Union: Texans in the U.S. Army." *North and South: The Magazine of the Civil War Conflict* 3 (November, 1999).

Meiners, Fredericka. "The Texas Border Cotton Trade, 1862–1863." *Civil War History* 23 (December, 1977).

Mendoza, Alex. "'For Our Own Best Interests': Nineteenth-Century Laredo Tejanos, Military Service, and the Development of American Nationalism." *Southwestern Historical Quarterly* 115 (October, 2011).

Morris, Leopold. "The Mexican Raid of 1875 on Corpus Christi." *Quarterly of the Texas State Historical Association* 4 (1900–1901).

Oates, Stephen B. "John S. 'Rip' Ford: Prudent Cavalryman, C.S.A." *Southwestern Historical Quarterly* 64 (January, 1961).

———. "Texas under the Secessionists." *Southwestern Historical Quarterly* 67 (October, 1963).

Quiroga, Miguel Gonzalez. " Mexicanos in Texas During the Civil War." *Mexican Americans in Texas History* (Austin: Texas State Historical Association, 2000).

Schoonover, Thomas. "Confederate Diplomacy and the Texas-Mexican Border, 1861–1865." *East Texas Historical Journal* 11 (Spring, 1973).

Shearer, Ernest C. "The Carvajal Disturbances." *Southwestern Historical Quarterly* 55 (October, 1951).

Shook, Robert W. "The Battle of the Nueces, August 10, 1862." *Southwestern Historical Quarterly* 66 (July, 1962).

Smith, Mitchell. "The 'Neutral' Matamoros Trade, 1861–1865." *Southwest Review* 36 (Autumn, 1952).

Smyrl, Frank H. "Texans in the Union Army, 1861–1865." *Southwestern Historical Quarterly* 65 (October, 1961).

———. "Unionism in Texas, 1856–1861." *Southwestern Historical Quarterly* 68 (1964).

Thompson, Jerry. "A Stand Along the Border: Santos Benavides and the Battle for Laredo." *Civil War Times Illustrated* 26 (August, 1980).

———. "Mutiny and Desertion on the Rio Grande: The Strange Saga of Captain Adrian J. Vidal." *Military History of Texas and the Southwest* 11 (1975).

———. "Drama in the Desert: The Hunt for Henry Skillman in the Trans-Pecos, 1862–1864." *Password* 3 (Fall, 1992).

———. "Adrian J. Vidal: Soldier of Three Republics." *Hispanic Genealogical Journal* 14 (1996).

Thompson, William G. "Letters from Commanding Officer in Area in 1863." *Port Isabel Press,* (March 31, 1881).

Trudeau, Noah Andre. "The Story of the War's Final Days." *Civil War Times Illustrated* 29 (July–August, 1990).

Tyler, Ronnie C. "Cotton on the Border, 1861–1865." *Southwestern Historical Quarterly* 73 (April, 1970).

———. "Santiago Vidaurri and the Confederacy." *The Americas* 26 (July, 1969).

Tyson, Carl Newton. "Texas: Men for War; Cotton for Economy." *Journal of the West* 14 (January, 1975).

Weinert, Richard P. "Confederate Border Troubles with Mexico." *Civil War Times Illustrated* 3 (October, 1964).

White, William W. "The Disintegration of an Army: Confederate Forces in Texas, April–June, 1865." *East Texas Historical Journal* 26 (1988).

Wilson, D. M. "The Last Battle of the War." *Confederate Veteran* 18 (1910).

Unpublished Material

Ash, Bette Gay Hunter. "The Mexican-Texans in the Civil War." MA thesis, East Texas State University, 1972.

Broussard, Ray F. "Ignacio Comonfort: His Contributions to the Mexican Reform, 1855–1857." PhD diss., University of Texas at Austin, 1959.

Calderón, Roberto Ramón. "Mexican Politics in the American Era, 1846–1900: Laredo, Texas." PhD diss., University of California, Los Angeles, 1993.

Callahan, Manuel. "Mexican Border Troubles, Social War, Settler Colonialism, and the Production of Frontier Discourses, 1848–1880." PhD diss., University of Texas at Austin, 2003.

Cowling, Annie. "The Confederate Cotton Trade with Mexico." MA thesis, University of Texas, 1926.

Dickeson, Sherrill L. "The Texas Cotton Trade during the Civil War." MA thesis, Texas Tech University, 1967.

Farías, Hector, and José Roberto Juárez. "Juan Francisco Farias Residence Historical Narrative." Author's files.

Fielder, Bruce M. "The Mexican Connection: Confederate and Union Diplomacy on the Rio Grande, 1861–1865." MA thesis, North Texas State University, 1978.

Gallegos, J. J. "Santiago Vidaurri: Regional Power, Trade and Capital Formation in Northern Mexico." Author's files.

García, Luis. "Santiago Vidaurri and Santos Benavides: A Relation between Mexican Leaders across a Borderland," Paper presented at the Texas State Historical Association, March 2010.

Graf, LeRoy P. "The Economic History of the Lower Rio Grande Valley, 1820–1875." PhD diss., Harvard University, 1942.

Gray, Ronald Norman. "Edmund J. Davis: Radical Republican and Reconstruction Governor of Texas." PhD diss., Texas Tech University, 1976.

Greer, Viola Ann. "Santiago Vidaurri, Cacique of Northern Mexico: His Relationship to Benito Juárez." MA thesis, University of Texas at Austin, 1949.

Irby, James A. "Line of the Rio Grande: War and Trade on the Confederate Frontier, 1861–1865." PhD diss., University of Georgia, 1969.

Kitchen, Carr P. "Mexican Depredations in the Lower Rio Grande Valley, 1835–1885." MA thesis, Baylor University, 1933.

Moreno, Joe. "Laredo's First International Bridge." Author's Files.

Moseley, Edward H. "The Public Career of Santiago Vidaurri, 1855–1858." PhD diss., University of Alabama, 1963.

Nichols, James David. "The Limits of Liberty: African-Americans, Indians and Peons in the Texas-Mexico Borderlands, 1820–1860." PhD diss., University of New York at Stony Brook, 2001.

"Reconstruction of Past Drought across the Coterminous United States from a Network of Climatically Sensitive Tree-Ring Data." National Oceanic and Atmospheric Administration, Washington, DC.

Riley, Denny. "Santos Benavides: His Influence on the Lower Rio Grande, 1823–1891." PhD diss., Texas Christian University, 1976.

———. "Santos Benavides: True Confederate." Paper presented at the Texas State Historical Association, March 1978.

Ryle, Walter Harrington. "The Political Career of Don Santiago Vidaurri." MA thesis, Northeast Missouri State Teachers College, 1956.

Romo, Rolando M. "The Rise of the Laredo Ranching and Mercantile Elite: A Case Study of A. M. Bruni." Texas A&M International University, 2005.

Salinas, Horacio Jr., "Santos Benavides: The Making of a Confederate Officer along the Rio Grande Frontier, 1861–1864." Texas A&M International University, 1996.

Sutton, Jared Paul. "Ethnic Minorities and Prohibition in Texas, 1887–1919." MA thesis, University of North Texas, 2006.

Townsend, Stephen A. "The Rio Grande Expedition, 1863–1865." PhD diss., University of North Texas, 2001.

Valerio-Jimenéz, Omar Santiago. "'Indios Barbaros,' Divorcees, and Flocks of Vampires: Identity and Nation on the Rio Grande, 1749–1894." PhD diss., University of California at Los Angeles, 2001.

Villarreal y Talamantes, Armando. "Intervention and Conflict in the Trans-Nueces, 1755–1850." PhD diss., University of Texas at Arlington, 2003.

Wagner, Leslie Alice Jones. "Disputed Territory: Rio Grande/Rio Bravo Borderlands, 1838–1840." PhD diss., University of Texas at Arlington, 1998.

Webster, Michael G. "Texan Manifest Destiny and the Mexican Border Conflict, 1865–1880." PhD diss., Indiana University, 1972.

Government Documents

"Heirs of Santos Benavides." 64th Congress, 1st Session, House of Representatives, Report No. 231 (February 21, 1916).

"Heirs of Santos Benavides." 64th Congress, 1st Session, Senate, Report No. 271 (March 18, 1916).

INDEX

SB = José de los Santos Benavides

abolition: Benavides family on, 75. *See also* slavery
Adams, W. H.: in Laredo Election Riot (1886), 296
African Americans. *See* blacks
Agustín of Mexico. *See* Iturbide, Agustín de
alcohol. *See* prohibition
Alderete, Pablo, 175
Alderete, Rafael, 271
Allen, Laura, 328
Alleyton, Texas: cotton smuggling in, 139
Alvarado, Francisco, 155
Álvarez, Juan, 106
amnesty. *See* pardon
Ampudia, Pedro de, 18
Anderson, H. B., 260
Appomattox Court House, Virginia: Confederate surrender at, effect in South Texas, 198
Arguëlles, Pedro, 322
Arguindegui, Mariano: pardon of, 312
Arista, Mariano, 18
arms: smuggling of, in Civil War, 126, 143–44, 181, 188; smuggling of, SB and, 68, 315
Arthur, Chester A., 274
Atlee, E. A., 276; in Laredo Election Riot (1886), 304; as mayor of Laredo, 304; as state representative, 290; as senate candidate, 305
Austin, Stephen F., 8–9; on Laredo, 9
Austin, Texas: Confederate veterans' home in, 312, 314; SB's last visit to, 318, 320
Bagdad, Texas, 306; Abraham Lincoln's death celebrated in, 205; cotton smuggling in, 138, 139, 141; described, 138
banditry: in South Texas, 62, 102, 118, 122, 217–21, 223; 245–46
Banks, Nathaniel P., 144–45; Union strategy in South Texas of, 160
Barrett, Theodore H., 199, 201, 203
Bartlett, J. L.: on Laredo City Council, 294
baseball: in Laredo, 234, 237
Bee, Barnard, 57, 216
Bee, Hamilton P., 46; on Benavides brothers, 133; Brownsville surrender by, 134, 148–50; Bourland Commission and, 42; in Civil War, 112, 113, 118, 124, 126, 128, 130, 133, 134, 141, 142, 146–50, 151, 190, 196; on Confederacy's collapse in South Texas, 208; corruption of, 141; cotton smuggling and, 141, 142; desertion and, 118; on Lipan Apache incursions, 51; mails and, 58, 64; Octaviano Zapata raids and, 124, 126; pictured, 57; political career of, 58; post-Civil War life of, 216–17; on SB, 133; SB on, 152; Somervell Expedition (1842–1843) reparations and, 32; Union invasion of South Texas and, 146–50; wagon train of, captured by Lipan Apaches, 51–52; as Webb County clerk, 56, 58
Bee, Lamar. *See* Benavides, Lamar Bee de
Belden, Fred: mails and, 64
Bell, Peter H., 42, 46

Benavides, Agustina (adopted daughter of SB). *See* Garza Ayala, Agustina Benavides

Benavides, Agustina Villarreal del (wife of SB), 69: beauty of, 26; business acumen of, 25; in Civil War, 157; death of, 328; infertility of, 70; marriage of, 24, 26; pictured, 25; travels of, 306, 309–10, 315; wills and testaments of, 325–26

Benavides, Basilio (uncle of SB): as alcalde of Laredo, 10–12, 16; as businessman, 113; in Canales rebellion, 16; on Catholic Church, 62; Comanches and, 10, 11–12; death of, 188, 214; as Democratic State Convention (1861) delegate, 83; early life of, 10; English (language) and, 77; Federalist principles of, 15, 26; illness of, 188; as justice of the peace candidate (1847), 37; Lipan Apaches and, 10; as mayor of Laredo, 32, 59; on Native Americans generally, 9; pictured, 16; political career generally, 2; Santiago Vidaurri and, 61–62; on secession, 80; on slavery, 80; Somervell Expedition (1842–1843), effect on, 30; Somervell Expedition (1842–1843), reparations for, 32; as state representative, 60, 77, 81, 260; on US rule in Laredo, 39–40; vagrants in Laredo and, 48; as Webb County judge, 59, 214

Benavides, Encarnación (Carmen). *See* García, Encarnación (Carmen) Benavides de

Benavides, Eulalio (illegitimate son of SB), 71

Benavides, Feliz (daughter of Basilio). *See* Rodríguez, Feliz Benavides de

Benavides, José Cristóbal (Cristóbal, half-brother of SB): Alanis, role in lynching of, 229; birth, 6; as businessman, 62–63, 63–64, 113, 232–34, 268, 327; *City of Laredo v. Raymond Martin Et Al.* testimony of, 244–45; as city treasurer in Laredo, 240; in Civil War, 84, 96, 104, 113, 125, 132, 133, 150, 171, 184, 186, 191, 196, 211; death of, 328; as Dog Town bandit posse member, 219; as ferry operator, 243, 244–45; Ft. McIntosh building purchases by, 96; gravesite pictured, 327; Hamilton P. Bee on, 133; in Laredo Election Riot (1886), 299; mails and, 113; marriage of, 327; as Native American fighter, 222; Native American threat to Laredo and, 78–79; pictured, 136, 140; as rancher, 72; Sebastián Lerdo de Tejada, support for, 250; as smuggler, generally, 232–34

Benavides, José de Jesús (father of SB), 2, 6; death and legacy, 6–7; second marriage, 6

Benavides, José de los Santos (SB): appraisal of, 324, 331; as arms dealer, 66, 68, 143–44; baptism of, 6; binational loyalty of, 112, 113, 144, 154, 331; birth of, 2, 6; border control and raids and, 121–23, 125–26, 127–28, 129–30, 132; at bridge over Rio Grande dedication (1890), 321–23; as businessman, 60–61, 66, 68, 69–70, 70, 113, 232–34, 234, 236, 268, 324; in Canales rebellion, 16; in Casteñeda expedition, 26; children of, listed, 24; *City of Laredo v. Raymond Martin Et Al.* testimony of, 244; in Civil War, 2, 84–207; Confederacy, loyalty to, 104; Confederate rank of, 84, 132, 151–52; Confederate veterans' home (Austin, Texas) and, 312, 314; in constitutional convention election (1875), 258; on corruption, 282; cotton smuggling and, 143, 151, 153, 164; death and funeral of, 323–24; disqualification from public office of, 214; as Dog Town bandit posse member, 219–21; education of, 9; English (language) and, 116, 260–61; in 1884 Webb County election, 288, 290; as ferry operator, 61; "frontier troubles," testimony about, 245–46; gravesite pictured, 330; on Guadalupe García, 106; on guerilla war, 152; on Hamilton P. Bee, 152; Hamilton P. Bee on,

133; health of, 170, 171, 175; Ignacio Comonfort, escort of, 106–8; John S. "Rip" Ford, memoirs of, 317–18; John S. "Rip" Ford, relationship with, 166, 178, 191–92, 192–95; in Laredo Election Riot (1886), 298, 301, 302, 302–4; legacy, 325; mails and, 64, 70, 113; Mariano Arguindegui pardon and, 311; Mariano Escobedo, relationship with, 248, 250; marriage of, 24, 26; as mayor of Laredo, 50, 59–60; in Mexico, 252, 306–7, 308–9, 315, 321; Mirabeau B. Lamar, interview with, 39; as Native American fighter, 222, 223; Native American threat to Laredo and, 53–54, 55, 78–79; on Native Americans, 9; as notary, 212, 214; pardon of, 234; "People of the Frontier" letter of, 156–57; pictured, 25, 88, 239, 264, 272, 275; on police reform, 292; political influence of, 276, 277; political principles of, 262, 274; on Porfiriatio, 309; Porfirio Díaz, compared to, 254; Porfirio Díaz, relationship with, 248, 251, 252, 306–7, 314–15, 315; on Porfirio Díaz's reelection (1888), 315–16; Porfirio Díaz's visit to Texas (1883) and, 273–74; prohibition and, 263, 265, 316–17; property ownership of, 234, 236, 270–71; railroads, support for, 254–55, 265–67; as rancher, 23, 61, 68, 70, 72, 236, 323; Reform Party and, 281; remains of, 331; reputation of, 278; Rio Grande City riot (1888) and, 321; runaway slaves and, 76, 96; on sanitation in Laredo, 60; Santiago Vidaurri, relationship with, 66, 68, 69, 69–70, 71–72, 77–78, 94, 104–5, 106–8, 108, 110, 112, 113–14, 126–27, 180, 180–81, 210; Sebastián Lerdo de Tejada, support for, 250; as smuggler, generally, 232–34; Somervell Expedition (1842–1843), effect on, 30; as state representative, 229, 259–63, 265, 271, 273–74; as state representative, defeated for, 240, 257, 258; on streets in Laredo, 60; Texas legislature, praise from for, 133–34; as Texas Senate candidate, 304–5; at Texas State Capitol dedication, 318, 320; as voter (1847), 37; Unionists and, 96; US Army, rumored turning to, 154–55; as US House of Representative candidate potentially, 279–80; as US Minister to Mexico, potentially, 318; US-Mexican amity and, 254, 255, 268–69, 276, 306–9, 311–12, 314–16, 318; as Webb County judge, 60; wills and testaments of, 325–26; as World's Industrial and Cotton Centennial Exposition (1884) commissioner, 277; writings of, 254, 255, 276, 302, 307, 309, 311, 315

Benavides, José del Refugio (Refugio, brother of SB): as alderman of Laredo, 59, 242; birth, 6; Cherokee and, 55; in *City of Laredo v. Raymond Martin Et Al.*, 244, 245; in Civil War, 103, 113, 124–25, 125, 133, 150, 168, 173, 184, 185, 186, 188, 188–89, 189, 190, 196, 202, 206; coal mining operation of, 267; death of, 326, 328; as Dog Town bandit posse member, 219; English (language) and, 245; Hamilton P. Bee on, 133; illness of, 188; John S. "Rip" Ford, relationship with, 192; mails and, 64, 113; as mayor of Laredo, 59, 60, 225, 240–41, 256; as Native American fighter, 222, 225; Native American threat to Laredo and, 78–79; as notary, 214; pictured, 136; Reform Party and, 281; Somervell Expedition (1842–1843), effect on, 30; on Tejano enlistment, 100; as Texas Ranger, 225–26, 228–29; as voter (1847), 37

Benavides, José Eulalio (Eulalio, half-brother of SB), 270, 298, 325; birth of, 6; as businessman, 113; as district clerk, 241; as leader of search party for SB, 74; as rancher, 63; Sebastián Lerdo de Tejada, support for, 250; as Webb County inspector of hides and animals, 237

Benavides, Juan V. (adopted son of SB), 70, 71; at Agustina's death, 328; as city

attorney of Laredo, 328; death of, 328; education of, 281–82; in 1884 Webb County elections, 284, 286–90; in 1886 Laredo municipal elections, 292, 294; Guarache Party and, 287; in Laredo Election Riot (1886), 302; later life of, 328; Reform Party and, 281; at SB's funeral, 323–24; as SB's interpreter, 269, 282; in SB's will, 325; as Webb County Democratic chairman, 304
Benavides, Lamar Bee de (wife of Cristóbal), 236, 299, 327
Benavides, Lorenzo, 60
Benavides, Margarita Ramón de (mother of SB), 2; death of, 6
Benavides, María Andrea (half-sister of SB). *See* Leyendecker, María Andrea Benavides
Benavides, María del Patrocinio (sister of Basilio): as SB's godmother, 6
Benavides, Maria Encarnación García de (wife of Basilio), 10
Benavides, María Francisca (half-sister of SB). *See* Farías, Francisca Benavides
Benavides, María Juliana (half-sister of SB). *See* Leyendecker, María Juliana Benavides
Benavides, María Ricarda (sister of SB): birth, 6
Benavides, María Seferina (sister of SB): birth, 6
Benavides, Petronilo (illegitimate son of SB), 24
Benavides, Tomasa Cameros de (stepmother of SB), 6; SB, relationship with, 7
Benavides, Santos (subject of biography). *See* Benavides, José de los Santos
Benavides, Santos (son of Refugio, nephew of SB): arrest of, 241
Benavides, Santos (US Army sergeant): pictured, 326
Benavides, Santos, Jr. (adopted son of SB), 71; later life of, 328–29; in SB's will, 325
Benavides, Santos Eraclio (Eraclio, adopted son of SB): death of, 270; in SB's will, 325
Benavides, Teresa, 113
Benavides Lópes, Francisco Baez, 2
Berlandier, Jean Louis, 5
Bernard, Ruben F.: in Laredo Election Riot (1886), 300–1
Bettina colony, 279
"Black Bean Incident" (1843), 34
blacks: US troops, in Laredo, 212. *See also* slavery
Blaine and Logan Republican Club, 283
Blücher, Felix von, 189
border raids: in Civil War, 121–28, 129–30, 132. *See also specific raids and raiders*
Botas: control of Laredo politics after 1886 by, 329; in 1884 Webb County elections, 287–90; in 1886 Laredo municipal elections, 291, 292, 294–95; in Laredo Election Riot (1886), 295–96, 298–304; origins of, 287
Botello, Victor, 51
Bourland, William H., 42
Bourland Commission, 42
Boyard, Stephen, 291–92, 294; in Laredo Election Riot (1886), 304
Brackett, Albert: on Laredo, 50; on Native American threat to Laredo, 52
Branson, David, 199, 201, 212
Bravo Villaso, Calixto, 22, 27, 28
Brazos Island: US Army on, 144–45, 147, 187, 189, 193, 200, 202, 203
Broadwater, Guy B., 305
Brown, John Henry: on Somervell Expedition army, 27
Brownsville, Texas: 1863 Confederate surrender of, 134, 148–50; 1863 Confederate surrender of, pictured, 149; 1864 Confederate recapture of, 184–87; 1865 Confederate surrender of, 205; cotton smuggling in, 137, 138, 188; market in, pictured, 117. *See also* Fort Brown
Buena Vista, Battle of (1847), 39
Bureau of Foreign Supplies, 143
Burleson, Edward, 46
Burlington, Iowa, SB in, 310

Butcher, H. B.: as Dog Town bandit posse member, 219

Callaghan, Charles, 236; in Civil War, 84, 92, 98; coal mining operation of, 267; Fort McIntosh, assumption of control over, 83; mails and, 64; as Native American fighter, 223
camels, 179
Cameron County, Texas: secession in, 82; tax exemption for, bill sponsored by SB, 263
Cameros, Tomasa. *See* Benavides, Tomasa Cameros de
Camp, W. W., 175
Camp Crawford, 43–44. *See also* Fort McIntosh
Campbell, Francis M.: mails and, 58
Canales, Antonio: uprising of (1838–1840), 15–19
Canales, Servando, 306, 308
Cardenas, Jesús, 17
Cardenas, Meliton, 96
Cardis, Louis, 257, 258
Carleton, James Henry, 145, 160, 162, 176
Carrera, Pedro: murder of, 48–49
Carrizo, Battle of (1861), 90–94, 104, 106; aftermath of, 125
Carrizos (Native Americans), 17, 52
Carrington, W. H. D., 202, 203
Carroll, W. C., 216
Cart War (1857), 142
Carvajal, José María de Jesús, 104, 115, 122, 143; filibustering expedition of, 63; at Matamoros siege (1862), 108, 110–12; pictured, 109; scheme to raise Confederate regiment of, 113–14; on slavery, 75; as Tamaulipas governor, 210
Castañeda, Francisco, 26
Catholic Church: Basilio Benavides on, 62; Mexican Constitution of 1857 and, 107; Santiago Vidaurri on, 62, 69
cattle rustling: bill about, sponsored by SB, 261–62
Caven, William John, 273
Cazneau, William Leslie: mails and, 58
Centro, Achilles, 48–49
Cervantes, Casiano, 179
Chacon Creek, Battle of (1837), 14, 19
Chapman, George, 171
cholera: in Laredo, 44, 48, 188
Christen, L. J.: on Laredo City Council, 294; in Laredo Election Riot (1886), 302
City of Laredo v. Raymond Martin Et Al., 243–45
Civil War, 2, 84–207. *See also individuals in and specific engagements*
Clark, Edward: as governor, 83; Mexico, flight to, 206, 209; on SB, 94; on Tejano enlistment in South Texas, 97, 102
Cleveland, Grover, 318
climate: in South Texas, 165–66, 179
Club Azul Independiente Mejico-Tejano, 283
coal: industry near Laredo, 267–68
Cochran, A. M., 316
Cochran, John Hughes, 260, 273
Cockerel, Samuel, 186
Coke, Richard, 317; in 1873 gubernatorial election, 238; lawlessness on US-Mexican border and, 225–26; railroads and, 265
Comanches: Laredo, threat to, 9, 10–12, 15, 36, 46, 47, 52–55, 78–79, 222; Stephen F. Austin and, 9
Comonfort, Ignacio, 65–66; death of, 183; on SB, 107; SB escorts, 106–8
Confederate States of America: end of, 207, 208; Mexico and, 111, 182; SB, loyalty to, 104; Texas joins, 83. *See also* Civil War
Confederate veterans' home (Austin, Texas), 312, 314
Conrow, Aaron H.: Mexico, flight to, 209
Corpus Christi, San Diego and Rio Grande Narrow Gauge Railroad Company, 265–66
Cortina, Juan Nepomuceno: Ádrian J. Vidal and, 147, 148; at Battle of Carrizo (1861), 90–94; Confederacy, threat

to, 146, 148, 185, 193; cotton smuggling and, 151; as Juarista, 202; Laredo, threat to, 85; Octaviano Zapata and, 123; pictured, 83; raiding activity of, 104, 108, 128, 190, 224, 226–27, 228; Santiago Vidaurri, threat to, 71–72; SB, attempts to arrest of, 104–5; SB, meeting with, 155; Tejanos, popular appeal to, 85; US Army, alliance rumored with, 89;
Cortina War (1859–1861), 62, 71, 81; beginnings of, 85; José Ángel Navarro appointed to investigate start of, 165; SB praised for role in, 103, 105
Cos, Martin Perfecto de, 9–10
cotton: as defensive tool, 171; as diplomatic tool, 135–36; on Mexican border, pictured, 111, 149, 120; as payment, 183; SB's seizure of, 191, 192; smuggling of, 55, 99, 101, 111, 115, 136–43, 148–51, 152, 153, 154, 155, 163–64, 168, 169, 170, 171, 177–78, 181, 183, 188, 198–99, 204, 206; in South Texas, 135, 136–39, 141–43; tax on, 111; Union strategy in South Texas and, 145, 160, 162, 166, 167, 171–72. *See also* World's Industrial and Cotton Centennial Exposition (1884)
Cox, Noah, 259
Crawford, William Harris, 43
Cruz, Pedro, 223
Cuellar, Remal, 268

Dana, Napoleon Jackson Tecumseh, 160, 176; on SB, 154
Daniell, Lewis E., 317, 324
Davis, Edmund J., 52, 271; in *City of Laredo v. Raymond Martin Et Al.*, 243–44; in Civil War, 133, 144, 145, 146, 152, 154, 154–55, 170, 205; in 1873 gubernatorial election, 238; 1872 Webb County election and, 237; mails and, 58, 64; pictured, 213; political influence of, 214; SB, rumored turning of by, 154–55; SB, influence on of, 259; secession and, 83
Davis, Jefferson, 53, 190–91; cotton and, 135
Davis, Henry Clay, 197
Davis, Henry T., 147
Davis Landing, Texas, 197. *See also* Rio Grande City, Texas
de la Garza, Juan José, 51
de la Garza, María Hilaria, 197
Dean, Harrison L., 204
Delafield, Richard, 47
desertion: in Civil War, 118, 165, 191, 195, 198
Devine, Thomas J., 163–64
DeWitt, Bartholomew J., 63
Días, Antonio Abad, 153
Diaz, Vivian: Somervell Expedition (1842–1843), effect on, 30
Díaz, Agustín, 86
Díaz, Martina, 223
Díaz, Pedro, 86, 89
Díaz, Porfirio, 323; Confederate veterans' home (Austin, Texas) and, 312, 314; conspiracies in Texas against, 314–15; fall from power of, 328; first presidential term of, 251–52; Manuel González, rumored rift with, 311; Mariano Arguindegui pardon and, 311; Mariano Escobedo, opposition from, 248, 250–51; Nuevo Laredo, attack on (1876), 247; pictured, 313; political ideals and methods of, 252, 254; reelection of (1888), 315–16; Rio Grande inspection tour (1878) of, 276; SB, compared to, 254; SB, relationship with, 248, 251, 252, 306–7, 314–15, 315; SB on, 309; Sebastián Lerdo de Tejada, rebellion against, 248; Texas State Capitol cornerstone laying and, 315; Texas visit to (1883), 273–74; Treviño–González feud and, 276–77; on US-Mexico relations, 307; at World's Industrial and Cotton Centennial Exposition (1884), 277
Dimmit County, Texas: border adjustment bill sponsored by SB, 261
diseases: bill about, sponsored by SB, 261; at Fort Brown, 146. *See also specific diseases*
Dobie, J. Frank, 228
Dodd, Thomas, 322

Dohoney, Ebenezer Lafayette, 316
Dog Town, Texas: banditry in, 217–18
Dovalina, Agustín: Somervell Expedition (1842–1843), effect on, 30
Ducatet, Felix, 163–64
Duff, James, 147, 178
Dunn, James, 186
Duran, José María, 262
Durango, Mexico: cotton mills in, 141
Durkee, W. C., 202
Dwyer, Thomas B., 173, 175; on SB, 170

Eagle Pass, Texas: arms smuggling in, 68, 181; Confederate battle flag buried at, 209; cotton smuggling in, 111, 120, 139, 141, 142–43, 145, 150–51, 151, 152, 162, 163, 164, 166, 167, 167–68, 170, 188; guerilla operations around, during Civil War, 176–78; mails in, 58, 64, 70; Mexican consulate opened in, 252; pictured, 55
Edger, E. S., 310
education: of Agustina Garza Ayala, 117; of Juan V. Benavides, 281–82; in Laredo, 240; of SB, 9; SB and, in state legislature, 263
elections: 1847 Laredo, 37; 1849 Webb County, 56; 1860 statewide, 77; 1866 Laredo, 212, 214; 1872 Webb County, 237–38; 1873 Laredo, 238, 240; 1873 statewide, 238, 257; 1874 Laredo, 241; 1875 Laredo, 242; 1875 state constitutional, 258; 1876 Laredo, 256; 1878 statewide, 259–60; 1880 statewide, 263; 1882 statewide, 271; 1884 statewide, 276; 1884 Webb County, 284–90; 1886 Laredo, 291, 292, 294–95; bill about, sponsored by SB, 261. *See also* Laredo Election Riot (1886); politics
Elizario, Guadalupe: murder of, 223–24
Emory, William H.: on smuggling in Laredo, 230
Encinal County, Texas, 41, 261; prohibition in, 317; Reform Party in, 283–84; SB property in, 236
English (language): Basilio Benavides and, 62, 77; Cristóbal Benavides and, 62; José María Rodríguez and, 63, 77; in Laredo, 56, 59, 215, 282, 303; Porfirio Díaz and, 315; Refugio Benavides and, 244, 245; SB and, 116, 240, 269, 273, 278, 280, 282, 322
Escandón, José de, 2, 6
Escobedo, Mariano, 54, 209, 227; pictured, 249; Porfirio Díaz, opposition to, 248, 250–51; SB, relationship with, 248;
Escuela Amarilla (Laredo, Texas), 240
Etchison, Emanuel D.: refugees and, 119–20
Evarts, William M.: SB letter to, 307–8

Farías, Francisca Benavides: birth, 6; pictured, 20
Farías, Francisco, 20; as Dog Town bandit posse member, 219
Farías, George, 324
Farías, Juan, 55
Farías Chronicles: A History and Genealogy of a Portuguese/Spanish Family (Farías): SB profiled in, 324
Fernandez, José María, 130
Fernández Iazguirre, José Antonio, 11, 12
ferry: over Rio Grande, 61, 242–45; over Rio Grande, pictured, 251
Finlay, George Preston: as interpreter for SB, 262; seeks SB's electoral support, 276
Fish, Hamilton, 226
Flores, Anselmo: at Battle of Carrizo (1861), 92
Ford, John S. "Rip": at Battle of Carrizo (1861), 90; on Benavides brothers' military prowess, 125; on Cherokees, 11; in Civil War, 84, 105, 106, 110, 112–13, 142, 145, 159–60, 165, 165–66, 172–73, 174–75, 178, 179, 184, 188, 190, 190–95, 196, 198–99, 200, 203; on climate in South Texas, 165–66; as commander in Rio Grande valley, 190; on Confederate morale, 165; as constitutional convention (1876) delegate, 258; cotton smuggling and, 142, 145; in 1878 statewide election, 259; "frontier troubles," testimony about, 245; on

Guadalupe García, 106; illness of, 188; in Laredo, 45–46; at Matamoros siege (1862), 110–12; memoirs of, 317–18; on Native Americans, 45; Ochoa insurrection and, 87; pictured, 161; Refugio Benavides, relationship with, 192; on SB, 93–94, 174–75, 175–76; SB, relationship with, 166, 178, 191–92, 192–95; on Tejanos and secession, 81–82; on Tejanos and slavery, 74; on trade with the enemy, 179; as US House of Representative candidate, 280
Forey, Elie Frédéric, 180
Fort Brown, 43; as Confederate headquarters in South Texas, 87, 105, 114, 146, 147, 188, 192, 193, 196, 200, 203; Confederate surrender of (1863), 148–49; desertion at, 118; illness at, 146; supply train from attacked, 123; as US Army headquarters in South Texas, 84, 166, 168, 205, 210, 212; US Army surrender of (1864), 185, 187. *See also* Brownsville, Texas
Fort Chadbourne: John Z. Leyendecker and, 63
Fort Duncan, 43, 52; in Civil War, 153, 168, 177, 180, 197; pictured, 55. *See also* Eagle Pass, Texas
Fort Inge, 53, 177
Fort McIntosh: banditry and, 218–19, 246–47; baseball team from, 234; Confederate enlistments at, 97; economic effects on Laredo of, 47–48, 244; established, 44; Evaristo Madero visit and, 269; fortifications at, 47; garrison of, 47; Hamilton Bee at, 57, 58; James Slaughter at, 47, 99; John Z. Leyendecker and, 63; Native Americans and, 48, 51, 52, 53, 222–23, 224, 225; pictured, 322; reputation of, 49; sale of buildings of, 94, 96; sanitation in Laredo and, 214–15; as SB's Civil War headquarters, 87, 89; smallpox at, 236–37; Texas Rangers at, 45–46; US closure of (1859), 61; US reoccupation of (1865), 211–12, 214; US surrender of (1861), 83–84; Walter W. Hudson death at, 45
Fort McKavett: John Z. Leyendecker and, 63
Fort Worth Gazette: SB's obituary in, 324
Foster, John W., 274, 306
France: Mexico, invasion of, 180–83, 210
Franklin, Billy, 220
Frederick Probst and Company, 248
Fredericksburg, Texas: Leyendeckers in, 63, 64, 120, 121; SB in, 72, 74
Fremantle, Arthur James Lyon: on Bagdad, Texas, 138

Galveston, Harrisburg, and San Antonio Railway, 308
Galveston, Texas: in Civil War, 101, 131, 195, 205; James Slaughter in, 99; Leyendeckers in, 63; Porfirio Díaz, potential visit to, 273; SB, letter to citizens of by, 273
Galveston and Camargo Railroad, 265
Galveston Daily News, 268; SB's writings in, 276, 302, 307, 309, 311, 315
Galveston News, 245; SB's writings in, 254, 255
Galveston Weekly News: SB profiled in, 277–78
Ganado, Francisco, 20
García, Bartolomé (Bartolo), 241, 242; as mayor of Laredo, 94; Somervell Expedition (1842–1843), effect on, 30
García, Benito: as Webb County judge, 214
García, Encarnación (Carmen) Benavides de (wife of Bartolomé), 241
García, Encarnación (murdered laborer), 127–28, 129
García, Francisco (comandante at Piedras Negras), 177
García, Francisco (Guarache), 298
García, Guadalupe, 104–6, 108, 110
García, Higinio: as Laredo city Marshall, 294
García, Ignacio, 20
García, José Antonio, 10
García, José María, 6, 22
García, José Trinidad, 24, 26

García, Julian, 187, 197
García, María Encarnación. *See* Benavides, María Encarnación García de
García, Maria Gertrudis Ramirez de, 10
García, Tirza. *See* Martin, Tirza García de
García Ramirez, Jesús, 126
García Soto, Juan: in Civil War, 84, 93; as Native American fighter, 223
Garza, Carlos: murder of, 224
Garza, Catarino Erasmo, 320, 321
Garza, Cayetano de la, 170; as ferry operator, 243, 244; as Webb County surveyor, 237
Garza, Eugenio, 184
Garza, Jesus, 54
Garza, Juan G.: at Battle of Carrizo (1861), 91
Garza, Juana, 68
Garza Ayala, Agustina Benavides: adoption, 70; death of, 269; education of, 117–18; marriage of, 71, 269; in SB's will, 325
Garza Ayala, Lázaro, 250, 270, 314; at Agustina's death, 328; marriage of, 71, 269; pictured, 319; Texas State Capitol dedication and, 318
Garza Ayala Benavides, Francisco (grandson of SB): at Agustina's death, 328; birth of, 269; in SB's will, 326
Garza García, Genero, 311
Garza González, Manuel, 77
Geiger, Harriel G., 260
German Texans: in Civil War, 119, 120
Getty, George Washington, 210
Gibson, George A., 196
Giddings, George H., 167, 173, 180, 185, 193; at Battle of Palmito Ranch (1865), 199, 200, 201; Refugio Benavides, relationship with, 190
Gil, Cesario, 11
Gil, Lorenzo: Somervell Expedition (1842–1843), effect on, 30–31
Gilgan, Thomas, 232–33
Gillespie, Richard Addison: death of, 36; US sovereignty over Laredo and, 35–36
Glorieta, Battle of (1862), 115, 121
Goliad, Texas, 23, 74
Gomez, Francisco, 71
Gonzales, Anastacio, 246
Gonzales, Aniceto, 262
Gonzales, Darío, 172; in Laredo Election Riot (1886), 296, 298, 302; Reform Party and, 280; as Webb County sheriff, 237
Gonzales, Felipe, 224
Gonzales, José María: Somervell Expedition (1842–1843), effect on, 30; on US rule in Laredo, 39–40
Gonzales, Martin, 129, 166
Gonzales, Texas: cotton smuggling in, 143; runaway slaves in, 74
González, Manuel: on border disturbances, 254–55; Geronimo Treviño, feud with, 276–77; international railroad and, 254; pictured, 253; political ideals and methods of, 255; Porfirio Díaz, rumored rift with, 311; Sebastián Lerdo de Tejada, in rebellion against, 248; SB, relationship with, 251, 255, 308; SB, visit with, 252, 306, 307; SB on, 254, 255
González, Juan Severiano, 262
Gossett, Malachi, 217–18, 219–21
Gossett, Richard (Dick), 217–18; death of, 220
Gould, Jay, 266, 266–67
Grant, Ulysses S., 198; 1873 Texas gubernatorial election and, 238
Green, Thomas F., 217–18, 219, 220–21
Green, Thomas Jefferson, 31, 32
Gregory, William, 200
Griffin, Charles: on SB, 221
Guadalajara, Mexico: cotton mills in, 141
Guarache Party: absorption of, 329; in 1884 Webb County elections, 286–90; in 1886 Laredo municipal elections, 291, 292, 294–95; in Laredo Election Riot (1886), 295–96, 298–304; origins of, 286. *See also* Reform Party
guerrilla warfare: Mariano Escobedo's use of, 248; Porfirio Díaz's use of, 251; SB on, 150, 151, 152; by US Army in

South Texas, 143, 155–56, 176–78. *See also* McManus, T. P.

Hall, Edward F.: death of, 305; as ferry operator, 243, 245; in Laredo Election Riot (1886), 301; O. M. Watkins, altercation with, 290–91; as state senator, 276, 290
Halleck, Henry W.: on US Army strategy in South Texas, 162
Hamilton, Andrew Jackson, 96, 214
Hamilton, Alexander J., 119
Haskins, R. F., 133
Hayes, Rutherford B., 224; Porfirio Díaz, recognition of, 252
Haynes, James J.: in Laredo Election Riot (1886), 302; Pablo Quintana crossing (1876) and, 246; Reform Party and, 283
Haynes, John L., 80, 246, 283; in Civil War, 144, 146, 152–53, 154–55, 167, 176, 182; SB, rumored turning of by, 154–55
Hays, John Coffee: in Laredo, 14, 19, 20–21
Hébert, Paul O., 102, 159
Herrera, Antonio, 20
Herrera, Concepcion ("Chono"): in Laredo Election Riot (1886), 298
Herrera, Natividad, 133, 220, 221; in Laredo Election Riot (1886), 299
Herron, Francis J., 185
Hidalgo County, Texas: secession in, 82
Hinojosa, José María: at Battle of Carrizo (1861), 91
Hinojosa, Juan, 74
Hinojosa, Pedro, 312
Hinojosa, Rodrigo, 74
Hogan, Andrew J.: as Dog Town bandit posse commander, 218, 218–21
Holabird, Samuel Beckley: Tonkawa horse theft and, 44
Holt, Alfred E., 170, 172
Hord, James R., 96
House of Representatives (Texas). *See* Texas House of Representatives
House of Representatives (United States). *See* US House of Representatives
Houston, Sam, 19, 39; in 1860 gubernatorial election, 77; on Erastus "Deaf" Smith's raid on Laredo (1837), 14; secession and, 80, 83; Somervell Expedition and, 26, 27, 32; Texas, reputation in, 62
Houston, Temple, 318, 320
Houston and Great Northern Railroad, 236
Hudson, Walter W.: Tonkawa horse theft and, 44–45
Hunt, A. C.: coal mining operation of, 267–68
Hunter, John Warren: on cotton smuggling, 137
Huster, William, 119, 124
Hutcheson, Joseph Chappell, 262

Ibarra, Juan, 172, 175
Independent Club, 329
Indians. *See* Native Americans
international bridge: in Laredo, 281
International–Great Northern Railway (I&GN), 265, 266, 267, 301; John Ireland, opposition to, 275; SB riding on, 271, 277, 308, 309
interpreter: for Basilio Benavides, in Texas House of Representatives, 63, 77, 284; Juan Benavides as, for SB, 269, 282; for SB, in Texas House of Representatives, 260–61, 262
Ireland, John, 273; Laredo Election Riot (1886) and, 301, 302; SB electoral support for (1884), 274–75
Iturbide, Agustín de, 7–8
Iwonski, Carl G. von: sketches by pictured, 90

Jackson, Richard Henry, 212
Jarvis, Samuel M.: as ferry operator, 243; as Laredo mayor, 215, 238, 265; Benavides's smuggling and, 232–33; 1873 statewide election and, 238; 1872 Webb County election and, 237–38; railroads and, 265, 266; as Republican Party stalwart in Laredo and Webb County,

238, 257; street leveling of, 240
Jennings, N. A.: on smuggling in Laredo, 231
Jiménez, Ángel: at Battle of Carrizo (1861), 92, 93
Johnson, Andrew, 234
Johnson, Otis, 262
Johnston, Joseph E.: surrender of, effect in South Texas, 198
Jones, Alexander C., 192, 194, 195, 197
Jones, Anson, 34
Jones, O. G., 200
Juárez, Benito, 66, 107; during French invasion of Mexico, 180–83, 210; on Ignacio Comonfort's return to Mexico, 108; Santiago Vidaurri and, 108, 110; SB and, 232, 233
Juárez-Lincoln International Bridge, 325

Kenedy, Mifflin, 110, 150, 155; Corpus Christi, San Diego and Rio Grande Narrow Gauge Railroad Company and, 266; cotton and, 136, 138, 141, 183, 198
Kennedy, Thomas W., 263
Kickapoos: Laredo threat to, 103, 223–24, 225, 246; in Remolino Raid (1873), 224
Kimmey, Myndert M., 137, 151, 162
King, Richard, 110, 150; Confederate loyalty of, 155; on Confederate morale, 198; Corpus Christi, San Diego and Rio Grande Narrow Gauge Railroad Company and, 266; cotton and, 136, 138, 141, 183, 198
King Ranch, 180; cotton smuggling at, 139, 149–50, 155; US Army capture of, 155

Lamar, Mirabeau B., 16; Canales rebellion and, 17, 18; in Laredo, 36–37, 39–40; on Laredo, 37, 40; pictured, 38; Quinoñes raid and, 20; SB, interview with, 39; Texan Santa Fe Expedition and, 22
Lambert, Will: Confederate veterans' home (Austin, Texas) and, 312, 314
land titles: after Mexican-American War, 41–42
Lane, Lydia Spencer: on Laredo, 49
Lane, Walter P., 41
languages: in Laredo, 56, 59. *See also specific languages*
Laredo Guard: in Laredo, 36–37, 39–40; oppressions of, 40
Laredo, Battle of (1864), 170–74
Laredo, Texas: baseball in, 234, 237; Benavides family departure from (1863), 157–58; city hall, pictured, 270; cotton smuggling in, 139, 141, 142–43, 164; described, 9, 37, 40, 44, 49–50, 64, 84; as disputed territory (1836-1848), 13, 15; election violence in, 287; finances in, 94; founding of, 6; growth of, post-Civil War, 234; hunger in, 116; incorporation of, 56; international bridge in, 281; Iturbide Street, pictured, 283; languages in, 56, 59; lawlessness in, 48; mail in, 58, 64, 70, 113; map of, pictured, 285, 293; Mexican-American War (1846–1848) in, 34, 35–41; Native Americans, threat to, 9, 10–12, 15, 33, 36, 42–43, 46, 47, 50–56, 62, 74, 78–79, 85, 96, 102–3, 116, 118, 162, 212, 221–2, 224–26, 246; Mexican consulate opened in, 252; newspapers in, 215–16, 268, 282, 290, 314–15; order in, after Civil War, 221; pictured, 216, 251, 283; police reform in, 291–92; political parade in, route pictured, 295; politics in, 56, 58–60, 237–45, 256–60; railroad in, 234; Salinas Avenue, pictured, 310; sanitation in, 60, 214–15; SB born in, 2; SB as mayor of, 50, 59–60; schools in, 40; slaves in, 75–76; smallpox epidemics in, 214–15, 236–37, 304; smuggling in, generally, 230–34; Somervell Expedition (1842–1843) in, 27–32; Stephen F. Austin on, 9; streetcars in, 281; streets in, 60, 215, 240; surrender to US Army of (1865), 211; Texas Rangers in, 19–21, 45–46, 3012; Texas Revolution in, 9, 10–12; US Army in, 43–45, 47–48; US sovereignty over established, 35–36; as

Webb County, Texas seat, 40–41
Laredo Bridge and Street Railway Company, 281
Laredo Daily Times, 282; as pro-SB paper, 280
Laredo Election Riot (1886), 295–96, 298–302; inflammatory flier, pictured, 297; legal ramifications of, 302–4; map of, 293; reaction to, 302
Laredo Ferry Company, 243–45
Latham, F. W., 191
Lee, Robert E., 116, 134, 205; John Bankhead Magruder and, 131; surrender of, effect in South Texas, 198
Leo, Alejandro J., Jr., 271
Lerdo de Tejada, Sebastián, 248
Level, David M., 75
Lewis, Gideon K. ("Legs"), 41
Leyendecker, Bonnie: on Laredo Election Riot (1886), 300
Leyedecker, Isabella: pictured, 65
Leyendecker, Jacob: in Civil War, 121
Leyendecker, John (Johann), 63
Leyendecker, John Zirvas, 59; in Civil War, 84, 100, 120, 121, 126, 188, 193, 206, 211; death of, 328; early life of, 63–64; in 1886 Laredo municipal elections, 292; home of, 234; on Laredo, 64; in Laredo Election Riot (1886), 302; marriages of, 64, 65; pictured, 136; as postmaster, 292; on streets in Laredo, 60; as Webb County treasurer, 214, 237
Leyendecker, María Andrea Benavides: birth of, 6; death of, 65; on German Texan Unionists, 120–21; homesickness of, 72, 74; marriage of, 64; pictured, 65
Leyendecker, María Juliana Benavides, 210; birth of, 6; later life and death of, 328; marriage of, 65; pictured, 329
Lidwell, Michael, 75–76; as ferry operator, 244
Lincoln, Abraham, 78, 79, 80; assassination of, 198, 205; Mexican policy of, 145; Texas strategy of, 144–46
Lipan Apache, 5, 23; defeat of, 55–56; Laredo, threat to, 9, 10, 15, 33, 50–54, 222, 246; in Remolino Raid (1873), 224; warrior pictured, 33
Littleton, John, 174
Loomis, Gustavus, 48
López, Albino, 118, 124, 126, 128, 129–30, 132
Lopez Montalbo, Fernando: murder of, 290
Lopez Montalbo, José: murder of, 290
Lott, Uriah: Corpus Christi, San Diego and Rio Grande Narrow Gauge Railroad Company and, 266
Lovell, D. D.: murder of, 227
Løvenskiold, Charles Grimus Thorkeli de, 97–98, 100, 102; on Tejanos as soldiers, 100, 103
Lubbock, Francis Richard, 111; on SB, 104; on Tejano enlistment, 98, 102
Luckett, Philip Noland, 81; early life of, 103–4; in Civil War, 114, 125

MacDonell, Christopher M.: as ferry operator, 243, 244–45
Mackenzie, Ranald Slidell ("Bad Hand"), 224
Madero, Evaristo, 164; reception for, 268–69
Magruder, John Bankhead, 132, 134, 174; 182, 192; Alexander C. Jones and, 195; arms smuggling and, 181; Confederate strategy in South Texas of, 159; corruption of, 141, 153; cotton smuggling and, 141, 142, 143, 151, 152, 153, 164, 177–78, 183, 191; John "Rip" Ford named commander in Rio Grande valley by, 190; Mexico, flight to, 206, 209; pictured, 131; Santiago Vidaurri and, 180; on SB, 187
mail: in Laredo, 50, 58, 64, 70, 113, 234
Major Brown: in Laredo, 36
Maltby, Henry A., 81
Maltby, William, 75
Manning, Thomas Courtland, 318
Mansfield, Battle of (1864), 184
Mansfield, Joseph K. F.: on smuggling in

Laredo, 230
Marcy, Randolph Barnes: on Laredo, 49–50
Martin, Raymond: biography of, 241–42; 1884 Webb County election and, 290; 1872 Webb County election and, 237–38; as entrepreneur, 234, 281; as ferry operator, 243, 244, 245; marriage of, 59, 241; as political opponent of SB, 238, 241, 242, 256–57, 259, 280, 282; pictured, 235; on prohibition, 316–17; on streets in Laredo, 60
Martin, Tirza García de, 241
Martin Democrats. *See* Botas
Martines, Andrés, 36, 37, 41; corruption of, 66
Martinez, Vicente, 290
Matamoros, Mexico: arms smuggling in, 204; Charles Russell flight to, 150; cotton smuggling in, 137, 138, 139, 188; evacuation of, by Mexican imperial forces (1866), 209–10; Juan Cortina, capture of, 151, 185; money smuggling at, 163; Mosby Monroe Parsons in, 209; refugees in, 119–20, 188, 198; SB in, 306; siege of (1851), 104; siege of (1862), 110–12; US Army recruitment at, 123, 126; US attack from rumored, 147–48
Maxey, Samuel Bell, 255, 316
Maximilian of Mexico, 183; execution of, 210
McIntosh, James Simmons: as Fort McIntosh namesake, 44
McKean, Clug, 96
McKinney, Thomas F., 163–64
McLane, Albert L.: in 1878 election, 260; as state representative, 256, 258
McLane, Charles A.: as Laredo city attorney, 294
McManus, T. P., 160, 162, 176, 177
McNelly, Leander H., 228
Mejía, Thomás, 181, 203, 205, 209–10; execution of, 210
Mendiola, Benardo: as Native American fighter, 223
Mendiola, Hypolito, 225
Merchants' War: José María Jesús Carvajal in, 104
Merriam, Henry: Pablo Quintana crossing (1876) and, 246–27
Mescalero Apaches: Laredo, threat to, 103, 162; in Remolino Raid (1873), 224
Meuly, Alexander: in 1886 Laredo municipal elections, 294
Mexía, Enrique Guillermo Antonio, 321
Mexican-American War (1846–1848), 34; Gustav Schleicher during, 279; Laredo in, 35–41. *See also* Treaty of Guadalupe Hidalgo
Mexican Boundary Commission (1828), 5
Mexican Central Railroad, 308
Mexican National Railway, 267, 269, 309
Mexican Revolution, 328
Mexico: Abraham Lincoln, policy toward, 145; Confederates flee after Civil War to, 206, 209, 216; French invasion of, 112, 180–83; independence of, 7; refugees from Texas to, 118–20; refugees to Texas from, 121–22, 208; Porfiriato in, 246–48, 250–52, 254–55; SB, loyalty to, 112; SB in, 252, 306–7, 308–9, 321; United States, relationship with, 224, 252, 254, 306–9
Mexico City: during French invasion, 180, 183; Mariano Escobedo imprisoned in, 251; in Mexican-American War, 39, 41; Porfirio Díaz captures, 248; Santiago Vidaurri captured and executed in, 210; SB in, 252, 306–7, 308–09, 315
Mier Expedition (1842–1843), 32, 34
Miller, Dick: saloon of, 129
Miller, James B., 42
Mills, Roger Quarles, 318
Milmo and Company: cotton smuggling of, 138–39
Milmo Hall: anti-prohibitionist meeting at (1887), 316–17; Evaristo Madero, banquet for at (1883), 269; Reform Party (Guaraches) and, 281, 282, 284, 286, 287

Milmo National Bank: Reform Party (Guaraches) and, 281, 284, 301
Milmo O'Dowd, Daniel, 236; in Laredo Election Riot (1886), 302; Reform Party and, 281
Milmo O'Dowd, Patricio, 150, 157; Confederate bank notes stolen by, 162–64; cotton and, 137, 138–39; early life of, 139; Reform Party and, 281
Mimbres Apache, 162
Miramón, Miguel: execution of, 210
Mitchel, N. A., 197
Monterrey, Battle of (1846), 36
Monterrey, Mexico: Agustina Garza Ayala in, 71, 117; Benavides family evacuated to, 157; Charles Russell, flight to, 150; cotton smuggling in, 138, 141, 151, 153; disorder in, 311; Francisco Baez Benavides Lópes as alcalde of, 2; during French invasion of Mexico, 181, 183; Mariano Arguindegui imprisoned in, 312; Mexican National Railway reaches, 267; Pendleton Murrah, death in, 209; Santos Eraclio Benavides y Villarreal, death in, 270; SB in, 66, 113, 211, 269, 270, 274, 321; Unionists in, 162; during the War of the Reform, 65
morale: of Confederate troops, 92, 164–65, 166, 183–84; 190, 198
Murphy, Patrick Francis ("Pat"), 257, 258
Murrah, Pendleton, 151; death of, 209; Mexico, flight to, 206, 209
Mussett, Fenis, 76, 81
Mussett, John D., 86; at Battle of Carrizo (1861), 91, 92; on Tejano enlistment, 98

Napoleon III, 112, 145, 210
Naranjo de la Garza, José Francisco, 307; SB writings about, 255
Native Americans: Basilio Benavides on, 9; John S. "Rip" Ford on, 45; Laredo, threat to, 42–43, 46, 50–56, 62, 74, 96, 102–3, 116, 118, 212, 221–22, 224–26; SB on, 9. *See also individual confederations and tribes*
Navajos, 162
Navarro, Ángel. *See* Navarro, José Ángel, III
Navarro, Antonio (son of José Antonio Navarro), 69
Navarro, Francisco (governor of Nuevo León), 308
Navarro, José Ángel, III (son of José Antonio Navarro), 69, 110, in Civil War, 165, 196; SB's will and, 325; as state representative, 81
Navarro, José Antonio (Texas Revolution statesman), 69, 165
Navarro, Sixto Eusebio (son of José Antonio Navarro): in Civil War, 165, 196, 202; SB's will and, 325
Neighbours, Robert S., 53
New Orleans, Louisiana: Cristóbal Benavides in, 211; James Slaughter in, 99; José María Rodríguez in, 63; Raymond Martin in, 235, 241; US capture of, 115; World's Industrial and Cotton Centennial Exposition (1884) in, 277
Newsom, W. L., 192
Nolan, Matthew, 156, 167, 179–80, 193–94; Ochoa insurrection and, 87, 89; pictured, 88
Norton's Union Intelligencer: SB profiled in, 278
Nueces County, Texas, 37; Matthew Nolan as sheriff of, 88; secession in, 81
Nueces Massacre (1862), 119
Nueces Strip: land titles in, 41–42; lawlessness in, 13, 15, 223
Nuecestown Raid (1875), 226–27
Nuevo Laredo, Mexico: baseball team from, 237; cotton smuggling in, 115, 191; created, 41; Cristóbal Benavides business in, 232, 234–35, 268; Porfirio Díaz, attack on (1876), 247, 251; SB business in, 232, 234–35, 268, SB, invasion of (1863), 127–28, 130

O'Brien, J. F., 309
Ochiltree, Thomas P., 276
Ochoa, Antonio, 105: at Battle of

Carrizo (1861), 90, 91; insurrection of, 86–87, 89
Odin, Jean Marie, 69
Olguin, Bernardo, 262
Olivares, Juan, 77
Ord, Edward O. C., 224
Ortiz, José: as Dog Town bandit posse member, 218
Ortiz, Juan (doctor), 108
Ortiz, Juan (teamster): murder of, 218
Ortiz, Plutarco: as Dog Town bandit posse member, 218; in in Laredo Election Riot (1886), 298

Palmer, William Jackson, 309
Palmito Ranch, Battle of (1865), 199–203
pardon: of Mariano Arguindegui, 312; of SB, 234
Parsons, H. R., 212
Parsons, Mosby Monroe: Mexico, flight to, 209
Partido Viejo. *See* Independent Club
Pease, Elisha Marshall, 52; on protection for Laredo from Native American attacks, 52–53
Peña, Agustín de la, 320
Peña, Federico, 325
Peña, Silverio de la, 320
Peñaloza, Joseph M., 195, 196
Penn, James Saunders, 275, 284; anti-Martin poetry of, 282, 288; early life of, 280; on 1886 Laredo municipal elections, 292; on Guarache defeat in 1884 Webb County elections, 290; Reform Party and, 280; on SB, 280, 282; on voting irregularities in 1884 Webb County election, 289
"People of the Frontier" letter (1863), 156–57
Pérez, Antonio, 20–21, 133
Peterson, Hamilton: 1872 Webb County election and, 237
Pfeiffer, George, 166–67
Pierce, Charles C.: Reform Party speech of, 286–87
Pierce, Gardner W.: in Civil War, 103; on Laredo, 84; on Tejano enlistment, 100, 102; on refugees from Mexico, 208
Pierce, Leonard, Jr., 146, 154, 164; on cotton smuggling, 137; recruitment efforts of, 118–19, 126, 133
Plan de Ayutla, 61, 106
Plan de Iguala, 7
Plan de Tacubaya, 107
Pleasant Hill, Battle of (1864), 184
police reform: in Laredo, 291–92
politics: in Laredo, 56, 58–60, 237–45, 256–60, 279–84, 286–92, 294–96, 298–305, 329, 331. *See also* elections
Polk, James K., 34
Porter, William J., 75
post office. *See* mail
Powers, Stephen: political machine of, 257–58, 259, 260, 271
Prime, Nathaniel, 214; as Native American fighter, 222
prohibition: SB and, 263, 265, 316–17; in Texas, 316
Prohibition Party, 316
Puebla, Siege of (1863), 180, 249, 253, 306
Pyron, Charles, 183, 194, 195, 196

Querétaro, Mexico: cotton mills in, 141; imperial executions at, 210
Quinoñes, Agatón, 19–20, 21, 23
Quintana, Pablo: border crossing of (1876), 246–47
Quintero, José, 181
Quiroga Villarreal, Julian, 54, 223, 236; Benavides smuggling and, 232

Rabb, Thomas, 132
racial animosity: against Tejanos, 22–23, 29, 156, 165, 166, 227–29
Ragsdale, Samuel Gabriel, 196
railroads: international, 254–55, 308; in Laredo, 234, 265–67, 271; SB as advocate for, 308, 309. *See also specific railroads*
Ramirez, Jesús, 242
Ramon, Ildefonso: Somervell Expedition (1842–1843), effect on, 30
Ramón, José María, 19; on US rule in Laredo, 39–40

Ramón, Margarita. *See* Benavides, Margarita Ramón de
ranching: Raymond Martin and, 242; SB and, 23, 61, 68, 70, 72, 236, 323
Rancho Clareño, 87, 104, 123, 125; Isidro Vela hung at, 124; massacre at (1861), 88, 89, 91, 106
Rancho Davis, 197. *See also* Rio Grande City, Texas
Reagan, John H., 317; on prohibition, 316
Reconstruction: in South Texas, 208–29
Redmond, Henry, 46; at Battle of Carrizo (1861), 90, 91, 92; biography of, 85–86; as cotton smuggler, 115; Ochoa insurrection and, 87
Reeves, George R.: death of, 273
Reform Party: constituencies of, 283, 285; in Encinal County, Texas, 283–84; established, 280, 281–82; miners in, 285; rallies of, 284. *See also* Guarache Party
refugees: from Texas to Mexico, 118–20; from Mexico to Texas (Rojos), 121–22, 208
Remolino Raid (1873), 224
Republic of the Rio Grande, 17–19; Antonio Zapata in, 39, 86; capital of, 39
Republican Party: in Laredo and Webb Counties, 238
Reséndez, Abraham, 320
Reyes, Bernardo, 311
Reyna, Pedro: at Battle of Carrizo (1861), 92
Ringgold Barracks, 43, 99, 197, 320; in Civil War, 103, 114; 118, 123, 152, 154, 174, 176, 180, 184, 187, 188, 190, 192, 194, 196, 206; cotton smuggling at, 206; desertion at, 118; pictured, 43; US Army in, 152, 154, 174, 211, 212. *See also* Rio Grande City, Texas
Ripley, Eliza Moore Chinn McHatton: on cotton smuggling, 137
Rio Grande: bridge over, at Laredo, 266–67, 321–23; flood of (1842), 24
Rio Grande and Eagle Pass Railway, 267, 269
Rio Grande and Pecos Railway, 268
Rio Grande City, Texas, 197, 259, 263; in Civil War, 148, 152, 154, 164, 166, 175, 184, 187, 188, 206; cotton smuggling in, 111, 139, 141, 142, 188; Juan Cortina and, 72, 85, 92, 104; Mexican consulate opened in, 252; pictured, 43; railroads in, 265; riot in (1888), 320–21; secession vote in, 80; US Army in, 152, 154, 156, 166, 174, 211, 212. *See also* Ringgold Barracks
Rio Grande Valley. *See* South Texas
Rios, Antonia, 70
Rivers, Robert Jones, 42
roads. *See* streets
Roberts, Oran Milo, 271, 307
Rockport, Fulton, Laredo, and Mexican Pacific Railroad, 215, 265
Rodríguez, José María, 214, 242, 304; early life of, 63; in 1884 Webb County elections, 284; in 1876 state representative election, 258; as interpreter for Basilio Benavides, 77; in Laredo Election Riot (1886), 296, 304; on Native Americans, 103; political realignment of, 256–57; railroads and, 265
Rodríguez, Feliz Benavides de, 63
Román, José San, 139
Ross, Lawrence Sullivan ("Sul"), 323; Mexico City, prospective visit to, 316; on prohibition, 316; Rio Grande City riot (1888) and, 321; Texas State Capitol dedication and, 318
runaway slaves: in Laredo, 75–76, 96; SB and, 76, 96; Tejanos and, 74–75
Runnels, Hardin Richard: in 1860 gubernatorial election, 77
Rusk, Thomas J., 42
Russell, Charles, 102, 163; cotton smuggling and, 142, 153–54; flight of, 150–51
Russell, John C., 292; in *State of Texas, Ex. Rel. Daniel Milmo, Santos Benavides, et al. v. Darío Sánchez*, 303–4
Russell, William H., 238, 259

Salinas, Agustín: as ferry operator, 243, 244; as Laredo mayor, 238, 240; as state representative, 256, 258
Salinas, Monico: death of, 132–33

San Agustín Church (Laredo, Texas), 188; Agustina Benavides wedding at, 269, 319; baptismal records at, 24; constructed, 234; John Z. Leyendecker's funeral mass at, 328; John Z. Leyendecker's wedding at, 64; Lone Star flag hung on, 28; pictured, 216; SB's funeral mass at, 323–24; SB's wedding at, 24–25
San Antonio, Texas: cotton smuggling in, 139; during Vásquez expedition (1842), 22; during Woll expedition (1842), 23–24; SB in, 68–69, 113, 115; secession in, 83
San Antonio Express, 299; interpreter for SB, support expressed in, 260–61
San Jacinto, Battle of (1836), 12; Alexander Somervell at, 27; Erastus "Deaf" Smith at, 14; John Coffee Hays at, 19; Mexican deaths at, compared to Nuecestown Raid, 228
Sánchez, Darío: in 1886 Laredo municipal elections, 294; in Laredo Election Riot (1886) and aftermath, 296, 298, 302, 303, 304; as mayor of Laredo, 281
Sanchez, Eugenio, 186
Sanchez, Margarito, 96
Sánchez, Nicolás, 58, 182
Sánchez Barrera y de la Garza, Tomás (great-great-grandfather of SB), 5–6, 10, 236, 244
Sandoval, Ruiz, 314
sanitation: in Laredo, 60, 214–15
Santa Anna, Antonio López de, 26, 106, 321; Santiago Vidaurri and, 61–62; in Texas Revolution, 9–10, 12, 13, 18; invasion of Texas of (1842), 21–23
Santa Fe Trail, 21–22, 121
Santa Gertrudis, Battle of (1866), 209, 249
Schleicher, Gustav, 275, 279, 280
Schmitt, George H.: Laredo Election Riot (1886) and, 301, 302
Schott, Arthur Carl Victor: sketch by, pictured, 8, 13, 33
Scott, Winfield, 39, 41
Sebree, Victor, 320
secession: of Texas, 78, 79, 80–83; Basilio Benavides on, 80; SB on, 82; in South Texas, 80–82
Sedgwick, Thomas D., 212
Seguín, Juan N., 23; as military recruiter, 66
Seminoles: Laredo, threat to, 54
Senate (Texas). *See* Texas Senate
Serna, Jésus de la, 110
Settle, J. A., 97
Shafter, William R., 212
Shaw, Owen, 46
Shelby, Joseph O.: Mexico, flight to, 209
Shelby, W. W., 320
Sherman, William T., 198; in Laredo, 266
Showalter, Daniel, 174, 185, 188, 189, 197
Sibley, Caleb Chase, 83–84
Sibley, Henry Hopkins, 115, 121, 194
Skillman, Henry, 162, 198
Slaughter, James Edwin: in Civil War, 151, 169, 185, 194, 203, 204, 205, 206; on filibusters in Laredo, 48; as Fort McIntosh quartermaster, 47; Mexico, flight to, 206; pictured, 99
slavery: in South Texas, 74–77; Basilio Benavides on, 80; Benavides family and, 75. *See also* runaway slaves
smallpox: 1872 epidemic in Laredo, 214–15; 1879 epidemic in Laredo, 236–37; 1886 epidemic in Laredo, 304
Smith, Edmund Kirby, 151–52, 192, 198, 312; Civil War surrender of, 99, 205; cotton smuggling and, 141, 142, 143, 163; Mexico, flight to, 206, 209; pictured, 101
Smith, Erastus "Deaf": in Laredo, 14, 19
Smith, M. S., 200
Smith, Persifor, 53
smuggling, 230–34; pictured, 231. *See also under* arms; cotton
Sociedad Mutualista Union Mexicano, 283
Somervell, Alexander, 26–27
Somervell Expedition (1842–1843), 26–32, 34, 41
Soto, Agustín, 37
South Texas: banditry in, 217–21; climate

in, 165–66, 179; communications difficulties in, during Civil War, 160, 162; Confederate collapse, effect in, 208–9; Confederate strategy in, 159–60, 167, 176, 178–80, 189; cotton in, 135, 136–39, 141–43; early history of, 1–2; lawlessness in, 118, 217–221; 245–46; map of, pictured, 95; pictured, 8, 13; Reconstruction in, 208–29; secession in, 80–82; slavery in, 74–77; Union invasion of, 144–57; Union strategy in, 160, 162, 168–69, 176, 182

Spanish (language): Agustina Benavides Garza Ayala and, 117; Charles C. Pierce and, 286; George Preston Finlay and, 262, 276; José María Rodríguez and, 63; in Laredo, 56, 59, 216, 296; Leonard Pierce Jr. and, 119; newspapers, 268, 282, 290, 314–15; Randolph Barnes Marcy and, 50; SB and, 262; 269, 316, 322; in South Texas, 261, 263, 273; Thomas Courtland Manning and, 318

Speed, James, 155

Starr County, Texas: secession in, 80, 82

State of Texas, Ex. Rel. Daniel Milmo, Santos Benavides, et al. v. Darío Sánchez, 302–4

Steffan, Peter, 236

Sterling, Mark, 36

Stevens, Clem, 216

Stillman, Charles, 110, 185

streetcars: in Laredo, 281, 320

streets: in Laredo, 60, 215, 240, 283; in Laredo, pictured, 283

Sutton, Warren P., 306

Swope, J. S., 172, 175

Taylor, Richard, 184; surrender of, effect in South Texas, 198

Taylor, Zachary: in Mexican-American War, 34, 35, 36, 37, 257

Tejanos: in Civil War, pictured, 90; cotton smuggling, role in, 141–42; desertion of, in Civil War, 118; enlistment of, in Confederate Army, 96–98, 100, 102–4; racial animosity against, 22–23, 29, 156, 165, 166, 227–29; recruitment of, in US Army, 123, 133; secession and, 81–82; slavery and, 74–77

Texan Santa Fe Expedition, 21–22

Texas: annexation to United States of, 34; constitution (1876) of, 258; prohibition in, 316; refugees from Mexico to, 121–22, 208; refugees to Mexico from, 118–20; secession in, 78, 79, 80–83. *See also* South Texas *and individual municipalities and counties*

Texas Cotton Bureau, 164, 181, 183, 191; end of, in Laredo, 198; established, 141; on Mexican conscription, 142; SB, criticism of, 143

Texas House of Representatives: Basilio Benavides in, 77, 260; Eighteenth Legislature, members pictured, 272; SB in, 3, 229, 259–63, 265, 271, 273–74; SB praised in, for Civil War service, 133–34

Texas Mexican Railway, 266, 267

Texas Rangers, 103, 260; funding bill for, amended by SB, 263; John Cortina and, 71, 85, 110; in Laredo, 19–21, 45–46, 3012; in Laredo Election Riot (1886), 301–2; Native Americans and, 223; pictured, 226; Refugio Benavides in, 225–26, 228–29; reputation among Tejanos in Laredo, 19, 21, 41, 228–29; violence against Tejanos by, 227, 228

Texas Revolution, 9–12; Basilio Benavides as Laredo alcalde during, 16; Tejanos in, 23, 69, 165; veterans' pension bill, supported by SB, 263

Texas Senate: Edward F. Hall elected to, 290; SB as potential candidate for, 271, 276, 304–5

Texas State Capitol: cornerstone laying of, 315; dedication, 318, 320

Texas State Lunatic Asylum: funding bill for, sponsored by SB, 263

Texas Union Expedition, 144–46

Thaison, Andrew Hans, 329

Thayer, Clarence C., 163

Thompson, Benjamin: in Laredo, 128–29
Thompson, C. W.: cotton smuggling and, 164
Throckmorton, James W., 221
Tilden, Bryan P., 36
Tilden, Texas. *See* Dog Town, Texas
Tonkawas: horse theft by, 44
translator. *See* interpreter
Treaty of Guadalupe Hidalgo (1848), 41, 230; Native American raids and, 225
Treaty of Velasco (1836), 13
Treviño, Geronimo, 274; Manuel González, feud with, 276–77 pictured, 256; SB writings about, 255
Treviño, Teodocio: as SB's godfather, 6
Treviño, Tomás, 52, 191
Tucker, L. T., 37
Twiggs, David E.: Fort McIntosh closure by, 61; in secession crisis, 82–83, 104
Tyler, John, 34
Types of Successful Men of Texas (Daniell): SB profiled in, 317, 324

Underground Railroad: in Laredo, 74; Tejanos and, 74–77
Unionists: SB and, 96. *See also* Davis, Edmund J.; Haynes, John L.
United Confederate Veterans, 312
United Daughters of the Confederacy, 312
United States: Mexico, relationship with, 224, 252, 254, 306–9. *See also* US Army
Upson, Christopher Columbus, 280
Uribe, Blas María, 86; as political power broker of Zapata County, 259
Uribe, Fernando, 86
Ursuline Convent (Laredo, Texas): pictured, 216
US Army: in Laredo, 43–45, 47–48, 211–12, 214; Native Americans, conflicts with, 224–26; in South Texas, during Civil War, 144–57, 160, 162; Tejano recruitment of, 123, 133. *See also* Fort McIntosh
US House of Representatives: SB rumored as candidate for, 279–80
US Senate: Sam Houston speech on floor of, 32; Thomas Rusk speech on floor of, 42;

Valenzuela, Andres, 124
Valerio, Cecilio, 155–56, 180
Valerio, Juan, 155
Valera, Ramón: Texas invasion of (1842), 23
Van Dorn, Earl, 97; on SB, 96
Vargas, Felipa, 24
Vásquez, Ráfael: Texas invasion of (1842), 21–23
Vasquez, Tómas, 179
Vela, Crisento, 51
Vela, Isidro, 124; at Battle of Carrizo (1861), 90, 91, 92; Ochoa insurrection and, 87, 89; secession and, 80–81, 86
Vela, José María, 283
Vela, Nepomuceno, 89
Vela, Santiago, 89
Vidal, Ádrian J.: mutiny of, 147–48; SB on, 156
Vidal, Jesús, 125
Vidaurri, Atanacio: ferry concession and, 245; as mayor of Laredo, 245; pictured, 136
Vidaurri y Valdez, José Santiago: Basilio Benavides and, 61–62; on Carvajal's scheme to raise a Confederate regiment, 114; on Catholic Church, 62, 69; cotton smuggling and, 153–54, 163; death of, 210; early political career, 61; during French invasion of Mexico, 181–82; John Bankhead Magruder and, 180; Laredo, support for, 116; Lipan Apaches and, 51, 53, 54, 55–56; Mexican politics and, 65–66, 108; Octavio Zapata raids and, 124; pictured, 67; SB, relationship with, 66, 68, 69, 69–70, 71–72, 77–78, 94, 104–5, 106–8, 108, 110, 112, 113–14, 126–27, 180, 180–81, 210
Vidaurri y Valdez, Prudencia, 139
Vielé, Egbert Ludovicus, 43–44; on Lar-

edo, 44; Tonkawa horse theft and, 44
Villarreal, Agustina. *See* Benavides, Agustina Villareal del
Villarreal, Feliciano, 68
Villarreal, Felipe, 234
Villarreal, Florencio: as alcalde of Laredo, 37; Somervell Expedition (1842–1843) and, 27, 29
Villarreal, Manuel: death of, 132–33
Villarreal, Perez, 124
Villarreal de Ugarte, Josefa, 234
Vineyard, Jesse, 200
Vino, Guillermo, 124; death of, 132–33
Voz del Pueblo, La: as Martin paper, 282

Ware, James A., 177
Washington, DC: Gustav Schleicher dies in, 279; Porfirio Díaz in, 274; SB in, 310; Texas Unionists in, 144
Watkins, O. M.: Edward F. Hall, altercation with, 290–91
Watson, Pleasant B., 197
Watson, William: on cotton smuggling, 138
Webb, James, 41
Webb County, Texas: border adjustment bill sponsored by SB, 261; created, 40–41; financial problems in, 221–22; secession in, 81–82, 82; slavery in, 75
Weisenger, W. J., 191–92
Wells, James Babbage, Jr., 305: political machine of, 257–58, 259, 260, 271
Western Union Telegraph and Cable Offices (Laredo): pictured, 305
Weyman, J. B., 177
Whitehead, J. P. C., 291
Wilkinson, James A.: on languages in Laredo, 56; on Native Americans, 42–43; as Webb County judge, 56
Williams, George H., 226
Williams, John J., 203
Witten, Henry F., 52
Wood, Albert, 193
Wood, George Tyler, 42, 45
Wood, Peter C., 217
Woll, Adrían: Texas invasion of (1842), 23–24, 26
Woman's Christian Temperance Union, 316
World's Industrial and Cotton Centennial Exposition (1884), 277

Yturria, Francisco, 206

Zamora, Teodoro: at Battle of Carrizo (1861), 90
Zampano, Trinidad, 86
Zapata, José Antonio de: in Canales rebellion, 15–16, 16–17; death of, 17–18; SB, influence on, 16, 18, 39; as Zapata County, Texas namesake, 15–16, 86
Zapata, Nicanor, 227
Zapata, Octaviano: border raids of, 123–25, 126–27; death of, 132–33, 220
Zapata County, Texas: naming of, 15–16, 86; politics in, 85–86; secession in, 80–81, 82, 86; slavery in, 75
Zaragoza, Ignacio, 306
Zardeneta, Juan, 315
Zavala County, Texas: border adjustment bill sponsored by SB, 261; created, 262–63
Zertuche, Miguel, 129
Zuazua, Juan Nepomuceno: death of, 71